T0311611

# BUSINESS WITH PURPOSE

## ADVANCING SOCIAL ENTERPRISE

# BUSINESS WITH
# PURPOSE

## ADVANCING SOCIAL ENTERPRISE

## MELODENA STEPHENS

Mohammed Bin Rashid School of Government, UAE

**World Scientific**

EW JERSEY · LONDON · SINGAPORE · BEIJING · SHANGHAI · HONG KONG · TAIPEI · CHENNAI · TOKYO

*Published by*

World Scientific Publishing Co. Pte. Ltd.

5 Toh Tuck Link, Singapore 596224

*USA office:* 27 Warren Street, Suite 401-402, Hackensack, NJ 07601

*UK office:* 57 Shelton Street, Covent Garden, London WC2H 9HE

**British Library Cataloguing-in-Publication Data**
A catalogue record for this book is available from the British Library.

**BUSINESS WITH PURPOSE**
**Advancing Social Enterprise**

ISBN 978-981-120-517-0
ISBN 978-981-120-408-1 (pbk)

Desk Editor: Sandhya Venkatesh

Printed in Singapore

# CONTENTS

Cases: White Helmets (emergency services: Syria), M-Pesa (mobile payment: Kenya), Aravind Eye Hospital (healthcare: India), Narayana Hrudayalaya Hospital (healthcare: India), Chid Liberty's L&J (fair-trade certified clothing and handbags: Liberia), and TOMS (One for One model: USA).

Cases: Visayan Forum Foundation (human trafficking: Philippines), The Akshaya Patra Foundation (free mid-day meals: India), The Ibrahim Prize (governance: Africa), Zipline International Inc. (medical drone delivery: Impact Africa), International Consortium of Investigative Journalists (corruption: USA) and Peace Works & KIND Inc. (health, kindness, tolerance: USA).

Cases: BeadforLife (entrepreneurship: Uganda), Sulabh International Organization (sanitation: India), Gavi, the Vaccine Alliance (vaccines, innovative financing: impact of 70+ countries), Vestergaard LifeStraw Water Campaign (drinking water, innovative financing: Kenya), and Tree Change Dolls (recycling and upscaling: Australia).

Cases: Grameen (Microfinance: Bangladesh), Vision Spring (eyecare: India, El Salvador), Deloitte MicroLoan (microfinance: Malawi), and Invisible Children (activism: Uganda).

# FOREWORD

In my over a 1,000 close encounters with founders across the globe, one thing is uniformly shared — the founder and team's ability and passion for solving the next massive complex opportunity. You can slow them down, but you cannot stop them. No matter what you ask them, no matter what obstacles you raise, they keep honing in on their obsession to solve.

At the same time, these builders can fail if they don't see the changing landscape or understand the ecosystem and players in which they work. They will often fail if they aren't also able to ask and address the tough questions that data and experience raise, or if they do not surround themselves with boards and advisors who do the same.

This is true in any entrepreneurial experience in any setting.

This book zooms in on core examples in the social enterprise venture space from around the world and it highlights seven key points in each dedicated chapter.

(1) *Perseverance is foundational*: Entrepreneurship is tough and lonely. To persevere, one needs much more than passion. Social enterprises, in particular, operate in gray areas where there are no established norms or models to easily imitate. They must take the lead in especially harsh conditions with limited resources. Perseverance and steely focus on purpose often decide who succeeds or fails.

(2) *Know the lay of the land and be flexible to change*: Who are the players that can influence their goals and how can they leverage them to help and not hinder? Most start-ups find this a complicated thing to do. And it gets tougher in emerging markets where only recently there has been an increase of investors and talent that has done this before. The ability to find resources, not only in their market but also in other rising markets where people have successfully solved similar problems, can separate a good founder from a great one. The social enterprise venture (SEV) must be able to manage various stakeholder expectations and balance them with their own goals.

(3) *Understand the path to scale*: The fact that many start-ups face the so-called "valley of death" in their lifecycle means that they need to be aware of the resource crunch that can hit them and plan for the next spurt of growth. Understanding the time to scale and the bottlenecks may help a team ride the next growth curve. There are great examples in Chapter 3 and you can see what the role innovation plays in service delivery and financing (not always in the final product)! The SEV Business Initiative Canvas is a good tool to be used along with the list of other business models SEVs can use.

(4) *Build a strong support system*: The coping strategies put into place may be essential for the survival of the firm and the founder sanity. Often the support systems are closer than you think — friends, family, workspace, investors — and building your personal board

of directors is an often under-appreciated tool. Chapter 4 highlights the importance of developing networks and good governance.

(5) *Broaden the definition of access to resources*: To identify and leverage networks to get access to resources are skills that need to be developed, especially as a crisis is always looming on the horizon.

(6) *Manage and control resources for growth*: This is vital for internationalization and scaling. Chapter 6 presents a list of finance methods with their pros and cons, and tools to help young teams develop their brand story, brand strategy, and media strategy. An interesting tool to help identify future networks and communication for crisis management is also presented.

(7) *Measure, measure, measure — and communicate it (repeatedly)*: When creating change, founders are tasked with the responsibility of ensuring that the interventions must be for the better. The Intervention Change Strategy tool is a good method to monitor and track the changes *vis-à-vis* the firm objectives and its impact.

Melodena Stephens has been working on this project for years but has dedicated her profound studies to these issues from the beginning of her career. Few have the pattern recognition across industry and geography as she. Few ask tougher questions. She mixes her academic insights with practical observations. This book is no academic study. It is a practical, accessible, and provocative look at what allows great enterprises to solve great challenges and opportunities in real time.

We are living in an era of unprecedented problem-solving, with the tools to speed and scale solutions that were unimaginable a few years ago. We have tremendous assets and knowledge at our fingertips to help us achieve this. This book is a wonderful contribution and will help entrepreneurs build and change their worlds.

Christopher M. Schroeder
Co-founder, Next Billion Ventures
Author, *Startup Rising: The Entrepreneurial Revolution Remaking the Middle East*

# REVIEWS

This book was written with great passion by Professor Melodena Stephens, and provides a comprehensive view on Businesses for Purpose. With the world today facing complex challenges, social entrepreneurs have been tackling these head on whilst addressing the UN Sustainable Development Goals. In this book, you will find a variety of exciting cases that will inspire you. It will help you navigate your way in this ecosystem in order to create a positive impact in the world."

Sheikha Shamma Bint Sultan Bin Khalifa Al Nahyan
CEO and Founder
Alliances for Global Sustainability, UAE

Melodena's traits for successful social entrepreneurs — passion, perseverance, purpose, plan, people, path — greatly resonate her own personality, which led to produce this masterpiece: Business with Purpose. A great effort and resource capturing the true examples and values of social entrepreneurship, public-private partnership and innovation.

This book is a classic case of encompassing global landscape and challenges, highlighting ground realities and showcasing successes — from across the markets as well as key issues — to propose innovative solutions for a sustainable world.

Melodena has read the pulse well and convincingly captured the need for innovations and innovative financing, engagement of the public sector and the entrepreneurial mind-set to resolve international humanitarian aid and development challenges in order to achieve the SDGs.

Are Social Enterprises the new norm/future and problem solvers for a developed, thriving and sustainable world? Or NGOs have to change the way they operate? Readers have abundant material and varied examples to ascertain successful mechanisms for better and sustainable international humanitarian aid and development.

Finally, Melodena's deep understanding and simple narration of how social enterprises are envisaged, set up, governed, managed, run, with example from various sectors, is super authentic. She also gave justice to her work through clearly reminding the challenges, risks and failures social entrepreneurs face. This honesty, with facts and figures, makes it a great source to anyone who is willing to pick up even a loose chance or idea and drop a very strong impact on humanity. Questions at the end of each chapter are great re-cap and rethink source.

Faisal Gilani
Senior Manager for Middle East & Africa Resource Mobilisation
Private Sector Partnership & Innovation Finance
Gavi, The Vaccine Alliance, Switzerland

I congratulate the author, Melodena Stephens, for providing fresh and informative insight into the challenges of setting and operating social enterprises venture. The case studies encapsulated in the book is based on highly erudite research which will hopefully inspire future generation of social entrepreneurs.

Dr. Bindeshwar Pathak
Founder
Sulabh Sanitation and Social Reform Movement, India

The logic of the social enterprise, its focus on purpose and meaning, is going to become the dominant rationale for organizations and their management. Within these pages, management practitioners and scholars alike will find a plethora of examples and insights how to apply this logic to their own fields of practice as well as research.

Prof. Dr. André Reichel
Professor for International Management & Sustainability
International School of Management, Germany

This book provides invaluable insights on the intricacies of building and running a social enterprise and the enabling environment for a thriving ecosystem. At a time where no government on its own can tackle the complex economic, social and environmental challenges we are facing, this book is providing us with real life examples on how businesses can and must play an instrumental role in the economic and social progress of our societies.

Reem Khouri
Co-founder and CEO
whyise, an impact analytics software solution, Jordan
Founding Partner at Kaamen, an impact design firm, Jordan

# ACKNOWLEDGEMENTS

This journey began in 2010 when my life was going through significant bouts of change. You realize life does not treat everyone fair and many people are left behind — because they are out of sight and therefore we are blind — we don't know; they are out of reach, and we give up because we feel helpless, or we know, and we don't care because we are blinded by our own viewpoints. I was inspired by the people who dedicated their lives to solving other people's problems, often at considerable personal cost. I began to read up and study them. I saw the cost of good intentions that solved the wrong problems, or the communities that thought they were getting a hands-up, when they were actually learning to become dependent on their problem solvers. Was there something we were missing in education — between the good intentions and relevant solutions? This question was the genesis for my many years of research into this topic.

I would like to thank the many people who were with me on this journey. First of all, my children. They had the unconventional bedtime stories — about the entrepreneurs who wanted to change the world. Growing up with such an unusual background has made them change makers. They are changing my world because they are wonderful young human beings who have shown with quiet endurance, how you can be exceptional. They are changing the world around them. My children have been my constant inspiration and have supported me.

Thank you my friends — you know who you are — you have stood by me in difficult times and pushed me into the spotlight from the shadows. I want to thank my research assistants — Sadaf and Mohit. I do a million things at one time, and they have helped me with the essential details in managing projects of this size. My thoughts sometimes flow faster than my fingers can capture.

My thanks to the UAE National Research Foundation that allowed me to research Social Enterprise Ventures in depth and see first-hand the changes they were making. Many of the research cases are mentioned in this book. My thanks to my mentors in the investing world, you shared the for-profit world candidly with me to help me find the space between the for-profit and the not-for-profit worlds. My thanks to my fellow researchers with whom I have bounced ideas. Of course, a big thanks to John Stuart, my Editor; Cornell Coelho, my graphic designer and Sandhya Venkatesh from World Scientific Publishing.

A big thanks to Sheikha Shamma Bint Sultan Bin Khalifa Al Nahyan, Christopher M. Schroeder, Fadi Ghandour, Dina Al Sherif, Reem Khouri, Faisal Gilani, Prof. Dr. Andre Reichel and Dr. Bindeshwar Pathak — for mentorship, support and critical insights.

Thanks to the people who shared their inspirational stories of the SEV ventures written about in this book...

There are three different audiences I have tried to cater to in one book and hope you will find something for each of you. While the theory boxes may appeal to the more advanced researcher, the cases are for everyone who is learning and the worksheets for the practitioner. I wish you the very best in your journey to change the world to be a better place to live in.

# SOCIAL ENTERPRISE VENTURES: AN INTRODUCTION

## Chapter Objectives

➢ Justify the need for social entrepreneurs.

➢ Identify the gray areas and white spaces social entrepreneurs operate in.

➢ Explain the challenges that social entrepreneurs will face in the developmental sector.

➢ Define a social enterprise venture (SEV) and identify the boundary conditions for social entrepreneurship and its key assumptions.

➢ Give examples of types of social entrepreneurship ventures which have created scalable business models.

➢ Debate the importance of internationalization and its impact on social entrepreneurship.

➢ Identify impact areas that social entrepreneurs can operate in.

➢ **Cases:** White Helmets (emergency services: Syria), M-Pesa (mobile payment: Kenya), Aravind Eye Hospital (Healthcare: India), Narayana Hrudayalaya Hospital (Healthcare: India), Chid Liberty's L&J (Fair-trade certified clothing and handbags: Liberia), and TOMS (One for One model: USA).

## 1.1. Social Enterprise Ventures: Business with Purpose

A business or an organization with purpose looks at more than just profits and organizational objectives. A business with purpose is bold, making big bets, taking risks, learning from failure, reaching beyond the comfort zone, and most importantly letting urgency conquer fear.[1] There is nothing conventional in the challenges the world is facing and it requires unconventional organizations to create change. Global debt is at a record high. According to the International Institute of Finance (IIF), it hit US$255 trillion in first half of 2019.[2] This includes the debts of all governments, households, and financial and non-financial corporates. This is 320% of global gross domestic product (GDP). US and China accounted for 60% of this increase. To achieve the 17 sustainable development goals (SDGs) that the United Nations has outlined by 2030 is not an easy feat, as the predicted cost is US$3.9 trillion per year with an estimated gap of US$2.5 trillion.[3] This is a conservative estimate, by any standards.

Yet, there is money easily available in cash savings.[4,5] A recent IMF paper, consolidated the global value of assets under management in pension funds, insurance funds, mutual funds, sovereign wealth funds, private equity, as well as hedge funds, and concluded that there was enough money (US$922 trillion at the end of 2012) available to invest in long-term infrastructure projects.[6] Bain & Company in its report, *A World Awash in Money*, estimates that the size of global capital markets will be US$900 trillion by 2020.[7] This will mean that the value of total capital will be 10 times the total global output of goods and services and three times the base of non-financial assets — highlighting the huge potential role of this sector in financing the SDGs. Jeffery Sachs highlights that war, violence, conflict (security and military spending), and loss of lives cost the world US$15 trillion in 2017, but the cost of achieving SDGS would, by some estimates, only be US$3–4 trillion a year.[8]

We are living in a crisis-prone world. What the developmental sector needs now more than ever is endurance. Haiti is a great example. When the earthquake hit Haiti in 2010, the UN was on the forefront of a life-saving mission, but unknown at that time, some of the UN troops accidently introduced the cholera virus into the Haiti ecosystem. Haiti, along with the international aid and medical organizations operating at that time, were not prepared for this situation, leading to a cholera epidemic. This led to an estimated death count of over 30,000 people, compounding the humanitarian crisis. There were other immediate and subsequent global crises that the UN needed to focus on, and it took them 6 years to acknowledge responsibility for the additional crisis introduced to the fragile Haiti ecosystem. This complex issue highlights the fact that the problem was not about the urgent need for help that was vital, nor that the subsequent events could have been foreseen, and hence avoided (hindsight is always easy), but that all crises call for drastic intervention and an ability to stay and help long term till the system stabilizes. This is one of the main shortcomings of the humanitarian sector and the development sector today. There is a simple reason behind this — resource scarcity and lack of interconnectedness.

The humanitarian sector and the development sector today often run out of funding. To make choices on which humanitarian crisis to focus on, for example, feeding those starving in Somalia or the refugees from Syria or invest in prevention or containment of Ebola, should not be a choice at all. All should be equally important, but we don't seem to have the capacity to focus on all of them, even if we do have the resources to manage our combined efforts. To achieve the SDGs, we need innovative funding, we need the private sector to work with the public sector, and we need entrepreneurial mind-sets to find solutions.

Another shortcoming of the humanitarian sector and the development sector today is the lack of interconnectedness with like-minded organizations necessary for the supply chain, power brokers, and resources. This is highlighted by the refugee migration and asylum challenge in Europe. In 2015, the EU saw 1 million refugees and migrants cross EU borders. It was estimated that one-third of the arriving refugees were children and 17% were women. While humanitarian assistance is short term, and emergency based, the impact of the efforts can only be felt when you consider working with the developmental sector to achieve SDGs. There is a thin line between humanitarian relief and long-term developmental work.[9] In this book, we look at what a social enterprise venture (SEV) is, the ecosystem it operates in, its lifecycle, dynamics that support it, and finally the measurement of impact of a social enterprise.

Further, there are other spillovers that must be considered, like harmonizing integration, utilizing potential human capital amid the rise of right-wing extremist, and creating solidarity among member states with the Brexit Leave Campaign, for example, to name a few issues.

Social entrepreneurs who run SEVs lie between the continuum of for-profit entrepreneurs with some purpose and non-profit organizations. Non-profits can be direct service organizations, intermediary or capacity-building organizations, or policy or advocacy organizations or foundations that provide financial and technical resources to non-profits.[10] Much of the academic and public debate on what is a social enterprise centers around the adequacy of the social motives of *Profit with Purpose* or *Purpose with Provisions* organizations. At the simplest level, a social entrepreneur engages in *entrepreneurial activity with an embedded social purpose*.[11] SEVs can be mapped across a combination of value creation (*for* social mission versus *with* social mission) and the other value monetization (funds *required for* social mission versus social mission *generates* funds) (see Exhibit 1.1).[12]

Exhibit 1.1: **Social Enterprise Hybrid Spectrum**

| **Purely philanthropic** | **Social enterprise venture** | **Purely commercial** |
|---|---|---|
| Social value | Social and economic value | Economic value |
| Mission driven | Market and mission driven | Market driven |
| Appeal to goodwill | Mixed motives | Self-interest |

*Source*: Adapted from Dees.[13]

Iman Bibars, Regional Director of Ashoka Arab World[14] identifies three types of for-profit models being used interchangeably with social entrepreneurship. The first is called *Business with a Heart*, which is, according to her, a for-profit organization with a strong CSR component. The second is a *Social Business* where the primary purpose is making money but at the same time contributing to the community, which is an integrated by-product of the business. The third category, *Inclusive Business*, also has a primary focus on making money, but the business model is structured to embed community members that maybe marginalized — by employing the deaf or blind, for example. Further, there are other spillovers that must be considered, like harmonizing integration, utilizing potential human capital amid the rise of right-wing extremist, and creating solidarity among member states with the Brexit leave campaign, for example, to name a few issues.

Zahra *et al.*[15] identify three types of social entrepreneurs: *Social bricoleur, social constructionists,* and the *social engineer.* The *social bricoleur* typically acts at a local level solving local issues and works with a lean resource problem-solving approach. The *social constructionist* identifies, builds, launches, and operates a business model at a larger market scale (local, regional, and even international), by leveraging opportunities or exploiting "market failures" through the development of products and services, using collaborative methods with key stakeholders to address social needs that governments, agencies, and businesses cannot. Last is the *social engineer,* who operates at a national to international level, challenging existing social structures and bringing about revolutionary change, which means creating legitimacy for long-term success. The Dalberg Global Development Advisors report for the Asian Bank looks at three criteria for classification of social enterprises. The criteria are social impact (looking also at scalability in terms of reach and/or depth), financial viability (can the business fund operations on the revenues it generates), and bankability (can the business generate favorable returns to investors).[16] This report estimates that social enterprises are less than 3% of total registered companies/organizations.

Ideally, SEVs are organizations that are run using business principles and stakeholder accountability, they have a strong social mission, should generate sufficient funds to survive or ideally are self-financing, and will reinvest the profits into the social cause. There is always a debate on how much profit generated for the cause should be deemed enough to classify an organization as a social enterprise. Exhibit 1.2 presents the range of businesses that can lie in the spectrum of social enterprises.

Exhibit 1.2: **Social Enterprise Spectrum**

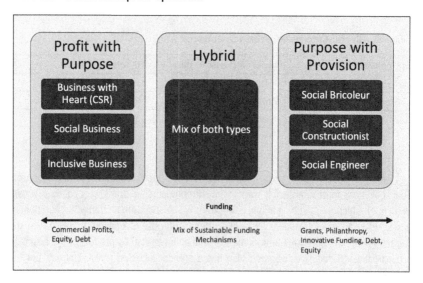

There have been several meta-analyses in the field of social entrepreneurship. Hill *et al.*[17] looked at 465 articles on the topic published between 1968 and 2007 and found that only 212 scholarly articles explored the topic from a theoretical point of view. They conclude that social dislocation in technological, social, political, institutional, and economic infrastructure creates opportunity for new ventures though their local knowledge and social networks. Short *et al.*[18] conducted a meta-analysis of 152 academic articles on social entrepreneurship spanning 20 years, published in the *Strategic Entrepreneurship Journal*, and found that social entrepreneurship research remains in an embryonic state because the conceptual articles outnumber empirical studies, and empirical efforts often lack formal hypotheses and rigorous methods. Both papers cite the overwhelming number of qualitative case studies being presented. Part of the challenge lies in the fact that social entrepreneurs theoretically intersect three fields of study — non-profit/public management, commercial entrepreneurship, and social issues in management[18] — at the very least.

A social entrepreneur must be able to embrace both business and non-profit values, and work with both a commercial and public mind-set. They must have a variety of traits as highlighted in Exhibit 1.3. This diagram explores the boundary and exchange conditions for a successful social entrepreneur. Overall, they must be risk-takers, see the big picture, solve problems, and manage stakeholders. At a more detailed level, they must be able to focus on value creation versus value appropriation, empower people and communities, develop a business model that is replicable, scale a business, find sustainable financing, and as a change maker, they must be able to measure impact for their targeted beneficiaries and the communities of operation. All this needs to be done while embedding good governance in operations (see Exhibit 1.4).

Exhibit 1.3: **What is a Social Entrepreneur? Boundary and Exchange Conditions**

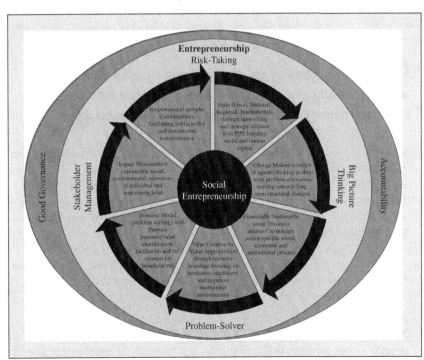

*Source:* Compiled from Santos,[20] Bibars,[21] Desa,[22] Hill *et al.*,[23] and Zahra *et al.*[24]

Gives a definition of an SEV adapted by the proposed conceptual framework suggested by a meta-analysis study by Hossain *et al.*[19]

Exhibit 1.4: **Definition of Social Enterprise Venture**

SEV is defined as an organization, initiative, or start-up that has a strong social innovation characteristic focusing on a scalable and sustainable social wealth creation or sustainable living at the individual or community level; the SEV is entrepreneurial in solving problems at an organizational, community, market, and policy level — using innovation in the space it operates, whether products or services, resource management, systems and processes development or collaborative partnership management, focusing on positive impact for all its stakeholders, using good governance principles and transparency in motives.

## 1.2. **Gray Areas and White Spaces Social Entrepreneurs Operate In**

As a concept, social entrepreneurship is not new. The topic developed in response to the inability of any one of the players like civil society, state, religious orders, market, and international aid to solve public and society problems.[25] Motives often were a guise for soft power. The concept of soft power has formally been around since the 1990s when Joseph Nye published his book *Bound to Lead: The Changing Nature of American Power.* Nye described soft power as follow:

> ❝ When one country gets other countries to want what it wants... might be called co-optive or soft power in contrast with the hard or command power of ordering others to do what it wants. ❞[26]

Development aid has been used as a channel of soft power not just for governments but also for multinational corporations (MNCs), often being routed through civil society organizations (CSOs), of which non-profit organizations (NGOs) are a subset (see Exhibit 1.5). In 2015, the UK took a strategic decision to invest £85 million, much of it coming from the Official Development Aid (ODA) budget, in the BBC World Service, focusing on supporting initiatives in Russia, North Korea, the Middle East, and Africa.[27] BBC in many ways, is the voice of the UK and its foreign office. In 2014, one in seven of the then current world leaders had studied in the UK.[28] The reach of BBC and the British influence is high, as according to the 2016 Portland Soft Power 30 Index, UK ranks number two (trailing USA before the Trump Administration came to power).[29] The British Council report describes soft power as follows:

> ❝ A country's soft power is its ability to make friends and influence people — not through military might, but through its most attractive assets notably culture, education, language and values. In short, it

**is the things that make people love a country rather than fear it; things that are often the products of people, institutions and brands rather than governments. 〞**[30]

Exhibit 1.5: **Why is Developmental Aid Important?**

ODA can be classified into two types: developmental and non-developmental aid. Development aid can be defined as "aid expended in a manner that is anticipated to promote development, whether achieved through economic growth or other means".[31] Non-development aid does not necessarily promote development or involves a grant element of less than 25%.[32] Of the two types, Minoiu and Reddy[33] find that developmental aid promotes long-run growth — usually with a time lag of 15 years. Clemens *et al.*[34] find that a US$1 increase in short-impact aid raises income, on average, by US$1.64 (in present value) for aid allocated to supporting budgets and balance of payments commitments, infrastructure investments, agriculture, and industry. With the increasing number of disasters, as of October 2018, high-income countries can apply for ODA if the economy falls below the World Bank threshold due to disaster.

Soft power has been considered as both the savior and a foe in the developmental space. Take for example, Kenya, a remarkable country, often described as the cradle of humanity with its civilization being dated back to 3.3 million BC. Aid has been flowing into Kenya for a long time. While it is erratic, it currently forms a small percentage of overall ODA (3–5%), with about 70% being derived from bilateral donors in the form of grants, of which 60% is directly funneled into projects rather than through the exchequer system.[35,36] The many years in which aid has been channeled into development projects has resulted in a country with aid impact fragmentation and a deep suspicion of the hidden agenda of aid organizations. In Kenya, a 1% increase in aid unpredictability decreases economic growth by 0.7% according to a study by Ojiambo *et al.*[37] In 2014, Kenya had 9,728 registered NGOs but only 7,258 were active.[38] This deep concern about NGOs and their impact was captured in 2013, by a mockumentary on the NGO sector called the "Samaritans". This concern about operational motives, transparency of agenda, and capability extends to the CSOs too.

CSOs are defined as voluntary organizations with governance and direction coming from citizens or constituency members, without significant government-controlled participation or representation.[39] NGO is sometimes used interchangeably with "CSO", but NGOs should be properly understood as a subset of CSOs involved in development cooperation, albeit often one with no clear boundaries. Constituency-based organizations, such as trade unions or professional associations, for example, often do not self-identify as NGOs, but rather as CSOs.[39] Intergovernmental organizations (IGOs) are a special category composed primarily of sovereign states, or of other intergovernmental organizations, and are established by treaty or other agreements that act as a charter for creating the group. Examples include the United

Nations, the World Bank, or the European Union.[40] IGOs are different from NGOs as IGOs are within governmental scope and NGOs are normally private organizations though they can receive funding from governments.

For Liberia, ODA in 2011 was US$765 million according to OECD, which at that time was 73% of its gross national income. Much of the aid is earmarked for education, but in 2013, of the 25,000 students who took the entrance exam for the University of Liberia, all failed, highlighting the questionable impact of aid on education.[41,42] The angst at the inadequacies of the NGO sector and visible inequalities of the privileged expats and local employees is resulting in a backlash across Africa. Kenya now insists that one-third of all Board members in foreign-based NGOs must be Kenyan, Uganda has made it difficult to hire foreigners, and Ethiopia does not allow more than 10% of NGO funds to come from abroad.[43]

> 🍀 **Social Entrepreneurs often operate in gray areas of neglect and failure: between government jurisdiction, public welfare, and private business enterprise. Sometimes, these are white spaces — "a place where a company might have room to maneuver in a crowded playing field. 🍀**[44]

The world as we know it, is a place with serious problems. In 2018 alone, there were 850 recorded natural disasters, which left 10,400 people dead, and caused up to US$160 billion of economic damage.[45] According to the 2017 report by the Business & Sustainable Development Commission, the top two global burdens — violence and armed conflict (9.1%), and biodiversity and ecosystem (3.1%) impact — had a combined economic shock of 12.2% of 2014 GDP.[46]

According to The UN Refugee Agency, in 2019, there were 70.8 million people, who were displaced from their homes by conflict and persecution.[47] This is the largest displacement in the history of mankind, four times that of a decade earlier. Take the extreme case of Syria, where the exacerbated civil war has resulted in a displaced population of over 6.5 million within the country, with an estimated 9 million people leaving the country leaving many children out of school, for over 6 years.[48] There is a total breakdown in the country, out of the reach of even humanitarian aid. The UN Under-Secretary-General Stephen O'Brien said, "*We continue to be blocked at every turn, by lack of approvals at central and local levels, disagreements on access routes, and violation of agreed procedures at checkpoints by parties to the conflict.*"[49]

Citizens for Syria, a CSO established in Berlin, mapped the CSOs working in Syria.[50] In the first phase, they identified over 800 CSOs (excluding social media projects that were in excess of 3000 Facebook pages). The key domains of operation were as follows: "Relief", "Media", "Civil and Advocacy Organizations", "Development", "Health", and "Education and Research" followed by others domains like "Social Services", "Human Rights", and "Culture and Arts" in that order. Protracted refugee situations lead to longer repatriation times — which is on an average, 17 years.[51] We need to rethink our global strategy about conflict zones and the people trapped in these situations (see Case Study 1.1). Articulating a long-term resolution to the crisis seems oxymoronic, but besides being given life-saving basic necessities and getting

## Case Study 1.1: **White Helmets**

White Helmets (or the Syrian Civil Defence) is a group of volunteers from all walks of life, operating in war-torn areas in Syria and Turkey. They were operating in 2012 as a group of civilians responding to emergency situations of evacuation in areas subject to repeated bombing. In 2013, they received a boost when UK, Denmark, and Japan began funding them. Selected groups were sent to Turkey, where an international contracting firm, ARK, trained the civilians using props representing downtown Aleppo and information culled from 1947 British manuals written to save Londoners from air raids. Initially, the equipment was primitive battery-powered hand tools, but as funding increased, their equipment became more modern — seismic listening devices, ambulances, fire engines, and hydraulic tools. These were much needed equipment, necessary to operate in the harsh and dangerous conditions of the civil war in Syria.

Raed al-Saleh is the founder of the White Helmets. Before the Syrian uprising, he was an electrical supplies salesman. He says their moto is *to save one life is to save humanity*. White Helmets were formalized as an organization in 2014. They operate with a strict code of conduct — no guns, strict neutrality, and no sectarianism — and then, after training, volunteers are given a white uniform and helmet and sent on their first mission. As of 2017, they had over 3,000 volunteers and were said to have rescued over 80,000 people. They have a funding of US$30 million from various donors, and each volunteer receives a stipend of US$150 per month. It is estimated that one in six of these volunteers have been killed or badly wounded, and in many cases by the "double-tap", a second wave of Russian and Syrian airstrikes, which occurs on the same site as volunteers frantically searched for survivors and bodies. White Helmets were nominated for the 2016 Nobel Peace Prize. That year, the prize was awarded to Juan Manuel Santos, President of Columbia.

Angelina Jolie said in her speech to the UN Security Council in 2015, "*We cannot look at Syria, and the evil that has arisen from the ashes of indecision, and think this is not the lowest point in the world's inability to protect and defend the innocent*". Raed, in his 2015 address to the UN Security Council said, "*Ladies and Gentlemen, what do you expect a simple Syrian citizen like me to ask from this council? Do we ask for more ambulances that the Syrian Regime will soon destroy anyway? Do we ask for more digging tools to recover bodies and limbs and bury them? Or do we ask for new resolutions condemning these acts to be added to the previous list of resolutions that you've signed, while some of you are still supporting the Syrian Regime politically, materially and militarily, including with spare parts for the aircraft used to drop these barrel bombs and kill more Syrians? The international community has lost its credibility for Syrians in the absence of any political will to end the killing in Syria, and the UN Security Council has been transformed from the Security to the Insecurity Council in the eyes of the downtrodden because it has failed to uphold its own resolutions.*" Syria still remains an unresolved issue in 2019.

equipped with lifesaving equipment and medical aid, they need psychological support, and need to rebuild their lives again through infrastructure support and education and retraining for their livelihoods.

The attainment of the SDGs is no guarantee for sustainability. The graph (see Exhibit 1.6) maps the United Nations Human Development Index (HDI) which measures a country's average achievements in the areas of health, knowledge, and standard of living against each country's ecological footprint. Ideally, an HDI higher than 0.8 is considered "very high human development" and an ecological footprint of less than 1.7 global hectares per person is advisable. Most countries have a long way to go — indicating a huge area for further development. This includes "developed" countries. There should be a symbiotic relationship between humans and the environment they live in. How do we manage both? At what pace of development and where does a consumption society figure? The same debate applies if the society is dependent on profits from companies or resources like oil wealth. When do the "global" needs outweigh the "country" or "regional" needs? These are negotiated positions. There is a trend to focus on the triple bottom line in the corporate sector, but this concept is itself evolving (see Exhibit 1.7).

Exhibit 1.6:  **Ecological Footprint per Person and HDI with SDGI Ranking**

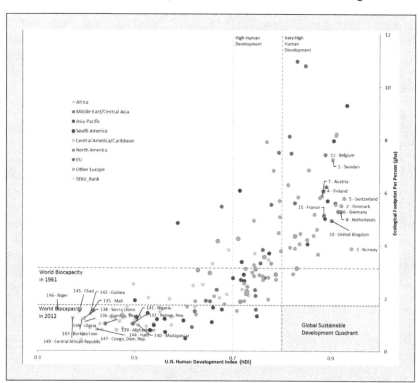

*Source*: http://www.footprintnetwork.org/content/images/efhdisdgi.jpg

Exhibit 1.7: **Theory Synopsis on Sustainable Development**

In addition to the discussion of the sustainability agenda which focuses on economy, environment, and society, there needs to be a reframed approach, moving away from the traditional approaches shown in Figures A and B. According to Giddings *et al.*,[52] we need to break down the boundaries between the three and embed human activity and well-being as central, in the context of the environment (Figure C).

Figure A   Common three-ring view

Figure B   Nested sustainable development

Further adapting from Haughton,[53] we should be focusing on the following five equity principles: (i) futurity — inter-generational equity; (ii) social justice — intra-generational equity; (iii) transfrontier responsibility — geographical equity; (iv) procedural equity — people treated openly and fairly; and (v) inter-species equity — importance of biodiversity.

Figure C   Breaking down boundaries

*Source*: Giddings *et al.* (see Footnote 54).

## 1.3. **Do Good and Do Good Well: Finding the Balance**

Consider the accidental negative impact of doing good. Douglas Durst says, "The road to poverty is paved with good intensions."[54] Kenya in the past, like much of Africa, has been the recipient of the West through donated secondhand goods. Kenya imports close to 100,000 tons of secondhand clothes or *mitumba* (bundles wrapped in plastic), shoes, and accessories per year — most of which were donated to charity shops in the west.[55] Changes in trade agreements, followed by years of charitable "dumping" of clothes from USA and Europe resulted in a lucrative secondhand clothes market. Because the prices were so affordable, the local textile retailers, especially those producing local textiles like *khanga* and *kitenge*, were unable to be competitive and soon ran out of business.[56] This resulted in the cotton mills closing down as they could not supply textiles manufacturers. This led to the cotton farmers losing their livelihood.[57] This is a problem not only for Kenya, but for Africa, as 70% of donated clothes end up in Africa. The problem was that well-meaning charity givers were not thinking of the future implications on the recipients and about creating sustainable livelihoods. I was asked a question by a school child in rural Kenya in 2015, about why they needed to wear western clothes to school and were the local clothes not good enough. We need to do good but do good well. This can be done with a little bit of foresight and the power of public private partnerships (PPP) (for example, see Case Study 1.2). Jacqueline Novogratz, the Founder and CEO of Acumen said,

**❝ Today's world needs more than humanitarians. We need individuals who know to listen and who have real and tangible skills to share. We will succeed only if we fuse a very hardheaded analysis with an equally soft heart. ❞[58]**

Case Study 1.2: **M-Pesa**

In 2000, UK's Department for International Development began the Financial Deepening Challenge Fund. Its purpose was to encourage private sector-led projects to improve access to financial services in markets where the uncertainty of the outcome made it impossible to make a business case to invest alone. Vodafone which owned a 60% share of Kenya's Safaricom was awarded a grant of approximately £1 million (of which they were required to match the amount) to begin developing a product that would leverage mobile phone technology to help deliver financial services in East Africa. In 2005, a pilot of M-Pesa was ready to be rolled out. It was a collaboration among Safaricom, Vodafone, the Commercial Bank of Africa, Faulu Kenya — a Kenyan microfinance program — FSD-Kenya, and MicroSave. The final product was introduced in March 2007 with a focus on the product "Send Money Home". In less than a year, they acquired 2 million customers in Kenya. By 2015, there were 19.9 million M-Pesa active users, with over 237 million person-to-person transactions, an increase of 18% from 2013 to 2014, and more importantly 43% of Kenya's GDP was estimated to flow through M-Pesa. While this project began as a private public partnership (PPP), it is now a profitable enterprise for Safaricom, and revolutionizing mobile financial services at the grassroots levels.

**❝** Social Entrepreneurs need to operate with a public–private partnership model mind-set and must think of possible reach (scale of business). Technology is a key driver in achieving scale as it can document impact, monitor change, and reduce costs. **❞**

In 2015, India had over 3.1 million NGOs and as one newspaper report put it, "more than double the number of schools in the country, 250 times the number of government hospitals, one NGO for 400 people as against one policeman for 709 people".[59] Take Indian healthcare, for example, where the government contributes to 30% of the total country's health expenditure[60] and foreign aid contributes 1.6% of India's total healthcare spend.[61] In 2014, India had the largest number of unimmunized children in the world, equaling 6.8 million or roughly a third of the world's total.[62] Even by 2015, less than 20% of the total Indian population was covered by health insurance, with 80% of the out-of-pocket expenditure being in rural India, mostly being spent on medicine.[63] Reducing the cost of healthcare is an area of key consideration for social entrepreneurs working in this field. The Aravind Eye Hospital (see Case Study 1.3) and Dr. Devi Shetty's Narayana Hrudayalaya Hospital (see Case Study 1.4) have revolutionized cataract and cardiac surgery, by using assembly-line surgery models and frugal supply chain systems to bring down costs. Using differential pricing, where the poor pay close to nothing, these organizations are able to deliver global healthcare standards. Frugal innovation and Jugaad innovation are concepts that are being embraced worldwide (see Exhibit 1.8).[64] Social entrepreneurs are working in areas where few multinational corporations (MNCs) have wanted to go because the margins are so slim. There are many such cases that will be highlighted in this book.

Exhibit 1.8:  **Theory Synopsis Jugaad versus Frugal Innovation**

*Jugaad* as a concept has existed in the Indian subcontinent and across the world as *gambiarra* or *jeitinho* in Brazil, *jua kali* in Kenya, *zhizhu changxin* in China, *Made in Jinjira* in Bangladesh, *DIY* (do-it-yourself) or *hacking* in USA, or *Systeme D* in France.[65] It was popularized by the book *Jugaad innovation: Think frugal, be flexible, generate breakthrough growth*[66] and refers to the frugal, flexible, and inclusive approach to innovation and entrepreneurship[66] and uses creative improvisation.[67]

*Frugal innovation* focuses on the approach of taking the cost out of the entire innovation process, from the generation of ideas, to the development of products and services, to their commercialization, and is often perceived as a functional adaptation strategy to scarce resources. It can be defined as *means and ends to do more with less for more people.*[68] While both concepts are similar, *jugaad* innovation is perhaps broader in concept and more applicable to social entrepreneurs.

When Ebola impacted West Africa in 2014 and posed a risk of a global pandemic, the world was unprepared. In Guinea, Liberia, and Sierra Leone, besides the 11,312 deaths, and the US$2.2 billion economic loss,[69] there was also an impact on health, education, and society. Regular

## Case Study 1.3: **Aravind Eye Hospital**

Dr. Govindappa Venkataswamy established the Aravind Eye Hospital in 1978. Almost 50% of its customers get treatment free as care is made available to those who cannot pay and for the rest they are given affordable eye care services. Cataract surgeries form 70% of all operations. Cataract is the leading cause of blindness in India. Aravind Eye Hospital uses a unique *assembly-line* setup where an average surgeon can do six to eight operations per hour, supported by a team of internally trained technicians. In

2015–2016, they performed 408,220 surgeries versus the global average of 500. Of these, 206,130 were paying, 86,325 were free, and the rest subsidized. Aravind Eye Hospital works with many women from villages, who haven't had the opportunity to go to college. They are trained in a two-year course and get an opportunity to work as mid-tier technicians or Mid-Level Ophthalmic Personnel. By end of 2016, it had trained 2,200 mid-tier technicians.

Normally, in eye surgeries, the cost of a surgery is 80% dependent on fixed costs, and by increasing the number of surgeries Aravind Eye Hospital was able to bring down the average cost of the surgery. It also pursued innovations to reduce the variable cost. In the 1990s, the cost of intraocular lens was still too high for the average Indian customer who could barely afford to pay US$10 for the lens. At that time, the market price of a lens was US$70. In 1992, it set up Arulab, a non-profit charitable trust that makes intraocular lenses and other ophthalmic consumables. Arulab was able to bring down the lens pricing to US$2, and by 2011 had a 7% share of the global intraocular lenses market covering over 120 countries.

Total direct and indirect cost for each cataract surgery procedure in 2013 was US$29.02, of which fixed cost was US$6.79 and variable cost was US$22.23. The largest variable cost categories were consumables at US$10.76 and direct labor at US$7.06. The surgeon's cost was US$2.25 and other labor costs were US$4.81. In USA, the direct ophthalmic medical costs are between US$2,653 and US$3,392 and surgeon fees alone are US$761 per surgery. Aravind has also created Vision Centers to increase access and Aravind Eye Banks.

vaccines were interrupted, and due to quarantine, 5 million children were denied school access.[70] Over 16,600 children lost both or one parent or a primary caregiver to the disease,[71] and the world is still unable to quantify the mental and social costs associated with the disease and its stigma. Social entrepreneurs like Chid Liberty from Liberia and his workers who owned 49% of the company were caught unprepared for Ebola. Chid says, *Ebola was not in our business plan* (see Case Study 1.5).

## Case Study 1.4: **Narayana Hrudayalaya Limited**

Dr. Devi Shetty is known as the Henry Ford of cardiac surgery. Dr. Shetty founded the Narayana Hrudayalaya in 2001, with the motto *None shall be turned away because they can't pay.* He approached the Indian market to fill a gap. He says that India needs about 2 million cardiac surgeries a year and only 130,000–140,000 were being performed by all the hospitals. Dr. Shetty estimates that 12% of all cardiac surgeries are done in his hospitals, which allows them economies of scale in purchasing supplies. This is around 35 major heart surgeries a day, considered one of the largest number of heart surgeries in the world.

The cost of an average surgery was above an average Indian's price range. Dr. Shetty directly negotiates with suppliers to bring down costs and in some cases, uses frugal innovation to reduce the prices. In 2002, Narayana Hrudayalaya worked with the Indian Space Research organization's (ISRO) Karnataka Telemedicine Project to help connect rural health centers via the INSAT satellites with urban super specialty hospitals for medical consultations and treatment. Narayana Hrudayalaya used telecardiology consultations and this brought down the cost for rural patients. They tied up with Texas Instruments to reduce the cost of X-rays taken in a government hospital, which were essential for diagnoses, switching to digital X-ray, and producing affordable digital X-ray plates — costing about INR 37,000 apiece. By 2012, they had treated over 53,000 heart patients, becoming the world's largest telemedicine program. By these methods and creating a unique assembly-line process, Dr. Shetty has brought down the price of a cardiac surgery.

The poor are treated on a charity basis. The payment model is called the sliding scale payment model which allows multiple price points based on the customer/beneficiaries' circumstance. In the case of the hospital which has a world-class reputation, over 60% of the patients are rich who subsidize the cost of the poorer patients. In 1989, the cost of a cardiac surgery in India was INR 140,000 but by 2010 using these methods, he was able to bring it down to INR 75,000 (around US$800–2000 compared to USA where the cost is over US$100,000).

The company, Narayana Hrudayalaya Limited, went public in 2016 and was valued at US$1 billion. According to Dr. Shetty, this movement in India is the beginning of the removal of affluence as a determinant of access to quality healthcare. In 2003, Dr. Shetty also designed a comprehensive insurance scheme called Yeshasvini Co-operative Farmer's Health Care Scheme, which for an annual premium of INR 60 (US$1.50) provides cover to poor farmers for over 1,600 surgical procedures.

By 2019, Narayana Health had 23 hospitals across India, was running a profit of US$8 mn in 2017 with affordable prices and international care. An endoscopy cost was US$14, a lung transplant US$7000 and heart transplant US$11,000.

Case Study 1.5:
## Chid Liberty's L&J: Ebola was not in Our Business Plan

Chid Liberty is the co-founder and CEO of Liberty & Justice (L&J), a fair–trade-certified apparel manufacturer based in Liberia. Liberia's 14-year civil war ended in 2003, but economic revitalization is slow. L&J began in 2009 but was registered in 2010. Their clients included brands like PrAna, FEED Projects, Haggar, and other large buyers in the U.S. Their factory was in Monrovia, Liberia. Their workers were paid a 20% higher wage than their peers. The workers own a 49% stake in the company and the company's stake was directed into community development. An amount equivalent to 2–10% of sales proceeds is channeled into a fund managed by the workers, and it has led to the construction of a school for some 200 students. L&J hired women, and that too a larger number of older women than most others companies. This required that they invest in training so that the women learnt the trade. In 2012, Chid expanded into Ghana. By 2014, he had planned a goal of employing 700 employees in Ghana and 500 in Liberia.

By early March 2014, Ebola broke out in Liberia. At the time, Liberia had a total of about 50 doctors and 5,000 full-time and part-time health workers for its population of 4.3 million people. The medical staff was first to be hit resulting in the few hospitals closing down. By July 2014, Liberia had closed most of its borders. By August 2014, Liberia declared a state of emergency in the place where the L&J factory was based and most of the 303 workers lived. Chid had just built a new factory to make uniforms, based on orders from contracts worth US$40 million, but with the Ebola outbreak no one wanted the products. They were ready to ship their first half a million orders out but instead had to shut the factory. They flew out every expat as no one knew how long the crisis would last. It is estimated that Ebola has cost Liberia, Sierra Leone, and Guinea more than US$2 billion over 2014–2015.

All employees were safe and well but there were no more orders. Chid knew the market potential in Liberia for school uniforms was huge. He estimates it was a US$5 million market and could be three times that size if every child went to school. Liberian parents did not have money to pay for uniforms. By May 2015, Liberia was declared Ebola free but still no one wanted to place orders yet.

Chid began researching and came up with a 45-day Kickstarter campaign that was launched on June 2, 2015 for his product UNIFORM, which used a "one-for-one" model. A longitudinal study in Kenya (Evans *et al.* 2009) found that donating school uniforms decreased absenteeism and increased test scores. Chid sold T-shirts on Kickstarter directly to customers for prices between US$48 and US$28 and donated US$5–10 for manufacturing school uniforms. The result was that he sold US$50,000 worth of T-shirts in the first 5 hours. He eventually raised a total of US$230,059 through 1,360 backers, and was able to put 8,000 kids back to school. He was also able to pay the wages of the women who worked in his factory, 98% of whom are mothers.

**❻** In a recent AT Kearney report titled Scaling Up: Catalyzing the Social Enterprise, it was found that social enterprises in the UK, for example, contributed up to 2% of the country's GDP and in the USA, it was 3–5% of the GDP. A paper by the British Council predicts that "by 2020 almost all charities and associations will be somewhere on the "social enterprise spectrum" — generating some if not all of their income through trading activities .... simply claiming to be doing good work will no longer be enough. Social enterprise will cease to be a label behind which to hide poor businesses. But equally the best social enterprises will deliver a better social return on investment than the best for-profit, public or charitable association. By generating an income and yet prioritising social over financial returns the best social enterprises will provide outstanding examples of what positive social impact really means. **❼**[72]

The *Better Business, Better World* report[73] looks at 12 global burdens and identifies a US$12 trillion market opportunity by 2030, linked to the four economic systems of food and agriculture; cities; energy and materials; and health and well-being, which are approximately 60% of the real economy and critical to delivering the SDG Global Goals. It is estimated that 50% of this value is located in developing countries. By including sectors like information communication technologies, education and consumer goods, a further US$8 trillion market opportunity can be opened up.[74] The value of achieving gender equality could contribute up to US$28 trillion to global GDP by 2025.[75] The opportunity value is translated in terms of employment — the creation of 380 million new jobs by 2030, with almost 90% of them in developing countries with affordable housing creating 70 million (20%) of these jobs. There is an opportunity to do good and be financially sustainable.

**❻** There is no alternative but to turn to social enterprises to fill the gap between governments at the national and international level and in areas like the development sector. However, the first key rule is "Do Good and Do Good Well. **❼**

## 1.4. Growing SEVs across the Border: What is Missing?

While impact can be at a local level and can be disruptive, research from international business shows that early internationalization of start-ups helps in scaling a business. While scalability has many meanings depending on the context, in this book, it refers to a business model that can grow (revenues and impact) by optimizing resources, using operation leverage, and with low marginal cost increase. Those organizations that internationalize during the start-up phase are called *born globals* or *international new ventures* and are narrowly characterized by entrepreneurship literature as those companies which exist in at least three continents, have between 25% and 75% of their sales revenue coming from outside their home base, and take at least a period of 2–6 years before going global.[76]

*Born globals* are rapidly increasing and by some estimates are 20% of the European Union (EU), benefiting the economy by fostering economic growth through innovation, creating resources of skills and knowledge, and enabling high-value-added activities.[77] There is negligible research on the internationalization of social ventures. First of all, the concept of scale may differ as working with disenfranchised communities means there is contextual adaption that cannot be easily replicable across three diverse continents. Second, sustainable development impact may take a longer period to be effective, more than that estimated for traditional for-profit start-ups. Third and most importantly, as returns are not always measured in terms of profits, the definition of *born globals* does not extend to SEVs.

In entrepreneurship literature, SME internationalization can be fostered by possession of specialized knowledge (especially for proprietary products, knowledge-intensive products, high-technology products, high-value products, and high-quality products). According to the EU, SMEs can be divided into three categories based on innovation: (1) technology developers (1–3% of the total SME population, smaller and younger companies), (2) leading technology users (10–15% of SMEs), and (3) technology followers (80–85% of the population).[78] How does this apply to social entrepreneurs who are rapidly adapting technology and are innovative in their own right? These are further areas of research.

The role of international networks has been linked to getting access to more resources[79] and it is well known that internationalizing of resources helps reduce risk. Impact can also be disseminated by leveraging strategic alliances.[80] While in the case of non-profits, the role of strategic alliances and working with public–private partnerships has been acknowledged, the research seems limited to cases studies.[81]

This book will explore how social entrepreneurs can use strategies to internationalize (Chapter 6) and will also present some benefits from research conducted on why they should internationalize and how it will differ from traditional SMEs.

**❰❰ SEV entrepreneurs who want to internationalize face many challenges: (1) geographic distance, (2) psychic distance, (3) finding synergies in local contexts, (4) resources optimization, (5) alliance and partner management, (6) managing media and fostering education, and (7) managing crisis at a more complex level. ❱❱**

## 1.5. Areas of Impact

The areas of impact a social entrepreneur may focus on are often influenced by his/her own personal passion, but they can be facilitated by the laws and regulations of the host country, observation of practical inefficiencies, or necessitated by the breakdown of existing systems and the need to create a coping strategy for the current situation. You can get inspiration for areas to work in by looking at SDGs. Each of the 17 SDG goals are further broken down into targets.[82] The Foundation

Center has created a taxonomy where grants are available which provides an exhaustive list of areas social entrepreneurs can work in.[83] You can get inspiration looking at the beneficiaries of non-profit organizations like Ashoka, Acumen, Endeavor, investment firms like Bamboo Finance, Echoing Green, The Unchartcd, Root Capital, Gray Ghost Ventures, and of course other impact investors.

Social entrepreneurs can work in areas of research, education, management, delivery, and control. They can work with people at the individual level or with groups at the community level or at a collective societal level locally, regionally, internationally, or globally. They can work with or through technologies, other organizations or governments. The field is very large (see Appendix 1). If you want to be a social entrepreneur and don't know where to start, begin with a passion point. This is something all entrepreneurs should ideally share.

Steve Jobs highlighted the need for passion with this quote

> 🕮 **There are many moments that are filled with despair and agony, when you have to fire people and cancel things and deal with very difficult situations . . . it's so hard (to build a company) that if you don't have a passion, you'll give up. 🕮**

While individual motives may be different, to build a scalable business you need to learn about the community and be unafraid to reach out to partners (see Case 1.6).

You need to be able to answer these simple questions as follows:

1. Who is being served — look at the lowest possible denominator (the individual) and aggregate it into a group (example, community, married women, etc.)?

2. What is the purpose of the organization? How is this articulated into your vision and culture?

3. Where will you start to test and fine tune your business model? What are the possible roadblocks?

4. How is the organization supported? What resources are necessary and have you evaluated the cost of those resources, how you will acquire them, and the cost of acquisition? What are some opportunities and market and structural synergies you can leverage?

5. Who is your start-up team — partners, employees, mentors, and advisers? What complementary knowledge and resources do they bring?

6. Where is the focus of the strategy? Your priority areas? What are areas you cannot afford to delegate and which you will have to make more time for — urgent priority areas?

7. Have you mapped your impact on stakeholders based on actions (conative), thinking (cognitive), or emotions (affective)? For more information on this topic, see Exhibit 1.9.

**Social or sustainable development impact has several characteristics: (1) it should be long term, (2) it should consider embedded context and be sensitive to the diversity of targeted beneficiaries, (3) it**

## Case Study 1.6: **TOMS**

TOMS's founder, Blake Mycoskie, is often credited with the *One for One* business model. Blake was traveling through Argentina at the end of 2005, to revisit the country and enjoy the culture. This was a place he had briefly stopped over during *The Amazing Race* competition in 2002. He took to wearing the local shoe, the *alpargata*. At the end of the trip, he met a woman in a Buenos Aires café who was working with volunteers to deliver donated shoes to poor children. Even in affluent places, there were pockets of poverty. She mentioned some of the challenges of the initiative. They were constrained by their supply, which was dependent on the donations of shoes. Even with a large stock of donated shoes, there was no guarantee that the donated shoes would be the right sizes for the children. Blake then went with them to donate shoes. He saw firsthand the joy of their actions and the sadness, when there was no shoe that could fit a child. This experience opened his eyes to the fact that many children in that country did not have shoes and hence were also unable to attend schools as it was a school requirement. He met two brothers who had one pair of shoes between them and hence took turns to attend school.

This was the inspiration for the logic behind TOMS, the logo he envisioned on February 26, 2006. TOMS stood for *Tomorrow's Shoes*, where Blake envisioned the concept where you buy one pair of shoes, and hence can donate a pair of shoes to a child in need. This removed the need for donations. He shared his vision with his polo instructor and his new friend, Alejo, who also helped him produce and source the shoes, initially working out of Alejo's family barn. Blake, who had no experience in this area, started working with local suppliers to produce prototypes of the traditional shoe made more acceptable for the American market. After US$5,000 and 3 months, Blake was ready for the next step.

With a sample of 250 shoes shoved into a few bags, he returned to USA. In Los Angeles, he showed the shoes to friends and eventually using their advice, approached retailers. One of the shoe buyers fell in love with the story behind TOMS, and placed their first order. A short time later an article ran in the *Los Angeles Times* on April 19, 2009. By the end of that day, his website went crazy, clocking 2,200 orders. The article by Booth Moore stated, "*The shoes — for men and women — come in more than a dozen colors, stripes and camouflage patterns, for just US$38. And for every pair purchased, the company will donate a pair to a village in South America or Africa. Go to www.tomsshoes.com.*" The challenge for Blake was that he had just 160 pairs left from his first sample stock. Blake had to scale-up production and creatively manage the shortfall in resources with his slim budget — stretching his working capital. When they reached a sale of 10,000, the initial TOMS team, family, and his intern went to Argentina for the first shoe drop which was at the end of the first year".

At the beginning, Blake thought of the initiative more as a project, not as a business. He feels the simplicity and unique design of the shoe, offered a moment for storytelling and helped promote the *One for One* model. By 2011, TOMS had an annual growth of 300%, with direct-to-consumer sales via the website accounting for one-third of the sales. Most of their promotion came from their 5 million social media followers who created strong positive word of mouth. Blake credits a lot of his growth to the success of storytelling. In his book, he retells the story of how AT&T became a great ally.

He also says growth came because he thought in incremental steps, testing his way and constantly seeking advice.

In 2014, Blake sold 50% of TOMS to Bain Capital. At that time, TOMS was estimated to be valued at US$625 million. He said at that time, "*I was CEO by default, but I never was a CEO. I mean I'm a founder, I love the beginning of things. I love working with the creative team, but running a business, dealing a lot with HR, dealing a lot with processes, that's never really been my strength. Once I was in a position where I could bring on and attract world-class CEO talent, like Jim, our CEO, I was super excited to do so.* He said in another interview, *I learned being a great CEO and being a great founder are two different things and I was better suited to being a founder. Being a CEO requires much more present management of people, whereas I prefer to give people space, and to have lots of space.*" After the new injection of funds, and the hiring of a new CEO, Blake said of his mission, "*We thought that "One for One" was why we do what we do, but we realized that it is just what we do.*" He says, "*The "why" of our mission is that we care for one another*". He realized his social entrepreneurship model could be broader and in 2015 ran a campaign *For One, Another*, to highlight their movement and their 100+ giving partners. In 2017, they went back to their *One for One* slogan. By 2017, TOMS products were available in over 70 countries.

In 2013, TOMs began producing one-third of their Giving Shoes in places like Ethiopia, Vietnam, India, and Kenya to create jobs and reduce their carbon footprint. They had created 700 jobs by 2017 in the countries they were donating to. TOMS has also been diversifying their product offering since 2006. Some statistics given on their website as of August 2017 show the following: since 2006, 60 million pairs of shoes have been given to children; since 2011, TOMS Eyewear restored sight to over 400,000 people; since 2014, TOMS Roasting Company provided over 335,000 weeks of safe water; and since 2015, TOMS Bag Collection supported safe birth services for over 25,000 mothers.

Blake has now created a US$150 million social ventures fund called Toms Social Entrepreneurship Fund (more: http://www.toms.com/social-entrepreneurship-fund). It was an early investor in Andela which attracted a Series A funding round from Spark Capital and a US$24 million Series B funding round led by the Chan Zuckerberg Initiative. The success of TOMS has spawned a host of *One for One* imitated and adapted business models.

Exhibit 1.9:  **Theory Synopsis — Attitudes and Social Impact**

Attitudes are defined as a response of a general and enduring positive or negative feeling toward or about the object of that attitude which could be, for example, some person, place, object, idea, or issue.[84] There are three types of attitudes first conceptualized by Allport[78]: conative, cognitive, and affective attitudes.[85] These terms are used across various types of studies from consumer behavior, learning, health, and entrepreneurship disciplines. Attitude is important as a concept as it has been found to be linked to self-interests, social identification, and value relevance, suggesting that if you want to change behaviors, you need to first link it to some pre-existing attitudes.[86]

Conative attitude (actions) or the behavioral component includes behavioral intentions and existing predispositions to behave in a given way toward the object.[87] Cognitive attitude consists of the subjective judgements based on beliefs, thoughts, and knowledge an individual has in his memory about an attitude object.[88] Affective attitude (emotions) can be defined as feelings associated with the object.[89] Morris *et al.* in their study, find that emotional response is a powerful predictor of intention and brand attitude.[90]

Attitudes can also be of two types (see Figure): implicit attitudes, which are affective reactions that are automatically triggered on encounter with a stimulus and don't require much cognition and need not be accurate, and explicit attitudes, which are evaluative judgements and focus on affirmation of validity.[91] This highlights the importance of understanding context or pre-existing biases and the associations relevant to the focus target group, to create social impact. Social impact theory can be defined as the influence (strength, immediacy, and number of sources) exerted on an individual's feelings, thoughts, or behavior by the real, implied, or imagined presence or actions of others.[92]

Figure:  Interplay of association in explicit and implicit reasoning

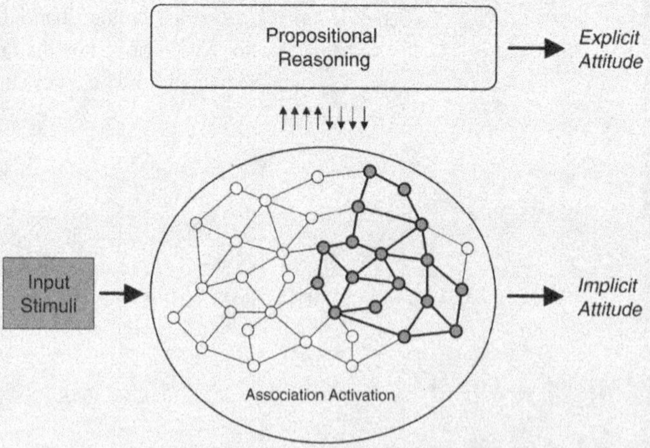

*Source:* Adapted from Gawronski and Bodenhausen.[93]

**should be monitored and evaluated often using lean data methods, (4) should be transparent, (5) should lead to the well-being of all involved, should ideally not hurt the environment, may involve structural changes at market, legal, economic, and technology levels, (6) needs acknowledgment that it is an iterative process, and (7) builds on partnerships.**

Social entrepreneurs can work with people at an individual level or a community level in a specific geographic area or across places. Social impact should not only change attitudes but behaviors as well. Ideally, investors in an SEV want quantifiable proof of change. As an entrepreneur working in sustainable development spaces, you need to have an accurate idea of the status before intervention and identify what factors or variables you will track. The information costs of acquisition, monitoring, and reporting are to be built into your operating model and cost structures.

The geographic areas of impact can be at the local, regional, national, international, or global level. The internet and rapid propagation of technology allows geographic areas to be compressed and far more easily accessed. Social entrepreneurs also have to build time commitments into their business models — by understanding realistically how long it will take to ensure impact takes place and for them to become self-sufficient. They need to assess how they want impact to take place and monitor and evaluate the adequacy of impact by their introduction of a portfolio of products and services (see Exhibit 1.10).

Exhibit 1.10:   **SEV Impact Areas**

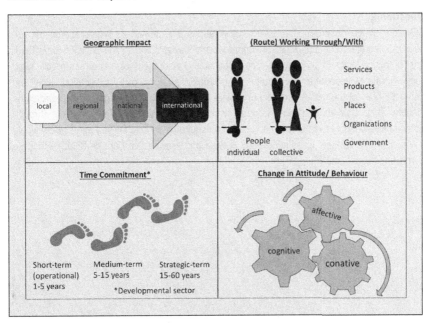

## 1.6. **The Way Ahead**

The journey of a social entrepreneur is a complex and difficult one. Good intentions will not help you scale and sometimes may hurt the beneficiaries and the cause you are trying to champion. This is why it is important to take a moment and think of strategy. Most books and literature available focus on for-profit entrepreneurs and this is beneficial. In this book, resources have been compiled from lesson learnt from for-profit, non-profit, and hybrid ventures. Chapter 2 helps you analyse the SEV ecosystem and find strategies to manage the multiple complex worlds that your cause may intersect. Chapter 3 goes through the stages of an SEV life cycle and presents strategies that an entrepreneur can use to help move across various stages. Chapter 4 helps you identify, build, and leverage your support system. An SEV founder needs all the help he or she can tap into. Chapter 5 helps you plan and manage your resources. Chapter 6 focuses on internationalization of an SEV and highlights the roles that brands, social innovation, and networks can play. Chapter 7 focuses on measuring impact and control and presents the Intervention Strategy Plan. Don't worry — SEVs are built on far less and the more equipped you are, the more likely you will succeed!

## 1.7. **Questions**

### Question 1

How would you define an SEV (see Section 1.4)? What are the existing gray areas of the definition that still exist today? Do you see a distinct need for social entrepreneurs? What happens between the two pillars of social and economic values? Why do we rely on two opposite ends of the spectrum to solve social and economic challenges?

### Question 2

SEVs are hybrid organizations. Hybrid organizations are defined as organizations that are able to integrate competing logics in unprecedented ways[94] and in the case of SEVs there are competing logics of social welfare or sustainable development logic and commercial logic. They sometimes become a movement — for example, Fair Trade or B-Certification. Jäger and Schröer[95] present the following model to explain the criteria for observing hybrid organizations' identity. They state that hybrid organizations create "functional solidarity" which, through communal solidarity is valued by the society, to acquire resources. Do you agree? How would you justify organizations or initiatives like M-Pesa and Aravind Eye Care or TOMS? What are competing logics? (see Table 1.1).

Table 1.1: **Competing Logics for a Hybrid Organization**

| Organizational identity dimensions | Fields of Hybrid organizations' identity | | |
| --- | --- | --- | --- |
| | Market identity | Hybrid identity | Civil society identity |
| Identification of individuals with organization | Organizational members' identity is to fulfill a function in society by acting primarily in their self-interest | Organizational member's identity is to execute a meaningful work | Organizational members' identity is to understand themselves to be a means to the higher goals of a collective |
| Structures that determine Organizational events | Organizational structures are part of markets as rational networks, which they use as a means for pursuing their goals | Organizational structures are dependent upon how valuable communal solidarity is to a society | Organizational structures are embedded in social networks |
| Practice of Organizational executives | Organizational actor's practice is to mobilize resources like volunteers, sponsors, donors, and others | Organizational actor's practice is to exchange solidarity for financial/ non- financial resources | Organizational actor's practice is to serve the public good |

*Source*: Adapted from Jäger and Schröer.[96]

## Question 3
Urban art and painting can create social impact. Listen to the TED talk of Haas&Hahn, *How painting can transform communities* (Available: https://www.ted.com/talks/haas_hahn_how_painting_can_transform_communities) and Edi Rama *Take back your city with paint* (https://www.ted.com/talks/edi_rama_take_back_your_city_with_paint). Would you call them social entrepreneurs? Why? Identify which SDGs these initiatives may fit in?

## Question 4
Take the case of the Lucky Iron Fish.[97] Read the article cited below (can be accessed from https://www.forbes.com/sites/robindschatz/2015/10/18/how-a-social-entrepreneur-overcame-his-arrogant-failure-and-won-kudos-from-oprah/). What are some of the gray areas that failing social entrepreneurs should watch out for? Why?

## Question 5
Do you see some challenges with the "Buy One and Give One" model? What are the gray areas? Look at organizations like The Body Shop before and after sale to L'Oréal in 2006 and then in 2017 to Natura Cosméticos and TOMS before and after partial sale to Bain Capital in 2014.

## Question 6
Look at the case study of White Helmets (Case Study 1.1), M-Pesa (Case Study 1.2), Liberty L&J Chid (Case Study 1.5), and TOMS (Case Study 1.6). Discuss whether you think SEV businesses differ from commercial business as researched by Shaw and Carter[98] who find differences in the following five areas:

(1) **Entrepreneurial process:** Similar to conventional entrepreneurs, social entrepreneurs focus on identifying and exploiting opportunities in the market, but unlike commercial entrepreneurs, they focus only on unmet social needs. However, unlike conventional entrepreneurs, social entrepreneurs must capture value in a two-stage process, first the beneficiary must realize the value and at the second stage, the perceived benefit must be converted to be realized by the indirect stakeholders or partners in the value delivery chain.

(2) **Network embeddedness:** For social entrepreneurs, this is an important activity as it is necessary to build relationships and gain trust and credibility with beneficiaries, patrons or investors, markets, and other key stakeholders. This activity allows them access to the local community and other key stakeholders, and gets the prerequisite knowledge and resources needed for success.

(3) **The nature of financial risk, reward, and profit:** Many social entrepreneurs are exposed to lower forms of their own financial risk as they use more diverse forms of funding. While this is unlike commercial entrepreneurs, social entrepreneurs also did not plan for long-term financial security. The often-unique environments where social entrepreneurs operate have no correlation between supply and demand functions and price of service (as beneficiaries are often unable or unwilling to pay for the service). This is the challenge over commercial entrepreneurs who first seek profits and then growth (though not always the case — see Uber).

(4) **The role of individual entrepreneurs in managing and structuring social enterprise:** Social entrepreneurs use a diversity of structures that are built around two focal points — local community and client beneficiaries — to build social value creation (social rents). This suggests that social entrepreneurship may be a collective rather than individual activity and the business structure, unlike the commercial start-up, does not revolve around the entrepreneur. They also have unique challenges for creating sustainable competitive advantage (SCA) or sustainable contributable advantage (SConA) — they need both value-creating and capturing strategies, as identified by Robb-Post et al.[99] "The heterogeneity of resources in place for a firm is the imperfect mobility of their resources. This allow ventures to keep their resources uniquely valuable to the firm. The additional cornerstones of ex post limits to competition (barriers in place after entering the market) and ex ante limits to competition (barriers in place prior to entering the market) speak to more of the external forces of the market".

(5) **Creativity and innovation:** It is assumed that social entrepreneurs may be more innovative than business entrepreneurs, particularly with regard to the management of their enterprises and the complexity of problems.

**Question 7**

Look at the various typologies of SEVs given in Exhibit 1.1 or 1.2. How would you classify TOMs, Unilever's Dove, Ben & Jerry's, and Grameen Bank?

**Question 8**

SEVs may need to address challenges like (1) beneficiary's inability or unwillingness to pay, (2) difficulty in accessing beneficiaries, and (3) power struggles with entrenched players who do not want disruption of the ecosystem. Even when SFVs get paying clients who can help fund beneficiaries, there are conflicts in motives. Look at M-Pesa (Case Study 1.2), Aravind Eye Hospital (Case Study 1.3), and Narayana Hrudayalaya (Case Study 1.4). What could be some challenges in introducing it to other countries? What are the conditions that would make it feasible?

**Question 9**

What are the other competitors or NGOs or IGOs or SEVs operating in similar areas? What are they doing well that you can adapt or adopt into your business model?

**Question 10**

For your SEV, or if you don't have one, chose a local one, what is your overall broad area of impact? Use Table 1.1 to help you find areas of impact.

**Question 11**

Look at beneficiaries, clients, and other stakeholders like employees, volunteers, investors, and partners. What is the change your SEV is trying to bring about in terms of qualitative and quantitative impact? Record this in Table 1.2. The difference of future status and current status will give you the change.

Table 1.2: Measurement of Future Impact

| Beneficiary | Current status | Future status |
|---|---|---|
| Individuals<br>    Factor 1<br>    Factor 2 | | |
| Society of impact<br>    Factor 1<br>    Factor 2 | | |
| Investors / Patrons / Donors<br>    Factor 1<br>    Factor 2 | | |
| Other Stakeholders<br>    Factor 1<br>    Factor 2 | | |

Appendix 1: **Areas of Impact for Social Entrepreneurs**

| Agriculture, fishing, and forestry | Arts and culture | Community and economic development |
|---|---|---|
| **Agriculture:** Farm viability; Farmlands; Irrigation and water management; Livestock and ranching. | **Arts services:** Artists' services; Arts administration; Arts councils; Arts education; Arts exchange. | **Business and industry:** Business promotion; Construction; Corporate social responsibility; Entrepreneurship; Manufacturing; Mining and resource extraction; Real estate; Social enterprise; Tourism; Trade; Transport and storage. |
| **Fishing and aquaculture:** Fish farms and hatcheries; Sustainable fishing. | **Cultural awareness:** Sacred sites — protection, restoration, education, exploration; Traditional knowledge — collection, preservation, interpretation, legal protection and education. | |
| **Food Security:** Community food systems; Food sovereignty; Subsistence farming; Sustainable agriculture; Agricultural productivity; Protection from exploitation of small farmers; Sustainable food production; Ecosystem management; Adaption to climate change or other disasters; Management of diversified seed and plant banks; Warehousing and storage; Rural infrastructure; and Management of food commodities market & food price volatility. | | **Community improvement:** Community beautification; Community organizing; Community service; Neighborhood associations; Sanitation infrastructure. |
| | **Folk arts and performing arts:** Various (preservation, promotion, education); Festivals. | **Economic development:** Employment; Rural development; Urban development. |
| | **Historical activities:** Commemorations; Genealogy; Historic preservation; War memorials; Education (humanities studies; museums). | **Financial services:** Anti-predatory lending; Banking; Credit unions; Development finance; Financial counselling; Home financing; Insurance and Investment services. |
| | **Public arts:** Various | |
| **Forestry:** Non-timber forestry; Sustainable forestry, and prevention of de-forestation. | **Visual arts:** Architecture; Art conservation; Ceramic arts; Design; Drawing; Painting; Photography; Printmaking; Sculpture; Textile arts | **Housing development:** Foreclosure prevention; Home ownership; Housing loss prevention; Housing rehabilitation; Public housing; Tenants' organization. |
| | Film and Documentary. | **Safety:** Access to mental and physical safety; Shelter; emergency aid; food and water; legal protection; rape, traffic accidents, trafficking, forced marriages, genital mutilation, forced domestic violence, etc. |
| | | **Miscellaneous:** Sustainable development. |

*Source:* Adapted from http://taxonomy.foundationcenter.org/subjects.

| Education | Environment | Health |
|---|---|---|
| **Adult education:** Basic and remedial instruction; Continuing education; ESL and second-language acquisition.<br><br>**Disability:** Access to education for people with various disabilities to help equip them for a productive and fulfilling independent life where capable.<br><br>**Education services:** New school forms like charter school education; Child development; College preparation; Computer literacy; Cooperative education; E-learning; Educational exchanges; Educational software; Educational testing; Multicultural education; Out-of-school learning; Access to primary and secondary educations; Vocational training; Internships; Parent–teacher involvement; Reading promotion; Student services & retention; Special needs education; STEM education, Tutoring; Teacher education; Safe; Non-violent and inclusive effective learning environments. | **Biodiversity:** Water; Land; and Sky.<br><br>**Climate change:** Carbon disclosure and auditing; Education; and Research.<br><br>**Clean Energy:** R&D; Education and management of renewable energy.<br><br>**Domesticated animals:** Care; Prevention of abuse.<br><br>**Environmental:** Education & monitoring; Research.<br><br>**Environmental justice**<br><br>*Natural resource:* Conservation and research.<br><br>*Water management:* Water efficiency; Water scarcity management including water harvesting; Recycling; Reuse; Water bio-diversity/ecosystem management and protection; Water pollution; and Disease prevention. | **Child health:** Premature babies; Vaccines, and safe drinking water; Nourishment.<br><br>**Diseases and conditions:** Prediction; Response and control; Vaccine and disease R&D; and Epidemic contagion.<br><br>**Healthcare access:** Facilities; Medical staff; Medicine and diagnostics; Education; Cost reduction; Healthcare administration and financing; Healthcare quality; Holistic medicine; In-patient medical care; Medical specialties; and Medical support services.<br><br>**Maternal Health:** Research; Management; Education.<br><br>**Mental healthcare:** R&D; Access; Treatment; Inclusion; Education; Management of violence; Nursing care; and Out-patient medical care.<br><br>**Public health:** Data management; Access; Control; security/privacy; Prevention of exploitation and discrimination based on data; Inclusion: and Malnutrition.<br><br>**Rehabilitation:** Access; Resources and training, disability inclusion and access to resources; Substance abuse treatment and management.<br><br>**Reproductive healthcare:** Family planning; Education and management; Affordable and safe medicine and services; Safety from sexually transmitted diseases.<br><br>**Research and development**<br><br>*Sanitation:* Education; Infrastructure; Prevention and development; Pollution control and monitoring.<br><br>**Traditional medicine and healing**<br><br>*Tropical diseases:* Example, malaria.<br><br>*Water-borne diseases:* Prevention; Research; and Treatment. |

*Source*: Adapted from http://taxonomy.foundationcenter.org/subjects.

Appendix 1: **(cont)**

| Human rights | Human services | Information and communications |
|---|---|---|
| **Antidiscrimination:** Children's rights, Disabled persons' rights, Immigrants' rights, Refugee rights, LGBTQ rights, Minority rights, Prisoners' rights, Rights of the aged, Women's rights, etc. | **Basic and emergency aid:** Food aid; Free goods distribution; Gift distribution; Thrift shops; Travelers' aid; Victim aid; Emergency food, health, shelter, sanitation, and security; Resettlement/ evacuation. | **Communication media:** Audio recording; Film and video; Mobile media; Publishing; Radio; Television; Web-based media. |
| **Individual liberties:** Freedom from slavery; Freedom from violence and torture; Freedom of association and expression; Freedom of religion; Reproductive rights; Right to die; Right to free movement and asylum; Right to life; Right to privacy; Empowerment. | **Family services:** Adolescent parenting/pregnancies; Adult day care; Child welfare; Family counseling; Family disability resources; In-home aid and personal assistance; Parent education; Single parent support; Domestic abuse. | **Information and communications technology:** Computer security; Software applications; Telecommunications.<br><br>**Libraries:** Academic libraries; Archives and special collections; Government libraries; Public libraries; School libraries and media centers. |
| **Justice rights:** Capital punishment; Due process; Equal rights. | **Job services and workforce development:** Job matching and (re) training; Sheltered workshops; Unemployment compensation; Vocational rehabilitation; Personal services; Shelter and residential care; Special population support; Youth development. | **Media access and policy:** Information and media literacy; Media democracy; Media justice.<br><br>**News and public information:** Journalism; Open data. |
| **Social rights:** Cultural rights; Economic justice; Environmental and resource rights; Freedom of information; Labor rights; Marriage equality; Traditional marriage; Voter rights. | **Poverty eradication:** Social protection systems for poor and vulnerable. | **Technology:** Access to information; Protection of privacy and security; Reduce cyber bullying/cybercrime; Technology literacy (digital divide); Education; and Cyber-currency. |
| **Miscellaneous:** Diversity and intergroup relations; Tolerance; Peace; Happiness. | **Miscellaneous:** Human services information and management. | |

*Source*: Adapted from http://taxonomy.foundationcenter.org/subjects.

Appendix 1: **(cont)**

| International relations | Philanthropy | Public affairs |
|---|---|---|
| Democracy and civil society development, | Foundations | **Democracy:** Civic participation and Elections; Public integrity. |
| Climate change, | Non-profits | **Leadership development national security:** Bioterrorism; Counterterrorism; Customs and border control; Cyber warfare; Immigration and naturalization; National defense. |
| Foreign policy, | Philanthropy and public policy | |
| Goodwill promotion, | Venture philanthropy | |
| International development, | Voluntarism | |
| International economics and trade, | | **Public administration:** Census; Government regulation; Public assistance; Public finance; Public work. |
| International exchange, | | |
| International peace and security: Arms control; Conflict resolution; | | **Public policy:** Equal rights and justice, Healthcare coverage, Access to education, Free media, etc. |
| Multilateral cooperation trade. | | |
| | | **Public utilities:** Electric utilities; Oil and gas utilities; Sewage utilities; Water utilities. |
| | | **Public/private ventures** |

*Source*: Adapted from http://taxonomy.foundationcenter.org/subjects.

Appendix 1: **(cont)**

| Public safety | Religion | Science and social sciences |
|---|---|---|
| **Abuse prevention:** Bullying; Child abuse; Domestic violence; Elder abuse; Sexual abuse. | Practice; Historical documentation; Practice, education, and choice. | STEM promotion and facilitation; Access to resources; Specific subject discipline areas; Interdisciplinary subject areas; Conservation and revival of traditional or ancient studies of languages and sciences (Chinese and Ayurvedic medicine). |
| **Consumer protection:** Drug safety; Food safety; Universal design. | | |
| **Corrections and penology:** Offender re-entry; Prison alternatives; Probation and parole; Rehabilitation of offenders; Services for offenders. | | |
| **Courts:** Dispute resolution; Family courts; Juvenile justice. | | |
| **Crime prevention:** Cybercrime; Gun control; Impaired driving; Law enforcement; Missing persons; Narcotics control. | | |
| **Disasters and emergency management:** Civil protection; Disaster preparedness; Disaster reconstruction; Disaster relief; Disasters; Internal resettlement; Search and rescue. | | |
| **Fire prevention and control** | | |
| *Legal services:* Child advocacy; Guardianship; Housing law; Immigration law; Intellectual property; Legal aid; Public interest law. | | |
| *Safety education:* First aid training; Home safety; Poison control; Traffic safety. | | |

*Source:* Adapted from http://taxonomy.foundationcenter.org/subjects.

Appendix 1: **(cont)**

| Sports and Recreation | Others | |
|---|---|---|
| **Community recreation:** Camps and Clubs; Festivals; Parks; Playgrounds.<br><br>**Access and promotion of sports:** Adaptive sports; Competitive and recreational sports like American football; Baseball and softball; Basketball; Combat/Martial arts sports; Cycling; Equestrianism; European football; Golf; Gymnastics; Outdoor sports; Racquet sports; Running; Sports training; Table tennis; Track and field; Volleyball; Water sports; Olympics; Paralympics; Special Olympics; Winter sports; Local indigenous sports/festivals. | | |

*Source*: Adapted from http://taxonomy.foundationcenter.org/subjects.

## Sources

### Case Study 1.1: White Helmets

Compiled from multiple sources: For more on The White Helmets (2017), Read: https://www.whitehelmets. org/en; di Giovanni, J. (2016), "Syria's white helmets save civilians, soldiers and rebels alike," *Newsweek*, dated 21 January, Available: http://www.newsweek.com/2016/01/29/white-helmets-syrian-civil-war-418001. html [Accessed 25 July 2017]; Al Saleh, S. (2015), "Stop the barrel bombs in syria," *Washington Post*, dated 27 March, Available: https://www.washingtonpost.com/opinions/stop-the-barrel-bombs-the-deadliest-weapons-in-syrias-civil-war/2015/03/27/c983d024-cf4e-11e4-8a46-b1dc9be5a8ff_story.html?utm_term=.871b865ad1fd [Accessed 25 July 2017]; Economist (2016), "The rise of syria's white helmets," dated 16 October, Available: https://www.economist.com/news/middle-east-and-africa/21708515-amid-chaos-and-destruction-ever-bloodier-civil-war-volunteer-rescuers [Accessed 25 July 2017]; The Guardian (2015), "Angelina Jolie criticizes UN security council for paralysis over Syria," Available: https://www.theguardian. com/film/2015/apr/24/angelina-jolie-un-security-council-syria-refugees [Accessed 26 July 2017]; Al Saleh, R. (2015), "As a patriotic syrian, I never imagined I would do this," dated 29 June, Available: https://diary. thesyriacampaign.org/as-a-patriotic-syrian-i-never-imagined-i-would-do-this/ [Accessed 25 July 2017].

### Case Study 1.2: M-Pesa

Compiled from multiple sources: Cook, T. (2015), "An overview of M-Pesa," *FSD Kenya*, Available: http:// fsdkenya.org/an-overview-of-m-pesa/ [Accessed 30 October 2016]; Cracknell, D. (2012), "Policy innovations to improve access to financial services in developing countries: Learning from case studies in Kenya," *Centre for Global Development*, Available: http://www.cgdev.org/doc/LRS_case_studies/Cracknell_Kenya.pdf [Accessed 15 March 2017]; Centre for Public Impact (2016), "Mobile currency in Kenya: The M-Pesa," dated March 21, Available: http://www.centreforpublicimpact.org/case-study/m-currency-in-kenya/ [Accessed 1 March 2017].

### Case Study 1.3: Aravind Eye Hospital

Compiled from multiple sources: Aravind (2011), "A case study on Aravind eye care systems," *Aravind.org website*, Available: http://www.aravind.org/content/Downloads/ACaseStudyonAravindEyeCareSystems.pdf [Accessed 10 January 2017]; Srinivasan, A. (2011), "Driving down the cost of high-quality care: Lessons from the Aravind eye care system," *Health International*, Available: http://www.aravind.org/content/ Downloads/draravindinterview.pdf [Accessed 10 January 2017]; Hutton, D. W. *et al.* (2014), "The cost of cataract surgery at the Aravind eye hospital, India," *IOVS*, 55(13), Available: http://iovs.arvojournals.org/ article.aspx?articleid=2266507 [Accessed 10 January 2017]; Segre, L. (2017), "Cataract surgery cost," *All About Vision*, dated 1 August, Available: http://www.allaboutvision.com/conditions/cataract-surgery-cost. htm [Accessed 7 August 2017]. Aravind Eye Care System (2016), "1976–2016 — 40 years," Available: http:// www.aravind.org/content/downloads/aecsreport201516.pdf [Accessed 19 August 2017].

### Case Study 1.4: Narayana Hrudayalaya Limited

Compiled from multiple sources: Altstedter, A (2019). "The World's Cheapest Hospital has to get Even Cheaper," *Bloomberg Businessweek*, dated 26 March. Available https://www.bloomberg.com/news/ features/2019-03-26/the-world-s-cheapest-hospital-has-to-get-even-cheaper. Das, A. (2016), "Henry ford of heart surgery," *Economic Times*, dated 7 January, Available: http://timesofindia.indiatimes.com/business/ india-business/Henry-Ford-of-heart-surgery/articleshow/50475335.cms [Accessed 17 April 2017]. ET Bureau (2012), "ET awards 2012 Devi Prasad Shetty is entrepreneur of the year," *Economic Times website*, dated 19 September, Available: http://economictimes.indiatimes.com/news/company/corporate-trends/et-awards-2012-devi-prasad-shetty-is-entrepreneur-of-the-year/articleshow/16457983.cms?intenttarget=no [Accessed 17 April 2017]; ET (2017), "Today US FDA approved stent is available for Indians for Rs 30,000: Devi Shetty, Narayana Hrudayala," *Economics Times*, dated February 15, Available: http://economictimes.indiatimes.com/ opinion/interviews/today-us-fda-approved-stent-is-available-for-indians-for-rs-30000-devi-shetty-narayana-hrudayalaya/articleshow/57163786.cms [Accessed 17 April 2017]; Balachandran, M. (2016), "How an Indian doctor built a billion dollar company by making heart surgeries affordable," *Quartz*, dated 7 January, Available: https://qz.com/587550/how-an-indian-doctor-built-a-billion-dollar-company-by-making-heart-surgeries-affordable/; ILO (2015), "Social security extension innovations in Asia," *ILO,* Available: http://www.social-protection.org/gimi/gess/RessourcePDF.action;jsessionid=sQ7TYBZQTXypJydPwdGpqJwLWWLflk51PGJ FlcdmjskpbykWp9C3!79209976?ressource.ressourceId=3810 [Accessed 7 August 2017]; ISRO (2002), "Inauguration of Karnataka telemedicine project," Available: http://www.isro.gov.in/update/08-apr-2002/inauguration-of-karnataka-telemedicine-project [Accessed 19 August 2017]; Menon, P. (2012), "Interview with Dr. Devi Prasad Shetty, cardiologist, founder, chairman, Narayana Hrudayalaya health city — part one," *Cure Talk website,* Available: http://trialx.com/curetalk/2012/04/02/interview-with-dr-devi-prasad-shetty-cardiologist-founder-chairman-narayana-hrudayalaya-health-city-part-one/ [Accessed 18 August 2017]; Business Line (2005), "ISRO, hospitals bet big on telemedicine," Available: http://www.thehindubusinessline.com/todays-paper/tp-economy/isro-hospitals-bet-big-on-telemedicine/article2171967.ece [Accessed 18 August 2017].

## Case 1.5: Chid Liberty's L&J: Ebola was Not in Our Business Plan

Compiled from multiple sources: Acumen (2016), "Ebola was not in our business plan — how this social entrepreneur defied bankruptcy," *Acumen website,* dated 8 March 2016, Available: http://plusacumen.org/blog/ebola-not-business-plan-social-entrepreneur-defied-bankruptcy/ [Accessed 10 June 2017]; Bastian, M. (2014), "Ebola-hit liberia on brink of societal collapse — experts," *Rappler,* dated 30 September, Available: http://www.rappler.com/world/regions/africa/70583-ebola-hit-liberia-societal-breakdown [Accessed 8 June 2017]; Vickers, B. and Games, D. (2015), "The ebola crisis: Implications for trade and regional integration," *International Centre or Trade and Sustainable Development,* dated 6 May, Available: http://www.ictsd.org/bridges-news/bridges-africa/news/the-ebola-crisis-implications-for-trade-and-regional-integration [Accessed 11 June 2017]; Alter, C. (2014), "Liberia closes borders to curb ebola outbreak," *TIME,* dated 28 July, Available: http://time.com/3046012/liberia-border-ebola/ [Accessed 11 June 2017]; Evans, D., Kremer, M. and Ngatia, M. (2009), "The impact of distributing school uniforms on children's education in Kenya." *World Bank,* Working Paper, November, Available: https://www.povertyactionlab.org/evaluation/impact-distributing-school-uniforms-childrens-education-kenya [Accessed 7 June 2017]; Kickstarter (2017), "UNIFORM," *Kickstarter website,* Available: https://www.kickstarter.com/projects/114851663/uniform-worlds-softest-tee [Accessed 10 June 2017]; Liberty & Justice website: http://libertyandjustice.com; Pastorek, W. (2013), "Africa's first fair trade garment manufacturer is a model for women's empowerment," *Fast Company,* dated 11 November, Available: https://www.fastcompany.com/3021131/change-generation/africas-first-fair-trade-garment-manufacturer-is-a-model-for-womens-empowe?partner=rss#5 [Accessed 11 June 2017]. Burke, L. (2012), "In Liberia, factory work is changing womens' lives — starting at home," *Good,* Available https://www.good.is/articles/how-factory-work-is-changing-liberian-womens-lives-starting-at-home [Accessed 1 August 2017]. Foote, W. (2014), "On the front lines of ebola: My interview with an entrepreneur in Liberia," Available: https://www.forbes.com/sites/willyfoote/2014/08/25/on-the-front-lines-of-ebola-my-interview-with-an-entrepreneur-in-liberia/2/#20fea90d194c [Accessed 11 June 2017].

## Case Study 1.6: TOMS

Compiled from multiple sources: TOMS website (2017), Available: http://www.toms.com/blakes-bio [Accessed 11 August 2017]. Lebowitz, S. (2016), "TOMS founder: 'I was CEO by default, but I never was a CEO'," *Business Insider,* dated 18 June, Available: http://www.businessinsider.de/toms-blake-mycoskie-why-he-stepped-down-from-the-position-of-ceo-2016-6?r=US&IR=T [Accessed 11 August 2017]. Quittner, J. (2016), "What the founder of TOMS shoes is doing now," *Fortune,* dated 8 September, Available: http://fortune.com/2016/09/08/what-the-founder-of-toms-shoes-is-doing-now/ [Accessed 11 August 2017]. Mykoskie, B. (2016), "The founder of TOMS on reimagining the company's mission," *Harvard Business Review,* Available: https://hbr.org/2016/01/the-founder-of-toms-on-reimagining-the-companys-mission [Accessed 11 August 2017]. Kachilife Editorial (2017), "One for one: An interview with toms founder blake mycoskie," *Khachilife website,* dated 5 May, Available: http://khachilife.com/one-for-one-an-interview-with-toms-founder-blake-mycoskie [Accessed 11 August 2017]; Mycoskie, B. (2011), *Start Something that Matters,* Random House: New York; Moore, B. (2006), "They're flipping for alpargatas," *LA Times,* dated 20 May, Available: http://articles.latimes.com/2006/may/20/entertainment/et-stylenotebook20 [Accessed 11 August 2017].

# ENDNOTES

1   Case, J. (2019), *Be Fearless: Five Principles for a Life of Breakthroughs and Purpose*, Simon & Schuster: NY.

2   El Sawy, N (2019), "Global debt set to hit record $255tn by end of year," The National, dated 16 November, Available: https://www.thenational.ael/business/economy/global-debt-set-to-hit-record-255tn-by-end-of-year-1. 938280 [Accessed 16 December 2019].

3   UNCTAD (2014), "Developing countries face $2.5 trillion annual investment gap in key sustainable development sectors," *UNCTAD website*, Available: http://unctad.org/en/pages/PressRelease.aspx?OriginalVersionID=194 [Accessed 18 April 2017].

4   World Bank (2016), "1977–2015 gross savings (% of GDP)," *World Bank website*, Available: http://data.worldbank.org/indicator/NY.GNS.ICTR.ZS [Accessed 18 April 2017].

5   Chen, P., Karabarbounis, L. and Neiman, B. (2017), "The global corporate saving glut: Long-term evidence," *CEPR's Policy Portal*, Available: http://voxeu.org/article/global-corporate-saving-glut [Accessed 4 April 2017]. Chen, P., Karabarbounis, L. and Neiman, B. (2017), "The global rise of corporate saving", *The National Bureau of Economic Research*, NBER Working Paper No. 23133, Available: http://www.nber.org/papers/w23133 [Accessed 4 April 2017].

6   IMF (2016), "From global saving glut to financing infrastructure: The advent of investment platforms," *International Monetary Fund website*, IMF Working Paper WP/16/18, p. 42, Available: https://www.imf.org/external/pubs/ft/wp/2016/wp1618.pdf [Accessed 4 April 2017].

7   Bain & Company (2020), "A world awash in money — global capital trends," *Bain & Company website*, http://www.bain.de/Images/BAIN_REPORT_A_world_awash_in_money.pdf [Accessed 5 April 2017].

8   Sachs, J. D. (2019), "How can we achieve the SDGs? strategic policy directions." *Dubai Policy Review*, 1(1): 30.

9   Anyangwe, E. (2015), "Is it time to rethink the divide between humanitarian and development funding?," *The Guardian*, dated 4 December, Available: https://www.theguardian.com/global-development-professionals-network/2015/dec/04/funding-humanitarian-assistance-development-aid [Accessed 13 August 2017].

10  NetImpact (2017), "Social sector: Philanthropy/nonprofit: types of organizations," *Net Impact website*, Available: https://www.netimpact.org/social-sector-philanthropy-nonprofit [Accessed 1 August 2017].

11  Austin, J., Stevenson, H. and Wei-Skillern, J. (2006), "Social and commercial entrepreneurship: same, different, or both?," *Entrepreneurship: Theory & Practice*, 30(1): 1–22.

12  Dohrmann, S., Raith, M. and Siebold, N. (2015), "Monetising social value creation — a business model approach," *Journal of Entrepreneurship Research*, 5(2): 127–154.

13  Dees, J. G., 1998. "Enterprising nonprofits." *Harvard Business Review*, 76: 54–69.

14  Bibars, I. (2016), "Social entrepreneurs as change makers," In: Balakrishnan, M.S. and Lindsay, V. (eds.), *Actions and Insights: Middle East North Africa (Vol. 5): Social Entrepreneurship*, Emerald Group Publishing, pp. 23–32.

15  Zahra, S. A., Gedajlovic, E., Neubaum, D. O. and Shulman, J. M. (2009), "A typology of social entrepreneurs: motives, search processes and ethical challenges," *Journal of Business Venturing*, 24(5): 519–532.

16  Asian Development Bank (2016), "Are social enterprises the inclusive businesses of tomorrow?," *Inclusive Business Hub website*, Available: http://www.inclusivebusinesshub.org/wp-content/uploads/2016/05/SE-as-IBs-of-the-future-2-2-for-web-2.pdf [Accessed 18 April 2017].

17  Hill, T. L., Kothari, T. H. and Shea, M. (2010), "Patterns of meaning in the social entrepreneurship literature: a research platform," *Journal of Social Entrepreneurship*, 1(1): 5–31.

18  Short, Jeremy C., Moss, Todd W. and Lumpkin, G. T. (2009), "Research in social entrepreneurship: past contributions and future opportunities," *Strategic Entrepreneurship Journal*, 3(2): 161–194.

19  Hossain, S., Saleh, M. A. and Drennan, J. (2017), "A critical appraisal of the social entrepreneurship paradigm in an international setting: a proposed conceptual framework," *International Entrepreneurship and Management Journal*, 13(2): 347–368.

20  Santos, F. M. (2012), "A positive theory of social entrepreneurship," *Journal of Business Ethics*, 111(3): 335–351.

21  Bibars, I. (2016), "Social entrepreneurs as change makers," In *Actions and Insights: Middle East North Africa (Vol. 5): Social Entrepreneurship*, Eds. Balakrishnan, M.S. and Lindsay, V. Emerald Group Publishing: 23–32.

22  Desa, G. (2012), "Resource mobilization in international social entrepreneurship: bricolage as a mechanism of institutional transformation," *Entrepreneurship Theory and Practice*, 36(4): 727–751.

23  Hill, T. L., Kothari, T. H. and Shea, M. (2010), "Patterns of meaning in the social entrepreneurship literature: a research platform," *Journal of Social Entrepreneurship*, 1(1): 5–31.

24  Zahra, S. A., Gedajlovic, E., Neubaum, D. O. and Shulman, J. M. (2009), "A typology of social entrepreneurs: motives, search processes and ethical challenges," *Journal of Business Venturing*, 24: 519–532.

25  Salamon, L. M. and Anheier, H. K. (1998), "Social origins of civil society: explaining the nonprofit sector cross-nationally," *Voluntas: International Journal of Voluntary and Non-profit Organizations*, 9(3): 213–248.

26  Nye, J. (1990), *Bound to Lead: The Changing Nature of American Power*, New York: Basic Books.

27  Burell, I. (2015), "Government invests £85m in BBC world service in soft power U-turn," *BBC News*, dated 23 November, Available: http://www.independent.co.uk/news/uk/politics/government-invests-85m-in-bbc-world-service-in-soft-power-u-turn-a6745736.html [Accessed 31 October 2016].

28  Coughlan, S. (2014), "One in seven countries has leader who studied in UK," *BBC News*, dated 25 September, Available: http://www.bbc.com/news/education-29361704 [Accessed 29 January 2017].

29  Soft Power 30 (2016), "A global ranking of soft power 2017," *USC Center of Public Diplomacy*, Available: http://softpower30.com/wp-content/uploads/2017/07/The-Soft-Power-30-Report-2017-Web-1.pdf [Accessed 13 August 2017]. This index is based on 6 sub-indices: digital, culture, enterprise, engagement, education and government.

30  British Council (2015), "How soft power can help meet international challenges," *British Council website*, dated September, Available: https://www.britishcouncil.org/organisation/policy-insight-research/insight/how-soft-power-can-help-meet-international-challenges [Accessed 29 January 2017].

31  Minoiu, C. and Reddy, S. G. (2009), "Development aid and economic growth: a positive long-run relation," *IMF Working paper*, p. 7, Available: https://www.imf.org/external/pubs/ft/wp/2009/wp09118.pdf [Accessed 3 April 2017].

32  For more questions on ODA read OECD (2008) fact sheet "Is it ODA?" Available: https://www.oecd.org/dac/stats/34086975.pdf [Accessed 6 August 2017].

33  Minoiu, C. and Reddy, S. G. (2010), "Development aid and economic growth: a positive long-run relation," *The Quarterly Review of Economics and Finance*, 50(1): 27–39.

34  Clemens, M. A., Radelet, S. and Bhavnani, R. (2004), "Counting chickens when they hatch: the short-term effect of aid on growth," *CGD Working Paper No. 44*, Washington: Center for Global Development.

35  Mwega, F. M. (2009), "A case study of aid effectiveness in Kenya volatility and fragmentation of foreign aid, with a focus on health," *Wolfensohn Center For Development at Brookings*, Working Paper 8, January, Available: https://www.brookings.edu/wp-content/uploads/2016/06/01_kenya_aid_mwega.pdf [Accessed 30 October 2016].

36  Kenya has had an on off relationship with the West. In 2004, EU froze £83m aid which was to be funded directly into Kenyan government budget for general spending.

37  Ojiambo, E., Oduor, J., Mburu, T. and Wawire, N. (2015), "Aid unpredictability and economic growth in Kenya," *African Development Bank Group*, Working Paper Series, No. 226, July, Available: http://www.afdb.org/fileadmin/uploads/afdb/Documents/Publications/WPS_No_226_Aid_unpredictability_and_Economic_Growth_in_Kenya_H.pdf [Accessed 30 October 2016].

38  Karanja, S. and Kilonzo, E. (2015), "NGOs received Sh6b funds from unknown sources – report," *Daily Nation*, dated 15 September, Available: http://www.nation.co.ke/news/NGOs-receive-funds-unknown-sources/1056-2871462-gka0bz/index.html [Accessed 15 December 2016].

39  This definition is from the 2007–2008 Advisory Group on CSOs and Aid Effectiveness and adopted by OECD DAC, UNDP (n.d.), "NGOs and CSOs: a note on terminology," *UNDP website*, Available: http://www.cn.undp.org/content/dam/china/docs/Publications/UNDP-CH03%20Annexes.pdf [Accessed 16 December 2016].

40  UIA (2017), "What is an Intergovernmental Organization (IGO)?," *Union of International Associations*, Available: http://www.uia.org/faq/yb3 [Accessed 7 August 2017].

41  Acemoglu, D. and Robinson, J. A. (2014), "Why foreign aid falls and how to really help Africa," *Spectator*, dated 25 July, Available: http://www.spectator.co.uk/2014/01/why-aid-fails/ [Accessed 31 October 2016]

42  Denham, J. (2013), "Epic fail: all 25,000 students fail university entrance exam in liberia," *Independent*, Available: http://www.independent.co.uk/student/news/epic-fail-all-25000-students-fail-university-entrance-exam-in-liberia-8785707.html [Accessed 31 October 2016].

43  Kuo, L (2016), "Kenya is pressuring thousands of expat NGO workers and volunteers to go home," *Quartz*, Available: http://qz.com/716518/kenya-is-pressuring-thousands-of-expat-ngo-workers-and-volunteers-to-go-home/ [Accessed 30 October 2016].

44  Johnson, M. W. (2010), "Where is your white space," *Harvard Business Review*, dated 12 February, Available: https://hbr.org/2010/02/where-is-your-white-space [Accessed 29 January 2017].

45  Low, P. (2018), "The natural disaster of 2018," *Munich RE website*, Available: http://www.unisdr.org/files/47804_2015disastertrendsinfographic.pdf [Accessed 27 April 2019].

46  Business & Sustainable Development Commission (2017), "Better business – better world," Available: http://report.businesscommission.org/uploads/BetterBiz-BetterWorld.pdf [Accessed 18 January 2017].

47  UNHCR (2016), "Global forced displacement tops 70 million," *UNHCR website*, dated 20 June, Available: https://www.unhcr.org/news/stories/2019/6/5d08b6614/global-forced-displacement-tops-70-million.html [Accessed 12 December 2019].

48  World Population Review (2017), "Syria population in 2017," *World Population Review website*, Available http://worldpopulationreview.com/countries/syria-population/ [Accessed 25 July 2017].

49  AP (2017), "UN aid chief accuses Syrian government of blocking aid to most needy," *ABC News*, dated 27 January, Available: http://www.abc.net.au/news/2017-01-27/un-aid-chief-accuses-syria-of-blocking-help-to-most-needy/8218148 [Accessed 29 January 2017]. White Helmets (2016), Documentary, *Netflix*, Available on YouTube: https://www.youtube.com/watch?v=3wj4nclEDxw [Accessed 29 January 2017].

50  Citizens for Syria (nd), Available: http://citizensforsyria.org/OrgLiterature/CfS-mapping-phase1-EN.pdf [Accessed 29 January 2017].

51  UNCHR (nd), "The state of the world's refugees – protracted refugee situations: the search for practical solutions," Available: http://www.unhcr.org/4444afcb0.pdf [Accessed 29 January 2017]. The Free Thought Project (2015), "Average stay in a refugee camp is 17 years, UN expert says camps are 'The cities of tomorrow'," *The Free Thought website*, Available: http://thefreethoughtproject.com/average-stay-refugee-camp-17-years-expert-camps-the-cities-tomorrow/ [Accessed 29 January 2017].

52  Giddings, B. and Hopwood, B. and O'Brien, G. (2002), "Environment, economy and society: fitting them together into sustainable development." *Sustainable Development*, 10: 187–196.

53  Haughton G. (1999), "Environmental justice and the sustainable city," *Journal of Planning Education and Research*, 18(3): 233–243.

54  Durst, D. (1992), "The road to poverty is paved with good intentions: social interventions and indigenous peoples," *International Social Work*, 35(2): 191–202.

55  Kubania, J. (2015), "How second-hand clothing donations are creating a dilemma for Kenya," *The Guardian*, dated 6 July. Available: http://www.theguardian.com/world/2015/jul/06/second-hand-clothing-donations-kenya [Accessed 1 May 2016].

56  Mangieri, T. (2006), "African cloth, export production, and secondhand clothing in Kenya," Available: http://www.cggc.duke.edu/pdfs/workshop/Kenya%20cloth%20&%20clothing.pdf [Accessed 1 May 2016].

57  Frazer, G. (2008), "Used-clothing donations and apparel production in Africa," *The Economic Journal*, 118(532): 1764-1784.

58  Novogratz, J. (2009). *The Blue Sweater: Bridging the Gap Between Rich and Poor in an Interconnected World*, Rodale Inc.: USA.

59  Anand, U. (2015), "India has 31 lakh NGOs, more than double the number of schools," *The Indian Express*, dated 1 August, Available: http://indianexpress.com/article/india/india-others/india-has-31-lakh-ngos-twice-the-number-of-schools-almost-twice-number-of-policemen/ [Accessed 21 December 2016].

60  Nagpal, S. (2015), "How is india improving its healthcare system?," *WEF*, dated 17 December, Available: https://www.weforum.org/agenda/2015/12/how-is-india-improving-its-healthcare-system/ [Accessed 31 October 2016].

61  Nagarajani, R. (2013), "Foreign aid 1.6% of India's total health spend: study," *The Times of India*, dated 25 February, Available: http://timesofindia.indiatimes.com/india/Foreign-aid-1-6-of-Indias-total-health-spend-Study/articleshow/18668317.cms [Accessed 31 October 2016].

62  Gavi (2014), "India to introduce four new vaccines," *Gavi website*, dated 4 July, Available: http://www.gavi.org/library/news/statements/2014/india-to-introduce-four-new-vaccines/ [Accessed 30 October 2016].

63  Deyl, S. (2015), "Less than 20% of population under health insurance cover: report," *The Times of India*, dated 24 September, Available: http://timesofindia.indiatimes.com/india/Less-than-20-of-population-under-health-insurance-cover-Report/articleshow/49082784.cms [Accessed 4 January 2017].

64  Radjou, N., Prabhu, J. and Ahuja, A. (2012), *Jugaad Innovation: Think Frugal, Be Flexible, Generate Breakthrough Growth*, Josey-Bass: San Francisco, USA.

65  Prabhu, J. and Jain, S. (2015), "Innovation and entrepreneurship in India: Understanding jugaad," *Asia Pacific Journal of Management*, 32(4): 843–868.

66  Radjou, N., Prabhu, J. and Ahuja, A. (2012), *Jugaad Innovation: Think Frugal, Be Flexible, Generate Breakthrough Growth*, Josey-Bass: San Francisco, USA.

67  Krishnan, R. T. (2010), *From Jugaad to Systematic Innovation: The Challenge for India*, Utpreraka Foundation: Bangalore.

68  Bhatti, Y. A., Khilji, S. E. and Basu, R. (2013), "Frugal innovation," In: Khilji, S. and Rowley, C. (eds.), *Globalization, Change and Learning in South Asia*, Chandos Publishing: Oxford, pp. 123–144.

69  The World Bank (2016), "World bank group ebola response fact sheet," *World Bank website*, dated 6 April, Available: http://www.worldbank.org/en/topic/health/brief/world-bank-group-ebola-fact-sheet [Accessed 30 October 2016].

70  Mundasad, S. (2015), "How ebola changed the world," *BBC News*, dated 23 March, Available: http://www.bbc.co.uk/news/health-31982078 [Accessed 30 October 2016].

71  UNICEF (2014), "Impact of ebola," *UNICEF website*, Available: http://www.unicef.org/emergencies/ebola/75941_76129.html [Accessed 30 October 2016].

72  British Council (2014), "What will social enterprises in Europe look like by 2020?," *British Council website*, Available: https://www.britishcouncil.org/sites/default/files/what_will_social_enterprise_look_like_in_europe_by_2020_0.pdf [Accessed 2 April 2017].

73  Business & Sustainable Development Commission (2017), *Better Business Better World*, Available: http://report.businesscommission.org/report [Accessed 30 March 2017].

74  Based on analysis by the Business and Sustainable Development Commission team. Projections are based on data from AlphaBeta, 2017, Valuing the SDG prize: Unlocking business opportunities to accelerate sustainable and inclusive growth.

75  Woetzel, J., Madgavkar, A., Ellingrud, K., Labaye, E., Devillard, S., Kutcher, E., Manyika, J., Dobbs, R. and Krishnan, M. (2015), "The power of parity: How advancing women's equality can add $12 trillion to global growth," *McKinsey Global Institute*, Available: http://www.mckinsey.com/global-themes/employment-and-growth/how-advancingwomens-equality-can-add-12-trillion-to-global-growth [Accessed 29 January 2017].

76  Zahra, S. A., Ireland R. D. and Hitt, M. A. (2000), "International expansion, technological learning, and new venture performance," *Academy of Management Journal*, 43(5): 925–950; McDougall, P. P., Oviatt, B. M. and Shrader, R. C. (2003), "A comparison of international and domestic new ventures," *Journal of International Entrepreneurship*, 1(1): 59–82; Knight, G. A. and Cavusgil, S. T. (2004), "Innovation, organization capabilities, and the born-global firm," *Journal of International Business Studies*, 35(2): 124–141; McKinsey and Co. (1993), *Emerging Exporters. Australia's High Value-Added Manufacturing Exporters. Melbourne*, McKinsey and Company and the Australian Manufacturing Council; Oviatt, B. M. and McDougall, P. P. (1994), "Toward a theory of international new ventures," *Journal of International Business Studies*, 25(1): 45–64.

77  Eurofound (2012). *Born Global: The Potential of Job Creation in New International Businesses.* Luxembourg: Publications Office of the European Union; OECD (2013), *Fostering SMEs' Participation in Global Markets: Final Report.* Paris: Organisation for Economic Co-operation and Development, Centre for Entrepreneurship, SMEs and Local Development; Knight, G. A. and Liesch, P. W. (2016), "Internationalization: From incremental to born global," *Journal of World Business*, 51: 93–102; OECD (2000), *Enhancing the Competitiveness of SMEs Through Innovation*, Available: http://www.oecd.org/cfe/smes/2010176.pdf [Accessed 23 April 2017].

78  Clarysse, B., Lockett, A., Quince, T. and Van de Velde E. (2002), "Spinning off new ventures: A typology of facilitating services," Working Paper No. 41 IWT Institute for the Promotion of Innovation by Science and Technology in Flanders, Brussels, December.

79  For example, see: Sharma, D. D. and Blomstermo, A. (2003), "The internationalization process of born globals: A network view," *International Business Review*, 12(6): 739–753; Zhou, L., Wu, W. P. and Luo, X. (2007), "Internationalization and the performance of born-global SMEs: The mediating role of social networks," *Journal of International Business Studies*, 38(4): 673–690; Sullivan Mort, G. and Weerawardena, J. (2006), "Networking capability and international entrepreneurship: How networks function in Australian born global firms," *International Marketing Review*, 23(5): 549–572.

80  Dees, J. G., Anderson, B. B. and Wei-Skillern, J. (2004), "Scaling social impact", *Stanford Social Innovation Review*, 1(4): 24–33.

81  Patrinos, H. A., Barrera-Osorio, F. and Guaqueta, J. (2009), "The role and impact of public-private partnerships," *World Bank*; Lund-Thomsen, P. (2007), *Assessing the Impact of Public-Private Partnerships in the Global South: The Case of the Kasur Tanneries Pollution Control Project*, UNRISD Publication, Geneva.

82  For more information on UN Sustainable Goals, see: http://www.un.org/sustainabledevelopment/sustainable-development-goals/.

83  For more information on Foundation Centre grant taxonomy: see: http://taxonomy.foundationcenter.org.

84  Ajzen, I. (1982), "On behaving in accordance with one's attitudes," In: Zanna, M. P., Higgins, E. T. and Herman, C. P. (eds.), *Consistency in Social Behavior: The Ontario Symposium*, Vol. 2, Hillsdale, NJ: Erlbaum, pp. 3–15.

85  Allport, G. W. (1935), "Attitudes," In: Murchison, C. (ed.), *Handbook of Social Psychology*, Clark University, MA: Worcester, pp. 798–884.

86  Boninger, D. S., Krosnick, J. A. and Berent, M. K. (1995), "Origins of attitude importance: Self-interest, social identification, and value relevance," *Journal of Personality and Social Psychology*, 68(1): 61–80.

87  Robinson, P. B., Stimpson, D. V., Huefner, J. C. and Hunt, H. K. (1991), "An attitude approach to the prediction of entrepreneurship," *Entrepreneurship Theory and Practice*, 15(4): 13–31.

88  Robinson, *et al.*, (1991), *Op. cit.* p. 17; Boninger, D. S., Krosnick, J. A. and Berent, M. K. (1995), *Op. cit.*

89  Morris, J. D., Woo, C., Geason, J. A. and Kim, J. (2002), "The power of affect: Predicting intention," *Journal of Advertising Research*, 42(3): 7–17.

90  *Ibid.*

91  Gawronski, B. and Bodenhausen, G. V. (2006), "Associative and propositional processes in evaluation: An integrative review of implicit and explicit attitude change," *Psychological Bulletin*, 132(5): 692.

92  Latan, B. (1981), "The psychology of social impact," *American Psychologist*, 36: 343–365; Nowak, A., Szamrej, J. and Latané, B. (1990), "From private attitude to public opinion: A dynamic theory of social impact," *Psychological Review*, 97(3): 362.

93  Gawronski, B. and Bodenhausen, G. V. (2006), *Op.cit.*

94  Scott, W. R. (2001), *Institutions and Organizations* (2nd ed.), Sage Publications: Thousand Oaks, California.

95  Jäger, U. and Schröer, A. (2014), "The evolution of the non-profit and voluntary sector," *Voluntas: International Journal of Voluntary & Nonprofit Organizations*, 25(5): 1281–1306.

96  *Ibid.*

97  Schaltz, R. D. (2015), "How a social entrepreneur overcame his 'arrogant failure' and won kudos from oprah," *Forbes*, dated 18 October, Available: https://www.forbes.com/sites/robindschatz/2015/10/18/how-a-social-entrepreneur-overcame-his-arrogant-failure-and-won-kudos-from-oprah/#778fd1720445 [Accessed 9 August 2017].

98  Shaw, E. and Carter, S. (2007), "Social entrepreneurship: Theoretical antecedents and empirical analysis of entrepreneurial processes and outcomes," *Journal of Small Business and Enterprise Development*, 14(3): 418–434.

99  Robb-Post, C. C. Stamp, J. A., Brännback, M., Carsrud, A. L. and Östermark, R. (2011) "Do gooders versus good doers: An empirical examination of growth versus efficiency in social entrepreneurship," *Frontiers of Entrepreneurship Research*, 31(19), Article 5, Available: http://digitalknowledge.babson.edu/fer/vol31/iss19/5 [Accessed 17 August 2017].

# THE SOCIAL ENTERPRISE ECOSYSTEM

## Chapter Objectives

➤ Understand the complex elements of the SEV ecosystem.

➤ Explain various frameworks that intersect the SEV ecosystem.

➤ Define stakeholders and prioritize them based on their impact on the SEV ecosystem.

➤ Find an appropriate strategy to balance the myriad worlds that create the complex SEV ecosystem.

➤ Give examples of SEVs and how they have handled their operating ecosystem.

➤ Questions/Workbook.

➤ **Cases:** Visayan Forum Foundation (human trafficking: Philippines), The Akshaya Patra Foundation (free mid-day meals: India), The Ibrahim Prize (governance: Africa), Zipline International Inc. (medical drone delivery: impact Africa), International Consortium of Investigative Journalists (corruption: USA), and Peace Works & KIND Inc. (health, kindness, tolerance: USA).

## 2.1. The Playground Social Entrepreneurs Work in: An SEV Ecosystem

Between 1987 and 1997, non-profit organizations grew by 31%, to 1.2 million in number, exceeding the 26% rate of new business formation.[1] A new fourth sector is evolving. One that is a multi-stakeholder collaborative ecosystem which is operating in the development sector and estimated to contribute to about 10% of the global GDP.[2] The last GEMS study on social entrepreneurship, which spanned 58 countries, found that the rate of starting an SEV activity lagged behind commercial startup activities (3.2–1.1% versus 7.6%).[3] Academic research on the SEV ecosytem is lagging, partly because of the problem of identifying SEVs, which are found in the first, second, and third sectors and are confused with *ethical businesses*.[4] This makes the understanding of the SEV ecosystem complex, as it intersects with the developmental sector ecosystem on the one end and the commercial business startup ecosystem on the other (see Exhibit 2.1).

Exhibit 2.1:   **Theory Synopsis — Understanding the SEV Business Ecosystems**

The concept of a "business ecosystem" was first proposed by James Moore,[5] who borrowed his thinking from biology. He looked at the microeconomics of various entities in the system and how they co-evolved from sources of innovation, by using partnerships, bargaining power, and competition. He suggested that business organizations should not be looked in isolation of an industry, but across various industries, as they were all vying for survival. Iansiti and Levien[6] took it one step further and concluded that the ecosystem could be called an interconnected business, whose health was dependent on three factors: productivity (average return on capital), robustness (number of firms in the ecosystem), and niche creation (uniqueness or differentiation). Peltoniemi[7] highlighted that this interconnectedness can be both competitive and cooperative and that organizations share a common fate, made more complex by the fact that the business ecosystem is still dependent on the external environment.

The complexity of SEV ecosystem comes from several factors, according to Berkes and Davidson-Hunt.[8] They are as follows: (1) a complex interaction between local actors, who are place-based, and global actors, who may not have an attachment to the place and hence may be opportunistic and more transient; (2) politics of resource access and control creating tensions that need to be managed; and (3) a need to engage in global processes in a very interconnected world that may include both conflict and accommodation management strategies. This is highlighted in the discourse by Johanisova *et al.*[9] that looks at the "economy" as a complex system of where SEVs operate in a liminal sphere between monetized and non-monetized zones. The tensions that arise in this ecosystem are of four types: performing tensions, organizing tensions, belonging tensions, and learning tensions.[10]

This ecosystem approach of management extends across different institutions (private and public) and can cross national borders, making the lines of ownership unclear. At the policy level, SEVs must work with governments and Inter-governmental Organizations (IGOs) to get their causes into the agenda for prioritization. Should maternal health come before child health? What happens when there are limited resources and you need to make trade-offs? You are still dealing with lives in both cases. To take it further, should the focus be for a mother and child from a developing country where the overall quality of life is perceived better than the impoverished living at the bottom of the pyramid? Does this hold true in urban pockets of deprivation? What happens in the case of the threat of a global pandemic — where should priorities lie? Should fighting the pandemic take precedence over a routine, but lifesaving health interventions like vaccines? Added to this complexity is media noise and citizen fears — as citizens have the power to vote governments out. SEV ecosystems are complex.

To take decisions by finding synergies and compromises between the various intersecting ecosystems requires an understanding of the scale (especially in policy formulation and implementation), the commonalities between various systems intersected, and the difference in the ways the ecosystems are managed.[11] This means breaking things down into smaller chunks for implementation. To succeed, SEVs must understand value co-creation (see Exhibit 2.2) and learn how to get various players to work together for a common purpose. A review of literature[12] finds the following key ecosystem frameworks SEVs must be aware of when designing their business models: (1) legal and regulatory framework, (2) cultural framework, (3) governance framework, (4) resource framework, (5) competition, (6) access to markets, and (7) policy changes.

**SEVs must be able to look at various intersecting ecosystems and take decisions by finding synergies and compromises between these often-contradictory ecosystems and understanding the potential of scale (especially in policy formulation and implementation).[13]**

Exhibit 2.2:   **Theory Synopsis — Value Co-creation and Theory of Change**

Value co-creation is a not a new concept and is often used in business. It refers to a process where both the organization and the customer (in the case of SEVs it is the beneficiary and other stakeholders) co-create value either jointly or individually, passively or actively, in real-time or in an iterative process, while interacting at some level.[14] The key for success is the participation of the user of the services/products or the beneficiary.

In business, assumption is a collaborative process for peers.[15] This can be translated into the SEV context — but here, the beneficiaries would have to be included in the process and be addressed at the peer level. Merz et al.[16] reiterate this point (albeit in the business context), suggesting that value is "*co-created through network relationships and social interactions among the ecosystem of all stakeholders*" (p. 338). Co-creation requires a space for dialogue, providing alternative perspectives, and information.[17] Since one of the most critical stages for an SEV is understanding the problem they face in order to develop a sustainable solution (see Figure 2.1), you will require beneficiaries as co-creators for value creation and value facilitation. Often this is because you need multiple perspectives for changing the structural environment, collaboration with facilitating entities, and changing of self.

Figure 2.1:   Problem-Solving Process

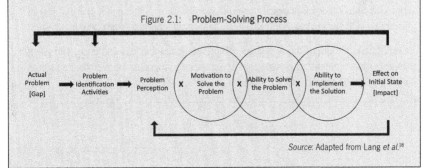

*Source*: Adapted from Lang et al.[18]

Exhibit 2.2:  **(cont)**

One useful tool for social change is the Theory of Change as put forward by Weiss.[19] It allows you to ask the question how and why change must occur, the beliefs you have about the process, what value you will provide by your intervention, and how you will measure the impact of this (goals). By working backward, the goals are tied to outcomes at various stages and the underlying assumptions of what works. Outcomes are tied to indicators that need to be measured. Indicators should come before the measurement of impact.[20]

Outcomes are defined as a condition that leads to clear goals.[21] This allows you to map the relationships of the goals and the activities and processes required to reach this. Weiss and the Annie E. Casey Foundation[22] stress that this does the following: (1) allows you to allocate key resources to vital parts of the program and develop core capacities (people, processes, supports, models, techniques, structures, plans, frameworks, and other inputs vital to bring, scale, and sustain change), (2) facilitates aggregation of knowledge at the program level through evaluation of results at various stages, (3) makes assumptions explicit, getting consensus on goals, and (4) helps address assumptions embedded on the program that can influence both policy and popular opinion.

Another way to look at the value creating process is borrowed from the social innovation playbook, *The Open Book of Social Innovation*.[23] You must first begin with the process of *evidentia*, to find the right problem. This requires a minimum of six mapping exercises as follows: (1) mapping needs of the community — this will allow you to find hierarchies, bottlenecks, and opportunities; (2) mapping capacities — this is needed for manpower planning and to increase synergy with entrenched players and leverage local talent; (3) mapping physical assets — this will help you plan finances for infrastructure and help in the management of resource-limiting liabilities; (4) mapping systems — SEVs operate in embedded contexts which may not be very formal hence understanding the complex systems allows you to manage design of the program, recruitments, governance, etc., that is required for reputation and legitimacy; (5) mapping flows — by mapping the flow of goods, people, and information you have a greater control on factors crucial to the SEV model; and (6) mapping expertise — expertise may lie outside the SEV and using partnerships and strong networks these capabilities and knowledge can be captured.

Once you have identified the right problem, you need to find the right solution. SEVs can look for sources of innovation (even using crowdsourcing if needed). They should co-create with key stakeholders to facilitate stakeholder participation and engagement.

Finally, SEVs should set up a method of monitoring, feedback, governance, and using impact measurement to ensure that the solutions suggested have the impact as outlined in their mission. More details are covered in Chapter 7.

## 2.2. **Legal and Regulatory Framework**

SEVs operate in unchartered territory, in gray areas where the legal and regulatory environment has either not adapted to accommodate such ventures or their objectives or are simply unwilling or unable to take responsibility when priorities may lie elsewhere. They need to understand the murky places they can be caught in when trying to create change. If you want to ban human trafficking, at a national or international level, you must start at a smaller scale — with vulnerable communities, local law enforcement, the participating public, and any other relevant organizations (see Case Study 2.1). Human trafficking is estimated to earn profits of US$150 billion, with a majority of the profits coming from commercial sexual exploitation (66%) and commercial forced labor (28%).[24] In the case of Visayan Forum Foundation, Inc. (VF), an anti-human trafficking non-profit, they worked with transportation companies which are the logistics point of trafficking. It is easy to make the mistake thinking that the key problem being solved was trafficking. While that was the main purpose of the organization, it was clear that rescuing a victim was not enough, as the core problem was to provide a sustainable livelihood, educate children, and at an even deeper level, tackle the buyers.

The VF case illustrates the ecosystem approach. It is a multi-jurisdiction case that crosses borders. To stop trafficking, you need to consider where victims are coming from, where they are being re-routed, and also where the victims are being sent. While profits per victim are highest in developed countries (US$34,800), followed by the Middle East (US$15,000), and then the rest of Europe (US$12,900),[25] the volume markets are Asia (11.7 million people in forced labor), Africa (3.7 million), South America (1.8 million), rest of Europe (1.6 million), the EU (1.5 million), and then the other developing countries.[26] To create sustainable impact, VF needs to reintegrate and protect rescued victims, by creating halfway houses, and collaborating with vocational institutes to help rescued victims find a sustainable source of income. To stop the crimes and create more deterrents, VF pushes for changes in legislations. The initial problem of trafficking and recruitment has evolved to move online. While physical trafficking may be reducing, online pornography has become a bigger challenge. Hence, the problem keeps evolving.

In addition to the above discussed points, the regulatory framework, existing infrastructure (or lack of it), and other support systems in the ecosystem like the impact investment climate may either impede or facilitate the growth of SEVs. Though it is difficult, depending on the area of impact, SEVs often find themselves co-constructing policy frameworks to change barriers in the ecosystem. Founders may need to take the role of a policy entrepreneur, which is a person who has the political will to advocate a solution that can tackle a problem and get it on the agenda or the list of problems or subjects that government officials or other related constituents are paying attention to.[27] Policy entrepreneurs must be able to articulate the mismatch in resources like funding, explain where resources need to be deployed, and prioritize where it is needed first.[28] In this journey, SEVs will have to be able to give facts to justify return on investment, and this needs impact measurement. Larger well-established development agencies have traditionally focused on short-term processes and used their accrued social capital with funding stakeholders to justify process results (conferences on poverty, fund-raising dinners, and reports published on the topic), rather than results itself.[29] The social entrepreneurship ecosystem climate is changing and there are more demands for transparency and accountability in this sector. For example, Charity Navigator (which is a

Case Study 2.1: **Visayan Forum Foundation (Philippines)**

Cecilia Flores-Oebanda is the founder and Executive Director of Visayan Forum Foundation (VF). The organization began in 1991 in Manila, Philippines. Human trafficking is illegal in Philippines. The country is considered a source country. The underlying root causes can be attributed to the following: (1) a subsistence economy (36.8% live below the poverty line with close to 47.5% earning  less than US$2/day); (2) unemployment (17.4% unemployed between ages 15 and 24); (3) a large undocumented population (900,000 people lack identity documents), and (4) corruption (according to the 2016 Corruption Perception Index, Philippines ranks 101 out of 176 countries). More than 10 million Filipinos work abroad, and in 2016, remittance was 10.2% of the Philippines economy. Of the estimated 800,000 said to be working in the illegal sex industry, a majority are thought to be children. Most of the young girls are promised employment across Asia in countries like Singapore, Taiwan, Hong Kong, Japan, and the Middle East.

Philippines has more than 700 islands, and victims are moved mostly by using shipping as the transportation mode. The transit points are urban areas like Manila, Cebu, Olongapo, Puerto Galera, Boracay, and Surigao. VF anti-trafficking strategies are implemented by working with the government and the private sector at eight major seaports and three airports, in partnership with 52 inter-island shippers, two airlines, and 2,000 bus companies. VF operates with over 200 local and international socio-civic groups, non-governmental organizations (NGOs), government agencies, and private institutions. They have put up shelters and similar projects in 13 places along strategic trafficking routes. Rescued women often have debts to pay and need to be rehabilitated to find alternative sources of employment. VF's Theory of Change is based on the following four pillars: (1) policy advocacy (focusing on evidence and research for policy reforms and sustainable change); (2) protective care services (to protect and transform the lives of victims, survivors, and vulnerable persons to prevent exploitation and explore opportunities for a better life); (3) ventures for freedom (strengthen and enable community watch to get involved); and (4) iFight movement (a youth movement aimed at creating awareness about and to prevent exploitation from human trafficking and slavery).

In 2012, USAID filed fraud charges against VF for allegedly using false documentation to list beneficiaries and misappropriate grant funds to the tune of US$2.1 million. These were difficult years for VF as funds were frozen and Cecilia battled to save her reputation and the credibility of the organization. Over 80% of the employees resigned or were let go, and rescuing children and the vulnerable came to a literal standstill. Cecilia denied any wrongdoing but acknowledged poor bookkeeping. She said, "*For me, the battleground now has actually shifted. It's shifted from the port. It's shifted from the battlefield of trafficking to all this paper. To hell with all this paper.*" In February 2013, Cecilia filed perjury charges against her former bookkeeper and the independent auditor hired by USAID. This was with the assistance of the Skoll Foundation of which she was made a fellow in 2008. In 2016, The Department of Justice (DOJ) cleared the NGO of the charge. It is estimated that VF has rescued and supported more than 18,000 trafficking cases.

registered as a charity) evaluates charitable organizations based on their stewardship of the money collected. This allows donors to see how much of their dollar donated goes to the cause versus administration and other expenses along with ratings in accountability and transparency.

**SEVs operate in unchartered territory, in gray areas where the legal and regulatory environment has either not adapted to accommodate such ventures or their objectives or are simply unwilling or unable to take the responsibility, when priorities may lie elsewhere.**

## 2.3. Cultural Framework

Culture is an amalgamation of goals, beliefs, values, norms, and representations of the group.[30] There are two cultural frameworks to be considered — the cultural background of the operating environment itself and the SEV cultural mind-set. SEVs operate in cultural spheres where there are different interpretations of truth, contracts, time, ethics, common sense, gossip, and silence that affect communication, etiquette, and behavior.[31] While the cultural ecosystem can be influenced, it cannot be controlled as easily as the SEV culture.

At the end of 2017, with the increasing number of sexual harassment cases in USA being revealed and the strengthening #MeToo Twitter campaign, Matt Damon, the actor, said in an interview, "*I think we're in this watershed moment. I think it's great. I think it's wonderful that women are feeling empowered to tell their stories, and it's totally necessary ... I do believe that there's a spectrum of behavior, right? And we're going to have to figure — you know, there's a difference between, you know, patting someone on the butt and rape or child molestation, right? Both of those behaviors need to be confronted and eradicated without question, but they shouldn't be conflated, right?*"[32]

The response on social media was violent with women protesting that sexual harassment was still harassment and could not be put on a scale. It resulted in a signed petition by over 19,000 fans to drop Matt Damon from the film Oceans 8.[33] Alyssa Milano, a strong proponent of the #MeToo campaign[34] commented about the interview, "*We are not outraged because someone grabbed our asses in a picture. We are outraged because we were made to feel this was normal. We are outraged because we have been gaslighted. We are outraged because we were silenced for so long.*"[35] Matt Damon eventually apologized and said, "*I really wish I'd listened a lot more before I weighed in on this.*"[36] Cultural situational context matters. In 2017, *Time* recognized the people behind the #MeToo movement for the Time Person of the Year. In 2018, Gillette offended many of its customers (591K dislikes versus 225K likes) with #TheBestMenCanBe advertisement, which was supporting the movement.[37]

**Organizational culture is a combination of visible artifacts (what you can see), values (your beliefs), and underlying assumptions (your perceptions of what is true).[40]**

An SEV founder must have a clearly articulated framework for the culture of the organization. Organizational culture is a combination of visible artifacts, values, and underlying assumptions.[38]

Patagonia is an activist company that reflects its cultural heritage of protecting the wild outdoors, not just in the products it offers but in its employees, who are passionate about its cause.[39] Patagonia is a high-quality outdoor brand that prides itself on its ethics, both in terms of sourcing its raw material and its policy toward human capital in the organization. Its mission statement asserts, *Build the best product, cause no unnecessary harm, use business to inspire and implement solutions to the environmental crisis.* They devote 1% of sales (approximately US$10 million) to environmental groups and try and reduce their carbon and toxic waste footprint as far as possible.

On December 4, 2017, when Patagonia, a specialist clothing retailer, adopted the cause of protecting the environment, it not only updated its North American website with the black webpage stating, *The President Stole Your Land*, but also released a press statement in response to the Trump Administration's shrinkage of the Bears Ears National Monument-protected lands by 85%, stating, "*The Administration's unlawful actions betray our shared responsibility to protect iconic places for future generations and represent the largest elimination of protected land in American history. We've fought to protect these places since we were founded and now, we'll continue that fight in the courts.*" — Rose Marcario, President and CEO, Patagonia (see Exhibit 2.3). On December 11th, they released another press statement saying that they had, with a coalition of other concerned parties, sued the Trump administration.[41] It went on to donate US$10 million, saved from unexpected tax cuts toward environmental causes.[42] This requires courage and a culture of support.

Exhibit 2.3:  **Patagonia Campaign**

Source: Property of Patagonia, Inc. Used with permission.

Managing cultural exchanges requires an understanding of culture and management of knowledge flows. An SEV can use both push-and-pull knowledge strategies to manage the cultural divide[43] (see Exhibit 2.4). This requires SEVs to pull knowledge to get a better understanding of context and push knowledge to help bridge the gap. For years, the Government of India wanted more rural children to attend school, but the challenge was that many parents preferred their children working in the fields to supplement household income to ensure basic needs of food and shelter were met. The solution that was espoused was that by attending school, children would get a free meal. This was a powerful incentive. It solved

Exhibit 2.4:   **Ecosystem Management: Cultural Framework**

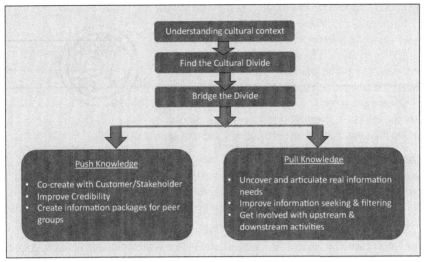

Source: Adapted from Roux *et al.* (see footnote 44).

malnutrition, child labor, and illiteracy. The diversity of cultural and political barriers across the respective states resulted in challenges with implementation due to lack of alignment within the central government, state government, and the implementing bodies.[44]

There was room for other organizations to step in. The Akshaya Patra Foundation is an NGO based in India that runs the world's largest mid-day meal program, serving more than 1.66 million lunches to public school students daily, across 12 states in India (see Case Study 2.2). To serve the large volumes of meals per day from their 34 kitchens, they redesigned their kitchen, managed logistics to save costs, and ensured a "just-in-time" fresh meals. To ensure all of this, they coordinated with schools, the government, donors, and volunteers. In 2003, The Akshaya Patra Foundation became the first organization to form a public–private partnership with the Government of India.[45]

**Finding and articulating real informational needs require SEVs to understand the cultural frame of reference in which they operate, which may reflect the social identities of groups.[46]**

One of the challenges that The Akshaya Patra Foundation faced (Case Study 2.2) was the recruitment and training of women in socially conservative regions for their decentralized kitchens. Many of the women were not educated nor had any work experience. They were taught counting to manage jobs like accounting and inventory management and even taught basic hygiene.[47] Rural areas often had power outages, and delivery trucks could be delayed. The women needed to know how to buy vegetables with longer shelf lives.[48] Another challenge was the mixing up of the perceived social classes among children, so that they could have their meals together in school.[49] SEVs must understand cultural frames and this means the social identities of the groups they work with, if they are to create a meaningful, long-lasting change.

Case Study 2.2: **The Akshaya Patra Foundation**

All over India, over 113 million children are served a free mid-day meal each day across 1.265 million schools. In 2001, the Supreme Court of India passed an interim order that a cooked mid-day meal became a right for children studying in schools run or aided by the government, even though this order was enacted in 1995 by the Indian federal government. The Mid-Day Meal (MDM) guidelines are set by the Government of India. The cost for the program ranges from (Indian Rupee) INR 4.13 to INR 6.18/meal minus the cost of honorariums to the cooks and the cost of monitoring and evaluation assistance.

The Akshaya Patra Foundation is an NGO based in India that runs the world's largest mid-day meal program, serving more than 1.66 million lunches to government school students daily, across 12 states in India. They began in 2000, serving 1,500 children in five schools. In 2010, their goal was to reach 5 million children by 2020. They feel that feeding a child is not a work of charity but rather one of social responsibility.

The Akshaya Patra Foundation manages the preparation of the meals in 34 kitchens, of which 13 are ISO certified (global quality benchmark). For a donation of INR 950 (US$30), a child can be provided a mid-day meal for the year. The centralized kitchens are automated to cook up to 100,000 meals a day. The numbers are boggling, considering that the meals are customized to local dietary habits. In North India, *roti* (flat breads)-making machines produce 200,000 *rotis* from 6,000 kg of wheat flour. *Roti* machines of that capacity were not available and had to be sourced from Holland. Rice cookers were sourced from Germany, with each rice cauldron cooking at least 500 L in 20 min. Each *dal* or *sambar* (lentil) cauldron has the capacity to cook 1,200–3,000 L of *dal*. *Dal* was made for North and West India and in South India, children were served *sambar*. Vegetables are procured on a daily basis, and the cooked food is packed in steam-sterilized vessels.

The cost of the mid-day meal provided by The Akshaya Patra Foundation is INR 10.23 of which INR 6.2 is provided by the Government of India. Around 40% of the funds for The Akshaya Patra Foundation comes from private donors, and it is essential to optimize funds to ensure supplies to schools are uninterrupted. They have been able to manage these costs by working with engineers to expand the centralized kitchens for handling the large quantities of material, working with vendors to ensure quality supplies of the volumes required, reduce food waste, and also ensure safe transportation and handling of the meals through efficient logistics and IT infrastructure. Inflation and food price volatility in India is high. To manage this better, The Akshaya Patra Foundation signs long-term contracts for procurement with commodity brokers.

Knowledge-pull strategies assume that knowledge is dynamic, often lying as tacit information in the ecosystem, and should be actively captured through networking.[51] Tacit knowledge when mobilized can be a competitive advantage.[52] Complex tacit knowledge is best transferred through face-to-face meetings or firsthand experiences, which minimize transmission errors.[53] This is important as many SEV founders operate in unfamiliar marketplaces. When Jacob Korenblum, founder of Souktel[54] first traveled to Palestine in 2005, to work on an economic growth project for the US Agency for International Development (USAID), he was told that there was a huge unemployment rate among the Palestinians. He assumed it was merely a supply problem that there were not enough qualified people.

To his surprise, after holding several interviews and focus groups, he found out it was a problem of matching demand and supply. Though there were many qualified young Palestinians, and there were many jobs available, the problem was not creating more qualified people but that prospective employees were unaware of the opportunities because of the poor infrastructure and internet connectivity. There was no way for the information to flow freely. Even if candidates were called for interviews, there were security problems associated with traveling, especially across the West Bank checkpoints. As of January 2017, there were 98 fixed checkpoints and an average of 310 monthly flying checkpoints in the West Bank restricting movements of the Palestinians.[55]

Souktel found a solution that plugged this communication and physical movement gap by offering m-technology. Using simple SMS texts not only were they able to cater to the job-matching market but they were also able to build other digital solutions for emerging markets for education and emergency services. Jacob was able to harness the information available in the market for good, using his experience in the aid sector, his language skills (he spoke Arabic), networks in his university (Harvard Business School), and his unique market knowledge to get enough funding to start, pilot, and sustain his business. In 2015, *Wall Street Journal* named Souktel one of *Five Apps Bringing the Next Billion People Online*.[56] By 2017, Souktel's clients ranged from aid organizations, non-government organizations, and governments to the media and individuals, and they had a reach of 200,000-plus people across 30 emerging market countries.

Knowledge-push strategies require the following: (1) co-creation with the customers of focus, (2) improving credibility with the stakeholders and in the public eye, and (3) creating information packages for peer groups, especially employees and key stakeholders, so that they can value the cultural differences, find common points of discourse, and bridge the divide. The Ibrahim Prize (see Case Study 2.3) requires co-creation at multiple levels. While the objective is to reward country leadership through an impartial review of governance indicators in the African nations, it has challenges to make this a reality. Through the dissemination of the ranking and award criteria that include important governance indicators, leaders of countries have data to work with, and board members have criteria for evaluation. They identify data that other NGOs and stakeholders must compile and publish these figures to rank countries. Value co-creation begins at the data collection stage. By presenting transparency of figures and to encourage leaders to co-create by first wanting to create change, this information is shared at the grassroots level. Knowledge credibility comes at two levels. The first is credence credibility — the perception that the people with the knowledge are experts[57] — and the second is safety credibility — the degree to which others trust and feel comfortable in the presence of the people with the knowledge.[58] Both are required to work in the ecosystem, and very often, the latter is neglected. Studies in psychology show that messages tailored to cultural frames are more persuasive than those that are not tailored.[59]

## Case Study 2.3: **The Ibrahim Prize**

The Ibrahim Prize was begun by the founder of Cel Tel, Mohamed Ibrahim in 2006. It is an attempt to try and keep elected government leaders honest through a US$5 million prize offered by the Mo Ibrahim Foundation. His experience building Cel Tel in Africa exposed him firsthand to the state of corruption in the continent. Being a strong believer in Africa's immense potential, he wanted to change the *status quo*. Ibrahim says, "*We are a very rich continent, the second-largest continent in the world, lush-green, plenty of resources. Everything we have. Yet we are the poorest people on earth. So, rich continent, poor people. After fifty years of independence, I don't think we can continue to blame the colonialists.*"[60] Ibrahim calls this award, a "*Prize for excellence in leadership.*"[61] This award exceeds the Nobel Peace Prize, which is valued at US$1.3 million. Ibrahim made his fortune selling Cel Tel, to MTC, Kuwait for US$3.4 billion (£1.8 billion) in 2005. The first year, they assessed 13 African former heads. Unfortunately, six of them took power back by staging coups.

By 2017, 53 African government leaders were evaluated using the Ibrahim Index of African Governance, which was originally developed with the Director of Program on Intrastate Conflict at the Harvard's Kennedy School of Government. It measured each government on 57 variables. By 2009, this Index had been expanded to 88 variables and again later to 100 variables, each of equal weightage and based on information publically available in 36 sources. The index measures safety and rule of law; participation and human rights; sustainable economic opportunity; and human development. The prize is awarded at the time of the leader's outgoing (cannot be more than two terms) and spread over 10 years (US$200,000 pa) with another US$200,000 pa, if they establish a charitable foundation. To push information to the people, Ibrahim regularly buys advertisement space in local newspapers.

The prize committee has its own research arm that publishes monthly reports. The board has had various luminaries like Kofi Annan, the former UN Secretary-General; Mohamed ElBaradei, the former head of the International Atomic Energy Agency and one of the icons of the Egyptian opposition; the former Finnish President, Martti Ahtisaari; Valerie Amos, former Under-Secretary General for Humanitarian Affairs and Emergency Relief Coordinator at the United Nations; Salim Ahmed Salim, former President of the United Nations Security Council and former President of the United Nations General Assembly; Jin-Yong Cai, former Executive Vice President and Chief Executive Officer of the International Finance Corporation (IFC); and other prominent African activists. Board members are paid US$30,000 to attend four board meetings annually. In 2017, there were 16 Board members.

The foundation does not feel pressurized to grant an award every year if there are no deserving candidates. Awards were given in 2008, 2009, 2011, 2014, and 2017. The award has its detractors who criticize the low impact of the prize on dictators, and the fact that when no prize is awarded, it may be considered too elitist to achieve. However, there is a competition between the nations and many leaders wish to win. This motivation alone is creating change.

## 2.4. **Governance Framework**

Governance is derived from the Latin root word *cybern* which means steering.[62] Governance can be defined as the *systems and processes that ensure the overall direction, effectiveness, supervision and accountability of an organization.*[63] An interesting document for all SEVs to read is presented by the Schwab Foundation for Social Entrepreneurship called *The Governance of Social Enterprises Managing Your Organization for Success.*[64] Governance involves the coordination, production, and implementation of collectively binding principles or rules to guide those interactions between relevant actors that is used to solve societal problems, create societal opportunities, and at the same time care for those institutions that enable them and/or provide collective goods.[65,66] In the corporate sphere, governance is essentially the separation of ownership and control, but in SEVs, the concept of shareholders may not exist, and this raises the question of stewardship and the way the SEV institutionalizes values.[67]

> **Governance involves the coordination, production, and implementation of collectively binding principles or rules to guide those interactions between relevant actors that is used to solve societal problems, create societal opportunities, and at the same time care for those institutions that enable them and/or provide collective goods.[68,69]**

Failure in governance often comes from the dependency of the success of the SEV on the individual, rather than the organization.[70] With the blurring of the lines that divides the public or government sector, private sector and non-profit or voluntary sector, governance is becoming more important. Governments were traditionally cast in a role where their job was to respond to market failures by providing public goods and services like water, national defense, social justice, and public education, and hence they were required to address the market-based inequalities through redistribution of resources using vehicles like unemployment benefits, disaster relief, etc.[71] The private sector focused on innovation and profits and hence also contributed to customer needs, providing employment and adding to a nation's wealth.[72] The non-profit or voluntary sector focused on social impact and was often self-governing. The merging of these three distinct areas, the rapid growth of the non-profit/voluntary sector, and the need for more transparency, have all highlighted that governance is a critical issue for SEVs. SEVs now need to have the speed, innovation, and accountability of the private sector and get involved in public policymaking and delivery.[73]

Take, for example, the high-profile case against Mohammed Yunus, the Nobel Laureate. Due to the politics of the situation, and more importantly the lack of transparency in funding and ownership between the various initiatives he was running at that time, he faced some backlash, first with the Danish documentary, "Caught in Microcredit", that in part arose when some of the funds purposed for Grameen Bank by the Norwegian government and other donors were transferred to Grameen Kalyan.[74] This was of the amount of NOK540 million, based on the exchange rate of that time. The matter was raised by the embassy in 1997, especially as at that time, they were not aware of Grameen Kalyan.[75] Based on a negotiation with the Norwegian government, the funds to the tune of NOK170 million were reimbursed in May 1998 to Grameen Bank and the funding formally concluded in 2003. Governance involves both an intentional and a structural dimension to various interactions.

(a) **Intentional Dimensions of Governance:** Intentional dimensions of governance[76] are conceptualized by the following elements: the philosophy, information pushed out, grant criteria agreed to, the regulations of operations, and finally the SEV actions themselves. These are explained in detail in what follows:

    (1) *Images or vision or guiding philosophy:* How clearly articulated are these? Is there a code of ethics? When decisions are taken — what is the plumb line used to especially look at the ethics of the situation? To look back at the example of Grameen Bank — one of the debates that has emerged is the data on the effectiveness of the intervention. While a majority of the funding was provided by donors that charged zero interest, the website of Grameen Bank claims interest was set at 16%,[77] and with the pressure to repay, the required savings, in retrospective, by one set of calculations, the interest rate could range anywhere from 20% to 24% making microfinance a very lucrative business.[78] So that *per se* should be considered while measuring the effectiveness of the program.

    (2) *Instruments like information, negotiation, and persuasion to regulations, grants, and sanctions:* With Grameen Bank, one of the challenges was that at one point of time, funds moved between the bank and Grameen Kalyan, Grameen Danone (a JV with Danone), and Grameen Phone. The Grameen Foundation had a list of all Grameen family organizations, which was in excess of 28 organizations as per the last compilation in 2014.[79] It is important that SEVs are cognizant about regulations, grant guidelines, and so do not misuse them. Ignorance is not a valid argument.

    (3) *Actions:* One of the challenges all SEVs face is that their actions speak louder than words. Rabee Zureikat, founded the Zikra Initiative in 2007[80] in the hope to promote tourism exchange between marginalized rural areas of Jordan and rich urban communities. When he began working in the Ghor Al Mazra'a community, there was a lot of skepticism by the people living there as the community had seen so many NGOs and well-meaning individuals with donations and ideas, but no long-term staying power. This was a community that was historically shunned by Jordanians because of their dark skin color. In fact, at the beginning, Rabee also began working in the traditional way with a donation of clothes. What made him different was that by listening to the community, he saw that what they wanted was acceptance and economic empowerment. He realized he had much to learn from them — their sustainable way of life and their cultural knowledge. There was a power imbalance of giver and taker in that situation, and he wanted to reframe it to an exchange of

learning. He did this by promoting tourism exchanges. Urban tourists are hosted in local people homes, and learn their way of life, which is now being saved from being forgotten. He facilitates microloans as the community earns through this "tourism exchange". More importantly, by showing his staying power, he demonstrated through his actions that he can walk the talk and that he cares about the community.

(b) **Structural Interactions of Governance:** Structural interactions of governance involve organizational setup elements. Very often, some of these elements are created haphazardly during growth and leave the SEV open to chaos, poor operations, and worse — fraud. They are explained in what follows:

(1) *Hierarchical governance vertical, top-down, steering, and control*[81]: One of the challenges SEVs face is that they are opportunistic and chaotic when scaling, and this stresses the system especially if they don't have a formal structure. UK-based Oxfam was rocked by scandal in 2018[82] when it emerged that in 2005, members of the organization held orgy-like parties with prostitutes and minors in Haiti. Oxfam quietly handled the matter in 2001, reporting the issue as a "serious misconduct" and then fired 11 people. But the media got hold of the story on February 9, 2018 exposing the story especially as one of those individuals was rehired in the aid sector. Oxfam added in a statement: "*With up to 10,000 NGOs working in Haiti alone in 2011, not to mention hundreds of thousands of aid workers in countries around the world, it was unfortunately not possible for Oxfam to ensure that those found guilty of sexual misconduct were not re-employed in the sector.*"[83] Oxfam at this time was bidding for UK government funding and had several contracts with the European Commission. It resulted in political upheaval in UK, a debate on expatriate aid workers and their perks,[84] transparency of the aid sector, and loss of donor support for Oxfam. Did Oxfam do good work? Yes — over their 75 years of history. Did they have a structure to prevent abuse? Yes, but it was not strong or transparent enough. By taking public funds (government grants) and private donations, accountability should have been to the public, its investors, and those affected.

What are the questions to be asked? Does the SEV have a clear management structure of reporting and roles? Do they have an advisory board or a supervisory board? How do they separate the management from the executive board and the advisory board? What competence do board members have? Are there conflicts of interests? A study on SEVs in India found that over 50% feel there is a shortage of adequate managerial and technical personnel especially at the junior and mid-management levels, compared to 10% or less of mainstream businesses.[85] When there is such a high flux and an overreliance on volunteers, you will have areas of vulnerability in the organization.

(2) *Self-governance*: This can happen in several ways: self-regulation by market actors, self-governance by communities, or even through co-governance using public and non-public actors.[86] Due to the rapid media attention of microfinance (including the Nobel Prize) and the huge sums in excess of US$9.4 billion committed to the concept, a number of independent research studies have tested the impact of the concept.[87] Among the many papers on the topic, a more recent paper, titled *Microfinance and*

*the Business of Poverty Reduction: Critical Perspectives from Rural Bangladesh*, adds to the debate on microfinance and finds there are systematic problems often leading to the increasing levels of indebtedness among already impoverished communities which exacerbates vulnerabilities at multiple levels: economic (rising indebtedness, loss of land), social (increased surveillance, shaming, and disempowerment), and environmental (shifting cultivation patterns).[88] How often do SEVs coordinate with research parties to understand the impact of the change they are making? This may be critical to ensure transparency of efforts and minimize negative consequences of doing good.

The 2016 Global Fraud Study by the Association of Certified Fraud Examiners found that the top reported non-profit fraud schemes include the following: corruption (29%), billing (25%), expense reimbursements (25%), check tampering (25%), and skimming (19%).[89] The critical reasons were the following: first, lack of internal controls; second, overriding of existing controls; and third, lack of management review. Good governance practices are further covered in Chapter 4.

## 2.5. **Resource Framework**

The availability of resources in the markets of operations affects an SEV. Significant resources for SEVs are access to finance, human resources, infrastructure, customer loyalty, brand value, organization culture, reputation, and legitimacy. According to the resource-based view (RBV) theory, firms with strategic resources, which are valuable, rare, inimitable, and non-substitutable, can generate a *sustainable competitive advantage* in the marketplace.[90]

Finance has always been a key resource that SEVs like many other startups find difficult to access. Ironically, it is estimated that funding for SEVs will reach US$6 trillion by 2052.[91] To access finance, SEVs need a track record of performance and hence need to validate their model and show impact.[92] A majority of SEVs tend to focus on grants for financing, but the problem is in this case that the grant objectives may not be the same as the purpose of the SEV, which means repurposing the organization or modifying the focus of operations. The GEMS 2015 study found that SEVs invested 30–60% of their personal funds into their own venture, with over 30% relying on government funding and the remaining sources being the family and banks.[93] Grant money allows ownership of the SEV to remain with the founders, but rarely can be used to build infrastructure and create strong long-term teams. This creates uncertainty in operations about continuity and focus. A study of technology firms spanning a 25-year period shows startups choose risky financing options when they want to access unique resources they are in need of, and they feel that they have suitable defense mechanisms in place to keep the balance of power in the investor relationship.[94] There is little evidence or studies conducted on why SEVs chose certain types of funding and the opportunities and risks of these methods.

Another big problem SEVs face is hiring talent. When scaling an enterprise, you need more qualified and professional teams with a range of skills.[95] Women seem more comfortable in this field than men. Men and women are rather evenly involved in social entrepreneurship (men

55% versus women 45%), compared to traditional entrepreneurship where men outnumber women by a ratio of 2:1.[96] Volunteers make up 46–69% of the manpower of SEVs, and most SEVs are small organizations with less than five employees (45-68%).[97] Founders of SEVs tend to spend so much time on the cause that they forget that their role of managing human capital within an organization revolves around three additional functions: (1) human capital acquisition, (2) human capital development, and (3) human capital retention.[98] Founders typically want more control, and this leads to less equity being distributed and less finance being raised.[99] A recent study finds that family and founder ownership are associated with superior performance, but family management is not.[101] So founders can become good CEOs, but it requires strong teams and a change in the perspective of working management styles. For example, venture caplitalists tend to encourage the founders to step down when the firm is underperforming at the pre-IPO stage.[100]

While reputation and legitimacy are not considered conventional resources, they are important and can be acquired, developed, or won. Reputation is the evaluation of a firm by its stakeholders in terms of affect, esteem, and knowledge of the firm over time.[102] A study on reputation through the RBV lens found that reputation cannot be bought by additive and independent investments, but it can be enhanced by careful nurturing *of* interdependencies and complex relationships.[103,104] When you begin with a strong organizational identity (collection of symbols) that asks the question *Who are we, as an organization?* and then finds ways to institutionalize this throughout the organization,[105,106] this leads to a consolidation of organizational image (impressions of an organization) that leads to organizational reputation.[107] Organizational image answers the following questions: (a) what do employees/ stakeholders think outsiders think about their organization, (b) what do outsiders think about an organization, and (c) what employees/stakeholders project about their organization to hence influence how others think about the organization?[108]

The concept of legitimacy differs from reputation in the fact that it is a social contract between firms and society showing acceptance,[109] and if this social contract is destroyed, then the consequence to the firm involved can lead to its extinction. Legitimacy can be defined by *a generalized perception or assumption that the actions of an entity are desirable, proper or appropriate within some socially constructed system of norms, values, beliefs and definitions.*[110] Legitimacy is dependent on many different types of stakeholders like media, regulators, investors, and advocacy groups, and may lead to different types of legitimacies like pragmatic legitimacy (based on audience self-interest), moral legitimacy (based on normative approval), procedural legitimacy, cognitive legitimacy (based on comprehensibility or what is taken for granted), consequences or outcome legitimacy, and for the founders — personal legitimacy.[111] Resources are further discussed in Chapter 5.

## 2.6. **Competition**

Competition is always an important part of the ecosystem. While SEVs may not always have direct competitors, there is always a fierce competition for limited resources. It may mean looking across industries for innovations, working between cooperation and competitive strategies to safeguard market spaces, and creating sustainable value to create high barriers for entry. Since competition is often an outcome of limited resources and the inability to exploit new opportunities, one strategy to minimize competitiveness is to come up with a new playground of operation. If the area of focus for all competitors is women empowerment, you can use three types of strategies: structural holes (networks); white spaces; or differentiation (see Exhibit 2.5).

Exhibit 2.5: **Theory Synopsis — Structural Holes and White Spots**

A structural hole is a gap in network that provides social capital.[112] Social capital allows actors to invest in social relations with an expectation of returns through information, influence, social credentials, reinforcement of mental health, and entitlement of resources.[113] Networks are associated with three types of flows: assets, information, and status, and these can be exploited through timing, control, and access (through referrals).[114] We can assume networks are not stable as they are trust based.[115] Networks relationships can be informal or formal and become avenues for signaling in a crowded marketplace.[116] When these structural holes between networks are exploited, it feeds competition,[117] through the inherent qualities of a structural hole. While competition is considered a process (not a result), it is an outcome of limited choice and negotiated power.[118]

Another type of structural hole is the *White spot* or *white space*.[119] White spot coverage is the strategy associated with finding opportunities associated with structural holes in the business model using strategic foresight that can enhance competitiveness of the organization.[120] Strategic foresight allows organizations to deal with early warning signals that recognize and give warning about threats and opportunities arising from sources of weak signals present in the ecosystem. Strategic foresight can be either (1) directed (monitoring, issue-driven) or (2) undirected (scanning).[121] An example can be searching for gaps in intellectual property within the portfolio.[122]

When identifying innovation opportunities for the business model, sources can come from (1) within the organization and (2) outside the organization. White spots are typically found outside the current organization's structure and could look at existing customers served in a different way or new customers for the same process or for new products.[123] The changes the organizations must undertake to seize these opportunities for growth are often substantial if not transformational and can mean redefining process, the value proposition, revenue model, source of sustainable competitive advantage and pivotal resources (including intellectual property), and key markets.

The first is finding *structural holes*, which are existing gaps in the network for social capital. You search the marketplace for assets, information, and status and then exploit networks through timing, control, and access (through referrals). Using the example of women empowerment it may not work unless you get the men in the community to adopt the concept; hence, you might first want to work with influential men in the community.

The second strategy is to look for white spaces or white spots, which are knowledge opportunities associated with structural holes in the business model. You can look in gaps in Intellectual

Property (IP) or any of the business model elements required to create replicability and scale. If women empowerment is tied to financial empowerment, and you live in a fragile place where men would appropriate a women's earnings, but the population is relatively uneducated, you could pay women in cryptocurrency. This is being done in Afghanistan through the Women's Annex started by Roya Mahboob. In addition, you could reframe a cause in an area where funds are more easily available. For example, if you work in the field of martial arts and you are passionate about using your skills to do good. At the simplest level, you may use the idea of self-defense (focusing on the vulnerable, women and children). You can focus on the preservation of the art form and look for funding in the arts or heritage sector. You can research health benefits and focus on well-being or elderly health, for example. These are the ways you minimize competition.

Another challenge of reducing competition is finding your differentiation. This may be through acquiring and developing resources that give you a strategic competitive advantage in the marketplace, like a patent for a technology or even high-profile networks. While drones are increasingly being considered for commercial purposes, Zipline International Inc., a California-based robotics company began working in the emergency medical supply delivery services in developing countries. Part of their competitiveness comes from combining innovative technology in the market space of on-demand logistics with the medical sector in developing countries (see Case Study 2.4). To ensure the best product, they hired some of the brightest minds from leading aerospace companies like SpaceX, Google, Boeing, and NASA. Their strategic networks have been acquired through funding partners and investors (Sequoia Capital, Andreesen Horowitz, Google Ventures, Yahoo founder Jerry Yang, Microsoft co-founder Paul Allen), clients (governments of Rwanda and Tanzania), and partnership organizations (UPS Foundation, Gavi, the Vaccine Alliance). UPS incidentally was the courier chosen to deliver the drones to Rwanda. Both co-founders Keller Rinaldo and Will Hetzle are Harvard alums. Keenan Wyrobek, another co-founder, is a graduate of Stanford University. These associations bring in further networks.

## 2.7. Access to Markets

SEVs operate in fragile places where access to markets may be regulated. Of the World Health Organization-recommended vaccines, many are given in the first 2 months of a baby's life. In many conservative rural places, a woman would give birth at home, which is considered normal. The nearest medical facility may be too far to reach. In these cases, SEVs working in this sector of healthcare can work with existing entrenched players, like local midwives. In Pakistan, the regular displacement of children due to natural disasters and security threats make immunization difficult.[124] Gavi, the Vaccine Alliance worked with women who were trained as health workers to cater to villages with a population of 2,000 people. The women underwent a 6-month training course preparing them to attend to the basic needs of women and children. They would inoculate 8–10 children a day in their village and in the surrounding community by going door to door and educating parents on the benefits of immunization against unfounded rumors about such vaccines leading to infertility.[125] As seen with the recent 2019 measles epidemic in USA, one cannot ignore the importance of education.

Markets can also be accessed through public procurement tenders.[126] This means scanning the market for opportunities, competitively bidding for projects, or getting invited to work on special projects like Better Shelter. Humanitarian shelters are mostly associated with tents.

## Case Study 2.4: **Zipline International Inc.**

Delivery of supplies is a challenge in rural Africa. Because of the remoteness of the locations and poor infrastructure, some of the rural health centers are understocked with critical medical supplies like emergency blood, snake anti-venom, vaccines, or medicines. This means a critical care patient can die waiting for medical supplies. It is estimated that the death toll from rabies (preventable with timely vaccines) in the continent is around 24,000/year. Keller Rinaudo,

Keenan Wyrobek, and Will Hetzle founded Zipline in July 2011. Keller was involved in a previous venture called Romotive (2011–2014) which produced the mobile-enabled toy called Romo, where Keenan was an advisor. Keller pivoted from this product and decided the company would focus on solving real-world problems. The inspiration for Zipline came in 2014, when Keller met a graduate student named Zac Mtema at the Ifakara Health Institute in Tanzania. Zac had created a mobile alert system for healthcare workers to text urgently required medical supplies to the government, but due to the poor infrastructure (90% of roads can be washed away during the rains), the supplies often never reached leading to deaths. Keenan said it was an area of passion (solving a major problem in health) and commercial opportunity (logistics — on-demand delivery). While in USA the drone or unmanned aerial vehicles (UVA) was a highly regulated market, in Rwanda the government was willing to work with Zipline.

Zipline recruited aerospace veterans from companies like SpaceX, Google, Boeing, and NASA to custom design the proprietary technology behind the Zip. Zipline is very customer-centric. They spent close to 3 years developing their first product using customer requirements to perfect their model. If they can't source off-the-shelf technology, they figure out how to make it happen internally. They began launching in Rwanda at a national scale in 2016, and by the beginning of 2018, they had completed approximately 10,000 flights, unlike other drone competitors. By then, Zipline had raised US$43 million in venture funding from companies like Sequoia Capital, Andreesen Horowitz, SV Angel, Google Ventures, Subtraction Capital, Yahoo founder Jerry Yang, Microsoft co-founder Paul Allen, and Stanford University.

The Zip drone (or electric plane) weighs about 10 kg. Zips can carry a payload of 1.5 kg for a roundtrip distance of 120–160-plus km on a single battery charge that could last over 45 min in 95% of weather conditions (rain, wind, lightening). They use a launch catapult and a fixed wing design rather than the quadcopter design many drones prefer to ensure they can fly long distances. The goal is to keep delivery times to 15–30 min. It is an all-electric vehicle to ensure reliability for 24/7 deliveries, keeping in mind that the same rural areas would not have regular deliveries of gasoline. They are operated from Drone terminals (droneports) called "Nests" that are modified shipping containers stationed next to existing medical warehouses. All local terminals are staffed by locals, and hence, Zipline International creates employability. Local children often gather to see the launch and landing of the drones or "sky ambulances", and Keller feels this itself will inspire the next generation of entrepreneurs and engineers.

Zips are programed and tracked through software installed on an iPad that coordinates GPS locations of other drones and flight paths using data from, for example, the Civil Aviation Authority in Rwanda for Rwanda. All their drones use SIM cards to communicate through cell towers. Their technology has been inspired by flight computers and the method used by aircraft carriers to "hook" planes on landings. Zips have specially designed landing mechanisms requiring pinpoint accuracy to capture the plane safely. Zips need to decelerate from 100 km/h to zero in half a second. The state-of-the-art software can use information on wind speeds to ensure the payload falls in a radius of four parking spaces. Zips airdrop medical supplies using a propriety paper parachute to drop supplies to the designated location, requiring no additional infrastructure.

Safety and reliability are key to their reputation as they operate in both dense and remote areas. For example, the drone could also fly in a worst-case scenario with a broken propeller and most parts can be replaced. Some of the hospitals in the cities they cater to serve populations of half a million. They also need to ensure the product reaches in a fast, timely, and viable condition. Another area of innovation is security, Zipline builds its own end-to-end encryption from scratch. Zipline invests heavily into its technology and has built the infrastructure for automated regression testing of hardware.

The Zips uses cell phone components to reduce costs. The payload is packaged in proprietary packaging which is dropped using a specially designed paper parachute that together cost less than 50 cents. Zipline's customers are governments, pharmaceutical companies, and large logistics networks. Their business model focuses on both the on-demand courier service and the fulfillment service. They don't sell their drones (similar ones can cost US$10,000–US$68,000) but charge for the service provided. They charge a minimum monthly recurring fee from operations and maintenance of infrastructure and a minimum number of guaranteed deliveries. Above the minimum number of deliveries are additional charges per delivery which is on par with the motorbike deliveries that were being used but are far more reliable. Other governments are waiting in line, and they are transitioning to scale. They plan to expand their customer base from national governments to private hospitals and charge via mobile payment platforms. Their customer-centric focus helps keep them stay true to their original purpose as Keenan says that when you have customers approaching you with a life-and-death situation, which is not an abstract problem but a concrete problem of how to save a life, other temptations to diversify get lost.

Zipline's first national customer was the Government of Rwanda. They began delivering blood products from October 2016 to 21 transfusing facilities and by the end of 2017 had over 12 million citizens within 30 minutes of any essential product. Keller says in his TED talk, "*In all of health care logistics, you are trading off waste against access.*" By using Zipline, Rwanda has been able break the cycle of wastage reducing, for example, blood wastage to zero. Health workers place delivery orders by text message and receive their package within 30 minutes on average. Keller says this allows Africa to leapfrog over the absence of legacy infrastructure and go straight to newer and better systems.

In May 2016, they began trial-testing using the Zips in Rwanda for vaccine delivery with Gavi, the Vaccine Alliance and the UPS Foundation. They received a US$800,000 grant from the UPS Foundation. In 2017, they began expanding to Eastern Africa entering into Tanzania. Zipline will measure impact of its drone delivery services in Tanzania (Dodoma) by tying up with the Ifakara Health Institute (where Zac works) and the University of Glasgow. Tanzania plans up to 2,000 deliveries per day for 2018. The research project would be funded by the Human Development Impact Fund, the Bill & Melinda Gates Foundation, and Saving Lives at Birth, an initiative led by the US Agency for International Development.

Future innovations would be quieter propellers a longer range, heavier payloads, and solar panels. This market has huge potential but is becoming more competitive. Google's Project Wing, Amazon, and Walmart are players with vast funding resources entering this space. DJI is the market leader. UVA startups like Matternet, Wingcopter Flirtey, Quantum Systems, and Vayu are also working in cargo delivery in the development space. Matternet works with Swiss Post. Global competitions like UAE's "Drone for Good", which was run in 2016 and 2017 further fuel the competition for funding. Plus there is the added complication of regulation in crowded airspaces. According to a recent report by FSD on where drones can be used in the humanitarian landscape, 89% of the organizations said for mapping, 68% for monitoring, 49% for search and rescue, and 36% for delivery.

Zipline's long-term mission is to build instant delivery for the planet, allowing medicines and other products to be delivered on demand and at low cost without using a drop of gasoline. Zipline was recognized in 2017 as Fast Company's Top 10 Most Innovative Companies in Social Good + Transportation and Index's Design to Improve Life Award.

This concept of shelter has not evolved much over the last few decades. As refugees spend longer times in temporary shelters, in some cases decades, something more long-lasting was required. Better Shelter is a project supported by the IKEA Foundation and UNCHR. They came up with a new degradable product that lasts longer than the classic canvas tent (3 years versus 6 months). Though it costs two times as much as the regular tent, at US$1,250, it still proves to be a more viable and durable solution.[127] Better Shelter was initially contracted to supply 30,000 shelters to UNCHR in 2015, and by the end of 2017, they had expanded to Africa, Asia, Europe, and the Middle East.[128]

A common problem SEVs face in the developmental sector is that their markets of operation may be low-margin markets requiring volumes for survival if they want to move away from grants and donations.[129] The question here is whether the market of impact *needs to be the same* as the market for funding. TOMS handled this well with their "One for One" model. Shoes are bought in markets by people who can afford the price, which in turn pays for the cost of a pair of shoes that can be donated to the markets of impact. Market access is a combination of seizing opportunity (like Zipline International Inc.), leveraging networks (like Gavi, the Vaccine Alliance — discussed in Chapter 3), and developing a market (like Vestergaard's Life Straw — discussed in Chapter 3).

## 2.8. A Stakeholder Approach

To understand the operating environment, you need to identify relevant stakeholders. A stakeholder is defined as any person, group, or institution that can affect or impact the organization behavior, process, direction or goals, and business outcomes. Various stakeholders have relationships or interactions with the SEV, and these can be negotiated positions based on the organization's response to them. Useful theoretical literature on this topic is provided by Thomas Donaldson and Lee Preston[130] and more recently John Hasnas.[131] Managing stakeholders requires a strategy to gain knowledge, create meaningful interactions, and influence action to get results that can have implicit value or be morally laden.[132] There are several stages toward achieving these results which are as follows:

- **Identify:** The first step to managing stakeholders is making a list of all stakeholders in your various ecosystems that may impact the organization and its goals. Stakeholders can be internal or external to the organization. They may be present in the community, the operating ecosystem, and across the value chain. Because SEVs often operate in gray areas, there is a need to identify stakeholders with a strong moral leadership. One approach is to look at the key decisions to be made, or implemented, and evaluate those relevant stakeholders that can help or hinder the process. This approach can be depicted using a simple 2 × 2 matrix table (see Exhibit 2.6). This method allows SEVs with limited resources to manage prioritization of stakeholders. Sometimes opportunities present themselves in the ecosystem. In the Visayan Forum Foundation case (2.1), a big support came for the cause when the USA government put Philippines on the watch list for human trafficking in 2009, jeopardizing aid to the country.

Exhibit 2.6: **Stakeholders Important for a Decision Point: Internal and External Drivers on a Social Performance Issue**

|  |  | Internal Drivers and Barriers | |
|---|---|---|---|
|  |  | Low | High |
| External Drivers and Barriers | High | Moral Dependence – Learn and Follow if appropriate | Moral Leadership – Learn, try and associate for leverage & legitimacy |
|  | Low | Non-participant - Observe | Observer - Monitor |

*Source*: Adapted from Kusyk and Lozano.[133]

People may belong to stakeholder groups either through mutual consent or by implicit or tacit consent.[134] Take, for example, media. It can have a high positive or negative impact on the SEV through its influence on SEV stakeholders. Jason Russel, founder of Invisible Children, directed a film called "Kony 2012" that went viral — 100 million views in 6 days.[135] The focus was on capturing Joseph Kony, the leader of a guerilla army accused of abducting child soldiers in Uganda. The continued coverage on social media and press, the controversies it raised in Uganda, and the fact that most of the funds went into administration and awareness, led to the founder having a breakdown. His wife, Danica Russell said on his hospitalization, "*We thought a few thousand people would see the film, but in less than a week, millions of people around the world saw it. While that attention was great for raising awareness about Joseph Kony, it also brought a lot of attention to Jason — and, because of how personal the film is, many of the attacks against it were also very personal, and Jason took them very hard.*"[136] Perhaps what is most sad is that the focus was diverted from capturing Joseph Kony and highlighting the need for safeguarding children to other issues. (Case study is discussed in Chapter 4)

- **Classify:** Once you identify your stakeholder in the SEV ecosystem, they need to be classified on how they can be affected or how they can influence or affect a problem or action or type of responsive actions they make take (see Exhibit 2.7).[137] SEV stakeholders can also be segregated as primary and secondary stakeholders. This can be visualized using concentric circles where the innermost circle includes those stakeholders who have the greatest impact.[138] Primary stakeholders are defined as having *formal, official or a contractual relationship with an organization, and without which the company could not survive.*[139] Secondary stakeholders are all other influencers and include social agents or public interest groups. Stakeholder action stems from two reasons, they are either rule-based (have a common identity — for example, workers versus management) or outcome-based (have a common interest — for example, save the environment versus oil drillers).[140]

Exhibit 2.7: **Scoping Out the SEV Ecosystem**

| Impact of SEV | Type of possible Impact | Affecting which Stakeholders? | Affected by which Stakeholders? |
|---|---|---|---|
| High | Positive | Impact measurement | Leverage associations |
| | Uncertain | Watch and Monitor | Watch and Monitor |
| | Negative | Protect, minimize, distance or find common agenda | Protect, minimize, distance or find common agenda |
| Moderate | Positive | Impact measurement, can it be increased, | Leverage associations, explore possibility of stronger alliance |
| | Uncertain | Watch and Monitor | Watch and Monitor |
| | Negative | Protect, minimize, distance or find common agenda, could it become a stronger threat? | Protect, minimize, distance or find common agenda, could it become a stronger threat? |
| Low | Positive | Watch and Monitor | Watch and Monitor |
| | Uncertain | Watch and Monitor | Watch and Monitor |
| | Negative | Watch and Monitor | Watch and Monitor |

*Source*: Adapted from Chevalier and Buckles.[141]

Stakeholders can be mapped along other dimensions.

(1) *How much power do they have?*

Power is the degree of influence and impact they have over the SEV to get the SEV to do something they may not want to do.[142] The quality of power is transitory. There are many types of power that a stakeholder could use to control an SEV as follows[143]:

- coercive power which is based on using force, violence, or restraint;
- utilitarian power, which uses material or financial rewards;

- normative power, which manipulates narrative and social symbolic resources;

- political power, which is formal and derived from control over the decision processes by transient coalitions, co-option, and institutionalization where temporarily the goals are aligned;

- personal power, which comes down to the strength of the individual relationships: This may overlap with referent power, expert power, networking or connections power, and political power where you will need to co-opt to win. Stakeholders should also be mapped according to the knowledge they hold as this may give them explicit and implicit power. Look for *who knows who* and *who knows what* that captures the knowledge of multiple viewpoints across time, people, and locations. This will help the SEV find the dominant flows of knowledge, knowledge bottlenecks, latent knowledge; and areas of knowledge seepage.[144]

- position power is derived from formal authority which gives the stakeholder control over rewards, punishments, information, and other resources. Information is often critical in today's world, and the holder of information often has a tremendous amount of power. This overlaps with coercive power and legitimate power. The jurisdiction between what is legal and what is not, is a fine line and in some markets difficult especially where there is breakdown in civil society.

(2)  *How much interest do they have?*

Analysis of stakeholders can be based on the various outcomes they are expecting.[145] Stakeholders may have a vested interest in an SEV — whether it is wanting the SEV to succeed or fail. This implies that an SEV must chart and organize in hierarchical order, the various interests they can afford to satisfy. A project owner for a well-known NGO narrated this particular story. A well-known MNC approached them and said they wished to donate a large sum of money about US$1 million to build a tech-enabled school in a conflict zone in rural Africa. They had 3 months in which to donate the amount as the year was ending and they wished to see the project started to share the news in their annual board meeting. The project team explained that this would be very difficult to execute especially as (1) there was no form of formal government in that area, (2) there was no infrastructure for electricity and also no Wi-Fi, and (3) there were not enough teachers willing to work there yet. At this point, they were told to accept the money or it would be given to someone else. The NGO accepted the money, hired a project team on a short 6-month assignment. They had to bribe outlaws to be allowed to set up the foundation of the school and for the project team to take pictures of proof of the initiative. The project team members never heard back whether the project was completed, nor did the MNC follow-up about the school. While everyone had a common interest on paper, that of rural education, the MNC was more motivated by tax returns and shareholder equity, the NGO by collecting the funds (since they only hired the project manager and team for 6 months), and the project manager itself never went public in the personal interest he would lose future job opportunities. SEVs need to manage various conflicting stakeholder interests. Exhibit 2.8 shows how stakeholders can be arranged according to their power and interest.

Exhibit 2.8:   **Power/Interest Stakeholder Matrix**

|        |      | Interest | |
|--------|------|------|------|
|        |      | **Low** | **High** |
| **Power** | **Low** | CROWD<br>Potential stakeholders.<br>Minimal Effort, Watch | SUBJECTS<br>Keep informed, Form coalitions, convert to supporting PLAYERS, neutralize negative |
|        | **High** | PLAYERS<br>Do not threaten unless ready for action, keep satisfied, managed attention | CONTEXT SETTERS<br>Key players, watch and anticipate. Raise awareness, convert into Advocate PLAYERS |

*Source*: Adapted from Ackermann and Eden.[146]

(3) *What is the urgency?*

Urgency refers to the importance of time that the stakeholder claims over the SEV[147] and a call for immediate action by the stakeholder (1) when a relationship or claim is of a time-sensitive nature, and any delay by the SEV becomes unacceptable to the stakeholder, and (2) when that relationship or claim is considered important or critical to the stakeholder.[148] When Hurricane Harvey, a Category 4 storm hit Houston, USA in September 2017, the floods made many people homeless and there was a need for emergency shelters. Houston has the third largest church in USA, a 16,500-seat church called Lakewood Church, which did not immediately open its doors to take in people who needed refuge. Social media picked up this fact, and what followed was a slew of negative press — a tweet shitstorm.[149] The church did eventually open its doors, but by then, the damage was done. The victims were upset as they felt prayer alone was not enough, though reports did suggest that the church was doing the right thing in being cautious as water had seeped into its foundation.[150] Hurricane Harvey's toll on an unprepared urban infrastructure was immense, resulting in over 30,000 displaced, US$20 billion in property damage with 75% of the population not covered under flood insurance. There was a direct impact on the oil industry resulting in rise of petrol prices (20% of the USA refining capacity was closed), and worse — toxic sites flooded with further possibility of groundwater contamination.[151] Harvey affected not just Houston but the whole state of Texas. The hurricane needed urgent responses, and time was not on the side of those affected or those required to help.

(4) *What is the level of legitimacy?*

Legitimacy, as described before, refers to *a generalized perception or assumption that the actions of an entity are desirable, proper, or appropriate within some socially constructed system of norms, values, beliefs, and definitions.*[152] This means a stakeholder often has multiple layers of acceptance at the individual, organizational, and societal level, based on how they use power, and whether stakeholders perceive that it is being responsible.[153] Legitimacy management strategies revolve around gaining, maintaining, or repairing legitimacy and differs based on the type of legitimacy being sought.[154]

Looking at the combination of power, urgency, and legitimacy, there are eight types of stakeholder combinations possible (see Exhibit 2.9) and they can be grouped into three categories according to Mitchell *et al.*[155] The first category of stakeholders are called Latent Stakeholders. These are those stakeholders with high power and no legitimacy or urgency (dormant), have legitimacy but no urgency or power (discretionary), or have urgency but no power or legitimacy (demanding).

Exhibit 2.9: **Types of Stakeholders**

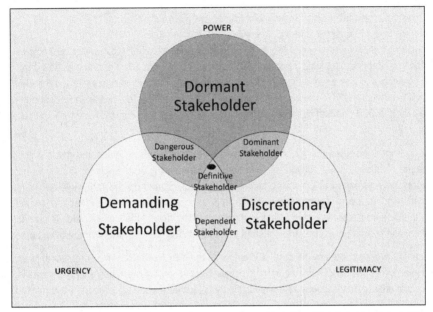

The second category of stakeholders are called Expectant Stakeholders. They can have power and legitimacy but no urgency (dominant), have urgency and power but no legitimacy (dangerous), or have urgency and legitimacy but are powerless (dependent).

The third category of stakeholders are those that have all three attributes and are called Definitive Stakeholders. Social agents like public interest groups can lobby for causes like environmental protection (Green Peace) or act as watchdogs (Charity Navigator, The International Consortium of Investigative Journalists) (see Case Study 2.5).

(5) *What is the level of predictableness?*

Stakeholders are composed of people and people are unpredictable. This may lead to explosive situations. It is important for an SEV to know who are dependable stakeholders, those that they can trust, and those that they can predict. It is the founder's responsibility to draw upon a mission, as a common reference point that brings together several stakeholders.[156] When you identify stakeholders, you will need to identify the frame of context and what boundary conditions are applicable to the relationships. Then you should be able to predict how they will behave, and this requires scenario analysis.

## Case Study 2.5: **International Consortium of Investigative Journalists (ICIJ)**

The International Consortium of Investigative Journalists (ICIJ), which is based in Washington D.C. was established in 1997 by the Center for Public Integrity. In 2017, ICIJ became a fully independent organization. The ICIJ is an organization that works with over 200 investigative journalists in 70-plus countries. They focus on cross-border topics like crime, corruption, and the accountability of power. In 2015, Bastian Obermayer and Frederik Obermaier, two German journalists from *Süddeutsche Zeitung*, received an anonymous
tip. Supported by their editor-in-chief Wolfgang Krach, they approached ICIJ in what is known as the Panama Papers. The data spanned 40 years of data from the Panamanian law firm Mossack Fonseca and was equivalent to 2.6 terabytes of data, 11.5 million documents, 4.8 million emails, in 25 languages, 107 media partners, and 400 journalists. The 5-year investigations of approximately 215,000 companies in 21 offshore jurisdictions led to a Pulitzer Prize for Explanatory Reporting in 2017.

The Panama Papers revealed the governance inadequacies in offshore holdings and made it possible to trace some of the elaborate network of shell companies used in some cases for money laundering. It resulted in the resignation of the Prime Minister of Iceland, Sigmundur David Gunnlaugsson, jail for the founders of the law firm, further exposed FIFA, and connected many people in the government and society with off-shore accounts and is hailed as a collaborative effort of the highest order. Secure forums, special database search programs, and constant communication were key in this integrative approach.

ICIJ needed to work in secrecy to protect the life of the whistleblower. They created a two-factor-authentication-protected search engine to help its investigative journalists, using encrypted emails, and finding ways to ensure that the data were accessible to its journalists but not leaked to the public — Wiki-Leaks style. Still there were casualties. Daphne Galiza, a journalist who worked in Malta uncovering corruption through the Panama Papers was killed by a car bomb on October 16, 2017. While 2017 was the year with the least number of journalists' deaths in 14 years, according to Reporters Without Borders, of the 65 who died on the job, 39 died as they were targeted for reporting on corruption or organized crime. However, 2017 was also the year in which the maximum number of journalists were imprisoned. According to the Committee to Protect Journalists, 262 journalists were imprisoned with 51% of them being in three countries — Turkey, China, and Egypt.

Scenarios should take into account three main contextual accounts: (i) description of a future end state in a horizon year, (ii) an interpretation of current events and their propagation into the future, and (iii) an internally consistent account of how a future world unfolds.[157] Despite all the predictions, there are some events that may not be predictable. Unexpected and unpredictable events are referred to as Black Swans.[158] In this case, you should be able to limit the impact of the crisis and adapt quickly.

The Failure Institute recently published some statistics of the failure of social enterprises in Mexico: 38.3% survived less than 1 year, 45.2% lasted between 1 and 3 years, 8.7% lasted 4–6 years, 2.6% lasted 7–9 years, and 5.2% lasted more than 10 years as a company.[159] Social enterprises in Mexico had a life expectancy 1 year longer than the commercial businesses. Top reasons for failure according to the institute were as follows: (i) lack of resources and infrastructure, (ii) environmental context, and (iii) board of directors. The fact that SEVs were unable to predict situations, whether it was a conflict between founders, funding drying up, political situations, or natural disasters, led to failure of the enterprise. Stakeholders can be plotted on a $2 \times 2$ matrix of predictability versus power.[160] When there is high power and low predictability, this is when the company can be exposed to great threats or can find great opportunities.

**Strategic failure is often caused by a crisis of perception, that is, the inability to see an emergent novel reality by being locked inside obsolete assumptions.[161]**

## 2.9. Balancing Myriad Worlds

An SEV must become an irritant, working in balancing different worlds that are already inhabited by large entrenched players like IGOs, government organizations, and private charities or foundations. SEVs dissect and connect these independent subsystems in a process called interpenetration.[162] To do the process successfully, it needs reciprocation by other systems, creating structural coupling for competencies,[163] and leading to a blurring of boundaries.[164] This process requires trade-offs by negotiation of the SEV goals with those of their stakeholders.[165] This process is also called bridging. [166]

Total S.A., a French transnational oil company, began a feasibility study of drilling for oil in Myanmar in July 1992. The study identified the least environmental damaging oil route and planned to sell 85% of its output to the Petroleum Authority of Thailand (PTT).[167] A consortium was set up comprising Total S.A. (32%), Unocal, a California-based multinational (28%), state-owned Petroleum Authority of Thailand (25%), and state-owned Myanmar Oil and Gas Enterprise (15%) and construction began in 1995 with delivery beginning in middle of 1998. In Myanmar, Thailand was considered the military regime, having ruled since 1988. The consortium set up a socio-economic program (SEP), spending US$5 million from 1995 to 1998 to manage the sensitivities.[168] Other oil companies, like Premier Oil of the UK, abandoned operations in Myanmar with mounting international pressure.[169] EU slapped sanctions against the military dictatorship in Myanmar in 1996, though Total S.A. as a French company continued to survive.[170] In early 2000, Total S.A. decided to forge partnerships with various UN agencies, in what may be seen as an attempt to increase legitimacy, though this was denied by the UNESCO.[171,172] The private sector company, run with full approval of its nation, tried to increase its legitimacy through its social initiative. In this case, there is an interaction of economic, political, governance, and legal and regulatory ecosystems.

To balance the various stakeholders' vested interests, there are several tensions the SEV must manage that broadly cover the following:

(1) *Identification of the social issue for intervention*[173]

In this case, SEVs not only must address the source of the problem but must also articulate their identity — as an insider or an outsider — and hence make a statement about their belonging.[174] There are two tools they can use: storytelling and anchoring.

Storytelling helps the audience reconstruct identities of both the stakeholders and the catalysts (SEV) involved.[175] The founder of Sulabh International, Dr. Bindeshwar Pathak came from a high-caste family (a hereditary class-based order that comes with privileges) in India. His mission to eradicate manual scavenging and improve sanitation in India is a journey of close to 50 years. His story of why he wanted to help, his sacrifices, and his ability to work with the community in the hardest of jobs, scooping sewage and disposing of it, made him an insider. Over 640 towns in India have been made scavenger free, and over 60 million government toilets are based on the Sulabh design which was provided free (this case is discussed in Chapter 3).[176] SEVs must be able to balance various and sometimes conflicting goals or demands across multiple stakeholders and be able to sustain its purpose over time.[177]

Anchoring is a statement of value belief, where people form judgments or take decisions based on information not directly retrieved from memory but constructed at the time of the query based on the prompt (anchor) provided. Suppose you wanted to help a community that had been just struck by a hurricane. How would you dress up? In designer clothes or would you wear "working clothes". This may provide an anchor by prompting a reminder of the purpose. Who so you think people would perceive more likely to help?

Ruwwad Al Tanmeya, The Arab Foundation for Sustainable Development, works in Jordan. When they began working in the Mohammed Amin refugee camp, an unofficial camp for Palestinian refugees set up in 1948, they were perceived with distrust and as an outsider. The community had seen many do-gooders come and go and very often for their own political motives. To gain trust, Ruwwad mapped both needs and assets through formal and informal dialogues with the community leaders and representatives of various interests. This process took over a year. They set up a list of priorities for the communities and fulfilled them — get a police station, restoration of a local school, a public library, a health center, and better garbage collection. They not only fulfilled all these demands but also set up an office in the heart of the community taking an insider approach — most NGOs had offices in better parts of Amman. From a hostile reception, Ruwwad is now welcomed as a part of the community.

(2) *Development of an appropriate organizational structure and estimation of all resources required*[178]

The first most important issue is that of the legal structure. Most social entrepreneurs (non-profits) begin their ventures as hobbies reaching out on social media to spread their cause. The moment you begin gathering funds, you risk an ethical issue of governance. One way to manage this tension is look at other players in the system across the world or in benchmark industries. Gavi, the Vaccine

Alliance was set up in 2000, hosted by UNICEF. Their goal was to help achieve UN Millennium Development Goal No. 4, which was to reduce the mortality rate for children younger than five by two-thirds through vaccines.[179] The realized then that they would be more effective working with other experts already present in the marketplace. In 2008, they became a formal independent foundation based in Geneva. Their unique public–private partnership model spans various sectors, developmental finance, funding institutions, vaccine manufacturers, health authorities, research partners, local country governments, civil society organizations, and those institutions with access to children. Their unique Board structure is a reflection of this. The complexity of stakeholder representation and goverance (Gavi, the Vaccine Alliance) as a case is discussed in greater detail in Chapter 3.

## (3) *Appropriate technology and product/service solution*[180]

Product innovations can focus on cost minimization. Aurolab Aravind Eyecare sells intraocular lens in India at less than 4% of the cost of a lens being sold in USA. Innovation can help find solutions in impossible situations. In the Zaatari refugees camp in Jordan, Refugee Open Ware 3D prints prosthetics.[181] Services can help bypass inadequacies in the market. Twiga Foods, a Kenyan business-to-business supply platform, uses mobile technology to connect urban retailers to the fresh produce market and hence benefits not just the retailers but also the farmers.[182] Voicebook or CGNet Swara is a social media platform for tribal areas of India, where a large proportion of people can't read or write. People can contribute to the "radio" program in their local dialect through Bluetooth, and the founder says it is a method to give voice to the voiceless, bypassing the tight regulation on radio licenses in India.[183]

## (4) *Ability to navigate the cultural and political landscape to manage the tensions of power and control*[184]

There are three useful skills SEV founders can use in managing stakeholder tensions. They are tagging, developing wisdom, and reframing.

Tagging is a method SEVs can use to create symbols of aggregation and define boundaries of interaction and identity through existing markers like brands, symbols, protocols, or rallying words.[185] Based on how you classify your stakeholders, SEVs must use any of the following strategies: inform, consult, involve, collaborate, and empower.[186] Those SEVs in the for-profit or hybrid sector will have the additional tension of justifying social values versus commercial values.[187] Very often, they will need to manage the disparities between cognitive understanding (knowledge, institutional goals, and tasks),[188] emotions, and existing behaviors already entrenched in the ecosystem.

Acacias for All, is a Tunisian reforestation project conceived by Sarah Toumi. She witnessed firsthand how the desert was claiming the date farms owned by her grandparents. In 2008, she began approaching the Tunisian government and banks for funding but was turned down. From there she went directly to female farmers, who were more open to adopt the idea. They were given the trees for free, joined the cooperative structure, and would earn an income of US$1,000 after 3 years through the sales of gum from the acacia trees and oil from the moringa trees.[189] Sarah has been recognized by Ashoka (2014), Echoing Green (2015), and Forbes 30 under 30 Social Entrepreneur (2016). Acacias for All is now a tale of empowered women farmers, working through cooperatives, a symbol of reforestation (fight against desertification) and the return to indigenous plants and trees.

Another skill SEVs must pick up is wisdom. Ecosystems are not just structures and rules but composed of people. SEVs must learn to balance interests at the (1a) intrapersonal, (1b) interpersonal, and (1c) extrapersonal level, and hence make decisions on when to (2a) adapt to existing environments, (2b) shape existing environments, or (2c) select new environment.[190] There is a need for wisdom as described by Sternberg (1992: 362), "*In terms of personality, the wise individual seeks to resolve ambiguities whereas the traditionally intelligent person excels in problems that have few or no ambiguities (and thus can be "objectively" scored as right or wrong)."*[191] This, according to the Berlin school of wisdom, means gathering knowledge about human nature and context of life problems from multiple perspectives (historically and socially), understanding relativism of values and life goals and differences (between individuals, group, and wider social/ cultural values and priorities), and collecting knowledge on how to handle uncertainty.[192]

Third, SEVS should be able to take a reframing approach, which is the ability to look at the problem or road block from multiple perspectives or frames. Roadblocks or the *einstellung effect* is a problem individuals face when they continue to solve a problem the same way even when a better solution presents itself.[193] The four reframing techniques posited by Lee Bolman and Terrence Deal[194] can be applied in such situations. Structural tensions revolve around how to allocate work (differentiation) and how to coordinate work that has been allocated (integration). The human resource frame looks at the tension of human needs and organization needs. The political frame looks at the tension from coalitions, the negotiation of power, and management of conflict. The symbolic frame looks at tensions that arise through meanings, faith, and belief that are given to make sense of what happened. Methods to manage these tensions from a leadership perspective are suggested by Lee Bolman and Terrance Deal in Exhibit 2.10.

Exhibit 2.10: **Reframing Leadership**

| | LEADERSHIP IS EFFECTIVE WHEN | | LEADERSHIP IS INEFFECTIVE WHEN | |
|---|---|---|---|---|
| FRAME | Leader is | Leadership Process is | Leader is | Leadership Process is |
| Structural | Analyst, Architect. Focuses on Excellence & Authorship | Analysis, design, build the process, implementation | Petty, bureaucrat or tyrant | Management by detail and flat, confusion |
| Human Resource | Catalyst, Enabler Focuses on Caring & Culture | belief in people, Support, empowerment | Weak, pushover | Abdication, uncertainty |
| Political | Advocate, negotiator Focuses on Justice & Power | Agenda alignment, analysis of political terrain, advocacy, arenas of negotiation, coalitions building, | Untrustworthy, Game Player | Manipulation, fraud |
| Symbolic | Hero/Heroine, Leads by Doing Focuses on Faith & Significance | Inspirational, meaning-making, identity, vision | Fanatic, Ritualist | Mirage, deception and lies, cling to the past |

*Source*: Adapted from Bolman and Deal.[195]

SEVs must learn to navigate the various ecosystems that their organizations intersect. While PeaceWorks had an initial agenda — to promote peace in the Middle East — this also intersected with the specialty food industry. Success in one sphere does not guarantee success in another. While the company did pivot and diversify to healthy snacks with a social cause focusing on kindness, to remain true to his mission, Daniel bought his company back to keep control of the direction it was moving towards (see Case Study 2.6).

## Case Study 2.6: **PeaceWorks and KIND Inc.**

PeaceWorks began in 1994 by Daniel Lubetzky, who was a lawyer by profession. He met Yoel Benesh in 1993, when on assignment in Tel Avi. Yoel was the manufacturer of the brand of sundried pesto paste Daniel loved, which was out of stock. Yoel explained he was driven to bankruptcy because his Palestinian employees frequently could not get to work from their homes on the West Bank, in the Gaza Strip.

This happened every time the borders closed as his factory was in the north of Tel Aviv. Daniel came up with the idea to work with Yoel and sell the sun-dried tomato pesto in USA to facilitate the idea of peace. He put in US$10,000 of his own funds and came up with the flavors of his spreads which he called "sprate" and personally sold in New York.

The product was made in Israel, but was sourced from around the Middle East — the glass jars from Egypt, sun-dried tomatoes from Turkey and olives, olive oil, and basil from Palestine. They branded the product as *Moshe and Ali's*, highlighting a fictional story of two people — Moshe Pupik, a Jewish chef and Ali Mishmunken, an Arab magician. The idea was to use food as a common bond to overcome conflict. The tag line was: *Cooperation never tasted so good.* Five percent of the Peace Works' profits were used at that time to fund workshops on tolerance, led by the Arab–Israel Institute for Economic Cooperation. Daniel put together an advisory board that included — for example, Ben Cohen, of Ben & Jerry's. By 2000, Yoel made profits of US$10 million, but he had to lay off all his Palestinian employees because the Israeli checkpoints prevented the employees from coming to work, though he still sourced from Palestinian farmers.

The brand eventually gave way to the Meditalia range. PeaceWorks managed to market to over 15,000 US retailers. Daniel learnt from the mistakes he made along the way. First by bringing in too many variations and not spending enough time on superior products and market understanding. New exotic flavors like Raging Raspberry Chipotle failed. Then Daniel tried to replicate the concept by producing salsa from the Chiapas region of Mexico, to draw attention on the discrimination of the Chiapas Indians. The product struggled as the differentiation was not clear with the other products nor did he promote the social cause. In 2001, Daniel began importing La Bici pasta chips from a Durban factory owned jointly by black and white South Africans but it was too expensive to ship, and at that time, the market in USA was focusing on the Atkins diet. The product was discontinued. In 2003, he launched Bali Spice, a range of products from Indonesia that focuses on peaceful relations among the Buddhists, Christians, and Muslims who work together in the factory near Jakarta.

In 2002, Daniel launched the One Voice Movement. PeaceWorks received a SKOLL award in 2008. From a steep learning curve based on many types of failure — inventory management, marketing, product management and strategy, KIND — a healthy food snack brand was born in 2003 and registered as a separate company in 2004 in New York. It reached sales of US$1 million in its first year. This time, not only did they talk of their social mission but also they made the product the focus. KIND Inc. was partially acquired by the private equity firm VMG Partners in 2008 and then bought back by Daniel in 2014. KIND's social mission is acts of kindness. The Kind Foundation was formed in 2004 and through it, a US$20 million initiative called Empatico was launched as a free online learning tool to connect students around the globe. The objective is to reach over one million students in 25 countries by the end of 2020.

Change is inevitable. An SEV's target communities may change, the problem may morph, stakeholders may change — either becoming dormant or aggressive or new ones may appear, and regulations or resources may not be the same — requiring a change in managing them. While crises are normal, an SEV must also keep an eye out for the black swans — those high-impact improbable events.[196] A study on the formation of human service organizations after natural disasters found that a local organizations capacity for a geographic area is dependent on the diversity of its voluntary models.[197] The study finds that associational diversity (a network of various skills of diverse types of organizations) has a positive effect on organizing capacity after a disaster, political diversity has a negative effect, and racial diversity has no significant effect. Managing during crises requires political coalitions (more on this topic in Chapter 6).

**To start, survive, and grow, an SEV must be able to think out of the box as the environment in which they operate in rarely stays constant.**

## 2.10. Mapping Your SEV Boundaries: A Recap

As discussed above, the ecosystem an SEV operates in may be complex and have many players with vested interests. By using the various frameworks presented above — legal and regulatory, cultural, governance, resource, competition, and access to markets — it is possible to assess various stakeholder viewpoints. You can map stakeholders based on their impact on your cause, their power, influence, interest, legitimacy, and how they can benefit you. The first step in a plan is to understand the conditions under which you operate. This will help you in your journey as an SEV founder.

## 2.11. Questions

**Question 1**

Take the case of Visayan Forum Foundation. Complete the visual map of various intersecting ecosystems. Do the same for your organization. How would you classify some of these stakeholders?

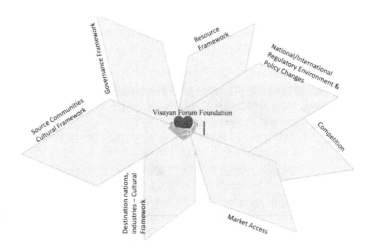

## Question 2

Take the example of the Ibrahim Prize, do you think incentivizing the market with monetary rewards and public recognition is a good way to change behaviors? Why? Behavioral economics or books offered by Jones, Pykett, and Whitehead,[198] Dan Airley,[199] or Kahneman and Tversky[200] may offer some interesting insights.

## Question 3

Armstrong et al.[201] define three roles the microfinance industry players can take. The first is the Connector. They act as intermediaries connecting the funds with the beneficiary. The second is the Interactor. Interactors build relationships with clients to help the information flow to connectors. The third is the Institutionalizer which disseminates data (innovation and best practices) to the relevant stakeholders to build confidence and fuel flow of funds. Discuss if this typology is valid for other industries? Why?

## Question 4

Waddock and Post (1991: 393, footnote 202) define social entrepreneurs as *"private sector citizens who play critical roles in bringing about "catalytic changes" in the public sector agenda and the perception of certain social issues. Although not involved in direct actions to solve public problems, their work sets the stage and context for policy making and policy implementation activities."* Do you agree? Take the case of the growing number of elderly in Europe, North America, or Japan. Find a structural hole to pitch a new idea for a product that will solve the societal needs of loneliness for the elderly.

## Question 5

SEVs need employees with organizational citizenship behaviors. This quality is described as positive behaviors outside the employee's formal job role.[202] In the case given above of ICIJ, with the Panama Papers — one journalist lost her life. There are three roles here — employees need to respect the boundaries of trust with confidential data and with each other, they need to ensure the research is impeccable as there are lives that can be affected, and lastly they need to balance their own safety and those involved with the quest for knowledge. How do you manage this based on Exhibit 2.7?

## Question 6

You are working in the Calais Camp in France. It is a transit refugee camp often referred to as the *new jungle*. At its height in 2015, it was hosting over 6,000 people from Syria, Iraq, Iran, Afghanistan, Ethiopia, and Eritrea, dependent on charity handouts. Many try to get over the border to Britain cutting through the wire fence or hiding in trains or the undercarriage of trucks passing through the Euro-tunnel. There are several issues — unaccompanied children disappear. This camp is not an official camp and hence has no one in charge. The donations are not always useful (they need tents, sleeping bags, functional clothes, food, medicines, etc., instead they get stale food, used wedding dresses, and old formal shoes).[203] In 2018, President Emmanuel Macron vowed that Calais will no longer be a transit point and the borders would remain closed. In 2017, France dealt with 100,000-plus asylum applications (17% increase on 2016) and 85,000 asylum seekers were refused entry to the country.[204] You need to approach the French government to negotiate a refugee solution — What is the leadership frame of reference you can use according to Bolman and Deal?[205] Research the background about the case. Which are the main stakeholders involved to resolve this? Classify the relationships between the stakeholders using the French and Granrose[206] framework: (1) exploitation, where one person uses another to achieve his or her own selfish objectives without considering any benefit to the other; (2) reciprocity, where two or more persons/stakeholders are using each other for mutual benefits based on give and take, and (3) mutuality, where the relationships go beyond exploitation and reciprocity as the parties involved do not see each other as a means but genuinely take an interest in the other's goals and needs.

## Question 7

The circular economy aims to create a systems innovation that redefines products and services to design waste out, while minimizing negative impacts on natural, social and, economic resources. To move toward a circular economy, an important part is recycling. While Germany, Austria, South Korea, and Wales lead in diverting waste from landfills (over 50%), in some countries, people like rag pickers or *Zaballeen* (garbage pickers in Arabic) do a good job in helping. Even in USA, the homeless were used to sort the garbage. Part of the challenge in this is classification of waste — commercial or household. There are ambitious targets being set — Wales plans to achieve zero waste by 2050 and EU plans 65% cycling by 2030. Garbage has also been exported for recycling and China plans to ban 24 types of garbage imports. More on this has been given in the report titled *Which countries recycle the most?*[207] Evaluate your country and identify the possible *einstellung effects* you may face.

# Sources

## Case Study 2.1: Visayan Forum Foundation (Philippines)

*Sources*: Anderson, L. (2016), "Trafficking foe cecilia flores-oebanda fights to clear her name," *Thomson Reuters Foundation News*, dated 16 May, Available: http://news.trust.org//item/20130516081452-xiw1f/ [Accessed 23 August, 2017]; CNN (2016), "DOJ clears visayan forum of charges in connection with USAID grant," *CNN website*, dated 3 December, Available: http://cnnphilippines.com/news/2016/12/03/department-of-justice-clears-visayan-forum-of-charges-in-connection-with-usaid-grant.html [Accessed 23 August, 2017]; CNN Documentary (2014), "The fighter," *YouTube*, Available: https://www.youtube.com/watch?v=8RXy97wAWfo [Accessed 23 August, 2017]; Coorlim, L. (2013), "Shadow threatens anti-trafficker's greatest moment," *CNN*, dated 16 May, Available: http://edition.cnn.com/2013/05/06/world/asia/freedom-fighters-activist/index.html [Accessed 23 August, 2017]; Corruption Perception Index (2016), *Transparency International*, Available: https://www.transparency.org/news/feature/corruption_perceptions_index_2016#table [Accessed 28 December, 2017]; Skoll (2017), "Visayan forum foundation," *Skoll website*, Available: http://skoll.org/organization/visayan-forum-foundation/ [Accessed 22 August, 2017]; Visayan Forum Official website: Available http://visayanforum.org; Lei Ravelo, J. (2012), "Philippine NGO faces fraud charges," *Devex*, dated 14 September, Available: https://www.devex.com/news/philippine-ngo-faces-fraud-charges-79133; World Bank (2017), "Personal remittances received (% of GDP)," Available: https://data.worldbank.org/indicar/BX.TRF.PWKR.DT.GD.ZS [Accessed 30 December, 2017].

## Case Study 2.2: The Akshaya Patra Foundation

*Sources*: Bansal, R. (2017), *God's Own Kitchen*, Manipal: Manipal Technologies Limited; The Akshaya Patra, Annual Reports from 2009-10 to 2016-17; Ministry of Human Resource Development India (2017), *Midday Meal Scheme*, Available: http://mdm.nic.in [Accessed 9 February 2018]; Center For Public Impact (2016), India's Midday Meal in School, dated 11 April, Available: https://www.centreforpublicimpact.org/case-study/indias-midday-meals-in-schools/ [Accessed 29 March, 2018]; The Akshaya Patra website, Available: https://www.akshayapatra.org [Accessed 30 December, 2017]; Interview with Chairman of the Akshaya Patra Foundation, *Madhu Pandit Dasa*, Available: https://www.akshayapatra.org/press-coverages/details/92?mode=popup [Accessed 30 December, 2017]; Keim, B. (2015), "Akshaya patra," *Stanford Social Innovation Review*, dated 9 November, Available: https://ssir.org/articles/entry/case_study_akshaya_patra [Accessed 30 December, 2017]; Upton, D., Ellis, C., Lucas, S. and Yamner, A. (2007), "Akshaya patra: Feeding India's schoolchildren," *Harvard Business Case Study*, Available: https://www.akshayapatra.org/sites/default/files/images/harvard_business_school_study.pdf [Accessed 30 December, 2017]. Interview with Vijay Kumar (2017), Director IT, *Enterprise IT World*, dated December 7, Available: https://www.akshayapatra.org/press-coverages/details/102?mode=popup [Accessed 30 December, 2017].

## Case Study 2.3: The Ibrahim Prize

*Sources*: Auletta, K. (2011), "The dictator index," *The New Yorker*, dated March 7, Available; http://www.kenauletta.com/2011_03_07_Mo_Ibrahim.html [Accessed 30 December, 2017]; BBC (2006), *Prize Offered to African Leaders*, dated 26 October, Available http://news.bbc.co.uk/2/hi/uk_news/6086088.stm [Accessed 30 December, 2017]; BBC (2007), *Mozambique Ex-leader Wins Prize*, Available: http://news.bbc.co.uk/2/hi/africa/7056159.stm [Accessed 30 December, 2017]; Mo Ibrahim Foundation, Available: http://mo.ibrahim.foundation

## Case Study 2.4: Zipline International Inc.

*Sources*: Boyle, A. (2016), "Zipline unveils drone delivery venture with a medical mission and big-name funding," *Geekwire*, dated 4 April, Available: https://www.geekwire.com/2016/zipline-drone-delivery-big-name-funding-rwanda-medical/ [Accessed 25 January, 2018]; Cook, J. (2012), "Romotive unveils new $150 smartphone-controlled robot, lands $5M from sequoia, others," *Geekwire*, dated October 16, Available: https://www.geekwire.com/2012/romotive-unveils-150-smartphonecontrolled-robot-scores-5m-sequoia/ [Accessed 25 January, 2018]; FSD (2016), "Drones in humanitarian action," Available: http://drones.fsd.ch/wp-content/uploads/2016/11/Drones-in-Humanitarian-Action.pdf [Accessed 25 January, 2018]; Hsu, J. (2018), "Africa's delivery drones are zipping past US," *Wired*, dated 13 September, Available: https://www.wired.com/story/africas-delivery-drones-are-zipping-past-the-us/ [Accessed 25 January, 2018]; Kolodny, L. (2016), "A test flight with zipline, makers of humanitarian delivery drones," *TechCrunch*, dated 13 October, Available: https://techcrunch.com/2016/10/13/a-test-flight-with-zipline-makers-of-humanitarian-delivery-drones/ [Accessed 25 January, 2018]; Recode (2017), "Full transcript: Zipline CEO keller rinaudo talks life-saving drones on too embarrassed to ask," *Recode*, dated 10 March, Available: https://www.recode.net/2017/3/10/14875324/transcript-zipline-founder-keller-rinaudo-delivery-drones-too-embarrassed-to-ask [Accessed 25 January, 2018]; Rinauldo, K. (2017), "How we are using drones to deliver blood and save lives," *Ted Talks*, Available: https://www.ted.com/talks/keller_rinaudo_how_we_re_using_drones_to_deliver_blood_and_save_lives [Accessed 25 January, 2018]; Robinson, M. (2016), "This secretive startup could save lives in the most remote places," *Business Insider*, dated 9 May, Available: http://www.businessinsider.com/zipline-drone-laboratory-2016-5?IR=T/#the-prototype-theyre-showing-off-today-can-fly-150-miles-round-trip-on-a-single-battery-charge-it-flies-between-50-and-85-miles-per-hour-6 [Accessed 25 January, 2018]; Stewart, J. (2016), "This startup wants to use drones to deliver blood, not bombs," *Wired*, dated 9 May, Available: https://www.wired.com/2016/05/zipline-drones-rwanda/ [Accessed 25 January, 2018]; Ulrich, K. (2017), "What's the drone doing? delivering blood: Interview with keenan wyrobek," *Saving Lives, SoundCloud*, dated 24 October, Audio https://soundcloud.com/user-634502599/drones-delivering-lifesaving-blood-karl-ulrich-talks-with-keenan-wyrobek-founder-of-zipline and Available: https://www.forbes.com/sites/karlulrich/2017/10/24/whats-that-drone-doing-delivering-blood-saving-lives/#371cc5e15a01 [Accessed 25 January, 2018]; Yakowicz, W. (2016), "Robots to the rescue: Blood delivery via drone is coming to the U.S.," *Inc.*, dated 4 August, Available: https://www.inc.com/will-yakowicz/zipline-blood-delivery-drones-rwanda-us.html [Accessed 25 January, 2018]; Zipline (2016), *Press release: Zipline announces world's first drone delivery service*, dated April 4, 2016 Available: http://www.flyzipline.com/uploads/Zipline%202016%20Launch.pdf [Accessed 25 January, 2018]; Zipline (2017), *Press release: Tanzania announces world's largest national drone delivery network partnering with zipline*, dated August 24, Available: http://www.flyzipline.com/uploads/Tanzania%20Announcement%20Press%20Release%20vFinal.pdf [Accessed 25 January, 2018]; Zipline (2018), *Our impact*, Available: http://www.flyzipline.com/our-impact/ [Accessed 25 January, 2018].

## Case Study 2.5: International Consortium of Investigative Journalists (ICIJ)

*Sources*: Clark, N. (2016), "How a cryptic message, 'Interested in data?,' led to the panama papers," *New York Times*, Available: https://www.nytimes.com/2016/04/06/business/media/how-a-cryptic-message-interested-in-data-led-to-the-panama-papers.html [Accessed 8 February, 2018]; Fletcher, P. (2017), "Number of journalists killed in line of duty down in 2017, number imprisoned this year a record," *Forbes*, dated 19 December, Available: https://www.forbes.com/sites/paulfletcher/2017/12/19/number-of-journalists-killed-in-line-of-duty-down-in-2017-number-imprisoned-this-year-a-record/#52e242d8605e [Accessed 9 February, 2018]; Greenberg, A. (2016), "How reporters pulled off the panama papers, the Biggest Leak in Whistleblower History," *Wired*, dated 4 April, Available: https://www.wired.com/2016/04/reporters-pulled-off-panama-papers-biggest-leak-whistleblower-history/ [Accessed 9 February, 2018]; Harding, L. (2017), "Panama papers investigation wins pulitzer prize," *The Guardian*, dated 11 April, Available: https://www.theguardian.com/world/2017/apr/11/panama-papers-investigation-wins-pulitzer-prize [Accessed 9 February, 2018]; ICIJ website: https://www.icij.org/investigations/; Paradise Papers (2018), Available: https://panamapapers.icij.org/video/ [Accessed 8 February, 2018].

## Case Study 2.6: PeaceWorks and KIND Inc.

*Sources*: KindSnacks Foundation website: Available: https://www.kindsnacks.com/foundation; Lubetzky, D. (1993), "Incentives for peace and profits: Federal legislation to encourage US enterprises to invest in arab-israeli joint ventures," *Michigan Journal of International Law*, 15(2): 405-457; Lubetzky, D. (2016),"From magic shows to KIND bars: One entrepreneur's unpredictable journey," *Medium*, dated 11 March, Available: https://medium.com/global-entrepreneurship-summit/from-magic-shows-to-kind-bars-one-entrepreneurs-unpredictable-journey-f32d334cc2d2 [Accessed 3 September, 2017]; Lubetzky, D. (2015), *Do the KIND Thing: Think Boundlessly, Work Purposefully, Live Passionately*, Ballantine Books; Pofeldt, E. (2004), "Food for peace – Daniel Lubetzky wants to promote ethnic harmony — one business deal at a time," *CNN*, dated 1 December, Available: http://money.cnn.com/magazines/fsb/fsb_archive/2004/12/01/8214531/index.htm

[Accessed 3 September, 2017]; Steinberg, J. (1998), "Making peace by making pasta sauces," *The Jerusalem Post*, dated 2 January, Available: http://www.peaceworks.com/press/libraryArticleMakingPeaceByMakingPastaSauces.html [Accessed 13 February, 2018].

## ENDNOTES

1  *The New Nonprofit Almanac & Desk Reference* (2002), San Francisco: Jossey-Bass.
2  Sabeti, H. (2017), "The fourth sector is a chance to build a new economic model for the benefit of all," *World Economic Forum*, dated 8 September, Available: https://www.weforum.org/agenda/2017/09/fourth-sector-chance-to-build-new-economic-model/ [Accessed 18 March, 2018]; FSMI (2018), "About the fourth sector," Available: https://www.mapping.fourthsector.org/about-fsmi [Accessed 18 March, 2018].
3  Bosma, N., Schøtt, T., Terjesen, S. and Kew, P. (2015), *Global Entrepreneurship Monitor 2015 to 2016: Special Report on Social Entrepreneurship*, Global Entrepreneurship Research Association, Available: www.gemconsortium.org [Accessed 2 December, 2017].
4  Allan, B. (2005), "Social enterprise: Through the eyes of the consumer (prepared for the National Consumer Council)," *Social Enterprise Journal*, 1(1): 57–77, Available: https://doi.org/10.1108/17508610580000707 [Accessed 22 November, 2017].
5  Moore, J. F. (1993), "Predators and prey: A new ecology of competition." *Harvard Business Review*, 71(3): 75–86; Moore, J. F. (1996), "The death of competition," *Fortune*, 133(7): 142; Peltoniemi, M. (2005). *Business Ecosystem: A Conceptual Model of an Organization Population from the Perspective of Complexity and Evolution*, Tampere, Finland, Tampere University of Technology and University of Tampere, p. 83.
6  Iansiti, M. and Levien, R. (2004), *The Keystone Advantage: What the New Dynamics of Business Ecosystems Mean for Strategy, Innovation, and Sustainability,* Boston: Harvard Business School Press, p. 225.
7  Peltoniemi, M. (2005). *Business Ecosystem: A Conceptual Model of an Organization Population from the Perspective of Complexity and Evolution*, Tampere, Finland, Tampere University of Technology and University of Tampere, p. 83.
8  Berkes, F. and Davidson-Hunt, I. J. (2007), "Communities and social enterprises in the age of globalization," *Journal of Enterprising Communities: People and Places in the Global Economy*, 1(3): 209–221.
9  Johanisova, N., Crabtree, T. and Fraňková, E. (2013), "Social enterprises and non-market capitals: A path to degrowth?," *Journal of Cleaner Production*, 38: 7–16.
10  Smith, W. K., Gonin, M. and Besharov, M. L. (2013), "Managing social-business tensions: A review and research agenda for social enterprise," *Business Ethics Quarterly*, 23(3): 407–442.
11  Hauck, J., Görg, C., Varjopuro, R., Ratamäki, O. and Jax, K. (2013), "Benefits and limitations of the ecosystem services concept in environmental policy and decision making: Some stakeholder perspectives," *Environmental Science & Policy*, 25: 13–21.
12  OECD (2015), *Building Enabling Ecosystems for Social Enterprises*, Moderator's Report, 22–23 April, Brussels, Available: http://www.oecd.org/cfe/leed/CBS-ecosystem-22-23-Apr15-Sum-report.pdf [Accessed 23 August 2017].
13  Hauck, J., Görg, C., Varjopuro, R., Ratamäki, O. and Jax, K. (2013), *Op.cit.*
14  Larivière, B., Joosten, H., Malthouse, E. C., Van Birgelen, M., Aksoy, P., Kunz, W. H. and Huang, M. H. (2013), "Value fusion: The blending of consumer and firm value in the distinct context of mobile technologies and social media," *Journal of Service Management*, 24(3): 268–293.
15  Galvagno, M. and Dalli, D. (2014), "Theory of value co-creation: A systematic literature review," *Managing Service Quality*, 24(6): 643–683.
16  Merz, M. A., He, Y. and Vargo, S. L. (2009), "The evolving brand logic: A service-dominant logic perspective," *Journal of the Academy of Marketing Science*, 37(3): 328–344.
17  Prahalad, C. K. and Ramaswamy, V. (2004), "Co-creation experiences: The next practice in value creation," *Journal of Interactive Marketing*, 18(3): 5–14.
18  Lang, J. R., Dittrich, J. E. and White, S. E. (1978), "Managerial problem solving models: A review and a proposal," *Academy of Management Review*, 3(4): 854–866.

19 Weiss, C. H. (1995), "Nothing as practical as good theory: Exploring theory-based evaluation for comprehensive community initiatives for children and families," In: Connell, J. P., Kubisch, A. C., Schorr, L. B. and Weiss, C. H., *Roundtable on Comprehensive Community Initiatives for Children and Families*, Washington DC: The Aspen Institute, pp. 65–92.

20 Montague-Clouse, L. and Taplin, D. (2011), The Basics of Theory of Change, Available: http://www.theoryofchange.org/wp-content/uploads/toco_library/pdf/2011_-_Montague-Clouse_-_Theory_of_Change_Basics.pdf [Accessed 19 March 2018].

21 Clark, H. (2010), *Keynote address delivered at HIPPY Canada conference* (*Home Instruction for Parents of Preschool Youngsters*), Ottawa, November.

22 Weiss (1995), *Op. cit.*, and Annie E. Casey Foundation (2004), Theory of Change: A Practical Tool for Action, Results and Learning. Available: http://www.focusintl.com/RBM020-aecf_theory_of_change_manual.pdf [Accessed: 13 February 2019].

23 Murray, R., Caulier-Grice, J. and Mulgan, G. (2010), *The Open Book of Social Innovation*, The Young Foundation: NESTA; Organizational Research Services (2004), *Theory of Change: A Practical Tool for Action, Results and Learning*, Annie E. Casey Foundation;

24 Human Rights First (2017), "Human trafficking by the numbers," dated 7 January, Available: http://www.humanrightsfirst.org/resource/human-trafficking-numbers [Accessed 23 August 2017].

25 Luscombe, B. (2014), "Inside the scarily lucrative business model of human trafficking," *TIME*, dated 20 May, Available: http://time.com/105360/inside-the-scarily-lucrative-business-model-of-human-trafficking/ [Accessed 23 August 2017].

26 ILO (2017), "Statistics on forced labour, modern slavery and human trafficking," Available: http://www.ilo.org/global/topics/forced-labour/statistics/lang—en/index.htm [Accessed 23 August 2017].

27 Kingdon, J. W. (1984), *Agendas, Alternatives, and Public Policies,* Boston: Little, Brown.

28 Harji, K. and Jackson, E. T. (2012), *Accelerating Impact*, NY: Rockerfeller Foundation.

29 J. Katzenstein and Chrispin, B. R. (2011), "Social entrepreneurship and a new model for international development in the 21st century," *Journal of Developmental Entrepreneurship*, 16(1): 87–102.

30 Sherif, M. (1966), *In Common Predicaments: Social Psychology of Intergroup Conflict and Cooperation*, Boston: MA: Houghton-Miffin.

31 Lewis, R. D. and Gates, M. (2005), *Leading Across Cultures,* Nicholas Brealey.

32 Valiente, A. and Williams, A. (2017), "Matt damon opens up about harvey weinstein, sexual harassment and confidentiality agreements," *Entertainment*, dated 14 December, Available: http://abcnews.go.com/Entertainment/matt-damon-opens-harvey-weinstein-sexual-harassment-confidentiality/story?id=51792548 [Accessed 10 January 2018].

33 Armstrong, K. (2017), More Than 25,000 People Have Signed a Petition to Have Matt Damon Cut from 'Ocean's 8', Lifestyle, dated 24 December, Available: https://www.yahoo.com/lifestyle/more-25-000-people-signed-202043150.html [Accessed 20 January 2018].

34 Milano, A. (2017), Tweet dated 15 October, *Twitter*, Available: https://twitter.com/Alyssa_Milano/status/919659438700670976 [Accessed 8 February, 2018]. The #MeToo movement was named the *Time* magazine's Person of the Year for 2017.

35 Celebrity News, (2017), "Minnie driver slams 'tone deaf' ex matt damon as alyssa milano tries to school him on sexual assault," *News.com.au*, dated 18 December, Available: http://www.news.com.au/entertainment/celebrity-life/minnie-driver-slams-tone-deaf-ex-matt-damon-as-alyssa-milano-tries-to-school-him-on-sexual-assault/news-story/35cc8d227a7fcabac5c1c8acd55ee814 [Accessed 8 February 2018].

36 Desantis, R. (2018), "Matt damon apologizes for controversial #metoo comments: 'I should get in the backseat and close my mouth for a while'," *NY Daily*, dated 16 January, Available: http://www.nydailynews.com/amp/entertainment/matt-damon-apologizes-controversial-metoo-comments-article-1.3760344 [Accessed 22 January 2018].

37 Gillette (2019), We Believe: The Best a Man Can Be, YouTube, dated 13 January [Accessed 16 January 2019].

38 Schein, E. H. (1984), "Coming to a new awareness of organizational culture," *Sloan Management Review*, 25(2): 3–16.

39 Chouinard, Y. (2016), *Let My People Go Surfing: The Education of a Reluctant Businessman–Including 10 More Years of Business Unusual*, Penguin.

40  Schein, E. H. (1984), *Op. cit.*

41  Patagonia Works (2018), "Patagonia gives customers a way to fight for the planet," dated 6 February, Available: http://www.patagoniaworks.com/press [Accessed 9 February 2018].

42  AJ Willingham, C. (2019). *Patagonia got $10 million in GOP tax cuts. The company's donating it for climate change awareness.* [online] CNN. Available: https://edition.cnn.com/2018/11/29/business/patagonia-10-million-tax-climate-change-trnd/index.html [Accessed 26 December 2018].

43  Roux, D. J., Rogers, K. H., Biggs, H. C., Ashton P. J. and Sergeant, A. (2006), "Bridging the science-management divide: Moving from unidirectional knowledge transfer to knowledge interfacing and sharing," *Ecology and Society,* 11(1): 4 [online] URL: http://www.ecologyandsociety.org/vol11/iss1/art4/

44  BCG (2016), *India's midday meals in schools, Center for Public Impact,* Available: https://www.centreforpublicimpact.org/case-study/indias-midday-meals-in-schools/ [Accessed 25 March 2018].

45  The Akshaya Patra Foundation (2016), *Annual Report 2015-16:* 13.

46  Ogbu, J. U. (1994), "From cultural differences to differences in cultural frame of reference," In: Greenfield, P.M and Cocking, R.R. (eds.), *Cross-cultural Roots of Minority Child Development,* pp. 365–391.

47  Upton, D., Ellis, C., Lucas, S. and Yamner, A. (2007), "Akshaya patra: Feeding india's schoolchildren," *Harvard Business Case Study,* Available: https://www.akshayapatra.org/sites/default/files/images/harvard_business_school_study.pdf [Accessed 30 December 2017].

48  *Ibid.*

49  Bansal, R. (2017), *God's Own Kitchen,* Manipal: Manipal Technologies Limited.

51  Nonaka, I., Toyama, R. and Konno, N. (2000), "SECI, ba and leadership: A unified model of dynamic knowledge creation," *Long Range Planning,* 33: 4–34.

52  Klepper, S. and Sleeper, S. (2000), *Entry by Spinoffs,* Unpublished manuscript, Carnegie Mellon University, Pittsburg, PA.

53  Sorenson, O. and Audia, P. G. (2000), "The social structure of entrepreneurial activity: Geographic concentration of footwear production in the U.S., 1940–1989," *American Journal of Sociology,* 106: 424–462; Sorenson, O., Rivkin, J. W. and Fleming, L. (2004), *Complexity, Networks and Knowledge Flow,* Unpublished manuscript, Harvard Business School, Boston, MA.

54  Balakrishnan Stephens, M. (2016), "Soutkel: Using m-technology to impact emerging markets," In: Balakrishnan Stephens, M. and Lindsay, V. (eds.), *Actions and Insights: Middle East North Africa (Vol. 5): Social Entrepreneurship,* Emerald Group Publishing, pp. 271–287.

55  MIFTAH (2017), *Israeli Checkpoints in the Occupied Territories,* dated 13 July, Available: http://www.miftah.org/Display.cfm?DocId=14429&CategoryId=4 [Accessed 19 January 2018].

56  Rusli, E. M. (2015), "Five apps bringing the next billion people online," *WSJ Blog,* dated 21 April, Available: http://blogs.wsj.com/digits/2015/04/21/five-apps-bringing-the-next-billion-people-online/ [Accessed 28 February 2016].

57  Cullen, P., Cottingham, P., Doolan, J., Edgar, B., Ellis, C., Fisher, M., Flett, D., Johnson, D., Sealie, L., Stocklmayer, S., Vanclay, F. and Whittington, J. (2001), *Knowledge Seeking Strategies of Natural Resource Professionals,* Synthesis of a workshop held in Bungendore, New South Wales, 5–7 June, Technical Report 2/2001, Cooperative Research Centre for Freshwater Ecology, Australia.

58  Rogers, E. M. (1995), *Diffusion of Innovations,* New York: The Free Press.

59  Uskul, A. K. and Oyserman, D. (2010), "When message-frame fits salient cultural-frame, messages feel more persuasive," *Psychology & Health,* 25(3): 321–337.

60  Auletta, K. (2011), "The dictator index," *The New Yorker,* dated March 7, Available: http://www.kenauletta.com/2011_03_07_Mo_Ibrahim.html [Accessed 30 December 2017].

61  *Ibid.*

62  Pierre, J. and Peters, G. B. (2000), *Governance, Politics and the State,* Houndsmills Basingstoke: Macmillan Press Ltd.

63  Cornforth, C. (2003), *The Governance of Public and Non-profit Organisations: What Do Boards Do?,* Oxon: Routledge Taylor & Francis Group.

64  Schöning, M. and Heinecke, A. (2012), *The Governance of Social Enterprises Managing Your Organization for Success,* Switzerland: World Economic Forum, Available: http://www3.weforum.org/docs/WEF_Governance_Social_Enterprises_2106_light.pdf [Accessed 3 January 2018].

65  Kooiman, J. and Bavinck, M. (2005), "The governance perspective," In: Kooiman, J., Bavinck, M., Jentoft, S. and Pullin, R. (eds.), *Fish for Life. Interactive Governance for Fisheries,* Amsterdam: Amsterdam University Press.

66  Risse, T. (2011), "Governance in areas of limited statehood: Introduction and overview," In: Risse, T. (ed.), *Governance Without a State?: Policies and Politics in Areas of Limited Statehood,* New York: Columbia University Press.

67  Mason, C., Kirkbride, J. and Bryde, D. (2007), "From stakeholders to institutions: The changing face of social enterprise governance theory," *Management Decision,* 45(2): 284–301.

68  Kooiman, J. and Bavinck, M. (2005), *Op. cit.*

69  Risse, T. (2011), "Governance in areas of limited statehood: Introduction and overview," In Risse, T. (ed.), *Governance Without a State?: Policies and Politics in Areas of Limited Statehood,* New York: Columbia University Press.

70  Light, P. C. (2006), "Reshaping social entrepreneurship," *Stanford Social Innovation Review,* 4(3): 47–51.

71  Gruber, J. (2005), *Public Finance and Public Policy,* Macmillan.

72  Wolk, A. M. (nd), "Social entrepreneurship and government: A new breed of entrepreneurs developing solutions to social problems," Chapter 6, Available: http://www.rootcause.org/docs/Resources/Publications/Social%20Entrepreneurship%20and%20Goverment.pdf [Accessed 6 February 2018].

73  Bache, I. and Flinders, M. (2004), "Themes and issues in multi-level governance," In: Bache, I. and Flinders, M. (eds.), *Multi-level Governance,* NY: Oxford University Press.

74  Norwegian Government (2010), Available: https://www.regjeringen.no/en/aktuelt/report_grameen/id627366/ [Accessed 3 January 2018].

75  Norad (2010), *Review Commissioned by the Norwegian Ministry of Foreign Affairs of Matters Relating to Grameen Bank,* dated 6 December, Available: https://www.regjeringen.no/globalassets/upload/ud/vedlegg/utvikling/grameen_bank_main_report_eng.pdf [Accessed 3 January 2018].

76  Kooiman, J. and Bavinck, M. (2005), *Op. cit.*

77  Grameen Bank (2011), *Credit Delivery System,* dated 12 June, Available: http://www.grameen-info.org/credit-delivery-system/ [Accessed 3 January 2018].

78  Roodman, D. (2010), "Quick: what's the grameen bank's interest rate?," *Centre for Global Development,* dated 24 September, Available: https://www.cgdev.org/blog/quick-whats-grameen-banks-interest-rate [Accessed 3 January 2018].

79  Grameen Foundation (2014), *Grameen and Yunus Organization Network At-A-Glance,* Available: https://grameenfoundation.app.box.com/s/I64q5oylw88rm2jbfs9p [Accessed 3 January 2018].

80  More on the Zikra initiative: http://zikrainitiative.org

81  Risse, T. (2011), *Op. cit.*

82  Epstein, H. C. (2018), "Why British conservatives are salivating over the oxfam scandal," *The Guardian,* dated 23 March, Available: https://www.thenation.com/article/why-british-conservatives-are-salivating-over-the-oxfam-scandal/ [Accessed 25 March 2018].

83  Ratcliffe, R. and Quinn, B. (2018), "Oxfam: Fresh claims that staff used prostitutes in Chad," *The Guardian,* dated 11 February, Available: https://www.theguardian.com/world/2018/feb/10/oxfam-faces-allegations-staff-paid-prostitutes-in-chad [Accessed 25 March 2018].

84  Daniels, J. P. (2018), 'In Haiti, no one is surprised by the Oxfam scandal', Devex, dated 23 March. Available: https://www.devex.com/news/in-haiti-no-one-is-surprised-by-the-oxfam-scandal-92342 [Accessed 25 March 2018].

85  British Council (2016), *The State of Social Enterprise in Bangladesh, Ghana, India and Pakistan,* Available: https://www.britishcouncil.org/sites/default/files/bc-report-ch4-india-digital_0.pdf [Accessed 4 January 2018].

86  Risse, T. (2011), *Op. cit.*

87  Arp, F., Ardisa, A. and Ardisa, A. (2017), "Microfinance for poverty alleviation: Do transnational initiatives overlook fundamental questions of competition and intermediation?," *Transnational Corporations,* 24(3): 103–117, Available: https://www.researchgate.net/publication/320100413_Microfinance_for_poverty_alleviation_Do_transnational_initiatives_overlook_fundamental_questions_of_competition_and_intermediation [Accessed 10 January 2018].

88  Banerjee, S. B. and Jackson, L. (2017), "Microfinance and the business of poverty reduction: Critical perspectives from rural bangladesh," *Human Relations,* 70(1): 63–91,

89  ACFE (2016), *Report to the Nations on Occupational Fraud and Abuse*, Available: http://www.acfe.com/rttn2016/docs/2016-report-to-the-nations.pdf [Accessed 18 January 2018].

90  Barney, J. B. (1991), "Firm resources and sustained competitive advantage," *Journal of Management*, 17: 99–120.

91  Fulkerson, G. and Thompson, G. (2008), "Fifteen years of social capital: Definitional analysis of journal articles 1988–2003." *Sociological Inquiry*, 78: 536–557.

92  Open Capital Advisors (2013), *Toward an Ecosystem for Early-Stage Incubation of Social Enterprises in East Africa*, Available: https://assets.aspeninstitute.org/content/uploads/files/content/docs/resources/Early-Stage%20Social%20Enterprise%20Ecosystem%20Workshop%20-%20Full%20Paper.pdf [Accessed 18 January 2018].

93  Bosma, N., Schøtt, T., Terjesen, S. and Kew, P. (2015), *GEMS 2015 Report on Social Entrepreneurship*, Global Entrepreneurship Monitor, Available: http://gemconsortium.org/report

94  Katila, R., M.Rosenberger, J.D. and Eisenhardt, K. M. (2008), "Swimming with sharks: Technology ventures, Defense Mechanisms and Corporate Relationships," *Administrative Science Quarterly*, 53: 295–332.

95  Baird, R. and Desjardin, S. (2015), "Show me what you can do: Diagnosing the human capital challenge for social entrepreneurs and exploring emerging solutions," *Aspen Network of Development Entrepreneurs*, Available: http://c.ymcdn.com/sites/www.andeglobal.org/resource/resmgr/Metrics/SGB_Impact-Report_2015_digit.pdf [Accessed 13 January 2018].

96  Kelley, D., Singer, S. and Herrington, M. (2016), *Global Entrepreneurship Monitor 2015/2016 Global Report*, Global Entrepreneurship Monitor.

97  Bosma, N., Schøtt, T., Terjesen, S. and Kew, P. (2015), *Op. cit.*

98  Harris, D. and Kor, Y. (2013), "The role of human capital in scaling social entrepreneurship," *Journal of Management for Global Sustainability*, 2: 163–172.

99  Lane, W. R. and Mel, J. (1993), "Control preference and financial attributes: Founders as CEOs in small, Publicly Traded Firms," *Journal of Small Business Finance*, 3(1): 43–62.

100  Polat, B. and Wadhwa, A. (2008), "Can successful CEOs hold on to their seats after going public? the impact of venture capitalists of founder turnrover," *Review of Business Research*, 8(6): 32–40.

101  Block, J. H., Jaskiewicz, P. and Miller, D. (2011), "Ownership versus management effects on performance in family and founder companies: A bayesian reconciliation," *Journal of Family Business Strategy*, 2(4): 232–245.

102  Gotsi, M. and Wilson, A. M. (2001). "Corporate reputation: Seeking a definition," *Corporate communications: An International Journal*, 6(1): 24–30.

103  Boyd, B. K., Bergh, D. D. and Ketchen Jr, D. J. (2010), "Reconsidering the reputation – performance relationship: A resource-based view," *Journal of Management*, 36(3): 588–609.

104  Fombrun, C. (1996), *Reputation: Realizing Value from the Corporate Image*. Boston: Harvard Business School Press.

105  Barnett, M. L., Jermier, J. M. and Lafferty, B. A. (2006), "Corporate reputation: The definitional landscape," *Corporate Reputation Review*, 9(1): 26–38.

106  Whetten, D. A. and Mackey, A. (2002), "A social actor conception of organizational identity and its implications for the study of organizational reputation," *Business & Society*, 41(4): 393–414.

107  Barnett, M. L., Jermier, J. M. and Lafferty, B. A. (2006), *Op. cit.*

108  Whetten, D. A. and Mackey, A. (2002), *Op. cit.*

109  Gehman, J., Lefsrud, L. R. and Fast, S. (2017), "Social license to operate: Legitimacy by another name?," *Canadian Public Administration*, 60(2): 293–317.

110  Suchman M. C. (1995), "Managing legitimacy: Strategic and institutional approaches," *Academy of Management Review*, 20: 571–610.

111  Bitektine, A. (2011), "Toward a theory of social judgments of organizations: The case of legitimacy, reputation, and status," *Academy of Management Review*, 36(1): 151–179; Suchman, M. C. (1995), *Op. cit.*

112  Burt, R. S. (1992), *Structural Holes: The Social Structure of Competition*, Cambridge, Mass.: Harvard University Press.

113  Coleman, J. S. (1988), "Social capital in the creation of human capital," *American Journal of Sociology*, 94: 95–120; Lin, N. (1999), "Building a network theory of social capital," *Connections*, 22(1): 28–51.

114   Burt (1992), Op cit.; Gnyawali, D. R. and Madhavan, R. (2001), "Cooperative networks and competitive dynamics: A structural embeddedness perspective," *Academy of Management Review*, 26(3): 431–445.

115   Tsai, W. and Ghoshal, S. (1998), "Social capital and value creation: The role of intrafirm networks," *Academy of Management Journal*, 41(4): 464–476.

116   Dubini, P. and Aldrich, H. (1991), "Personal and extended networks are central to the entrepreneurial process," *Journal of Business Venturing*, 6: 306–313.

117   Gnyawali and Madhavan, (2001), *Op. cit.*

118   Zaheer, A. and Giuseppe S. (2009), "Network evolution: The origins of structural holes," *Administrative Science Quarterly*, 54(1): 1–31; Zaheer, A., Gözübüyük, R. and Milanov, H. (2010), "It's the connections: The network perspective in interorganizational research," *The Academy of Management Perspectives*, 24(1): 62–77.

119   Eckelt, D., Dülme, C., Gausemeier, J. and Hemel, S. (2016), "Detecting white spots in innovation-driven intellectual property management," *Technology Innovation Management Review*, 6(7): 34–47; Johnson, M. W. (2010), *Seizing the White Spaces: Growth and Renewal through Business Model Innovation*, Boston: Harvard Business School Publishing.

120   Eckelt *et al.* (2016), *Op. cit.*

121   Rohrbeck, R., Arnold, H. M. and Heuer, J. (2007). Strategic Foresight in multinational enterprises – A Case Study on the Deutsche Telekom Laboratories. Munich Personal RePEc Archive, Available: https://mpra.ub.uni-muenchen.de/5700/1/MPRA_paper_5700.pdf [Accessed 12 October 2017].

122   Eckelt *et al.* (2016), *Op. cit.*

123   Johnson (2010), *Op. cit.*

124   Gavi (2013), *Immunisation in Pakistan: Challenges and Perseverance*, Video, Available: https://vimeo.com/64635330 [Accessed 27 February 2016].

125   Balakrishnan Stephens, M. (2016), "Gavi, the vaccine alliance: Saving lives one vaccine at a time," In: Balakrishnan Stephens, M. and Lindsay, V. (eds.), *Actions and Insights: Middle East North Africa (Vol. 5): Social Entrepreneurship*, UK: Emerald Group Publishing, pp. 135–191.

126   OECD (2015), *Building Enabling Ecosystems for Social Enterprises*, Moderators Report, Brussels, 22–23 Available: http://www.oecd.org/cfe/leed/CBS-ecosystem-22-23-Apr15-Sum-report.pdf [Accessed 10 December 2017].

127   Wainwright, W. (2017), "Why ikea's flatpack refugee shelter won design of the year," *The Guardian*, dated 27 January, Available: https://www.theguardian.com/artanddesign/2017/jan/27/why-ikea-flatpack-refugee-shelter-won-design-of-the-year [Accessed 17 January 2018].

128   More about Better Shelter: http://www.bettershelter.org/about/

129   Jenkins, B. and Ishikawa, E. (2010), *Scaling Up Inclusive Business: Advancing the Knowledge and Action Agenda*, Washington, DC: International Finance Corporation and the CSR Initiative at the Harvard Kennedy School.

130   Donaldson, T. and Preston, L. E. (1995), "The stakeholder theory of the corporation: Concepts, evidence, and Implications," *Academy of Management Review*, 20(1): 65–91.

131   Hasnas, J. (2010), "Whither stakeholder theory? A guide for the perplexed revisited," *Journal of Business Ethics*, 112: 47–57.

132   Gregory, A. (2007), "Involving stakeholders in developing corporate brands: The communication dimension," *Journal of Marketing Management*, 23(1–2): 59–73; Phillips, R., Freeman, R. E. and Wicks, A. C. (2003), "What Stakeholder Theory Is Not," *Business Ethics Quarterly*, 13(4): 479–502.

133   Kusyk, S. M. and Lozano, J. M. (2007), "SME social performance: A four-cell typology of key drivers and barriers on social issues and their implications for stakeholder theory," *Corporate Governance: The International Journal of Business in Society*, 7(4): 502–515.

134   Phillips, R. A. (1997), "Stakeholder theory and a principle of fairness," *Business Ethics Quarterly*, 7(1): 51–66.

135   Wasserman, T. (2012), "Kony 2012, tops 100 million views, Becomes the most viral video in history," *Mashable*, dated 12 March, Available: https://mashable.com/2012/03/12/kony-most-viral/#0IHt2sGJXEqF [Accessed 13 February 2018].

136   NBC News (2012), "Wife blames exhaustion for 'Irrational' behavior by 'Kony 2012' filmmaker," *MSNBC*, dated 17 March, Available: https://web.archive.org/web/20120317145702/http://usnews.msnbc.msn.

com/_news/2012/03/16/10721745-wife-blames-exhaustion-for-irrational-behavior-by-kony-2012-filmmaker [Accessed 8 February 2018].

137 Chevalier, J. M. and Buckles, D. J. (2008), *SAS2: A Guide to Collaborative Inquiry and Social Engagement*, Sage Publications.

138 Burga, R. and Rezania, D. (2016), "Stakeholder theory in social entrepreneurship. A descriptive case study," *Journal of Global Entrepreneurship Research*, 6: 4, DOI https://doi.org/10.1186/s40497-016-0049-8

139 Mitchell, R. K., Agle, B. R. and Wood, D. J. (1997), "Toward a theory of stakeholder identification and salience: Defining the principle of who and what really counts," *Academy of Management Review*, 22(4): 853–886.

140 Rowley, T. I. and Moldoveanu, M. (2003), "When will stakeholder groups act? An interest-and identity-based model of stakeholder group mobilization," *Academy of Management Review*, 28(2): 204–219.

141 Chevalier and Buckles (2008), *Op. cit.*

142 Weber, M. (1947), *The Theory of Social and Economic Organization*, New York: Free Press.

143 Etzioni, A. (1964), *Modern Organizations*, Englewood Cliffs, NJ: Prentice-Hall; Yukl, G. A. (1998), *Leadership in Organizations*, Sydney: Prentice Hall; Greene, R. and Elfers, J. (1999), *Power and the 48 Laws*, London: Profile Books.

144 Wexler, M. N. (2001), "The who, what and why of knowledge mapping," *Journal of Knowledge Management*, 3: 249–263; Nissen, M. E. and Levitt, R. E. (2004), "Agent-based modelling of knowledge dynamics," *Knowledge Management Research and Practice*, 2: 169–183; Reed, M. S., Graves, A., Dandy, N., Posthumus, H., Hubacek, K., Morris, J. and Stringer, L. C. (2009), "Who's in and why? A typology of stakeholder analysis methods for natural resource management," *Journal of Environmental Management*, 90(5): 1933–1949.

145 Rowley, T. I. and Moldoveanu, M. (2003), *Op. cit.*

146 Ackermann, F. and Eden, C. (2011), "Strategic management of stakeholders: Theory and practice," *Long Range Planning*, 44(3): 179–196.

147 Mitchell, R. K., Agle, B. R. and Wood, D. J. (1997), *Op. cit.*

148 *Ibid.*

149 Bowler, K. (2017), "Here's why people hate joel osteen," *The Washington Post*, dated 29 August, Available https://www.washingtonpost.com/news/acts-of-faith/wp/2017/08/29/heres-why-people-hate-joel-osteen/?utm_term=.80695bced80c [Accessed 3 January 2018].

150 An, K. (2017), "Even if joel osteen did the right thing, he lost a chance to teach christianity," *USA Today*, dated 2 September, Available: https://www.usatoday.com/story/opinion/2017/09/02/joel-osteen-right-close-lakewood-church-but-he-lost-chance-teach-christianity-kirkland-an-column/622215001/ [Accessed 3 September 2017].

151 Deeren, J. and Biesecker, M. (2017), "Toxic waste sites near houston flooded by harvey, EPA not on scene," *Chicago Tribune*, dated 2 September, 2017, Available: http://www.chicagotribune.com/news/nationworld/ct-harvey-toxic-superfund-sites-20170902-story.html [Accessed 3 September 2017]; Kirby, J. (2017), "Will Harvey Make Houston's Boom Go Bust?," *Daily Intelligencer*, dated 31 August, Available: http://nymag.com/daily/intelligencer/2017/08/will-harvey-make-houstons-boom-go-bust.html [Accessed 3 September 2017].

152 Suchman, M. C. (1995), "Managing legitimacy: Strategic and institutional approaches," *Academy of Management Review*, 20: 571–610.

153 Wood, D. J. (1991), "Corporate social performance revisited," *Academy of Management Review*, 16(4): 691–718.

154 Suchman, M. C. (1995), "Managing legitimacy: Strategic and institutional approaches," *Academy of Management Review*, 20(3): 571–610.

155 Mitchell, R. K., Agle, B. R. and Wood, D. J. (1997), "Toward a theory of stakeholder identification and salience: Defining the principle of who and what really counts," *Academy of Management Review*, 22(4): 853–886.

156 Wickham, P. A., 2006. *Strategic Entrepreneurship*, Pearson Education.

157 Wright, G. and Goodwin, P. (2009), "Decision making and planning under low levels of predictability: Enhancing the scenario method," *International Journal of Forecasting*, 25(4): 813–825.

158 Taleb, N. N. (2008), *The Black Swan: The Impact of the Highly Improbable*, London: Penguin.

159  Gasca, L. (2017), "3 Reasons why social enterprises fail — and what we can learn from them," *World Economic Forum*, dated 8 June, Available: https://www.weforum.org/agenda/2017/06/3-reasons-why-social-enterprises-fail-and-what-we-can-learn-from-them/ [Accessed 3 September 2017].

160  Newcombe, R. (2003), "From client to project stakeholders: A stakeholder mapping approach," *Construction Management and Economics*, 21(8): 841–848.

161  Wack, P. (1985), "Scenarios, shooting the rapids," *Harvard Business Review*, Nov–Dec: 131–142.

162  Luhmann, N. (1995), *Social Systems*, Stanford CA: Stanford University Press.

163  Maturana, H. R. and Varela, F. J. (1992), *The Tree of Knowledge: The Biological Roots of Human Understanding*, Boston MA: Shambhala Publications.

164  Luhmann, N. (1995), *Social Systems*, Stanford CA: Stanford University Press. *Op. cit.*

165  LaFrance, J. and Lehmann, M. (2005), "Corporate awakening — Why (some) corporations embrace public–private partnerships," *Business Strategy and the Environment*, 14(4): 216–229.

166  Pache, A. and Chowdhury, I. (2012), "Social entrepreneurs as institutionally embedded entrepreneurs: Towards a new model of social entrepreneurship education," *Academy of Management Learning & Education*, 11: 494–510.

167  LaFrance, J. and Lehmann, M. (2005). *Op. cit.*

168  *Ibid.*

169  *Ibid.*

170  Gebert, K. (2013), "Shooting in the dark? EU sanctions policies," *European Council on Foreign Relations*, 71, Available: http://www.ecfr.eu/page/-/ECFR71_SANCTIONS_BRIEF_AW.pdf [Accessed 18 January 2018]

171  LaFrance, J. and Lehmann, M. (2005). *Op. cit.*

172  *Ibid.*

173  Katzenstein, J. and Chrispin, B. R. (2011), "Social entrepreneurship and a new model for international development in the 21st century," *Journal of Developmental Entrepreneurship,*16(1): 87–102; Selsky, J. W. and Parker, B. (2005), "Cross-sector partnerships to address social issues: Challenges to theory and practice," *Journal of Management*, 31(6): 849–873.

174  Smith, W. K. and Lewis, M. W. (2011), "Toward a theory of paradox: A dynamic equilibrium model of organizing," *Academy of Management Review*, 36(2): 381–340.

175  Ibarra, H. and Barbulescu, R. (2010), "Identity as narrative: Prevalence, effectiveness, and Consequences of Narrative Identity Work in Macro Work Role Transitions," *Academy of Management Review*, 35(1): 135–154.

176  Balakrishnan, M. S. and Khurshid, S. (2016), "Sulabh international service organization: Overcoming social barriers to create change," In: Balakrishnan, M.S. and Lindsay, V. (eds.), *Actions and Insights: Middle East North Africa (Vol. 5): Social Entrepreneurship*, UK: Emerald Group Publishing, pp. 93–123.

177  Smith, W. K. and Lewis, M. W. (2011), *Op. at.*

178  Katzenstein, J. and Chrispin, B. R. (2011), "Social entrepreneurship and a new model for international development in the 21st century," *Journal of Developmental Entrepreneurship,* 16(1): 87–102; Selsky, J. W. and Parker, B. (2005), "Cross-sector partnerships to address social issues: Challenges to theory and practice," *Journal of Management*, 31(6): 849–873.

179  For more on how Gavi, the Vaccine Alliance planned to achieve the Millennium Development Goals — read: http://www.gavi.org/about/ghd/mdg/ [Accessed 17 February 2018].

180  Katzenstein, J. and Chrispin, B. R. (2011), *Op. cit.*; Selsky, J. W. and Parker, B. (2005), *Op. cit.*

181  Bensen, R. (2017), "Asem Hasna lost his leg in Syria — Now he's 3D-printing a second chance for fellow amputees," *Wired*, dated 24 July, Available: http://www.wired.co.uk/article/asem-hasna-prosthetics-syria [Accessed 20 January 2018]

182  For more about Twiga Foods: http://twigafoods.com

183  Lloyd, A. (2014), "In jungles of India, new phone app helps indigenous tribes embroiled in maoist insurgency," *National Geographic*, dated 27 September, Available: https://news.nationalgeographic.com/news/2014/09/140926-naxalites-maoists-india-adivasi-phone-app-technology/ [Accessed 19 January, 2018]; Smith, R. (2014), "Shubhranshu Choudhary: Giving a voice to a ravaged, neglected region," *National Geographic*, dated 18 June, Available: https://news.nationalgeographic.com/news/innovators/2014/06/140617-shubhranshu-choudhary-india-maoists-citizen-journalism/ [Accessed 19 January 2018].

184  Katzenstein, J. and Chrispin, B. R. (2011), *Op. cit.*; Selsky, J. W. and Parker, B. (2005), *Op. cit.*

185 Boal, K. B. and Schultz, P. L. (2007), "Storytelling, time, and evolution: The role of strategic leadership in complex adaptive systems," *The Leadership Quarterly*, 18(4): 41–428.

186 Bryson, J. M. (2004), "What to do when stakeholders matter: Stakeholder identification and analysis techniques," *Public Management Review*, 6(1): 21–53.

187 Pache, A. C. and Chowdhury, I. (2012), *Op. cit.*; Phillips, N. and Tracey, P. (2007), "Opportunity recognition, entrepreneurial capabilities and bricolage: Connecting institutional theory and entrepreneurship in strategic organization," *Strategic Organization*, 5(3): 313–320.

188 Friedland, R., Mohr, J. W., Roose, H. and Gardinali, P. (2014), "The institutional logics of love: Measuring intimate life," *Theory and Society*, 43(3–4): 333–370.

189 Cordall, S. C. (2017), "'If the land isn't worked, it decays': Tunisia's battle to keep the desert at bay," *The Guardian*, dated 13 October, Available: https://www.theguardian.com/global-development/2017/oct/13/tunisia-battle-to-keep-desert-at-bay-acacias-for-all [Accessed 20 January 2018]; See Ahoka Changemakers: Available: https://www.changemakers.com/discussions/entries/acacias-all [Accessed 20 January 2018].

190 Sternberg, R. J. (1998), "A balance theory of wisdom," *Review of General Psychology*, 2(4): 347.

191 *Ibid*.

192 Baltes, P. B. and Staudinger, U. M. (2000), "A metaheuristic (pragmatic) to orchestrate mind and virtue towards excellence," *The American Psychologist*, 55(1): 122–136.

193 Luchins, A. S. (1942), "Mechanization in problem solving: The effect of einstellung," *Psychological Monographs*, 54(6): i; Mayer, R. E. (1995), "The search for insight: Grappling with gestalt psychology's unanswered questions," In: Sternberg R. J. and Davidson J. E. (eds.), *The Nature of Insight*, MIT Press, Cambridge, MA, pp. 3–32.

194 Bolman, L. G. and Deal, T. E. (2008), *Reframing Organizations: Artistry, Choice and Leadership*, San Francisco: Jossey-Bass.

195 *Ibid*.

196 Taleb, N. N. (2010), *The Black Swan: The Impact of the Highly Improbable*, 2nd edn., NY: Random House Publishing Group.

197 Dutta, S. (2017), "Creating in the crucibles of nature's fury: Associational diversity and local social entrepreneurship after natural disasters in california, 1991–2010," *Administrative Science Quarterly*, 62(3): 443–483.

198 Jones, R., Pykett, J. and Whitehead, M. (2013), *Changing Behaviours: On the Rise of the Psychological State*, Edward Elgar Publishing.

199 Airley, D. (2009), *Predictably Irrational: The Hidden Forces that Shape Our Decisions*, New York: Harper Collins Publishers.

200 Kahneman, D. and Tversky, A. (2002), *Choices, Values and Frames*, UK: Cambridge University Press.

201 Armstrong, K., Ahsan, M. and Sundramurthy, C. (2018), "Microfinance ecosystem: How connectors, interactors and institutionalizers co-create value," *Business Horizons*, 61: 147–155.

202 Waddock, S.A. and Post, J. E. (1991). "Social entrepreness and catalytic change," *Public Administative Review*, 393–401; Organ, D. W. (1988), *Organizational Citizenship Behavior: The Good Soldier Syndrome*, Lexington, MA: Lexington Books.

203 Gentleman, A. (2015), "The horror of the Calais refugee camp: 'We feel like we are dying slowly'," *The Guardian*, dated 3 November, Available: https://www.theguardian.com/world/2015/nov/03/refugees-horror-calais-jungle-refugee-camp-feel-like-dying-slowly [Accessed 25 February 2018].

204 Wilsher, K. (2018), "France will not allow another refugee camp in Calais, says Macron," *The Guardian*, dated 16 January, Available: https://www.theguardian.com/world/2018/jan/16/macron-visits-calais-before-migrant-crisis-meeting-with-may [Accessed 25 February 2018].

205 *Ibid*.

206 French, W. A. and Granrose, J. (1995), *Practical Business Ethics*. Englewood Cliffs, NJ: Prentice Hall.

207 Gray, A. (2018), "Which countries recycle the most?," *World Economic Forum*, Available: https://www.weforum.org/agenda/2017/12/germany-recycles-more-than-any-other-country/ [Available: 25 February 2018].

# THE SEV LIFECYCLE

## Chapter Objectives

➢ Find key inflection points for SEV survival.

➢ Identify various stages of the SEV lifecycle — Spark, Ignite, Flame, Fire, and Blaze.

➢ Create strategies for growth using relevant business models.

➢ Explain various policy implications for supporting and scaling SEVs.

➢ **Cases:** BeadforLife (entrepreneurship: Uganda), Sulabh International Organization (sanitation: India), Gavi, the Vaccine Alliance (vaccines, innovative financing: impact of 70+ countries), Vestergaard LifeStraw Water Campaign (drinking water, innovative financing: Kenya), and Tree Change Dolls (recycling and upscaling: Australia).

## 3.1. Startup Survival

Large firms face obsolescence due to industry, market, and mega trends. A study of Fortune 500 firms from 1955 to 2017 found that only 60 remain[1] in business due to creative destruction, globalization, and crises. The rate of failure for startups is also high as 75% of venture-backed startups fail.[2] Premature scaling limits startup growth, and this is responsible for a 74% likelihood of failure.[3] Failure also differs across various industries — with the highest rates of failure in the information sector (63%) and the highest rates of success in finance (58%), though 50% of the startups do not cross 4 years.[4] The main reasons for startup failure were incompetence (46%); inexperience (41%); and fraud, neglect, or disaster (1%). The rate of commercial startup activity (7.6%) is higher than social entrepreneurial activity (3.2%), with more women than men (45:55) involved in the social sector than in the commercial sector (1:2).[5] In the SEV category, the least number of enterprises are in the for-profit sector, followed by hybrid and then purely social ventures, with rate of innovation of 1.6% versus the commercial sector that has a rate of innovation of 19–31%.[6]

There are not much data in the SEV sector, but according to F*ckUp Nights, based on Mexico, 38.3% of the social enterprises survived less than 1 year, 45.2% lasted 1–3 years, 8.7% lasted 4–6 years, 2.6% lasted 7–9 years, and 5.2% lasted more than 10 years as a company. This means that in Mexico, the life expectancy of social enterprises is one more year than that of traditional businesses.[7] This was supported by another study comparing the top 100 SEVs versus the top 100 public limited corporations in UK over the period 1984–2014, which found that SEVs performed 8% better.[8] The main reasons for SEV failure were lack of resources and infrastructure, inability to manage in the context, and no strong board of directors. But what is unfortunate is that compared to private startups, (1) SEVs rarely grow in employee numbers and (2) have limited chances for acquisition.[9]

The "valley of death" for startup survival is the time between starting a business and finding a reliable, sustainable business model that can be successfully scaled.[10] This requires crossing a financial chasm with innovation.[11] There are few points of interest for SEVs — the first is that most SEVs are not into replicable or scalable models as they work with communities with distinct problems. Second, they often provide services, and therefore may misconstrue innovation. Third, the valley of death phase normally needs a serious injection of capital, which SEVs may find difficult to source.[12] To understand the pitfalls in SEV survival and growth, you would need to understand the various stages. This chapter divides the life of an SEV into five stages using the analogy of fire — Spark, Ignite, Flame, Fire, and Blaze. Each stage is described here based on their motives, resources, and networks, and also legitimacy, geographic scope, and impact (see Exhibit 3.1).

Exhibit 3.1:  **Lifecycle Stage of an SEV**

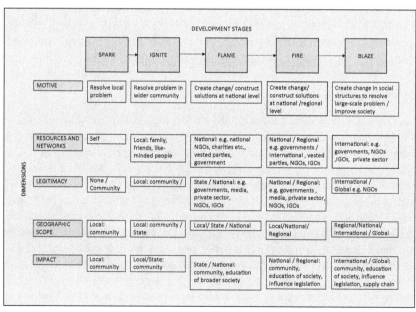

*Source*: Adapted from Stephens Balakrishnan *et al.*[13]

## 3.2. **Stage 1: Spark**

This stage is from ideation till the time of registration of the organization. Motives of entrepreneurs can begin as early as childhood and become a character trait, helping the founder get a perspective in life. For many social entrepreneurs, they begin pursuing their idea as a hobby, and hence, these informal ventures are often not counted in official statistics. The most common reason to start an SEV seems to be ethics and morals, followed by either a convenient opportunity, or the ability to discover or create an opportunity.[14] It has been found that the *How* and *Why* of motives are important for SEV founders, though there is little agreement on what percentage of their SEV should be focused on the business side of the motives.[15] Whatever the reason, an SEV venture cannot survive without a strong business model, and it needs to be self-sustaining through its own earned income, through market revenue, or through a combination of earned income, philanthropy, and subsidies.[16]

According to the GEMS 2017–2018 report, 75% of entrepreneurs are opportunity-driven. Serendipity has a big role to play in discovering opportunities. Take, for example, the origins of BeadforLife (see Case Study 3.1). In this case, the time from ideation to registration of the company took about a year. Part of the process was the discovery that other people were interested in the product (they had a saleable value) and the cause (helping other women succeed in Uganda). Motivation can also develop through the forced confrontation of issues by experiences (education or work).[17] Nobel Prize winner, Muhammad Yunus, who founded Grameen Bank, first lent money personally in 1976 to 42 women from the village of Jobra in Bangladesh, after taking his students on a field trip. He realized that a small microloan in terms of US dollars was a significant amount of money for the women who could use the funds to alleviate themselves from poverty and the vicious cycle of debt. Grameen was registered in 1989 as a non-profit and NGO. This process took about 13 years.

The Spark phase for Sulabh International Service Organization, an SEV dedicated to sanitation and eradication of the practice of night soil removal in India, was during the period 1968 to early 1970. For Dr. Bindeshwar Pathak, the founder, the seed for the idea that became Sulabh International Service Organization began in early childhood (see Case Study 3.2). He had a traumatic experience of being made to eat cow dung to purify himself after touching a person of lower caste in India. The "scavengers", removers of "night soil" or human feces, belonged to the lower caste. Dr. Pathak also saw a young bride weep because she was married into a scavenger family and was obliged to take up the family livelihood. Pathak also witnessed a young child die because people were unwilling to touch him because of his caste. All these experiences gave him the resolve to continue the work needed to eradicate the practice of night soil removal and bring sanitation to India to communities where it was not available.

Pathak had the ability to recognize an opportunity to do good. When he was presented a World Health Book on sanitation called "Excreta Disposal for Rural Areas and Small Communities" in 1968, he realized that to make a change, he would have to design a pour and flush pit toilet that would work in the Indian context, where there was no running water nor sufficient water pressure. Pathak largely depended on himself, extended family, and friends for additional resources (money and manpower). He received social validation from the community he was working with, the scavengers and colleagues from the organization that set him on the journey — the Gandhi Centenary Celebrations Committee. The cause itself did not have any valid form of legitimacy from the government. In those initial days, other than memos with good intentions, he had little official recognition. Pathak did not design a toilet till 1970, after he registered his NGO in the state (Bihar) from where he came from. In those early years, his impact was limited to the community he worked with.

## Case Study 3.1: **BeadforLife**

The three founders had prior experiences in this sector. Devin Hibbard, the CEO had a degree in public policy, had lived in India and Kenya and had been exposed to the developmental sector. She had been in Uganda visiting family. Torkin Wakefield (psychologist and public administrator) began her career in Peace Corps and formed many organizations to help marginalized people. Her husband is a doctor and treats patients with HIV and has worked in the slum areas. Ginny Jordan is a practicing psychotherapist and had worked with Torkin to create World Sits Down Dinner (hunger advocacy experience).

The SEV "BeadforLife" can trace its origin to a chance encounter in 2003 in Uganda between the three women founders who empathized with one Ugandan woman they met, Millie Grace Akena, whom they met in a Kampala slum. She was trying to sell bead jewelry made from rolled paper. Millie had been displaced by the atrocities of Joseph Kony. She was trying to support herself and her five children from the brutal work of quarrying, earning less than a dollar a day. The women bought some jewelry and wore it around the city and were instantly complemented on the jewelry. Millie had said she had no market, but the women realized there was potential for the recycled paper jewelry.

The women pooled their financial resources and bought a few bead necklaces from about 100 women in the neighborhood. They took the necklaces to USA and sold them using the concept of a "bead party" for a cause. They relied on friends and word of mouth to spread the story. Bead jewelry found a ready market, but the founders realized very quickly that the women in Uganda from whom they were buying beads were depending on them for money through their efforts. It would not be sustainable. BeadforLife was registered as a non-profit organization in Colorado, USA in September 2004, 1 year after the founders met Millie.

Within 10 years, BeadforLife had reached more than 1.2 million women with the story of the Ugandan women and raised millions of dollars to sustain the SEV. To increase sustainable livelihoods, they introduced the Street Business School program. It was born through constant trial and improvisation and is a 6-month mobile classroom program to help women get the necessary training to begin their own entrepreneurial venture. In terms of impact, BeadforLife has reached over 46,000 women in Uganda. Through the BeadforLife program, 3,250 women have begun a microenterprise. The women have higher success rates than the average startup in Uganda (80% versus 20%), and women graduating from the Street Business School have increased their income by at least 50%.

Like conventional entrepreneurs, SEV entrepreneurs may design their initiative out of necessity. Imran Khan, politician and Prime Minister of Pakistan and former Pakistani cricketer, helped establish the Shaukat Khanum Memorial Cancer Hospital & Research Centre in 1996. He explains his reason for starting the hospital: "*The motivation was my mother's illness from cancer, and suffering a very painful death. So watching her I began to realize that a) there is no cancer hospital in Pakistan because had there been a hospital she would have had a good chance of surviving, and secondly, what happens to a poor man who got cancer!*"[18]

## Case Study 3.2: **Sulabh International Service Organization**

Dr. Bindeshwar Pathak was born in 1943 to a higher caste, Brahmin family. Pre-independence, India was divided by a rigid caste system, where 70% of the population was considered "lower caste". The lowest level of this system was the "Dalit" or the "untouchables," and the most menial of jobs were reserved for them including that of scavenging, or removal of night soil. Though the caste system was officially banned in 1950 and quotas were introduced then and in 1989, Pathak observed that the lowest caste in his village the "Doms" or "Dalits" were considered untouchable as their job was to remove human waste or "night soil". They were called scavengers.

He was punished as a child for touching the lady who worked in their house from the caste. By some strange quirk of fate, in 1968 he started working for the Gandhi Centenary Celebrations Committee in Patna and he worked in the "Scavenger Liberation Cell." Mahatma Gandhi fought against this practice and called the people of this caste "Harijan" or "Children of God." Pathak realized that there was a need to find an alternative to the scavenging system. To build a toilet for rural areas, he needed to teach himself the necessary engineering required. He borrowed money from friends and family to fund his inventions. By the end of the 1970, he designed and built a two pit pour–flush water-seal toilet which he named Sulabh Shauchalaya and registered it as an NGO. Pathak applied for grants to construct toilets but was unable to get funding as the government changed or officials moved.

In 1973, Pathak got his first order from a municipal official at Ara. He also got a letter written to the then Prime Minister, Mrs Indira Gandhi, who recommended to the Govt. of Bihar to eradicate scavenging and untouchability. Soon the city of Patna, the state capital, followed suit. Though initially he had to use village influencers to get the community in villages to adopt the concept, women were his biggest champions. Pathak remembers how the women in his community had to wait till dark to go out for defecation and occasionally fell prey to snakes, scorpions and other beings. The first Sulabh public toilet complex was built in Patna and 500 people turned up the first day to use the toilet and pay Rs. 0.10 to use the toilet. In 1989, Sulabh was relocated to Delhi.

Based on the advice he had received long back, he decided to use a pay-and-use model to ensure he would always have funding. The land would be donated by the government for the case, and Pathak would then get 15–20% of the construction cost for overheads and consultation. The toilet would be built and maintained by the people from the community of impact. Sulabh then would maintain these complexes for 30 years, free of cost, by using the pay-and-use system where it charges 1 rupee (about 2 US cents) from each person who uses the community toilets. Sulabh uses revenues generated through a government-backed cleaning services contract to provide employment for former "scavengers". Sulabh also uses the cross-subsidies for its rural facilities or facilities in less-busy locations using the income from more popular locations.

Sulabh offers more than 40 types of toilets. Public toilets are also used for generating biogas. By 1978, Sulabh began getting international recognition. Pathak represents the government on goodwill assignments and acts as a consultant. Sulabh Public toilets are operated on 'pay and use' basis. The world's biggest toilet complex constructed by Sulabh International is in Pandharpur near Pune, Maharashtra. It has provisions of 2,848 toilet units with lavatories, bath cubicles, 39 toilets for physically challenged people and 382 toilets for VIPs. At present, 2 lakh people are using these facilites daily. From next year when fully completed, 4 lakh people will be able to use these facilities daily. It has amenities like lockers, dressing rooms and health centres for first-aid and para-medical services with doctors. Sulabh volunteers maintain these complexes round the clock and keep them spic and span for the use of the pilgrims. Some public toilets also act as public health centers with sanitary pad machines and educational drives to prevent HIV and AIDS. These toilets benefit local people, tourists, and foreigners who visit India. Pathak then worked on effluent treatment of biogas waste so that the water could be safely discharged into rivers or water bodies, without polluting them. He worked using dried water hyacinth to increase the gas production and later he experimented with duckweed in 1996. The duckweed-treated effluent was able to increase fish yield to 8–10 tons per annual harvest.

Pathak used a multi-prong approach to restore human dignity to those people who were rescued from the "scavenging life". The process has five stages: (1) liberation, (2) rehabilitation, (3) vocational training, (4) social elevation, and (5) proper education for future generations. In 1980, Pathak was able to get legal protection for the scavengers. This was extended in 1986 as a new law that was for the protection of Civil Rights and included scavengers also from other religions like Christians and Hindus. He needed to smash cultural mind-sets. He did this by encouraging people who were thought leaders to show the way. He had 10,000 families from these lower caste communities adopted by higher caste families. In 1988, for the first time Harijans were allowed into the Nathdwara temple in Udaipur to attend the puja and sit at a community meal with Brahmins. Pathak took women who were former scavengers to walk the ramp with the models who showcased their handiwork at the United Nations in New York on July 2, 2008. In 2013, Sulabh adopted "Widows of Vrindavan" and then extended this to Varanasi. The widows who lost their husbands are often shunned by their families and considered responsible for the death of their husbands. In 2015, Varanasi had over 38,000 widows living in the city. They are called the forgotten women and about 12,000 are between the ages of 20 and 45. Vrindavan had 6,000 widows in 2013, who lived their lives as an outcast. The widows who were adopted by Sulabh tied Rakhi to the Prime Minister of India, Narendra Modi.

Sulabh has its presence in 26 States and 4 Union Territories, 1784 local bodies, 1698 towns and 520 districts. There are nearly 50,000 voluntary social workers that are associated with Sulabh. It alone has installed more than 1.5 million toilets in individual houses and the Government of India has installed about 54 million toilets based on Sulabh design. Further, more than 9000 public toilets are maintained by Sulabh. Other countries like Bangladesh, Vietnam, China, Indonesia and others have also adopted the Sulabh toilet technology.

A total of 640 towns have been declared scavengers free with more than two million scavengers being liberated. They have been rehabilitated after being imparted vocational training and education. Sulabh acts as a consultant for international projects and even for human capacity-building for countries like Ethiopia, Mozambique, Uganda, Cameroon, Burkina Faso, Kenya, Nigeria, Senegal, Ghana, Zambia, Tanzania, Cote d' Ivorie, Mali, and Rwanda.

Pathak has received many awards (more than 90). The first was in 1984 — it was the KP Goenka Memorial Award. He received the Padma Bhushan (India) in 1991; the St. Francis Prize from Pope Paul John II in 1992; Global Best Practices by UN-Habitat/UNCHS in 1996; the Legend of the Planet award from the French Senate in 2013; and he was recognized as an Ashoka Fellow in 2008, and recently awarded with Gandhi Peace Prize-2016. Pathak says, *"I can explain the Sulabh way saying that it has four pillars viz truth, non-violence, ethics and morality coupled with vision, mission, commitment, capabilities, action and efficiency."*

In this field, there is still work to do as over 100 million people still don't have access to a toilet. India has a population of 1.2 billion, and of this total population, 70% live in rural areas; 50% have no access to toilets even though 75% of the Indian population has a mobile phone. In 2014, 2.4 billion people (90% rural) did not have access to basic sanitation facilities such as toilets or latrines with 13% having to use the open spaces or unsanitary facilities for defecating. Unsafe sanitation results in 8% of the global disease burden. By 2019, India wants to ensure that no one defecates in public for lack of adequate sanitation. A WHO study showed that every US\$1 invested in improved sanitation translates into an average return of US\$9. Prime Minister Narendra Modi has announced the goal of eliminating open defecation by 2019. At present, 45% of the households without toilets live in just five states — Bihar, Madhya Pradesh, Rajasthan, Haryana, and Uttar Pradesh, but the problem may be not just about building toilets but about education to create a cultural mind-set.

Sometimes motives are an outcome of *Zeitgeist* (the spirit of the time), a set of beliefs and ideals that are strongly held during that period. Bobby Sager an entrepreneur–philanthropist spends time living in disadvantaged areas. This period often ranges from a month to a year to find a business model that will provide a *"hand-ups and not hand-outs"* solution. The Sager Family Travelling Foundation acts as an incubator for these ideas.[19] Sager says, *"I go to a place and live in a place really long enough, to really understand what's going on in the ground ... usually that takes a month or two. I go to really difficult places because I'm looking for market opportunity, I am an entrepreneur. I want a real big return on my investment. Remember I said this is not feel good stuff .... I'm not going around the world to give people hugs; I'm going around the world to empower people so that they can change their lives and change the lives of their families, and their communities, and sometimes their countries. So I go to places that are really screwed up. Cause the difference between current reality and minimally acceptable, is really big — that is what I call market opportunity."*[20]

Amul, a milk cooperative, was founded in 1946 to empower poor local farmers in Gujarat, India to earn income and overcome unfair milk trade practices. Souk El Tayeb in Lebanon was created in 2004 to allow the country's small-scale producers to go directly to the buyers and hence champion local produce in a country torn by civil unrest. Twiga Foods was formed in Kenya in 2014 to help farmers go directly to the vendors, using a mobile technology platform.

## 3.3. **Stage 2: Ignite**

This phase of the SEV lifecycle is that point in time when an SEV becomes formally registered and starts developing its product offering, often experimenting with its minimum viable product (MVP). At this stage, the SEV begins looking at the wider community. They borrow resources from friends, family, and similar-minded people and may still not be ready to access formal capital, other than grants. They begin gaining legitimacy in the local community of impact, which is still a smaller geographic area. During this Ignite stage, SEVs focus on the process outlined by The Lean Startup method promoted by Eric Ries.[21] He says startups should focus on thinking big but starting small. They do this by using validated learning, where founders are making sense of their markets through the Build–Measure–Learn approach and pivoting (executing a change in strategy). There is constant experimentation, working actively with beneficiaries and other stakeholders to determine the value that is needed for success.

Legitimacy is critical at this stage, as it provides momentum to the cause. Since SEVs often act as change agents, they face resistance from the communities of impact. Mohammed Yunus stated, "*It is very difficult to change peoples' minds, the way they have grown, the way they have seen ... It is a social tradition that you are opposing, and it's not easy to turn the tide around.*"[22]

Often, manpower resources come from the local community or a close network of friends, family or like-minded people. Volunteering is the most common method SEVs with a dominant social motive use to tap into human resources. Gregory Dees, a pioneer of social entrepreneurship, stresses that it is hard to measure the *psychic income people get from giving or volunteering*.[23] One of the biggest challenges in the early stages is that volunteers are rarely recruited for their expertise in business management, and this will limit growth opportunities (see Exhibit 3.2).

Traditional forms of funding for SEVs are personal capital, family, and friends. Though banks offer smaller capital investments, they require guarantees. NGOs and governments provide grants, but they have strict criteria that must be met. Significant time can be taken in the initial years in applying for grants. Grants often come with their own objectives, which require applicants to modify their focus, and this may distract from the original purpose. To get larger amounts of funding, especially from angel investors, accelerators, incubators, and private equity firms, it is important to show commercial viability and potential to scale. A study on inclusive businesses found that only 32% were commercially viable and 13% had scale.[24] Firms need to be creative about funding. For example, Gavi, the Vaccine Alliance (see Case Study 3.3), used vaccine bonds in finance markets to get the necessary funds up front from long-term government commitments to help reshape the vaccine market. Vestergaard, a pioneer in the Humanitarian Entrepreneurship business model of "Profit with a Purpose" (see Case Study 3.4), used carbon credits to fund its LifeStraw water purifiers for Kenya.

Management of mobile resources like money and funding allows operations to continue. This choice is dictated by the organizational purpose and its values. The online tutoring website, Khan Academy, which was started in 2008 by Sal Khan, has a clear purpose — to be a non-profit. Sal began publishing on YouTube, and the videos became so popular worldwide (though the focus was initially family in 2005) that he quit his job in 2009 to focus on it full-time. The funding is entirely from donations (58% foundation and gifts, 13% corporate gifts, 10% donors), and they have spent over US$37 million in 2017.[25] They have 8 million

Exhibit 3.2:  **Capital Sources as a SEV Gets Scale**

**Investors**

| Traditional Philanthropy | Venture Philanthropy | Community Debt Financing | Community Development | Socially Responsible Capital | | | Socially Responsible Investment Funds | Traditional Capital |
|---|---|---|---|---|---|---|---|---|
| Personal Partners Family Friends | Foundations/Trusts Endowments Grants | Employee Equity Cooperatives Crowd Sourcing | NGO/ Government CSR Partnerships Managed Foundations | Angel investors | Incubators | Private Equity/ Venture Capitalist | Pension Funds/ Carbon Funds | Banks IPO Mutual Funds SWF |
| Less Institutional | | | | | | | | More Institutional |
| More tolerant of risk | | | | | | | | More risk averse [as stakeholders they are answerable increases and consequences of failure have wider impact ] |
| Investment time: early-stage | Early stage to international | Early stage | Early stage to international | Early stage | Seed funding | Seed funding | Growth, internationalization | Internationalization |
| No clearly defined social return | | | | | | | | Expect financial return and accountable social return |
| Investment with limited AUM | | | | | | | | Need AUM and track record of success, a management team, scalability |

*Sources:* Adapted from Stephens Balakrishnan and Lindsay; Emerson; and Suber et al.[27]

users a month, with 50 million registered users across 190 countries, and content available in 17 languages. There is potential to make money if they charged US$10/per year, as they have higher results in standardized learning, but that is not the intention, as the SEV feels strongly that anyone in the world should be able to access their content and they focus on the student who may not have access to financial resources.

Local communities provide local labor. In some cases, this is part of the social business model and sometimes, it is for reasons of convenience. Jamie Oliver, world renowned chef, established "Fifteen" in 2002 when he was 26 years of age. The purpose of Fifteen was to engage unemployed disadvantaged youth, focusing on behavior modification and skill development for a successful life. They run the Fifteen Apprentice Programme from where more than 500 young people have graduated across all the restaurants with 90% staying in the business. The business is profitable. Profits are donated to charities, and the concept is expanding around the world. Of the 200 applicants, 18 are chosen for an apprenticeship model. The trainees get a stipend of €100 per week. While all do not graduate (30%), those who stayed with the program had better financial literacy, reduction of the wage scar, and improved well-being and greater social mobility. The challenge is that the impact is seen over 5–10 years. The social return on investment (SROI) analysis found that each apprentice costs Fifteen about €30,000 per year, and the equivalent monetary value the youth, the families, the children, and the State received was calculated at €5 million per year, which is an SROI of 1:9.5.[26]

One of the challenges of testing MVP in social causes is that the impact may take time to be felt. This is where the theory of change (discussed in detail in Chapter 7) is important to track progress toward key goals. Even with commercial products, research shows that paying customers are unwilling to trade-off quality for good causes or ethical products, so the MVP must find the sweet spot between willingness to pay, promises made, and product value.

There is a constant need to fine-tune the proposed business model in this stage of the lifecycle (see Exhibit 3.1). Many SEVs also don't have a business model and are still trying to find a viable sustainable entity for their cause. In the SEV, BeadforLife, the founders quickly realized that the bead sellers were becoming dependent on the founders for sales, so they created a sustainable model where they created an entrepreneurial business school for the women, the Kampala Model. This is an 18-month program with a seed funding of US$4. This soon evolved in later stages to the "The Street Business School" a 6-month program, where they cover product making, planning, and money management and business sales. Through this, by 2017, they had reached 46,000 people in Uganda and found that 81% of the graduates of The Street Business School had started 3,250 microbusinesses, which were surviving 2 years later, despite the fact 80% of the business failed in the same period in Uganda. Their graduates went on living on US$1.35/day to US$4.19/day in two years.

Very often, founders make the mistake of trying to create the perfect product, when what they need is an MVP to get feedback and improve quickly. When Worldreader[28] was launched in 2010, their focus was to bring digital books to disadvantaged schools and families. But to take it from an idea to the next phase, they needed to get feedback from their constituents. Would they be able to read digital books on a device? Was there something that they were missing? They tested the MVP in one school in Ghana using what is known as a "concierge approach", using Kindle

Exhibit 3.3: **The SEV Lean Startup Process**

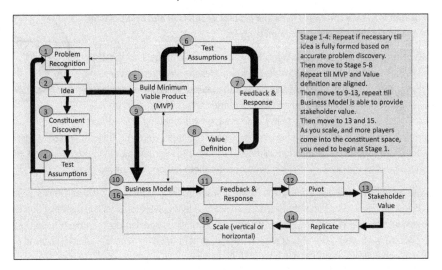

e-readers with 16 students, and the test was positive. They learnt that the Kindles were easily breakable as kids would unknowingly sit on them and hence approached the manufacturers to build a more durable machine. By 2011, mobiles were used by almost everybody and there was doubt about the need to adopt mobile apps. On the one hand, they could waste time and valuable resources chasing something that did not work on the field, but mobiles were becoming ubiquitous. What they did was to come up with a risky hypothesis and test it (rather than a paper MVP, a flyer or online sign-in sheet for a new product). They outsourced a simple app with a text reader and tested it in targeted communities and saw a huge increase in its usage (downloads and interaction time). They concluded it was a worthwhile product development and improved the functionality of the app. Currently, Worldreader has books, e-readers, and book apps which have reached over 7.6 million readers during the period 2010–2017. The SEV Lean Startup Process is Illustrated in Exhibit 3.3.

During the Ignite stage of lifecycle, SEVs must strengthen their networks and form advisory boards of experts. It is impossible that all of the knowledge required for success of an SEV lies with the founders. Strong networks can give access to funds, markets, management of the legal and political situations that arise, and business model optimization. Gavi, The Vaccine Alliance (see Case Study 3.3) was a new entrant into the development healthcare sector. It was formed in 2000 to help children in the developing world get the vaccines their counterparts in the developed world were getting and bridge the 15-year gap. Rather than fight the incumbents already entrenched in the market, they worked with them. Their board structure is a unique one, where the board members (each with equal votes) are UNICEF, World Health Organization, implementing country governments, Civil Society Organizations, Vaccine Manufacturers, Private Sector Partners, Research Agencies, donor country government, The World Bank, and the Bill & Melinda Gates Foundation. The CEO of Gavi has no voting rights. The association with the Bill & Melinda Gates Foundation, where Bill Gates personally champions the vaccine case, is an example of a strong champion in the network.

## Case Study 3.3: **Gavi, The Vaccine Alliance**

*Gavi's mission is to save children's lives and protect people's health by increasing equitable use of vaccines in lower-income countries*

The genesis of Gavi can be traced to a World Bank vaccine summit held on the 18th of March 1998. A key question asked was as follows: *How to start getting vaccines to children who needed those most?* At the start of the new millennium, the vaccine divide was huge: children born in industrialized countries were receiving an average of 11–12 vaccines but their counterparts in poor countries were getting around 50% of that number. Nearly 30 million children in developing countries were not fully immunized. There was a market-based scale problem of production volumes. Further, most vaccine manufacturers were not interested in producing expensive vaccines for children who needed them but couldn't afford them.

Gavi, the Vaccine Alliance (Gavi or the Vaccine Alliance) was launched in the year 2000 at the World Economic Forum in Davos. By 2019, Gavi had immunized 760 million children, averted 13 million deaths. For every US$1 spent on immunization, US$18 is saved by the prevention of illness-related costs in healthcare, lost wages and lost productivity. However, the absolute return on investment (ROI) estimated at US$48 is saved per US$1 invested if you consider the resulting healthier and longer lives.

How did they do it? First of all, Gavi is an alliance and that means they work with many partners who are experts in their fields. When you are dealing with researchers and markets that provide finance, local health and local customs, you need a different approach. By bringing all relevant stakeholders to the same table and transparently articulating goals, Gavi tries to create a sustainable impact agenda. This alliance approach is reflected in the unique composition of the Board and the 5-year strategic plans the organization lays out (see Figure 3.1).

The Gavi Business Model is an interesting example of how they reinvented aid. Vaccine development and research is a complex process. The wicked problem[1] Gavi faced on formation was that the existing vaccine manufacturers were simply not interested in manufacturing new vaccines for low-income markets. At that time, in 2000 the vaccine market was concentrated between five large multinational players, who controlled 85% of global sales, but with emerging market manufacturers controlling 86% of the volume. As a vaccine manufacturer, you were more likely to recover your R&D investment in developed countries when you could price the vaccines high, before the patent ran out. While the vaccine industry was a for-profit one, Gavi had a challenging task of finding a win–win situation, where philanthropy and profits could co-exist. By mid-2015, Gavi was able to source from 15 suppliers (8 of which were from emerging markets based in Asia, Latin America, and Africa).

One large gap in the vaccine market was that the R&D funds being allocated to the development of new vaccines for diseases affecting child mortality in low-income countries was not enough. The R&D cost of new vaccines can be anywhere between US$5–150 million in emerging markets and up to

---

[1] "Wicked problem" is a term often used in design thinking and refers to (by Rittel) the "class of social system problems which are ill-formulated, where the information is confusing. Here there are many clients and decision makers with conflicting values, and where the ramifications in the whole system are thoroughly confusing". Read more here: Buchanan, R. (1992). Wicked problems in design thinking. *Design Issues*, 8(2), 5–21; Rittel, H. W., and Webber, M. M. (1973). 2.3 planning problems are wicked. *Polity*, 4, 155–169.

US$200-700 million for multinational firms. Vaccine product development timelines can take 7–20 years depending on the results of large-scale clinical trials. New vaccines could have as many as 500 quality testing steps and required clinical trials in multiples of 10,000 subjects (see Figure 3.2). Investment in production facilities can take place as early as 5 years before product licensure. Because the R&D costs are so high, vaccine manufacturers tended to price the vaccines very high to recover product costs. Emerging manufacturers typically lagged 5–15 years behind multinational manufacturers in the production and licensing of new vaccines. For example, the pentavalent vaccine took 12 years between the first licensed vaccine from a multinational and the first licensed vaccine from an emerging manufacturer. The Meningitis Vaccine Project, which began in 2001, had a project cost of US$60 million and the first vaccine for use came out in 2010.

Figure 3.1: Gavi Board

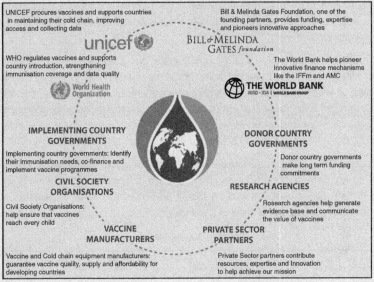

Source: Gavi.

Figure 3.2: Estimated vaccine R&D costs and chance of success (US$ million)

| Stage | Discovery[40] & Preclinical | Phases 1 & 2 | Phase 3 | Licensure | Total |
|---|---|---|---|---|---|
| Cost | 5 – 15 | 4 - 10 | 50 - 120 | 2 - 3 | 60 - 145 |
| Chance of success | 40% | 33% | 75% | N/A | 10% |
| Risk-adjusted cost | | | | | 135-350 |

Source: Wilson (2010).

2000, when Gavi was formed, the biggest barrier for vaccine manufactures for new vaccines is the unpredictable demand forecasts. The demand uncertainty in low-income countries, which could vary up to 80% between demand forecasted and vaccines purchased, resulted vaccine manufacturers suffering losses due to unused inventory. So, while low-income countries accounted for 88% of the volume of the global vaccine market, they were only worth 18% of the value. By pooling demand in those countries that were not able to afford the prices of vaccines, they were able to get buy-in from vaccine manufacturers who realized the market potential of the volumes of sales they could realize. Gavi aggregated the demand for the vaccine using a 15-year demand forecast that had an 80% accuracy. Gavi-supported countries represented over 60% of the world's birth cohort.

They were able to further incentivize vaccine manufactures by front-loading (paying a portion of the cost of vaccines up front) for R&D. This brought down the cost of nine key vaccines from US$1,100 (paid in USA) to US$28. The humanitarian aid and development space often suffer with short-term grants, which does not allow long-term commitments and plans, or long-term donor commitments. To better manage its fiscal responsibility and commitments to Gavi countries, Gavi uses innovative financing like the International Finance Facility for Immunization (IFFIm) *to help avert such [vaccine preventable] deaths by accelerating the availability and increasing the predictability of funds for immunisation, vaccine procurement and health systems strengthening programmes.*

IFFIm is a multilateral development public benefit entity that is registered as a private company in the United Kingdom and is independent from Gavi. It was launched in 2006 and was the first aid financing entity in history to attract legally binding commitments of up to 20 years from donors. IFFIm issues bonds or notes in the global debt market, which then converts long-term government pledges into immediately available cash resources. These vaccine bonds proved very popular with institutional and individual investors who wanted a market-based return and an ethical investment opportunity.

In the first 5 years (2001–2006), Gavi introduced four vaccines. In the next 5 years, 2007–2011, they introduced five more new vaccines. Between 2012 and 2016, they introduced another 16 vaccines and this resulted in 430 vaccine campaigns across the 73 Gavi countries. These 73 countries represented nearly two-thirds of under-immunized children (see Figure 3.3).

Figure 3.3:    Gavi Business Model

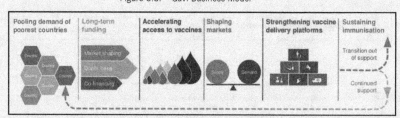

*Source*: Gavi.

But creating access to vaccines is not enough. On the ground, the reality was to reach out to every child, even to those in isolated remote areas. You need to reach out to civil society organization create a network of infrastructure to make sure vaccines were still viable, educate heal workers to give vaccines, ensure hygienic practices, and work with ministries and oth NGOs to ensure the cost of campaigns could be brought down. In emerging marke the poor who were afflicted with vaccine-preventable diseases were not treatab simply because their country's healthcare infrastructure was inadequa These facts indicated that prevention was required through safe a affordable vaccines. The Ebola epidemic is a great recent examp of the alarming consequences of the fact that there were no vaccines and also that there was insufficient healthcare facilities. Gavi supports innovations in the cold chain, data analytics, training, and even in identity as vaccines need to be tracked (for example, polio needs three timely doses to be effective).

Gavi uses a co-financing model. It encourages Gavi-supported countries to take accountability for their own citizens' health. For Gavi, there was still a long way to go. There were still 1.5 million children dying from vaccine-preventable diseases every year who were currently off the grid, and 19.5 million children who missed out on a full course of 12 basic vaccines recommended by the World Health Organization (WHO), 80% of which are in Gavi-supported countries.

Gavi is a successful example of private–public partnership. The UK's Department for International Development (DFID) has given Gavi the highest possible rating in its latest Multilateral Development Review, which ranks diverse organizations that DFID partners with on the global stage such as multilateral development banks, UN agencies, global funds, organizations that work with the private sector, inter-government organizations, and other humanitarian organizations. The Multilateral Organisation Performance Assessment Network (MOPAN), a network of 18 donor countries, reviewed Gavi for the period 2014 to mid-2016 and stated that Gavi is "*both 'strategic and nimble in meeting new vaccine challenges and countries' evolving needs, while keeping a clear focus on its mission goals.*" Gavi is also recognized as being a "strong model for sustainability". Some future areas for development were also identified in this report. They were need for clarification of Gavi's role and function at the country level; a clearer results framework for health system strengthening interventions; development of more systematic processes for recording and using evidence; and development of quality standards, follow-up, and use of evaluations.

Gavi began to publish results to help educate the public on the benefits of immunization at both the micro- and macrolevels. Between 2016 and 2020, through vaccines, Gavi plans to immunize 300 million children, avert 5–6 million future deaths, increase the under-5 mortality rate to 58/1,000 live births, avert 250 million future disability-adjusted life years (DALYs), and ensure that 100% of those countries that transition out of Gavi support continue provide recommended routine vaccines. How does Gavi plan for the future?

There are still challenges ahead. In spite of an 80% reliability in forecasting, of the planned 72 introductions expected in 2016, only 45 were achieved. Between 2016 and 2020, Gavi has planned over 190 vaccine introductions. The shortfalls were for a variety of reasons. Ebola set back the existing immunization program, and country uptakes were higher than predicted. There were supply shortfalls for the pentavalent vaccine, pneumococcal vaccine, and rotavirus vaccine.

There was also a need to focus on new vaccines. Gavi works with WHO to develop a vaccine priority list. For Gavi, 2016 was a particularly challenging year with outbreaks like Ebola and Zika virus, where there were vaccines. How does Gavi increase impact and create the capacity to handle outbreaks like Ebola? New epidemics were constantly evolving. The mass refugee migration crisis also increased fear about global health security as less than one-third of the world was prepared for an outbreak. Dr Seth Berkley, CEO of Gavi said, "… *global forces, such as climate change, human migration, conflict and urbanization, continue to impact and challenge our mission and threaten global health security in the process.*"

## 3.4. **Stage 3: Flame**

During this stage, an SEV begins to hire people to run the organization, as the organization is rapidly growing faster than the capabilities of the founders and the volunteers they are managing. Eric Ries says, *"Building a startup is an exercise in institution building. thus it necessarily involves management."*[29] In some cases, the concept begins spreading across states to the national level, and the organization must form partnerships with other stakeholders in the ecosystem, often working with the government for log-term change. There is a need to be financially viable and address new social value opportunities important for the business model, which now is more fine-tuned (see Exhibit 3.1).

The SEV "business model" describes the organizational structure and the mechanics of how the organization creates and captures value,[30] develops a sustainable competitive advantage in the communities of impact,[31] looks at value constellations,[32] and sustains itself over a long period of time.[33] An SEV business model must have the following qualities[34]:

(1) clear understanding of the organization's social mission (vertical or horizontal growth);

(2) access to specialized knowledge and resources that make impact viable and solve the root problem in a realistic time frame;

(3) access to external expertise that is necessary in the ecosystem context;

(4) ability to respond to the needs of clients and/or beneficiaries by pivoting and making adaptation to the MVP of business model;

(5) access to alliances and/or partnerships that give access to strategic resources.

Ideally for survival, revenues from commercial activities and funds must equal or exceed expenditure. When there is a shortfall, the SEV must be able to mobilize investors for social investment. This is the stage when an SEV should breakeven, but there are no fixed rules (see Exhibit 3.4). The Grameen Bank microfinance concept spilled over to 58 countries, but it took 17 years to breakeven, suggesting that the break-even points of pioneers in SEV sectors may have long incubation periods, like developmental projects requiring patient capital.[35] Based on the theory of change, SEVs must be able to document the impact. By 2012, Grameen Bank was serving 8.29 million borrowers (97% women) across 81,367 villages and on a single working day could collect weekly installments that averaged US$1.5 million, having a default rate lower than any other bank at that time (97% payback).[36]

SEVs need to work with media and influencers and find early champions. This is where a strong advisory board or strategic partnerships help. Nobel Laureate, Mohammed Yunus had a strong political network he developed in his early years, when he was in USA. He was there for his doctoral studies at the Vanderbilt University, USA (1965–1971), through his Fullbright scholarship. The university had many alumni active in the developmental sector. Mohammad Yunus was running the Bangladesh Information Center and campaigning actively in Washington DC when Bangladesh got its independence. When he returned to Bangladesh, he was appointed to the government's Planning Commission headed by Nurul Islam, his previous Professor, and took up an appointment in Chittagong University. These connections helped him get funding from the Ford Foundation (seed funding) and UN's IFAD and funding from Norway, Sweden, Japan, Holland, etc.

By the time Mohammad Yunus was awarded the Nobel Peace Prize in 2006 for founding the Grameen Bank, he had already won 60 different awards at both the national and international

Exhibit 3.4: **SEV Break-even Points: Microfinance**

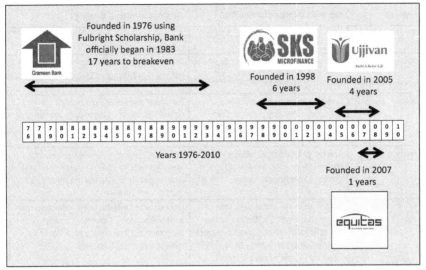

*Source*: Adapted from Koh *et al.*[37]

levels, though the Nobel Peace Prize further thrust the concept of microfinancing and social entrepreneurship into the global spotlight. Awards like those given by NGOs, governments, and foundations create legitimacy for the cause.

The irony of being the first one with an innovative idea is that market traction takes time. Managing the break-even point is critical, and for investors, the time taken for returns (patient capital) must be clear. Exhibit 3.4 shows you that copycats often take a much shorter time to breakeven and scale as the market may be more accepting of the new idea.

## 3.5. **Stage 4: Fire**

At this stage, SEVs are able to scale their impact beyond local geographic areas, across borders from national to regional context. This stage is characterized by scale and growth. Confusion exists as terms, scale, and growth, overlap. In the SEV context, scaling is about increasing impact (does not necessarily mean more resources), while growth is about organizational size and reach (more resources). There are two ways to scale. Go wide (horizontal scaling) or go deep (vertical scaling). Ironically, a strong SEV must prepare for its own obsolescence with respect to the initial problem as it has hopefully been solved, and this means it must be able to innovate, move on to a new problem, and use its existing resources to scale further impact (see Exhibit 3.5).

**Scaling is about increasing impact (does not necessarily mean more resources), while growth is about organizational size and reach (more resources). There are two ways to scale. Go wide (horizontal scaling) or go deep (vertical scaling).**

Exhibit 3.5:  **Scaling Strategies**

| Feature | Go Wide (Horizontal Scaling) | Go Deep (Vertical Scaling) |
|---|---|---|
| Impact | Many geographic markets and different types of customers. | One community or type of customer (often localized geographically). |
| Methods to replicate | Social franchising, organic growth, diversification based on market pull, strategic partnerships. | Trust, community organizing, co-creating, and working with entrenched players. |
| Tools | Disseminate information and tools for DIY, create affiliations among similar organizations, working across and in the same markets. Market pull and push. | Build trust and get legitimacy. Work with entrenched players. Market push and then pull. |
| Product/service | Adapted for local context with one strong core structure. Same or similar product concept across multiple markets. | Evolves with community needs and priorities. Many products for various target segments in one community or a narrow geographic area. Trust is a key product. |
| Reputation strength | National and international (work with media, governments, NGOs, government and other stakeholders). Creates awareness about cause and programs. Able to showcase success stories and impact. | More local and national (work with media and local stakeholders). Delivers on promises to the community that creates trust. Works with stakeholders to get legitimacy. |
| Governance (same for both) | Should have strong accountability, participation of stakeholders and transparency. | Should have strong accountability, participation of stakeholders, and transparency. |
| Manpower | Mix of professional and volunteers working in local markets with local people. | More volunteers and source from community of impact. |
| Impact measurement | Easier as the product is standardized. | Harder as each program may last a very short time. If able to replicate geographically, can think of changes in legislations, etc. |
| Funding | Grants, banks, impact investment, philanthropy, etc. | Grants, charity, crowdfunding, and self |
| Disadvantages | You lose control and need to invest in strong organizational practices. Need to work on adaptation and impact measurement. | Creates dependency on the venture and you become part of the community. |
| SCALE Factors: 5R[38] | Readiness (of organization, beneficiary, stakeholders, markets, and its transferability), Receptivity (what is the reception level in target communities), Resources, Risks, and Returns (social, regulatory, and economic). | |

*Source*: Author (first reproduced in Entrepreneurship, ME).[39]

To grow, you need to be able to reinvest profits or access funds. Unfortunately this is not easy. Only 52% of SEVs reinvest their profits back into the business.[40] Opportunities to grow and scale may come from other players in the market. Multi-stakeholder initiatives to scale up should not be ignored. In the developmental sector, the cost of an intervention campaign can be reduced if it is combined. Vestergaard (see case study 3.4) did this when it combined the distribution of LifeStraw with malaria nets and HIV awareness and testing. The distribution of bed nets would cost US$5 per net, but when it was integrated with other public health interventions, the cost was less than US$2 per net.[41]

**Success is not final, failure is not fatal, it is the courage to continue that counts. — Winston Churchill**

Case Study 3.4: **Vestergaard: *LifeStraw Kenya* Project**

Mikkel Vestergaard is the third generation of family entrepreneurs. What remains common from the first generation to the third is that they are all for-profit enterprises, but the business model Mikkel introduced is what he likes to call "humanitarian entrepreneurship." He wanted to find a vacant market space to operate in the interface between doing business and doing good by focusing on some of the major global gaps in the humanitarian sector.

One of their products is LifeStraw®. It was initially developed in 1998 for the Carter Center to prevent Guinea Worm infestation which causes blindness. It was distributed for emergencies like the earthquakes and floods that occurred in Pakistan and Haiti in 2009, though it could have been used for daily life. Consider the fact that 80% of diseases in developing countries are water-borne, killing a child every 8 seconds.[42] Water-borne diseases were rampant in Kenya at that time, with 42% of the people living below the poverty line. Boiling water was a convenient solution, but was contributing to deforestation by way of trees being cut for firewood. Mortality was high in Kenya, with the infant mortality rate at 47.5% per 1,000 live births and under-5 mortality rate at 70.7% per 1,000 live births. The healthcare infrastructure was also low with 0.2 doctors for 1,000 people, whereas most developed countries have a ratio of 3 or more per 1,000 people.

To work in the developmental sector, there are a lot of things you need to prepare for. The challenges that Vestergaard faced are as follows:

(i) **Technology:** Is the correct technology available? In this case they used their in-house R&D. The original LifeStraw was modified for households. Later in 2014 it was modified in terms of capacity for schools.

(ii) **Finance:** Mikkel wanted to give the LifeStraw water purifiers free to the communities that needed it most, but was not sure how they could source fund for achieving this goal. What they realized was that there was an opportunity for funding through the carbon markets. While it required an initial investment of US$30 million which the Board approved, they projected that they would be able to recoup the cost of investment over 10 years as the use of purifiers could be equated to the trees saved. When the plan was approved in 2011, carbon credits were trading at US$10–12, but soon after the market crashed, reduced to US$4–5. The market kept fluctuating, and though they were able to breakeven, they needed to finance additional educational campaigns and ensure that they had audits for carbon saved. The model was modified over 18 months, where consumer markets were tapped to help fund distribution of LifeStraw for schools in the "Follow the Liters" campaign in 2014, which is a type of cross-subsidization. This model was called *consumer-based responsibility crowdsourcing campaign.*

(iii) **Partnerships:** In Kenya, they worked with the Ministry of Health, Ministry of Education, Ministry of Gender, Ministry of Energy and Environment, and Finance Ministry to plan the launch. There were many CSOs also involved as well as the private sector.

(iv) **Data scarcity challenge:** They were planning to distribute to every household, but there was a huge discrepancy in population numbers: 3.2 million versus 4.5 million for the Western Region. They decided to take the higher number to be on the safe side. Because it was a carbon water project, they needed meticulous baseline data.

(5) **Coordination challenge:** It was one of the largest distributions done at a private level, eight times larger than any other carbon project in market at that time, and for the gold standard market, it was the first water project. It took 1 year to plan. To reach 877,505 households, they needed five area coordinators, 40 quality assurance supervisors, 40 district coordinators, 196 team leaders, and approximately 1,960 community health workers, who were hired with the help of the Ministry of Health. They needed to plan for yearly audits for 10 years and awareness campaigns as well. This campaign took 25.5 days for distribution. Vestergaard worked with about 8,000 workers to help with the distribution, education and installation of the LifeStraw® products. All this was accomplished with a core team of five people.

(6) **Data collection:** To ease data collection, they had mobile-enabled tech that allowed the community worker to install, record data, and problem-shoot. It also allowed real-time monitoring which was critical in places with remote access. They worked with the local telecom provider, Airtel, to increase the data capacity of their towers. During the first week of their campaign, they had over 40,000 uploads of data including photos, per day. Because there was no electricity infrastructure, the team took 5 days to charge and preinstall the mobile app using the hotel generator. Every night, they would charge the phones for the 26-day campaign. Later, they found out that for 20 shillings, they could have uploaded credit on the mobile through m-Pesa, and the employee could charge the phone at the neighborhood kiosks, which were operated using modified car batteries.

(7) **Crisis-shooting:** Of course, you need to be adaptable to what could go wrong. They ran out of sisal rope. Each LifeStraw needed 3–4 m. They required totally 900,000 m. Due to the shortage of sisal rope in the country, they had to source it from Mombasa.

(8) **Follow-up and audit:** Having got the baseline and having successfully distributed the product, auditing needed to continue for the next 10 years of the project, to earn carbon credits and it was important to ensure the products were being used as planned. They realized they needed to also teach beneficiaries how to store water (purified water could get contaminated if not stored properly), and they also needed to ensure the machines were being maintained. The filters could get choked with mud and needed cleaning. This meant creating repair centers, managing spares and replacement parts, and more training. To ensure usage frequent checks and education campaigns were continued.

(9) **Donor communication:** Donors and even the engaged customers want to know how the money is being used. Vestergaard used real-time data, visualization, and stories from the field, so donors all over the world could follow the distribution campaign "Follow the Liters".

Not only did Vestergaard have to modify their business model as the beneficiary markets evolved but also they needed to adapt it to each country, product and the local context. The challenge for the company will be the emerging fourth generation ledership, and the direction in which they will want to take the organization. Each generation has had their own impact on the company.

## 3.6. **Stage 5: Blaze**

At this stage, the SEV venture goes international. This means connecting to and "selling" to international markets.[43] For SEVs, connecting could also be in terms of media to gain legitimacy, access to more sources of finance, advisory board members, technical expertise, and new partners. Also, the concept of "selling" need not just be selling products, but even the idea to fund or change legislation for beneficiary impact. At this point, an SEV must also look inward at its team. Research shows that an internationally experienced management team increases the chances of getting funding.[44] To be effective, SEVs need high organizational adaptability, which comes from innovation in goals, team heterogeneity, collective credibility, active involvement of the boards, and the innovative ability to increase resources.[45] Shaw and Carter state, "*while for-profit and social entrepreneurs share a belief in the centrality of their role, social entrepreneurs more clearly must include and, indeed must share credit for success with, a collective of volunteers and beneficiaries* (p. 430)."[46] This is seen in the Gavi Case Study (Case Study 3.3), where to scale impact and grow, they developed a collective responsibility with key stakeholders and were able to connect with separate systems to create a mutually beneficial environment.[47]

The models developed for one location may not be replicable in another. There are challenges of managing "glocality" (how much of the model should be

ase Study 3.5: **Tree**
**:hange Dolls**

Sonia Singh began Tree Change Dolls in 2014 in Tasmania, soon after losing her job due to financial cuts. While the project began as a hobby — wanting to give her daughter a realistic looking doll to play with — it quickly grew. She repairs, recycles, and upcycles forgotten or discarded dolls and gives them a more child-
e appearance. She sources dolls at charity shops and then transforms them
 repairing, restoring, de-glamourizing (stripping them of paint), and upscaling
·painting and giving them new simple clothes). Sonia hand paints the faces of the dolls
d then make shoes from silicone which she considers more environmentally friendly
an plastic. Silvia, Sonia's mother, then sews and knits clothing for the dolls, making this
family business. Sonia initially posted the first picture of her "new" transformed Bratz
1l (before and after images) on Tumblr in 2015 and the response was so huge she had sold
)00 items in 6 months. The dolls are priced based on the work required and the price ranges
:ween $75–280 Australian dollars per doll. Each batch sold every month is of approximately
 dolls, and she uses social media to announce the sale. She is on Facebook, YouTube, Twitter, and
·tagram. The dolls are promoted on social media (or you can subscribe by email) and sold on Etsy
oatches. They sell out on the day of posting. She has DIY kits on Etsy. Etsy, which is based in NYC,
ognized Sonia Singh with the Community Choice prize at the Etsy Design Awards 2015 for Australia
J New Zealand. One of the main challenges is demand. Because of the limited supply, there are many
ators and hobbyists who are making their own dolls. Although she encourages it, she is protective of
 brand name. Sonia plans to hire more people to manage the global demand. Sonia believes, "*We can
· what we already have to create something unique and treasured by using our creativity.*"

globally standardized and what is locally adapted). Case study 3.5 follows the international growth of Tree Change Dolls through social media communities. SEV products may do more social harm rather than good, if introduced too quickly or without being adapted to the local context.[48] The topic of internationalization which deals with growth of scale-ups is covered in Chapter 6.

## 3.7. **Business Models**

A Business Model can be described as a blueprint or the organizational and financial "architecture" of a business[49] and it should be reusable in multiple markets. To retain a competitive advantage (why will investors or beneficiaries come to you?) and be sustainable, there are four threats SEVs may need to be aware of.[50]

(1) Imitation (can competitors imitate your success?);

(2) Holdup (can stakeholders use their power to stop the value process?);

(3) Substitution (can new products make you less relevant?);

(4) Slack (organizational complacency).

When business models don't work, it's because they fail either the narrative test (the story doesn't make sense) or the numbers test (the P&L doesn't add up).[51] There are several elements of a business model an SEV must plan and be mindful of. While most startups grow organically, and the process is chaotic, it helps to understand what works, and what does not. Especially, investors and donors like to know that the founding team has a sense of direction and control. The three key sections of a business model for SEVs are as follows: (1) impact, (2) market, and (3) business operations (see Exhibit 3.6).

Impact covers the following four sections: (1) problems you are solving, (2) beneficiaries, (3) impact of change, and (4) impact on beneficiaries and employees if you close down. Market covers the following fives sections: (1) value proposition, (2) current structural roadblocks, (3) current structural opportunities, (4) market forces and stakeholders opposing your idea, and (5) market forces and stakeholders supporting your idea. Business operations has eight sections as follows: (1) minimum working capital required, (2) where is your surplus revenues/profits for future contingency coming from, (3) resources missing, (4) resources at hand, (5) possible places of access for resources, (6) cost of attaining those resources, (7) possible partnerships, and (8) business models you can adapt.

- *Problem statement*: This will become your guiding star. SEVs cannot solve all the problems a community will face, and though you have secondary goals, it is vital to manage resources mindfully and state the key root problem you will solve in a simple statement so that everyone can understand. In some cases, this can be converted to a mission statement. This statement may change with time as impact increases or access to resources increase. Simple mission statements are more powerful and impactful. The objective of the problem statement (and hence the subsequent mission statement) is to tell everyone in simple terms, what you do. A problem statement addresses the *root cause of why you are introducing an intervention*. A mission statement articulates what your company is and does. Look at the examples in Exhibit 3.7 — what can be improved? Why? What clearly helps the organization plan for the future?

Exhibit 3.6:   **SEV Business Initiative Canvas**

| Impact | | Market | Business Operations | |
|---|---|---|---|---|
| **Problem You Are Solving** (statement) | **Value Proposition** *Beneficiary* <br><br> *Stakeholders* | **Market Forces and Stakeholders Opposing your idea** | **Minimum Working Capital Required** Monthly <br> Year 1 <br> Year 2 <br> Year 3 | **Possible Places of Access for Resources** |
| **Beneficiary** *Individual* <br><br> *Community* <br><br> *Other Stakeholders* | **Current Structural Roadblocks** | | **Where is your surplus revenue/profits for future contingency coming from?** | **Possible Partnerships** |
| **Impact of Change** (qualitative and quantitative terms) *Current Status* <br><br> *Future Status* Year 1 <br> Year 2 <br> Year 3 | **Current Structural Opportunities** | **Market Forces and Stakeholders Supporting your idea** | **Resources Missing** | **Business Models you can adapt** *(competitors or others)* |
| **Impact on Beneficiaries/Employees if you Close Down.** | | | **Resources at Hand** | **Cost of Attaining those Resources** |

Exhibit 3.7: **Examples of Mission Statements**

| SEV | What do you think is their problem statement? | Mission Statement |
|---|---|---|
| Gavi, the Vaccine Alliance | Through increasing equitable use of vaccines to (main focus of the organization)<br><br>(1) save children's lives (beneficiaries).<br><br>(2) protect people's health (beneficiaries) in lower-income countries (boundary condition). | Saving children's lives and protecting people's health by increasing equitable use of vaccines in lower income countries. |
| Khan Academy | Provide a free (condition), world-class education (main focus of the organization) for anyone, anywhere (beneficiaries). | Our mission is to provide a free, world-class education for anyone, anywhere. |
| Patagonia | | Build the best product, cause no unnecessary harm, use business to inspire, and implement solutions to the environmental crisis. |
| | | The High Commissioner for Refugees is mandated by the United Nations to lead and coordinate international action for the worldwide protection of refugees and the resolution of refugee problems.<br><br>UNHCR's primary purpose is to safeguard the rights and well-being of refugees. In its efforts to achieve this objective, the Office strives to ensure that everyone can exercise the right to seek asylum and find safe refuge in another state and to return home voluntarily. By assisting refugees to return to their own country or to settle permanently in another country, UNHCR also seeks lasting solutions to their plight.<br><br>UNHCR's Executive Committee and the UN General Assembly have authorized involvement with other groups. These include former refugees who have returned to their homeland; internally displaced people; and people who are stateless or whose nationality is disputed.<br><br>The Office seeks to reduce situations of forced displacement by encouraging states and other institutions to create conditions which are conducive to the protection of human rights and the peaceful resolution of disputes. In all of its activities, it pays particular attention to the needs of children and seeks to promote the equal rights of women and girls. |

Exhibit 3.7: **(cont)**

| SEV | What do you think is their problem statement? | Mission Statement |
|---|---|---|
| UNHCR | | The Office works in partnership with governments, regional organizations, and international and non-governmental organizations. It is committed to the principle of participation, believing that refugees and others who benefit from the organization's activities should be consulted over decisions which affect their lives. |

- *Beneficiaries*: All direct and indirect beneficiaries need to be identified. List the key stakeholders that may benefit either directly or indirectly from the SEV (you can use the knowledge you gained in Chapter 2). Consider families, communities, other SEVs operating in the market, and political and regulatory authorities. For example, for Gavi, governments, healthcare ministries, and communities benefit with healthier populations and decreasing child mortality rates (for children under 5). There are always primary, secondary, and tertiary beneficiaries. For SEVs, this is complicated. Gavi cannot access the children directly so it needs to work with UNICEF, Ministries of Health, WHO, and local community players — such as the Civil Service Organizations.

- *Impact of change*: Here you articulate the impact of your change intervention — what you hope to create. This means you have a good understanding of the baseline (what is the current scenario) and what you hope the intervention will be. This will help you keep control and make sure the intervention is the right one (more on this topic in Chapter 7).

- *Impact on beneficiaries if you close down*: This is critical and few SEV look at this. If you stop your operations, ask yourself — will you leave the community in a better state than you found them, or in a worse state? How can you mitigate risk? One way is by not expanding too quickly.

- *Value proposition for beneficiaries and stakeholders*: This is a statement that is derived from your problem statement and mission statement. It focuses on the customer (beneficiary) and states why they should "buy" your product or services. It may explain how your help might solve their problems or improve their situation (relevancy), how you are able to deliver these specific benefits (by quantifying value), and explain why they approach you and not others (unique differentiation). Take the example of Gavi. It measures its impact in saving lives, reducing workdays lost, or reducing medical bills. What is a relevant for a family may not be relevant for a community or at a national level. The days lost from sickness from vaccine-preventable diseases at the family level, may translate to increased poverty due to inability to pay medical bills. At a national level, it could aggregate as labor productivity and contribution to GDP or savings in paid sick leave. Value propositions are not tag lines or slogans. They are customer segment specific, so different beneficiaries may have variations of value propositions.

For writing a value proposition, more information is better than less, and clear bullet headlines help.[52] A good way to start is by writing a list of benefits and costs. Benefits can be social or emotional, from using the product or service (reliability, functional value) or trust. Cost is not just money, but time, effort, and resources. In some cases, target segments may to have to sacrifice reputation where the risks can be social ostracization, mental anguish (parents will be upset), etc.[53] This list will grow with time, so it is important to constantly update your cost–benefit analysis.

- *Current structural roadblocks*: Structural roadblocks can be regulations, infrastructure, or even technology. It could even be the ambiguousness of not knowing whose jurisdiction your SEV falls under. The more you are aware of this, the more market scanning you will do. This will help you develop mentors, networks, or strategic alliances.

- *Market forces and stakeholders for and against your SEV*: Do a review of Chapter 2 and get an idea of your ecosystem. This keeps you aware of threats and future opportunities.

- *Minimum working capital*: Running a business needs money, and you need to be able to audit the funds you receive. Create a plan for working capital. Be sure to quantify the value (cost) of volunteers and donated products and services (in-cash assistance). Most founders forget to value their time, and when they need to hire an operations manager, they struggle with the finances.

- *Contingency surplus*: In case of an emergency, do you have a contingency fund? What can you liquidate? Who will be your back-up financier? It is important to articulate this and also know how much surplus is available in cash, and if something needs to be liquidated, how much time will it take.

- *Resources missing*: This is a wish list of all the resources you would like to have. Keep in mind that grants and receivables may be delayed.

- *Resources in hand*: Maybe these are available but you can't tap into these resources because of time or other constraints. For example, from the beneficiaries you may get future manpower, or funding. Your networks could be partners who have access to technology, i.e., power brokers who can help you.

- *Possible places for access of resources*: The reality is irrespective of whether you are an SEV, non-profit, or a for-profit, you need money. Here you brainstorm and write a list of finances you can tap into — banks, grants, donors, etc. Resources can be manpower, technology, physical properties, or material. Very often, barter is used than cash and it is underestimated. This may be true especially in a market where currency devaluation is common. IRTA estimates that corporate barter is 30% of trade and retail barter at 20%.[54]

- *Possible partnerships*: Sometimes you cannot get cash, but in-kind donations may be equally useful. For example, UNICEF logistics in IHC (Dubai) is managed by the foundation arm of the private sector logistics group Kuehne + Nagel Group.

- *Cost of attaining the resources*: A critical resource is time, and then effort. But you may also need to learn new skills too. Do take these into account.

- *Business models you can adapt*: Rather than re-invent the wheel, spend some effort is seeing what models exist. Look for financially sustainable ones if you have a choice. While business models aren't only about money, here we focus on monetization or ability to generate some "funds" for sustainability or get active market traction. Payment can be subsidized for beneficiaries, pay as you go, peer managed, or "donated". This needs a clear differentiation between beneficiaries and benefactors. You must develop good governance. Some common business models used by SEVs (not those that depend entirely on donations or grants) are listed in Exhibit 3.8. This is not an exhaustive list but highlights the need for research to see what's out there that can be adapted.

Most SEVs use a combination model. For example, Warby Parker, (see Chapter 4). With the normal paying customer, they cut out the middleman, and hence have huge savings. They then donate an equivalent number of eyeglasses at a lower price to VisionSpring, which acts like a middleman and supplies them to local entrepreneurs who then sell the lower cost glasses to people within their community neighborhoods. They use cross-subsidization and the middleman business models.

Exhibit 3.8: **Some Examples of Financially Sustainable Business Models for SEVs**

| Model | Description | Example |
|---|---|---|
| Inclusive employment | Where revenues generated by the jobs provide funds to sustain the business model | Jamie-Oliver's Fifteen |
| Consumer cross-subsidization | Use the full-paying customer to subsidize for the low-income group | Aravind Eye Hospital |
| Creative cross-subsidization | Here, the objective is using innovative financing to subsidize the cost of intervention. | Vestergaard's carbon credits for the LifeStraw campaign; Gavi, the Vaccine Alliance's Vaccine Bonds. Grameen uses low-interest grants to give out microloans at a slightly higher (but still low) interest; Gavi uses many types of finance vaccine bonds. |
| Consumer-based responsibility crowdsourcing campaign | In crowdsourcing, the campaign is first and foremost so the customer chooses the product for the campaign first, and then for the product and service. | Vestergaard LifeStraw |
| Product-embedded value | Here, a portion of the products goes to a cause. | Body Shop |
| Barter and hands up | Here, the beneficiary committee commits to something for a hands up. | Volunteer hours for scholarship —Ruwwad Al-Tanmeya. |
| Waste to want | Here, the SEV may collect waste OR something that may be discarded and reuse it. | Example, food banks |
| Community-owned businesses/ cooperatives | Here, the objective is the beneficiary community has ownership in the product and hence is responsible for it. They succeed when the project succeeds. | Amul, in India, is an example of a cooperative which brought together dairy farmers and hence created milk cooperatives. |
| BOGO | Buy one, get one free or something proportional for those who cannot afford. Here, we are talking equivalency. | TOMS |

Exhibit 3.8: **(cont)**

| Model | Description | Example |
|---|---|---|
| Redefine the marketplace/ supply chain | The marketplace can be redefined to help. | Twiga Foods[55] works in Africa and they connect rural farmers in Kenya and deliver to urban vendors through an app to ensure transparent and fair pricing. FairTrade or ethical sourcing may be other examples most people are familiar with. |
| Consultancy and service leverage | Use the knowledge and technology you have already developed to leverage in the market place. | Souktel, a mobile platform using text messages to provide job opportunities in Palestine, realized they can use the technology for crisis communication and this led to a steady revenue stream.[56] In some cases, technology may be used to sell data insights but the ethics of this needs to be carefully evaluated especially if the participants don't know this. |
| Frugal engineering | Redesigning parts, components, and products to make them affordable. | Aravind Eyecare started Aurolab to manufacture intraocular lenses for only $4, which was costing US$150 at that time. |
| Find a third party that benefits | Here, the beneficiaries may not be able to pay but another entity may recognize the benefits. Many health interventions are funded by donor countries and ministries. | Zipline drone technology for the Rwandan government where the government becomes the first paying customer, not the users themselves. |
| MiddleMan | At times SEVs connect sellers and buyers. | BeadsforLife initially bought jewelry from Ugandan women to sell to consumers in USA. |
| Subscription model | Here, the subscription model allows you to earn a revenue. | Bookshare.org found that people who were blind or had learning disabilities had access to less than 5% of books. People had to scan books into computers with adaptive technology to convert the text into reader-friendly formats like speech or Braille. Beneficiaries subscribe to get access to the books. |

## 3.8. **The SEV Lifecycle: A Recap**

There are five stages in the lifecycle of an SEV. While most SEVs begin without a business model, it helps survival and growth to have a strategy. This strategy may change as the ecosystem and stakeholders change and as the community of focus evolves. SEVs may decide to focus on horizontal scaling or vertical scaling, or both, but the key is to ensure they have sufficient resources to do so. This may require finding new resources and leveraging a different set of strengths. The ability to change quickly may be a quality SEVs need in order to survive challenges thrown their way. The SEV Business Initiative Canvas is a good place to start.

## 3.9. **Questions**

**Question 1**
Read the book *Three Cups of Tea: One Man's Mission to Promote Peace* by Greg Mortenson and David Oliver Relin and follow the current news. What are the causes for the "Valley of Death" for this SEV? What stage was it in the lifecycle?

**Question 2**
Why is legitimacy important for SEVs? Read the paper titled, *Rhetorical Strategies of Legitimacy*, by Roy Suddaby and Royston Greenwood (2005).[57] Give an example of an SEV that uses the following types of legitimacy rhetoric strategy: ontological (what can and cannot co-exist); historical (appeals to history and tradition); teleological (focuses on a "divine purpose" or "final cause"); cosmological (emphasize its inevitability because of forces beyond the agency of immediate actors and audiences, stress it is a natural progression of the times); value-based (refers to normative authority outside the context drawn from the wider belief systems).

**Question 3**
Look at Exhibit 3.3 and fill in the canvas for an organization of your choice. What can be done for future growth?

**Question 4**
According to the model proposed by Eisenmann, Ries & Dillard (2012),[58] a startup has to decide once it tests its hypothesis whether to preserve, pivot, or perish. This topic has been studied under the headings of "grit" or "passion". [59] When do you think founders need to stop and realize they have reached the point of no return?

**Question 5**
What type of scaling has Vestergaard and Sulabh done? Look at Exhibit 3.5 to form your answer.

**Question 6**
How can Tree Change Dolls protect itself from imitation? In the case of Sulabh, the toilets are not patented, do you think their monetization model was a good one? Discuss.

**Question 7**
Create a mission statement for UNHCR.

**Question 8**
Create an SEV Business Initiative Canvas for UNHCR or any organization of your choice.

**Question 9**
You want to create an SEV creating tolerance in diverse and fragile focused on communities. This is in an inner-city ghetto where the youth high school dropout rate is high, communities tend to segregate themselves on their ethnicities, and there is a significant gender divide. You are approaching a large private sector organization to fund your activities. Create a value proposition statement based on cost–benefit analysis.

## Sources

### Case Study 3.1: BeadforLife

*Sources*: Interview on 15 June 2018, and information from website: https://www.beadforlife.org/our-story

### Case Study 3.2: Sulabh International Service Organization

*Sources*: Adapted from Stephens Balakrishnan, M. and Khurshid, S. (2016), "Sulabh international service organization: Overcoming social barriers to create change," In: Balakrishnan, M. S. and Lindsay, V. (eds.), *Actions and Insights: Middle East North Africa (Vol. 5): Social Entrepreneurs*, UK: Emerald Group Publishing, pp. 93-123; Balch, O. (2014), "From open defecation to toilets that produce biogas and fertilizer," dated 14 May, *The Guardian*, Available: http://www.theguardian.com/sustainable-business/india-compost-toilets-biogas-fertiliser-defecation [Accessed 15 December 2015]; Biswas, S. (2014), "Why India's sanitation crisis needs more than toilets," *BBC*, dated 6 October, Available: http://www.bbc.com/news/world-asia-india-29502603 [Accessed 10 February 2016]; Britannica (2016), *Untouchable: Hindu Social Class*, Available: http://www.britannica.com/topic/untouchable [Accessed 28 February 2016]; Denselow, A. (2013), "The Indian town with 6,000 widows," *BBC*, dated 2 May, Available: http://www.bbc.com/news/magazine-21859622 [Accessed 4 March 2016]; Economist (2014), *Sanitation in India: The Final Frontier*, Available: http://www.economist.com/news/asia/21607837-fixing-dreadful-sanitation-india-requires-not-just-building-lavatories-also-changing [Accessed 26 January 2016]; Smith, L. (2015), "City of Widows: The 38,000 forgotten women of Varanasi," *International Business Times*, dated 23 June, Available: http://www.ibtimes.co.uk/city-widows-38000-forgotten-women-varanasi-1505560 [Accessed 4 March 2016]; WHO (2008), *The Global Burden of Disease: 2004 Update*, Available: http://www.who.int/healthinfo/global_burden_disease/2004_report_update/en/ [Accessed 2 March 2016]; WHO (2015), *Sanitation*, Available: http://www.who.int/mediacentre/factsheets/fs392/en/ [Accessed 2 March 2016]; WHO (2016), *Lack of Water and Inadequate Sanitation*, Available: http://www.who.int/ceh/risks/cehwater/en/ [Accessed 2 March 2016].

### Case Study 3.3: Gavi, The Vaccine Alliance

*Sources*: Adapted from the following published case studies: Stephens, M. (2018), *Gavi, the Vaccine Alliance: Reshaping the Vaccine Market*, Karls Magazine, 1(1): 19–25; Stephens Balakrishnan, M. (2016), "Gavi: The vaccine alliance: Saving lives one vaccine at a time," In: Balakrishnan, M. S. and Lindsay, V. (eds.), *Actions and Insights: Middle East North Africa (Vol. 5): Social Entrepreneurship*, UK: Emerald Group Publishing, pp. 135–192.

Using data from Gavi website and other Gavi sources: Available https://www.slideshare.net/Gavi-Vaccine-Alliance/gavi-in-30-slides-129710585?ref=https://www.gavi.org/; Gavi (2005), *Delhi GAVI Boards meeting 6–7 December 2005, Doc AF.7. Supply Strategy*. Available: http://www.unpcdc.org/media/402758/gavi_supply_strategy_for_hib_and_hepb_dec05.pdf [Accessed 29 February 2016]; Gavi (2015), *CEO board report*, dated 10 June, Available: https://www.slideshare.net/Gavi-Vaccine-Alliance/gavi-ceo-board-report-10-june-2015 [Accessed 31 October 2017]; Gavi (2015), *CEO board report*, dated 10 June, Available: https://www.slideshare.net/Gavi-Vaccine-Alliance/gavi-ceo-board-report-10-june-2015 [Accessed 26 February 2014]; Gavi (2015), *CEO Board Report December 2015*. Available: http://www.gavi.org/Library/Audio-visual/Presentations/CEO-Board-Report-December-2015/ [Accessed 29 February 2016]; Gavi (2016), *Gavi facts and figures*. Available: http://www.Gavi.org/advocacy-statistics/ [Accessed 29 February 2016]; Gavi (2016), *Gavi Vaccine Supply and Procurement Strategy 2016–20*, Available: https://www.unicef.org/supply/files/VIC_2016_-_Day_1_-_Session_2_-_Gavi_SUPPRS_2016-20_final.pdf [Accessed 31 October 2017]. Gavi (2017), *Highlights of the Vaccine Alliance's 2016 Progress Report*, Available: http://www.gavi.org/progress-report/ [Accessed 29 October 2017].

*Additional Sources*: *2016 Pneumococcal vaccines AMC Annual report*; Bryant, A. (2015), "The secret of mali's ebola response success, and how it could transform child health," *Huffington Post*, dated 28 September, Available: http://www.huffingtonpost.com/andy-bryant/the-secret-of-malis-ebola_b_8208204.html [Accessed 20 December 2015]; Department for International Development (2017), "Raising the standard: The multilateral development review 2016," Available: https://www.gov.uk/government/uploads/

system/uploads/attachment_data/file/573884/Multilateral-Development-Review-Dec2016.pdf [Accessed 6 December 2017]; *IFFM (2016) Trustees Report and Financial Statements*; Gilchrist, S. A. N. and Nanni, A. (2013), "Lessons learned in shaping vaccine markets in low-income countries: A review of the vaccine market segment supported by the GAVI Alliance," *Health Policy and Planning*, 28(8): 838–846; GlaxoSmithKline Biologicals (nd), "Addressing developing world vaccine production technology transfer," *2009 Global Vaccines Public Policy Issues*, Available: http://www.gsk.com/policies/Technology-Transfer-Vaccines.pdf [Accessed 12 January 2012]; MOPAN (2016), *MOPAN 2015-16 Assessments*, Gavi the Vaccine Alliance, Available: http://www.mopanonline.org/assessments/gavi2015-16/Mopan%20GAVI%20[Executive%20Summary]%20[final].pdf [Accessed 6 December 2017]; Nguyen, A. (2016), *Gavi Vaccine Supply and Procurement Strategy 2016–2020* https://www.unicef.org/supply/files/VIC_2016_-_Day_1_-_Session_2_-_Gavi_SUPPRS_2016-20_final.pdf [Accessed 31 October 2017]; Sekhri, N. (2006), *Forecasting for Global Health: New Money, New Products and New Markets*. Background Paper for the Forecasting Working Group. Washington, DC: Center for Global Development. Available: http://www.cgdev.org/doc/ghprn/Forecasting_Background.pdf [Accessed 13 January 2012]; Sheridan C. (2009), "Vaccine market boosters," *Nature Biotechnology*, 27(6), 499–501; UNICEF (2009). *State of the World's Vaccines: Childhood Immunization at Record High*, dated 21 October, 2009. Available at: http://www.unicef.org/immunization/index_51482.html [Accessed 29 February 2016]; Wilson, P. (2010), *For giving developing countries the best shot: an overview of vaccine access and R&D*, Oxfam-MSF, Available: https://www.msf.org.uk/sites/uk/files/Vaccine_Report_201005111518.pdf [Accessed 24 February 2016]. [In the article, Wilson cites that these estimates were developed by Andrew Jones from published sources and consultations with experts and both developed and developing country firms. Published sources included André F.E. (2002), "How the research-based industry approaches vaccine development and establishes priorities," *Dev Biol* (Basel), 110: 25–39]; Whitehead, P. and Pasternak A. (2002), *Lessons Learned: New Procurement Strategies for Vaccines: 2002 Final Report to the GAVI Board*. Mercer Management Consulting.

## Case Study 3.4: Vestergaard: LifeStraw Kenya project

*Sources*: Adapted from: Stephens Balakrishnan, M. (2016), "Vestergaard: The humanitarian entrepreneurship business model: Where doing good is good business," In: Balakrishnan, M. S. and Lindsay, V. (eds.), *Actions and Insights: Middle East North Africa (Vol. 5): Social Entrepreneurs*, UK: Emerald Group Publishing, pp. 193–224; Other sources: Rural Poverty Portal — Kenya (nd), Available: http://www.ruralpovertyportal.org/country/statistics/tags/Kenya [Accessed 2 October 2015]; World Bank (nd), Physicians per 1000, Available: http://data.worldbank.org/indicator/SH.MED.PHYS.ZS [Accessed 2 October 2015].

## Case Study 3.5: Tree Change Dolls

*Sources*: Adapted from Khurshid, S. and Stephens Balakrishnan, M. (2016), "Tree change dolls: Creating a movement to recycle, repair and upcycle dolls," In: Balakrishnan, M. S. and Lindsay, V. (eds.), *Actions and Insights: Middle East North Africa (Vol. 5): Social Entrepreneurs*, UK: Emerald Group Publishing, pp. 429–438. Additional information from website: http://treechangedolls.com.au.

# ENDNOTES

1   Perry, M. J. (2017), "Fortune 500 firms 1955 v. 2017: Only 60 remain, thanks to the creative destruction that fuels economic prosperity," *AIE*, dated 20 October, Available: http://www.aei.org/publication/fortune-500-firms-1955-v-2017-only-12-remain-thanks-to-the-creative-destruction-that-fuels-economic-prosperity/ [Accessed 25 February 2018].

2   Ghosh, S. (2012) as cited in Gage, D. (2012), "The venture capital secret: 3 out of 4 start-ups fail," *The Wall Street Journal*, dated September 20, Available: https://www.wsj.com/articles/SB10000872396390443720204578004980476429190 [Accessed 25 February 2018].

3   Marmer, M., Herrmann, B. L., Dogrultan, E., Berman, R., Eesley, C. and Blank, S. (2011), "Startup genome report extra: Premature scaling," *Startup Genome*, 10: 1–56.

4   Statistic Brain Research Institute (nd), *Startup Business Failure Rate By Industry*, Available: https://www.statisticbrain.com/startup-failure-by-industry/.

5 GEMS (2016), *Global Entrepreneurship Monitor*, Available: http://gemconsortium.org/report/49542 [Accessed 1 March 2019].

6 *Ibid.* GEMS (2017), *Global Entrepreneurship Monitor*, Available: https://www.gemconsortium.org/report/49812 [Accessed 1 March 2019].

7 Gasca, L. (2017), "Why do social enterprises fail? new research reveals three reasons (And Some Surprises)," *Next Billion,* dated 19 May, Available: https://nextbillion.net/why-do-social-enterprises-fail-new-research-reveals-three-reasons-and-some-surprises/.

8 E3M (2014), *Who Lives the Longest? Busting the Social Venture Survival Myth*, Available: http://socialbusinessint.com/wp-content/uploads/Who-lives-the-longest_-FINAL-version2.pdf [Accessed 1 March 2019].

9 Gasca (2017). *Op. cit.*

10 Markham, S. K. (2002), "Product champions: Crossing the valley of death." In: Belliveau, A., Griffin, A. and Somermeyer, S. (eds.), *PDMA New Product Development Toolbook*, New York: John Wiley & Sons, pp. 119–140.

11 Moore, G. (1991), *Crossing the Chasm: Marketing and Selling Disruptive Products to Mainstream Customers*, New York: HarperCollins Publishers.

12 Murphy, L. M. and Edwards, P. L. (2003), *Bridging the Valley of Death: Transitioning from Public to Private Sector Financing. National Renewable Energy Laboratory*, NREL/MP-720-34036. http://www.nrel.gov/docs/gen/fy03/34036.pdf [Accessed 20 February 2019].

13 Stephens Balakrishnan, M. and Lindsay, V. (2014), "Development and internationalization of social entrepreneurial ventures: A conceptual framework," In: *56th Academy of International Business Annual Conference. Local Contexts in Global Business*, Vancouver, Canada, 23-27 June.

14 Ellis, P. D. (2011), "Social ties and international entrepreneurship: Opportunities and constraints affecting firm internationalization," *Journal of International Business Studies*, 42(1): 99–127; Fletcher, L. (2004), "International entrepreneurship and the small business," *Entrepreneurship & Regional Development: An International Journal*, 16(4): 120–121; Mair, J. and Marti, I. (2006), "Social entrepreneurship research: A source of explanation, prediction and delight," *Journal of World Business*, 41: 36–44.

15 Hervieux, C., Gedajlovic, E. and Turcotte, M. F. B. (2010), "The legitimization of social entrepreneurship," *Journal of Enterprising Communities: People and Places in the Global Economy*, 4(1): 37–67; Massetti, B. L. (2008), "The social entrepreneurship matrix as a 'tipping point' for economic change," *Emergence: Complexity and Organization*, 10(3): 1.

16 Boschee, J. (2009), "An introduction to affirmative businesses," *The Chronicle of Social Enterprise*, 1: 1–4.

17 Hockerts, K. (2015), "Determinants of Social Entrepreneurial Intention," *Entrepreneurship Theory and Practice*, 41(1): 105–130.

18 Khan, I. (2010), *Celebration of Entrepreneurship Conference*, Wamda Studio. November.

19 Sager, B. (2010), *Celebration of Entrepreneurship Conference*, Wamda Studio. November.

20 *Ibid.* and personal interviews With Bobby Sager.

21 Ries, E. (2011). *The Lean Startup: How Today's Entrepreneurs Use Continuous Innovation to Create Radically Successful Businesses.* Crown Books.

22 Ferraro, F., Etzion, D. and Gehman, J. (2015), "Tackling grand challenges pragmatically: Robust action revisited," *Organization Studies*, 36: 363-390.

23 Dees, J. G. (1998), "Enterprising nonprofits," *Harvard Business Review*, 76: 54–69.

24 Kubzansky, M., Cooper, A. and Barbary, V. (2011), *Promise and Progress: Market-based solutions to poverty in Africa.* Monitor group.

25 Khan Academy Annual Report 2017: https://khanacademyannualreport.org [Accessed 6 February 2019].

26 Dodd, T. (2010), "Fifteen london social return on investment (SROI) 2009/10," *Just Economics*, Available: https://issuu.com/fifteen/docs/fifteen_sroi_2011 [Accessed 23 April 2018].

27 Stephens Balakrishnan, M. and Lindsay, V. (2013), "The rise of the global social entrepreneur: A conceptual framework," In: *55th Academy of International Business Annual Conference. Bridging the Divide: Linking IB to Complementary Disciplines and Practice*, Istanbul, Turkey, 3-6 July; Emerson, J. (2000), "The nature of returns: A social capital markets inquiry into elements of investment and the blended value proposition," Working Paper. Available: http://www.blendedvalue.org/wp-content/uploads/2004/02/pdf-nature-of-returns.pdf [Accessed 1 March 2019]; Suber, R., Quartararo, J., McCurdy, P., and Rodriguez, V. H. (2010), "The spectrum of Investors for latin american hedge funds,"

*EurekaHedge*, Available: http://www.eurekahedge.com/Research/News/363/The_Spectrum_of_ Investors_for_Latin_American_Hedge_Funds [Accessed 1 March 2019].

28   For details on this example read: https://ssir.org/articles/entry/the_promise_of_lean_experimentation

29   Ries, E. (2011), *The Lean Startup*, Penguin: London.

30   Teece, D. J. (2010), "Business models, business strategy and innovation," *Long Range Planning*, 43(2–3): 172–194; George, G. and Bock, A. J. (2011), "e-business model in practice and its implications for entrepreneurship research," *Entrepreneurship: Theory and Practice*, 35(1): 83–111.

31   Morris, M., Schindehutte, M. and Allen, J. (2005), "e-entrepreneur's business model: Toward a unified perspective," *Journal of Business Research*, 58: 726–735.

32   Dees, J. G. (1998), "Enterprising non-profits – What Do You Do When Traditional Sources of Funding Falls Short?," *Harvard Business Review*, January–February: 55–67.

33   Stewart, D. W. and Zhao, Q. (2000), "Internet marketing, business models, and public policy," *Journal of Public Policy & Marketing*, 19(2): 287–296.

34   Adapted from Balan-Vnuk, E. and Balan, P. (2015), "Business model innovation in nonprofit social enterprises," In: Roos, G. and O'Connor, A. (eds.), *Integrating Innovation: South Australian Entrepreneurship Systems and Strategies*, University of Adelaide Press.

35   Grameen Bank (2012), *Biography of Dr. Muhammad Yunus*. Available: http://www.grameen-info.org/ index.php?option=com_content&task=view&id=329&Itemid=363 [Accessed 1 March 2019].

36   *Ibid.*

37   Koh, H., Karamchandani, A. and Katz, R. (2012), "From blueprint to scale: The case for philanthropy in impact investing," *Monitor Group-Acumen Fund*, Available: https://acumen.org/wp-content/ uploads/2017/09/From-Blueprint-to-Scale-Case-for-Philanthropy-in-Impact-Investing_Full-report.pdf [Accessed 1 March 2019].

38   Dees, G. and Anderson, B. B. (2004), "Scaling social impact," *Stanford Social Innovation Review*, Available: https://ssir.org/articles/entry/scaling_social_impact [Accessed 4 February 2019].

39   Stephens, M. (2018), "The how-to: Scaling social enterprise ventures," *Entrepreneur Middle East*, 16 August, Available: https://www.entrepreneur.com/article/318479 [Accessed 1 March 2019].

40   GEMS 2016. *Op. cit.*

41   Stephens Balakrishnan, M., (2016), "Vestergaard: The humanitarian entrepreneurship business model: Where doing good is good business," In: Balakrishnan, M. S. and Lindsay, V. (eds.), *Actions and Insights: Middle East North Africa (Vol. 5): Social Entrepreneurs*, UK: Emerald Group Publishing, pp. 193–224.

42   UN (2003), "Water-related diseases responsible for 80 per cent of all illnesses, Deaths In Developing World', Says Secretary-General In Environment Day Message," 16 May, Available: http://www.un.org/ press/en/2003/sgsm8707.doc.htm [Accessed 3 April 2012].

43   McDougall, P. P., Shane, S. and Oviatt, B. M. (1994), "Explaining the formation of international new ventures: The limits of theories from international business research," *Journal of Business Venturing*, 9: 469–487.

44   Bengtsson, L. (2004), "Explaining born globals: An organisational learning perspective on the internationalisation process," *International Journal of Globalisation and Small Business*, 1(1): 28–41; Li, L., Qian, G. and Qian, Z. (2012), "Early internationalization and performance of small high-tech "born-globals," *International Marketing Review*, 29(5): 536–561; Huang, Y. H. and Hsieh, M. H. (2013), "The accelerated internationalization of born global firms: A knowledge transformation process view," *Journal of Asia Business Studies*, 7(3): 244–261.

45   Diochon, M. and Anderson, A. R. (2009), "Social enterprise and effectiveness: A process typology," *Social Enterprise Journal*, 5(1): 7–29.

46   Shaw, E. and Carter, S. (2007), "Social entrepreneurship: Theoretical antecedents and empirical analysis of entrepreneurial processes and outcomes," *Journal of Small Business and Enterprise Development*, 14(3): 418–434.

47   Katzenstein, J. and Chrispin, B. R. (2011), Social entrepreneurship and a new model for international development in the 21st century, *Journal of Developmental Entrepreneurship*, 16(1): 87–102.

48   Rugimbana, E. and Spring, A. (2009), "Marketing micro-finance to women: Integrating global with local," *International Journal of Nonprofit and Voluntary Sector Marketing*, 14(2): 149–154.

49   Teece, D. J. (2010), "Business models, business strategy and innovation," *Long Range Planning*, 43: 172–194.

50   Ghemawat, P. (1991), *Commitment*, New York: The Free Press.

51  Magretta, J. (2002), "Why business models matter," *Harvard Business Review*, 86–92.
52  Labay, B. (2016), *The Presentation of Your Value Proposition Matters* [Original Research], Available: https://conversionxl.com/research-study/value-proposition-study/ [Accessed 6 February 2019].
53  Lin, C. H., Sher, P. J. and Shih, H. Y. (2005), "Past progress and future directions in conceptualizing customer perceived value," *International Journal of Service Industry Management*, 16(4): 318–336.
54  IRTA (2019), *The Barter and Trade Industry*, Available: https://www.irta.com/about/the-barter-and-trade-industry/ [Accessed 1 March 2019].
55  Read more about Twiga Foods: https://twiga.ke/marketplace/.
56  For more on Souktel read: Stephens Balakrishnan, M. (2016), "Soutkel: Using m-technology to impact emerging markets," In: Balakrishnan, M. S. and Lindsay, V. (eds.), *Actions and Insights: Middle East North Africa (Vol. 5): Social Entrepreneurs*, UK: Emerald Group Publishing, pp. 271–287.
57  Suddaby, R. and Greenwood, R. (2005), "Rhetorical strategies of legitimacy," *Administrative Science Quarterly*, 50(1): 35–67.
58  Eisenmann, T. R., Ries, E. and Dillard, S. (2012), *Hypothesis-Driven Entrepreneurship: The Lean Startup*, Harvard Business Publishing.
59  Duckworth, A. L., Peterson, C., Matthews, M. D. and Kelly, D. R. (2007), "Grit: Perseverance and passion for long-term goals," *Journal of Personality and Social Psychology*, 92(6): 1087; Jachimowicz, J. M., Wihler, A. and Galinsky, A. D. (2017), "The dual pillars of grit: The synergistic benefits of combining perseverance and passion alignment for job performance," PsyArXiv..[Epub ahead of print], *10*; Mueller, B. A., Wolfe, M. T. and Syed, I. (2017), "Passion and grit: An exploration of the pathways leading to venture success," *Journal of Business Venturing*, 32(3): 260–279.

# THE SUPPORT SYSTEM

CHAPTER
4

## Chapter Objectives

➢ Develop a strategy to build a support system.

➢ Use networking principles to leverage SEV resources.

➢ Identify good mentor characteristics.

➢ Design good governance into the SEV organization structure and operations.

➢ Highlight resilient strategies to cope in difficult times.

➢ **Cases:** Grameen (Microfinance: Bangladesh), Vision Spring (eye care: India, El Salvador), Deloitte MicroLoan (microfinance: Malawi), and Invisible Children (activism: Uganda)

## 4.1. Support Systems

SEVs look for unique solutions for problems that are intrinsically complex, and they work in gray areas where typical management models may not be applicable.[1] Founders who are passionate about the cause may find that they are losing steam and energy. Funding may be scare, donors may have their own objectives, beneficiaries may be hostile, the inability to help everyone may become emotionally draining, partners may run away, other players in the market may perceive you as a threat and refuse to collaborate, and worse, the regulatory and legal system may not be in your favor. The only way SEVs can survive in such hostile conditions is by creating a strong support system. In the business environment, the concept of networks has received extensive scrutiny. Aldrich and Zimmer[2] point out — "*it is not what you know but who you know,*" and this is about your social capital.

> **Social capital refers to the value of actual or potential assets and resources a person can acquire for an organization based on who he or she knows, what networks that person is associated with, as well as his or her reputation in certain communities.[3]**

Several organizations such as incubators, networking platforms, legal and financial advisors, and educational programs can form the backbone of the support system social entrepreneurs thrive upon. As most SEV founders come from a non-business background, they could leverage the expertise of their existing networks.[4] You would be surprised by how many people you know, and what skills they have. Studies find that the support a network can provide will increase the probability of a new firm's survival rate and growth, especially if they are able to develop strong ties or bonds with these "actors" who can be people or organizations.[5] Another study finds that the emotional support of a spouse can result in a 40% increase in earning than fellow entrepreneurs who experienced no support.[6]

**Strong ties are defined as "relationships with high emotional commitment and high frequency of contact, usually among socially homogeneous individuals."[7] Weak ties are defined as "relationships with low emotional commitment and low frequency of contact."[8]**

Weak ties are important especially when you work in a sector that requires market scanning. Support may come in many forms: emotional support, the added motivation to stay in the game, a means of tapping into current market information, or free advice. However, this support can also have a signaling effect, letting everyone know — they trust you, or back you up, or at least know you.[9] Networks are complex and layered (they show multiplexity). You can bond at multiple levels, at the informal level of friendship, the more casual information exchange or familiarity level, or more formal ties through formal business exchange.[10] Before looking outside for additional networks, start with your existing networks and their possible impact for your SEV.

Endeavour Foundation conducted a study looking at the networks of 2,000 technology entrepreneurs in six cities — Bangalore, Nairobi, Dhaka, Lagos, Dar Es Salaam, and Lahore, across various entrepreneurial ecosystems.[11] What they found was that ecosystems that produce a small number of companies that scale (growth is calculated in number of employees) and then reinvest the profits back into the community could create further growth for the ecosystem. In fact, those founders who received advice (formally or informally) or investment from an entrepreneur who had grown their own company to scale had approximately two times greater prevalence of top performance. These people of influence could be found in accelerators, incubators, business plan competitions, and other entrepreneurial firms. Not all local ecosystems have the required support systems, and it may be necessary to look outside at international support systems who can activate local actors, as seen in the case with Grameen Bank (see Case Study 4.1).

SEVs are also for-profit organizations, which may have more support available in larger metros. For example, in Silicon Valley, over 92 companies with a combined value of over US$2.1 trillion have created over 800,000 jobs and can be traced back to Fairchild Semiconductor. In fact, 70% of Silicon Valley's public firms are linked to Fairchild Semiconductor. Fairchild Semiconductor spun off 31 companies in 12 years. Finding mentors and employees from these star companies that act as connectors may be worth the extra cost of networking, relationship building, recruiting, and hiring. They come with vital knowledge and can act as bridges to potential investors, technology access, and political influencers.

Case Study 4.1: **Grameen Bank: Spark-Stage Support Systems**

Muhammad Yunus is the 2006 Nobel Prize winner in economics. He was born in Bangladesh, into a goldsmith's family. His early desire to help women was triggered by his mother. Even while studying for his Master's degree in Dhaka University, he was considered a bit of an activist, founding a nationally circulated magazine called *Uttaran* (Advancement). He was an entrepreneur, having founded a packaging company.

But his story begins a lot earlier. In 1965–1966, Yunus travelled for the third time abroad on a Fulbright scholarship for his masters. He soon began his doctoral studies, as he needed a PhD to begin teaching in Dhaka, a profession he loved. In 1970, he received his PhD in economics for his thesis titled, *Intertemporal Allocation of Resources – A Dynamic Programming Model* from Vanderbilt University GPED Program. By then, he had founded a citizen's committee and ran the Bangladesh Information Center, with other Bangladeshis in the United States, to raise support for liberation, actively campaigning in Washington DC. The Vanderbilt University and specifically the GPED program had alumni who were well connected, where many have taken positions in international development organizations, such as the World Bank, the International Monetary Fund, the Asian Development Bank, the Inter-American Development Bank, the African Development Bank, and the United Nations. Over the years, the program has benefited from the generous support of the United States Agency for International Development, the Ford Foundation, and the Rockefeller Foundation.

After Bangladesh's war for independence, he returned home and was appointed to the government's Planning Commission, headed by Nurul Islam, his previous economics professor, an activist and his mentor in 1972. In 1975, after the Great Flood and Famine, he began visiting villages near Chittagong and soon outlined the Grameen Bank scheme in his book *Give Them Credit* (1970s). Between 1974 and 1975, Muhammad Yunus was working on the feasibility of a research project, with farming – loaning money to farmers to buy the needed inputs for irrigation during a dry-season crop, even though he had been cheated of Tk13,000.

In 1976, he was teaching Economics in the University. His philosophy in teaching was getting the students out of the classroom into the real world. He and his students met Sufia Khatun in Jobra, whom they interviewed. They realized that the cost of her poverty was 25 cents and she earned 2 pennies a day. He loaned her at that time, the equivalent of US$12. When he sent a student to the village, he found 42 similar people who needed US$27. Yunus went to many banks, but no one willing to fund the idea of micro-loans.

Between 1976 and 1977, Yunus took a loan from Janata Bank, signing as guarantor. In 1976, the Ford Foundation gave aid worth US$12,000 and then he got an additional US$800,000 from the 1980s to the early 1990s. In 1981, IFAD provided US$3.4 million, payable in 25 years with a 17-year holiday at 3%. IFAD had in addition two more instalments till 1995. Clearly, Yunus had strong support at this stage of the SEV lifecycle. The Grameen concept was established in 1978, when the proposal to the Central Bank of Bangladesh to establish a bank to operate in rural areas was approved in 1976. Yunus became the Project Director of the Grameen Bank Project in 1976. By 1978, he received the Bangladesh President's Award for *Nabajug Tebhaga Khamar* (joint farming operation). Grameen Bank became independent only in 1983 and Yunus then became its Managing Director.

Because density and access to mentors and networks may be vital, when there is a choice, a second location for the organizations is beneficial. Gavi, the Vaccine Alliance has offices in Washington DC (near World Bank and donor countries) and Geneva (WHO and UNICEF). Zipline is based in Silicon Valley, but its area of impact is in Africa (see Exhibit 4.1).

Exhibit 4.1: **Silicon Valley Networks**

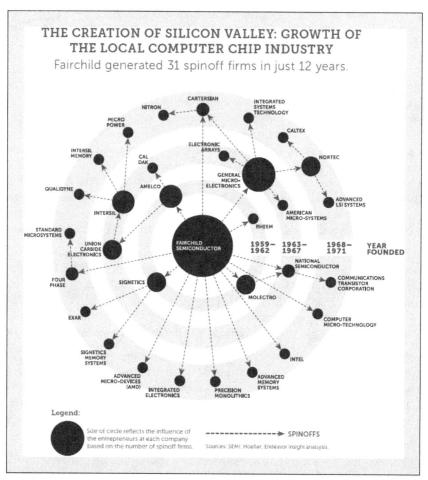

*Source*: Adapted from Endeavour Insights.[12]

## 4.2. **The Networking Process**

Networks are an active resource that can be accessed through the entire lifecycle of a venture. In the early stage, entrepreneurs test their business idea within the confines of their personal network. Most entrepreneurs finance their early ideas through friends and family. As they get more established and have a better idea of what resources they need, the networking process should progress to a more elaborate strategy where they look at acquiring skills, information and other resources.[13] When the venture is more established and running, founders move to a more exclusive network, and at this stage, a founder has a better idea of what they do and do not know and can seek what they need.[14]

The process of forming networks consists of three stages (see Exhibit 4.2).[15] The first stage is looking at structural holes and then identifying key contacts that will be beneficial to help bridge this gap. While this seems very transactional, it is also a function of opportunity. These contacts may lie within one or two degree of separation from family, friends, school or university alumni, and business contacts. Do not be afraid to use social media like LinkedIn, instagram, and Twitter. A study on alumni networks found that those universities with a strong alumni network also produced more successful founders.[16] Another study found that entrepreneurs actually spent over 5 hours per week to reach out to new people and maintain existing ones.[17] Reputed universities have more access to more successfully placed students (see Case Study 4.1). At some time, this "networking" may become exhausting, and you need to decide what is important for your business and for you personally and how much it can help you. To quote Martha Martinez and Howard Aldrich, *"cohesion through strong ties provides entrepreneurs with hard to find resources very early in the development of new ventures, but those resources are limited in scope and have a high cost. By contrast, diversity is more common and more important later in a venture's lifecycle."*[18]

Exhibit 4.2: **Three Stages of Networking**

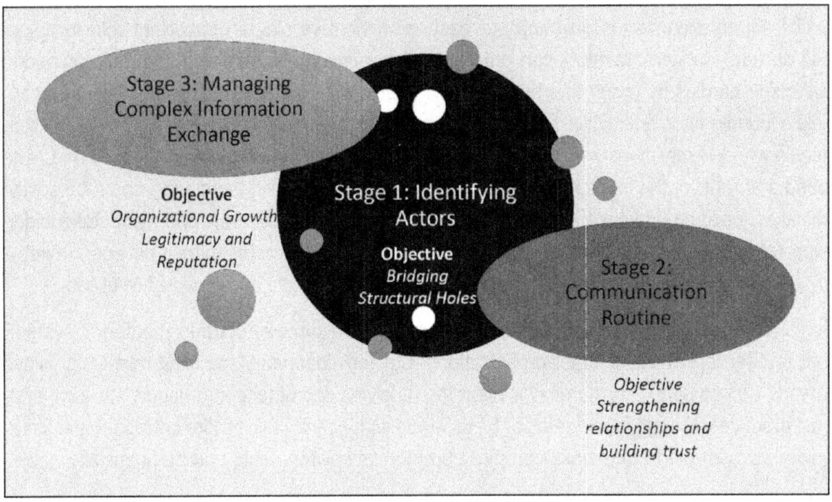

Stage 3: Managing Complex Information Exchange

Objective
*Organizational Growth Legitimacy and Reputation*

Stage 1: Identifying Actors

Objective
*Bridging Structural Holes*

Stage 2: Communication Routine

Objective
*Strengthening relationships and building trust*

*Source*: Author

The second stage is when these contacts will morph and become more complex, as the relationships become stronger. Social ties become stronger. The challenge is good governance practice. It is tempting to invite a friend to be a board member, but will your friendship stand the test when they do their job and are brutally honest? Most donors like to sit on the board, but how do you balance a donor's interest with the interest of the community and those of the organization? Often, additional co-founders are found at this stage and they will ideally complement existing founder skills.[19]

The third stage has the highest level of complexity and is based on the exchange of complex information between partners. The focus should be on scaling the SEV. Since stakeholders often have different levels of power and objectives, the more information that is exchanged, the higher the need for transparency, and hence greater management of diverse stakeholder needs. Managing information exchange is really about creation of new knowledge and gaining a space as a prominent actor in the ecosystem through legitimacy and reputation.

When reaching out to a contact that you have no relationship with, here are some guidelines. First be bold, gently persistent, and do your homework. Busy people have little time to spare, and time is what they value most. While it is good to start any relationship by being generous (doing something before asking something), influential people may already have "all their ducks in a row", so instead — appeal to their interests. Andrew Sobel advices us to think people not positions.[20] Maybe your intended contact loves Africa and that is where your SEV is based. Maybe they are foodies and you are trying to eliminate food waste. We call this "resonance", the ability to find something common on which to interact.[21] You are looking at many levels of compatibility — intellectual, social background, industry knowledge, education, interests, etc. In studies on mentorship, it has been found that the process of mentoring is a complex relationship based on mutual interests (professional and personal).[22]

### "Resonance is the ability to find something common on which to interact." — Barile and Polese[23]

Social entrepreneurship is anything but easy, and mentors play an important role to guide and nurture founders. Mentors can offer advice and encouragement and help entrepreneurs overcome hurdles by giving them inputs from their own experience.[24] The right mentors can help a founder learn and evolve to eventually be successful in their own venture. They are skilled people who leverage their own experiences or their expertise in their domain. A study on CEOs found that most of the mentees surveyed found mentorship helped them avoid common costly mistakes, become proficient in their roles faster, make better decisions, and meet stakeholder expectations.[25] In addition to their skills, mentors also open the doors to their network, thereby giving the entrepreneur access to a host of professional contacts and prospective clients.

Social entrepreneurs may not have all the benefits of a more structured mentoring system that is often prevalent in larger organizations, but their boundary-spanning roles may allow them to be in a better position for being at the receiving end of tacit knowledge, strategy, and best practices. Overall failure rates of SEVs would significantly fall if more entrepreneurs were guided by mentors to maneuver complex commercial environments and be financially viable.

What makes a good mentor? Studies show that formal mentorship is often more beneficial than no mentorship.[26] So far, there have been 21 formal mentor functions and 17 formal mentor traits identified: key behaviors being sought are as follows: as a trainer, where the mentor will provide vision, coaching, and modeling behavior; as an activist, where the mentor will actively intervene and sponsor; and as a supporter, where the mentor will accept and support the mentee through the process.[27]

Some other characteristics identified in former studies find that good mentors had personality traits like honesty and sincerity and interpersonal abilities like listening and professional status within the relevant community.[28] Like any relationship, these mentor–mentee interactions needed to be healthy and built on mutual respect to avoid exploitation of the vulnerable.

As confidential or personal information could be shared, it is important to trust each other. But finding a mentor is not enough, part of the onus of good transfer of knowledge lies with the mentee. Look for stakeholders that may be important for the growth of the SEV (see Exhibit 4.3). Another fact to be considered is that an SEV founder may also need to be a mentor to their subordinates. More than formal managers, entrepreneurs/owner CEOs were expected not only to be good managers and mentors but also to be visionaries and have the ability to articulate and pass on their vision to their followers to get commitment, motivate, and create satisfaction.[29]

Exhibit 4.3: **SEV Stakeholders**

| Community | Investors | Regulatory | Influencers |
|-----------|-----------|------------|-------------|
| Local/national/regional/international | | | |
| Individuals (impact/ influencers) | Banks | Commissions | Board |
| Family | Friends | Government Inspectors/ Auditors | Social Networks |
| Indigenous groups | Like-minded people (local/ regional/national/international) | NGO Auditors | NGO/Foundation |
| Civic authorities | NGOs | Local representatives of Authority | Business |
| Legal authorities | Foundations | Media | Community/Public |
| NGOs | Employees | Government | Media |
| Media | Suppliers/distributors (in-kind) | Government, Associations | Policymaker |
| Volunteers | Business | Government | Lobbyist |

*Source*: Adapted from Stephens Balakrishnan and Lindsay.[30]

In the SEV ecosystem, broad diffusion of information through connections with other SEVs allows for implicit coordination.[31] More formal networks can be created through strategic alliances. Strategic alliances are mutually beneficial relationships between organizations (private, public, and the third sector) over a period with defined outcomes. All parties involved seek a win–win agreement, where a common vision considers individual and team goals of each of the participating entities with shared responsibility founded on mutual trust and understanding. What does a social enterprise stand to gain from such an alliance? Why would a commercial entity or public agency collaborate with a social enterprise?

SEVs can benefit from such relationships, through enhanced legitimacy, being in a position to influence policy, and having access to a broad range of financial, creative, technical and human resources, firm survival, and greater organizational learning, even though it may take some time for this to show up.[32] In contrast, a commercial venture stands to gain a comparative edge over its competitors, have access to new markets and segments, possess enhanced brand value and reputation, build stronger and effective supply chains, and have opportunities for learning for employees to solve challenges. Despite an array of benefits, some organizations can be skeptical to collaborate for the fear of losing independence or identity.

Effective partnerships are multi-sectoral and include public, private, the third sector, and social enterprise ventures.[33] They are set up to resolve implementation challenges that organizations are unable to solve by themselves, and hence, they seek collaboration. These partnerships are becoming transnational, especially when you think of scale and impact.

One key caution area is to watch out for the dilution of values/aims, especially as the partnership is based on unequal power terms. This can be managed if there is a process to measure impact, profitability, roles of the organization, and an exit strategy. Since networks are fluid, governance is key.[34] To look at one example of a mutually beneficial partnership, look at Warby-Parker (see Case Study 4.2).

## Case Study 4.2: **Warby Parker — VisionSpring (India, El Salvador)**

Over 5 million pairs of glasses have been distributed by the Warby Parker's *Buy a Pair, Give a Pair* campaign. The business model uses the following two methods: (1) distributing a pair of glasses to children in schools when teachers spot a vision problem and (2) empowering adults by training them to conduct basic eye exams and sell glasses at affordable prices. The second model accounts for the majority of glasses distributed. Of the 2.5 billion people  that need prescription glasses, 624 million are unable to work or learn as they cannot access or afford glasses. Research has found that in emerging and pre-emerging markets, by giving a pair of glasses, productivity increases by 35% and income increases by 20%.

VisionSpring has been a partner from the beginning and most of its customers have never owned a pair of glasses in their life (50%). Based on a *Lancet* study, VisionSpring has created US$1.18 billion in terms of economic impact. Of course, the study was in the context of tea-pickers in India and numbers are just a proxy; the benefits of a pair of glasses to restore sight should not be underestimated. VisionSpring uses the hub and spoke model (vision entrepreneurs) or the partnership model (working with partners like BRAC in Bangladesh).

Both the founders of Warby Parker and VisionSpring had different journeys but were able to find a common ground. Fortunately, one of the Warby Parker co-founders worked in VisionSpring. VisionSpring, founded in 2001, is a non-profit social enterprise that sells low-cost glasses to people earning between US$1 and US$4 per day. Warby Parker, founded in 2010, is a for-profit B-Corp and sells affordable eyewear in the domestic market while donating a pair of frames to VisionSpring for each pair it sells.

When the co-founder of VisionSpring left in 2009, the board pushed to articulate the skills gap that would be left and considered a professional replacement. What is the role of professional management teams? Do you think this partnership would have materialized if one of the co-founders had not worked in VisionSpring? Is there a role for strong personal motivation in the cause that gives an SEV sustaining power? Should the Board have the same passion to prevent mission drift?[35]

**Mission drift can be defined as a process of organizational change, where an organization diverges from its main purpose or mission.**[36]

## 4.3. Governance

If networks are the fuzzy side of the business, good governance must be the backbone. Though governance is often related to governments, it is applicable to all institutions.[37] Corporate governance is a process of accountability, where an organization sets up a framework of rules, relationships, systems, and processes, through which authority is exercised and activities are controlled.[38] Due to the large number of scandals in the corporate sector involving large publicly traded companies such as Enron, WorldCom, Samsung, and Facebook, there is a substantial interest among policy workers in reforming governance across all the sectors. With globalization, concerns have grown over the lack of accountability of corporations.

Governance refers to both the structure which is institutionalized and the process or the means of social coordination.[39] Governance has three forms: hierarchical governance (which is often top-down), self-governance (which can be self-regulation by market actors or by communities), and co-governance (which is non-hierarchical and a negotiated form of governance between public and non-public actors).[40] The purpose of governance may lead to three types of governance orders: day-to-day problem-solving and opportunity creation (first-order governance, more interactive), maintaining, changing, and creating institutions (second-order governance), and the principles and norms guiding first- and second-order governance (third-order governance or policymaking).[41]

There are three elements of governance: image formulation, choice of instrument, and action.[42] We examine them briefly in what follows:

- *Image formulation*: This focuses on intentional governance (how and why) and can take the form of vision statements, convictions, facts, ends and goals, as well as knowledge, judgments, presuppositions, and hypotheses. The idea is to make them explicit to increase transparency.

- *Choice of instrument(s)*: This links the images to actions. Instruments are of two types: soft and hard. Soft instruments include intangible elements like information, negotiation, bribes, peer pressure, and persuasion to regulations, grants, and sanctions. These instruments may leverage networks. SEVs operate in gray areas, and the more they are prepared for the murkiness, the better the governance systems they can put into place. Hard instruments are based on statutory authority. These instruments are rooted in legal or financial contexts and may involve issues like legal litigation, taxes, permits, or fines.

- *Action*: Action is the method of putting the above instruments into effect. Typically, governance has been the function of shareholders, senior management, and the Board of Directors, all of whom have rights and obligations from a legal standpoint. In the third sector, the Board of Directors are not subject to the same scrutiny and legal purview as the private sector of

## Case Study 4.3: **Deloitte MicroLoan (Malawi)**

Over 85% of the population lives in rural communities where banking is not easily accessible, and there is a high illiteracy rate. There is a gender divide where women have difficulty in getting access to education, credit, land, and property. Women need a husband's approval to get access to credit from a financial institution. One area was need is in capacity-building of women. There is an increasing unemployment situation developing, and a need to set up more businesses. Deloitte 21 initiated an accredited training program that helps to develop the skills of the staff to increase the charity's professionalism and quality of services delivered.

Deloitte is a for-profit organization, working with The MicroLoan Foundation. Governance needs to be from both ends. The MicroLoan Foundation is based in UK and has published its Annual Reports since 2010, where the governance structure is clearly outlined. They meet at least once every 2 months. I operated in Malawi through the MicroLoan Malawi, a registered NGO in Malawi (this was changed to a limited company based on the requirements of the Malawi Reserve Bank in 2013). In 2010, Deloitte set up Deloitte 21, an educational initiative that focuses on developing the skills of young people fo economic success. The partnership with Deloitte 21 in 2010 was a CSR partnership, where they placed a UK director in Malawi and in addition gave 120K of consultancy services. The relationship has been in kind.

The role of the Board of the MicroLoan Foundation as outlined in the annual report is as follows: "*The Trustees ensure that the activities of the charity are consistent with its charitable objects and aim In agreeing our annual plans, the Trustees take into account public benefit as set out in th Charity Commission's general guidance on public benefit. The Trustees believe there is clee public benefit derived from the objectives and activities of the MicroLoan Foundation a set out below. The objectives are outlined as follows: The objectives of the Charity ar the relief of poverty, the advancement of education and the relief of sickness in th developing world by the provision of microloans. The principal activity of th Charity is the provision of grants and support to microfinance operatior predominantly established by MicroLoan (UK).*"

publicly traded companies. Since critical decisions are often made or approved at the board level it is imperative that the board members chosen have the right skills, expertise, and commitment to the enterprise. Many non-profit SEVs just have an advisory board. Many for-profit SEVs are not public. For SEVs, governance is a hybrid between non-profit democratic and commercial stewardship models.[43] In some cases, the model can be forced by regulations (see Case Study 4.3). Many SEVs work with for-profit partners — to increase the capacity for governance.

Do you think projects like the Deloitte–MicroFund Mala\ partnership need separate accountability?

## 4.3.1. *The Board*

For SEVs, governance is the mechanism to oversee compliance with policies and regulations and protect the mission and organizational objectives while meeting the demands of various stakeholders. A well-functioning board strengthens leadership and ensures the success of the SEV. Boards are steering committees and serve the purpose of stewardship and monitoring.[44] In addition to this, boards help management by providing strategic support, often compensating for lack of in-house expertise, giving access to external networks, helping in advocacy, and ensuring legacy by selecting individuals to carry out the organization's vision beyond the lifespan of its founders. Boards formulate strategy and challenge management. This helps develop an innovative and effective business model. Second, they provide access to networks they are associated with. This helps raise awareness of the social cause as well as fundraising and collaboration. Third, and perhaps the most important, board members function as ambassadors and provide a platform for advocacy. Finally, boards ensure the financial health of the organization to increase sustainability of the enterprise. The experience of a purposefully chosen board can help manage the tension between social and financial goals. When integrating social and financial goals, historically we have seen a tendency for social goals to be pushed aside to meet the business needs of the organization (think of Body Shop after acquisition by L'Oréal and of TOMS after acquisition by Bain Capital).

If not careful, social cause-based organizations will succumb to external forces and adopt principles and structures similar to those of a capitalist business to survive.[45] A board can be the organizational consciousness and help iron out convergences and divergences of their mission, values, actions, and norms. Many founders of SEVs may not have the management acumen to manage entrepreneurial and financial risk, and this can be compensated by strong board members. There must also be a demarcation in the responsibilities of the management and the board. The board should focus on guidance and oversight and should not be involved in the day-to-day workings of the enterprise. Similarly, management should ensure the board's decisions are implemented, though there can be conflicts between board members, as stakeholder interests creep in especially when trust and transparency are low.[46] It is important to know to what extent the board responsibilities overlap with management responsibilities.[47]

The two main responsibilities of the board are support and oversight which are complimentary, although mutually exclusive. This refers to primarily protecting the mission of the organization.[48] To keep mission drift minimal, besides the board, in some cases organizations seek external accreditation or manage this tension by separating the commercial and social mission activities.[49] Board members monitor the performance of management against benchmarks. This does include both business and financial performance, which are not mutually exclusive. Boards should help determine performance goals for the social mission and insist on external audits to enhance accountability, which in-turn increases transparency toward stakeholders and potential donors. In addition, the board is also duty bound to ensure that management complies with legal requirements and risk assessment. Every now and then, when the management takes strategic decisions, the board has to ensure that the decisions conform to the guidelines and broadly serve the mission of the organization. Some of these decisions that boards overlook are related to remuneration of the executive, changes in structure, annual budget, and those related to financing.

"Boards can significantly affect the trajectory of a start-up. A great board is a mixture of intellect, experience, personalities, ego, emotions, and aspirations that, when combined correctly, can be a strong net positive experience for the company. It can be magical when a diverse set of experiences among board members — including product development, business strategy, financial expertise, general management skills, and broad network reach — are joined effectively. In contrast, when the ingredients don't mix well, it can be disaster." — Brad Feld, co-founder of TechStars and the managing director of Foundry Group, and Mahendra Ramsinghani, founder of Secure Octane and Director of Venture Investments at Mubadala[50]

A diverse board benefits an organization as it brings together interests of different groups and creates value.[51] Stakeholders could include investors, customers, government, or members of the target group, minorities and caters to gender diversity. The idea behind having a diverse board is to legitimize the operations of the enterprise in front of these stakeholders. However, the multi-stakeholder approach is a potential for conflict and divergence of interests, with stakeholders seeking to act in the interest of their group.[52] SEVs often operate in the area of public goods, which may mean working with the government. There is a need for more active management of these boards when a stakeholder(s) pursues its(their) narrow interest.[53]

The most common problem for SEVs is the recruitment of board members with the right skills and experience.[54] Often, there is a limited supply of people available to serve on boards. This may require a founder to "pitch" to potential board members to convince them to join the SEV and if there is no monetary compensation, it would be of a voluntary nature, and function more as an advisory board. This could lead to a decline in the active interest.[55] The process of governance needs to be clearly articulated, and periodic updates and meetings need to be held, with the terms of membership and periods articulated. The advantage nowadays is that meetings can be done remotely using available technology till such time the SEV gains a suitable cash flow and reputation. One caution area is to clearly define the length of term for the board members upfront and also define the compensation and the duties to make sure there is no confusion later.

The right size of a board is variable to the needs of the enterprise. Typically, as the organization grows, so does the board size; however, you could also create several committees tasked with overseeing specific functions (audit, finance, recruitment, nomination, etc.). In the United States, for instance, large boards are typical and often constitute members with fundraising potential. For-profit enterprises have smaller boards that are manageable, and studies suggest they are more effective (see Exhibit 4.4).[56]

## 4.4. Resilience and Coping Strategies

Whether you have mentors, networks, or even a supporting board, the reality is that entrepreneurship is tough and those social entrepreneurs working in gray spaces find it harder than most. Burnout is common especially in those "valley of death phases". Arianna Huffington,

Exhibit 4.4: **Board Member Recruitment and Management Consideration**

| Individual member | Do they have the right skills and experience? |
|---|---|
| | What are the training and onboarding activities necessary for board membership? |
| | Do they have a strong network that you can leverage? |
| | Are the expectations of the responsibilities and remunerations (or even reimbursements) made clear? |
| | Is there conflict of interest? |
| Board as a collective group | Do you have a fair representation of "insider" and "outsider" viewpoints? |
| | Do you have a fair representation of social, financial, and political coalitions? |
| | Are you able to manage external stakeholder interests? |
| | How would you monitor agents? |
| | Is there clear division of responsibilities between the chairman and the chief executive officer? |
| | Accountability for what? Accountability to whom? |
| | Do they understand legal responsibilities — that of duty of loyalty and duty of care? |
| Protocols | Do you have the right legal and governance structure? |
| | Have you clearly outlined the membership terms, compensation, expectations, and membership period? |
| | Do you have formal and transparent procedures for the appointment of new directors? |
| | What is the reporting structure (accountability for what and to whom) and frequency of reporting? |
| | What are the reporting protocols and formats? What about sub-committees like audit, compensation, and nominating committees? |
| | Have you negotiated the power the board has to control management? When do they have the authority to step in and under what conditions? What about conflict resolution? |
| | How will you ensure that there is no mission drift? |

*Source*: Compiled from Brad Feld and Mahendra Ramsinghani.[57]

founder of the *Huffington Post*, candidly speaks of burnout that led her to found Thrive. While Arianna found success, the past is littered with suicides of many promising young founders who were unable to cope and did not reach out for help. In one of the few studies published, 30% of the founders surveyed struggled with depression and 27% struggled with anxiety.[58] While suicide is one extreme end of burnout, burnout impairs decision-making judgment, dissociates from reality and friends, and results often in the death of the venture itself. Those entrepreneurs who had a less flexible mind-set about their job roles and were obsessively passionate (of the status, money, or other rewards that it brings) about their job (versus harmoniously passionate — motivated by the job because it brings satisfaction and an important part of who they are) were more likely to face burnout.[59] As one blog writer postulated — burnout is an indicator you were solving the wrong problem. Of course, this is a very simplistic overview, but the question is, *can burnout be avoided and how?*

Burnout is often either a taboo topic (linked to serious mental illness) or glamorized for the wrong reasons. For it to be accepted with the same status as a common cold, society still has a long way to go. Part of the reason is that mental illness is not perceived on par with physical illness. Burnout is defined as "a syndrome of emotional exhaustion and cynicism that occurs frequently among individuals who do 'people-work' of some kind".[60] In humanitarian workers, for example, a longitudinal study found extraordinary stress was a major contributor to burnout.[61] People working with traumatized societies suffer from secondary traumatic stress.[62] Yet, very few health policies or even company policies actively handle this problem. The reality is that there are fewer mental health workers than physical health doctors. Mental health workers are nine per 100,000 population versus 140 per 100,000 of the all health workers.[63] While exhaustion and the feeling of inefficiency are common things all entrepreneurs and workers face, perhaps for an SEV depersonalization, the attempt to put distance between oneself and service recipients by actively ignoring the qualities that make them unique and engaging people[64] may be the worst thing to do for the cause and SEV. Here, the person may not be able to empathize with the mission of the organization. Help can take the forms of social support, organizational support, or even religion.[65] Social support has been found to reduce the levels of depression, psychological distress, burnout, lack of personal accomplishment, and greater life satisfaction.[66] We are looking at the quality of resilience increasingly in entrepreneurs.

Resilience is the ability of organizations or individuals to bounce back from a setback and continue to operate at least at normal states and is closely aligned with adaptation.[67] Resilience at an individual level is defined as the human capacity to face, overcome, be strengthened by, or even transformed by the adversities of life and is associated with a combination of three sources — I have, I am, and I can.[68] This can be translated to "comprehensibility (the extent to which an individual makes sense of adversity); manageability (the extent to which an individual perceives that resources are at her or his disposal to meet the challenges of inordinate demands); and meaningfulness (the extent to which an individual feels that the challenges faced are worth it)".[69] It is a *dynamic process of positive adaptation*.[70] Another study finds that higher the resilience (predicted with hardiness, resourcefulness, and optimism), higher the likelihood of success.[71] For the same study, optimism was found to be more important for women than men. A psychological study on entrepreneurs found that a high amount of psychological capital (a combination of self-efficacy, optimism, hope, and resilience) helped entrepreneurs experience lower levels of stress when running new ventures.[72] At an organizational level, resilience is collective — individuals, teams, structures, processes, and strategies. When structures are not adaptable to change, the stress will make itself felt on the individual.

While burnout may be inevitable, it can be managed, and a big part is knowing when to ask for help and when to step aside and hand over the operating reigns to others. Recently, there have been many high-profile burnout situations, that of Travis of Uber or Elon Musk and his tweets on Tesla that resulted in an SEC fine. The strengths a founder has — to think of an idea, concretize it, and build a fledgling organization — may not be the strengths required to grow and expand an organization. This realization itself is a painful one, especially if the founder did not plan for an exit. Many SEV founders are more passionate about the cause and may not have the skills to manage an organization, that too a rapidly growing one. Because many SEVs depend on volunteers, they don't have the needed specialists for the job. The case about the Invisible Children highlights the importance of managing stress. For some reason, when there is a problem with an organization or a founder, for-profit firms seem to have more public tolerance than non-profits (see Case Study 4.4).

## Case Study 4.4: **Invisible Children**

Invisible Children was formed in 2003 by three young filmmakers — Bobby Bailey, Laren Poole, and Jason Russell. They had witnessed firsthand the plight of the children subjected to the terror of the warlord Joseph Kony of *The Lord's Resistance Army*. Kony was known to abduct children and make them child soldiers. The first video was released in 2004 — *Invisible Children: The Rough Cut*. The team worked toward building traction for the cause through education  and awareness. In 2006, Global Night Commute saw 80,000 people sleeping in the city center to raise awareness of Ugandan children abducted by Kony. In 2010, President Obama said he was sending 100 military advisors to Africa to help in Kony's capture under the LRA Disarmament and Northern Uganda Recovery Act. The net revenues gained from donations were between US$8 and US$13 million between 2008 and 2011.

Invisible Children gained global fame after the Kony video, which was released in 2012. The video went viral and in 1 week had 112 million views. The hashtag #KONY2012 was tweeted 2.4 million times in March 2012 and was endorsed by many Hollywood celebrities. Fame was viral — Jason was interviewed by Oprah Winfrey. Ryan Seacrest was tweeting about the video. College students bought merchandise and contributed to the funding campaign and activist voice. The revenues in 2012 was US$28 million and was used to expand operations. The team was unprepared for the media onslaught and the website crashed. Criticism was inevitable on many issues — was the video simplifying a complex issue? What were they raising funds to do?

The fame opened the movement and the co-founders to intense scrutiny. It resulted in Jason having a very public nervous breakdown that was unfortunately captured on film. Viral causes focusing on university students are not uncommon — think of the TOMS Shoes and the Ice Bucket Challenge. While it may not be possible to predict why one cause becomes viral and another does not, it is necessary to know scrutiny is inevitable. For example, with the Ice Bucket Challenge, money was put into R&D to find a cure for ALS.

Meanwhile, Joseph Kony is still out there, hiding but free, though without the army he once had. He has been wanted for war crimes by the International Court of Justice since 2005. Invisible Children has learnt from their previous experience and moved away from public glare. USAID have an LRA crisis tracker (https://crisistracker.org), and they distribute high-frequency radios to create a civilian security system, working with Invisible Children.

Perhaps because public outrage at organizations focused on "doing good" is higher than "for profits". These are things to be watchful of. A strong support system may be helpful in this regard.

## 4.5. **Optimizing Your Support System: A Recap**

SEV entrepreneurs cannot survive nor scale without a strong support system. This means they need to develop a strong network to ensure they can overcome challenges in the market and powerful stakeholders with other vested interests. Thoughtfully curated networks on the board can be sources of good governance and competitive advantage through timely information, expertise, and market knowledge. Most important, entrepreneurship is a high-stress and lonely job. A support system can help with resilience and coping strategies.

## 4.6. **Questions**

**Question 1**

Are networks defined based on weak or strong ties? Which are helpful for innovations? Why? How has the role of the internet changed this? Do an analysis of your strong and weak ties using a similar diagram like the one that follows. What are the structural holes in your network that you need to bridge? For example, in the following diagram, would you hope to create a relationship with A?

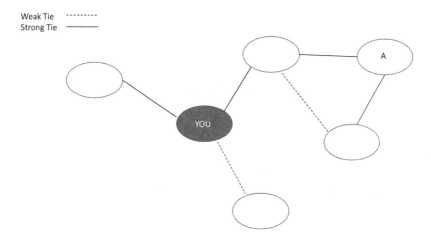

**Question 2**

What factors would you consider when recruiting for a Board of Directors for a social enterprise? Look at Gavi, the Vaccine Alliance board structure (https://www.gavi.org/about/governance/gavi-board/composition/) versus World Health Organization (https://www.who.int/governance/en/) versus The Global Fund (https://www.theglobalfund.org/en/board/). What can you learn? In your opinion, how would you treat shareholder voting rights (research voting rights of common stock shareholders) versus stakeholder voting rights?

**Question 3**

How would you define a mutually beneficial strategic alliance? Illustrate this with the use of a mutually beneficial strategic alliance using a cross-industry example.

**Question 4**

Should the board of an SEV accept the dilution of the organization's mission in favor of developing entrepreneurial potential? Do you think TOMS and Body Shop lost their way?

**Question 5**

Mission drift is not unusual. The case on Hershey's (read the article by Jones[73]) is an excellent example. Find more reasons with examples for mission drift that a strong governance structure should be mindfull of.

**Question 6**

As a fun exercise, take any founder and look at the networks they have developed during the various stages of their lifecycle that directly impact their business financials (currently or potential).

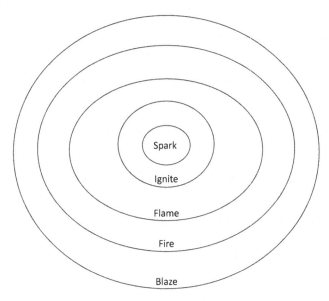

# Sources

### Case Study 4.1: Grameen Bank: Spark-Stage Support Systems

Compiled from multiple sources: American Foundation (2007), "Money does not go to the bank – often goes to the foundation," dated June, Available: http://www.american.com/archive/2007/may-june-magazine-contents/micro-man [Accessed 10 August 2014]; Bornstein, D. (1998), *The Price of a Dream: The Story of the Grameen Bank and the Idea That is Helping the Poor to Change Their Lives:* Simon & Schuster; Counts, A. (2008), *Small Loans, Big Dreams*; Dowla, A. and Barua, D. (2006), *The Poor Always Pay Back: The Grameen II Story.* Kumarian Press; ECA (2010), "Fullbright Alum Bangladesh Mohammad Yunus awarded Congressional Gold Medal," Available: http://eca.state.gov/highlight/fulbright-alum-bangladesh-muhammad-yunus-awarded-congressional-gold-medal#sthash.k6MxIgHS.dpuf [Accessed 10 August 2014]; James, Z. (2014), "Muhammad Yunus: Empowering the poor and marginalized," dated 30 July, https://www.wearesalt. org/muhammad-yunus-empowering-the-poor-and-marginalized/ [Accessed 29 March 2019]; Vanderbilt (2007), "Muhammad Yunus tells Vanderbilt seniors to help end poverty; Nobel Peace Prize winner accepts $100,000 Nichols-Chancellor's Medal," Available: https://news.vanderbilt.edu/2007/05/10/muhammad-yunus-tells-vanderbilt-seniors-to-help-end-poverty-nobel-peace-prize-winner-accepts-100000-nichols-chancellors-medal-58611/ [Accessed 29 March 2019]; Yunus, M. (2011), *CV of Professor Muhammad Yunus*, Available: http://www.muhammadyunus.org/index.php/professor-yunus/cv [Accessed 30 March 2019].

### Case Study 4.2: Deloitte MicroLoan (Malawi)

Compiled from multiple sources: Microloan Foundation – Australia (2010), *Impact Report 2009–10*, Available: https://www.microloanfoundationaustralia.org.au/wp-content/uploads/2011/04/MicroLoan-Impact-Review-2010.pdf [Accessed 2 April 2019]; Malawi (2004), *Malawi National Economic Empowerment Policy and Action Program*, Available: https://sarpn.org/documents/d0001262/P1496-policy-paper_malawi_May2004. pdf [Accessed 2 April 2019]; MicroLoan Foundation Annual reports: https://www.microloanfoundation.org. uk/about-us/our-impact/reports/; Top Consultant (2011), *Deloitte Supports Charity by Developing Employee Training*, dated 14 March, Available: http://news.top-consultant.com/US/Deloitte-supports-charity-by-developing-employee-training-7711.html [Accessed 2 April 2019].

### Case Study 4.3: Warby Parker & Vision Spring

Compiled from multiple sources: Stankorb, S. (2012), "Need blind, vision spring and Warby Parker shake up eyewear with impact," *Good*, dated 16 March, Available: https://www.good.is/articles/need-blind-vision-spring-and-warby-parker-shake-up-eyewear-with-impact [Accessed 3 April 2019]; TradeGecko (2018), "Warby Parker: How four students turned the eyewear industry on its head," *Blog*, dated 25 April, Available: https:// www.tradegecko.com/blog/warby-parker-eyewear-industry-disruption [Accessed 3 April 2019]; Warby Parker (2019), *Thank you X 5,000,000*, Available: https://www.warbyparker.com/buy-a-pair-give-a-pair [Accessed 3 April 2019]; Vision Spring (2018), "Landmark study proves and quantifies impact on worker's productivity," Available: https://www.visionspring.org/wp-content/uploads/2018/07/PROSPER-RCT-Study_ Lancet-2018.07.23.pdf and https://visionspring.org/why_eyeglasses/ [Accessed 3 April 2019].

### Case Study 4.4: Invisible Children

Compiled from multiple sources: Cruz-Enriquez, M. (2012), "Why Kony 2012 is bad public diplomacy, USC center on public diplomacy," dated 27 March, Available: https://www.uscpublicdiplomacy.org/comment/2385 [Accessed 7 April 2019]; Herbert, D. G. (2017), "Kony 2017: From guerrilla marketing to guerrilla warfare," *Foreign Policy*, dated 2 March, https://foreignpolicy.com/2017/03/02/kony-2017-from-guerilla-marketing-to-guerilla-warfare-invisible-children-africa/ [Accessed 8 April 2019]; Patringenaru, I. (2009), "Saving the 'Invisible Children'," *This Week at USCD*, dated 17 August, Available: https://ucsdnews.ucsd.edu/archive/ thisweek/2009/08/17_invisible.asp [Accessed 8 April 2019]; Invisible Children (2019), Available: https:// invisiblechildren.com/program/film/ [Accessed 8 April 2019]; Reuters (2012), "African union launches U.S.-backed force to hunt Kony," dated 24 March, Available: http://www.reuters.com/article/2012/03/24/ us-southsudan-kony-idUSBRE82N08T20120324 [Accessed 8 April 2019]; Schwartz, A. (2014), "Invisible

Children, the group behind Kony 2012, is shutting down," *Fast Company*, dated 15 December, Available: https://www.fastcompany.com/3039761/invisible-children-the-group-behind-kony-2012-is-shutting-down [Accessed 8 April 2019]; Taylor, A. (2014), "Invisible Children organization behind kony 2012 video to wind-down operations," *Washington Post*, dated 15 December, Available https://www.washingtonpost.com/news/worldviews/wp/2014/12/15/invisible-children-organization-behind-kony-2012-video-to-wind-down-operations/?noredirect=on&utm_term=.605d9e6f4a62 [Accessed 8 April 2019].

# ENDNOTES

1  Newman, W. H. and Wallender III, H. W. (1978), "Managing not-for-prof it enterprises," *Academy of Management Review*, 3(1): 24–31.

2  Zimmer, C. (1986), *Entrepreneurship Through Social Networks — The Art and Science of Entrepreneurship*, Ballinger, Cambridge, MA, pp. 3–23.

3  Envick, B. R. (2005), "Beyond human and social capital: The importance of positive psychological Capital for Entrepreneurial Success," *The Entrepreneurial Executive*, 10, 41–52.

4  Peters, L., Rice, M. and Sundararajan, M. (2004), "The role of incubators in the entrepreneurial process," *The Journal of Technology Transfer*, 29(1), 83–91.

5  Brüderl, J. and Preisendörfer, P. (1998), "Network support and the success of newly founded business," *Small Business Economics*, 10(3): 213–225.

6  Bosma, N., Van Praag, M., Thurik, R. and De Wit, G. (2004), "The Value of Human and Social Capital Investments for the Business Performance of Startups," *Small Business Economics*, 23(3), 227–236.

7  Martinez, M. A. and Aldrich, H. E. (2011), "Networking strategies for entrepreneurs: Balancing cohesion and diversity," *International Journal of Entrepreneurial Behavior & Research*, 17(1): 7–38.

8  *Ibid.*

9  Hoang, H. and Antoncic, B. (2003), "Network-based research in entrepreneurship: A critical review," *Journal of Business Venturing*, 18(2), 165–187.

10  Human, S. E. and Provan, K. G. (1996), "External resource exchange and perceptions of competitiveness within organizational networks: An organizational learning perspective," In: Reynolds, P., *et al.* (eds.), *Frontiers of Entrepreneurship Research*, pp. 240–252.

11  Endeavor Insight (2014), "How did silicon valley become silicon valley," *Endeavor Insights*, Available: https://endeavor.org/insight/new-endeavor-insight-report-analyzes-the-source-of-silicon-valleys-development/ [Accessed 8 February 2019]; Morris, R. and Török, L. (2018), "Fostering productive entrepreneurship communities," *Endeavor Insights*. Available: https://endeavor.org/content/uploads/2015/06/Fostering-Productive-Entrepreneurship-Communities.pdf [Accessed 1 April 2019].

12  Endeavor Insight (2014). *Op. cit.*

13  Hite, J. M. and Hesterly, W. S. (2001), "The evolution of firm networks: From emergence to early growth of the firm," *Strategic Management Journal*, 22(3): 275–286.

14  Greve, A. and Salaff, J. W. (2003), "Social networks and entrepreneurship," *Entrepreneurship Theory and Practice*, 28(1): 1–22.

15  Larson, A. and Starr, J. A. (1993), "A network model of organization formation," *Entrepreneurship: Theory and Practice*, 17(2): 5–15.

16  Nann, S., Krauss, J., Schober, M., Gloor, P., Fischbach, K. and Führes, H. (2010), *The Power of Alumni Networks — Success of Startup Companies Correlates with Online Social Network Structure of Its Founders*. MIT Sloan Research Paper. No. 4766-10.

17  Aldrich, H. and Reese, P. R. (1993), "Does networking pay off? A panel study of entrepreneurs in the research triangle," In: Churchill, N.S., *et al.* (eds.), *Frontiers of Entrepreneurship Research*, pp. 325–339.

18  Martinez, M. A. and Aldrich, H. E. (2011), "Networking strategies for entrepreneurs: Balancing cohesion and diversity," *International Journal of Entrepreneurial Behavior & Research*, 17(1): 7–38.

19  Spiegel, O., Abbassi, P., Schlagwein, D. and Fischbach, K. (2013), "Going it all alone in web entrepreneurship? A comparison of single founders vs. co-founders," In *Proceedings of the 2013 Annual Conference on Computers and People Research*, May: ACM, pp. 21–32.

20  Sobel, A. and Panas, J. (2014), *Power Relationships: 26 Irrefutable Laws*, John Wiley & Sons: New Jersey.

21  Barile, S. and Polese, F. (2010), "Linking the viable system and many-to-many network approaches to service-dominant logic and service science," *International Journal of Quality and Service Sciences*, 2(1): 23–42.

22  Sambunjak, D., Straus, S. E. and Marusic, A. (2010), "A systematic review of qualitative research on the meaning and characteristics of mentoring in academic medicine," *Journal of General Internal Medicine*, 25(1): 72–78.

23  Barile, S. and Polese, F. (2010), "Linking the viable system and many-to-many network approaches to service-dominant logic and service science," *International Journal of Quality and Service Sciences*, 2(1): 23–42.

24  Baker, E., Onyx, J. and Edwards, M. (2011), "Emergence, social capital and entrepreneurship: understanding networks from the inside," *Emergence: Complexity & Organization*, 13(3): 21–38.

25  de Janasz, S. and Peiperl, M. (2015), "CEOs need mentors too," *Harvard Business Review*, dated April. Available: https://hbr.org/2015/04/ceos-need-mentors-too [Accessed 26 November 2018].

26  Siebert, S. (1999), "The effectiveness of facilitated mentoring: A longitudinal quasi-experiment," *Journal of Vocational Behavior*, 54(3): 483–502.

27  Smith, W. J., Howard, J. T. and Harrington, K. V. (2005), "Essential formal mentor characteristics and functions in governmental and non-governmental organizations from the program administrator's and the mentor's perspective," *Public Personnel Management*, 34(1): 31–58.

28  Sambunjak, D., Straus, S. E. and Marusic, A. (2010), "A systematic review of qualitative research on the meaning and characteristics of mentoring in academic medicine," *Journal of General Internal Medicine*, 25(1): 72–78.

29  Papalexandris, N. and Galanaki, E. (2009), "Leadership's impact on employee engagement: Differences among entrepreneurs and professional CEOs," *Leadership & Organization Development Journal*, 30(4): 365–385.

30  Stephens Balakrishnan, M. and Lindsay, V. (2013), "The rise of the global social entrepreneur: A conceptual framework," In: *55th Academy of International Business Annual Conference. Bridging the Divide: Linking IB to Complementary Disciplines and Practice*. Istanbul, Turkey, 3–6 July.

31  Forno, A. D. and Merlone, U. (2009), "Social entrepreneurship effects on the emergence of cooperation in networks," *Emergence: Complexity & Organization*, 11(4): 48–58.

32  For example see: Elfring, T. and Hulsink, W. (2003), "Networks in entrepreneurship: The case of high-technology firms," *Small Business Economics*, 21(4): 409–422; Uzzi, B. (1999), "Embeddedness in the making of financial capital: How social relations and networks benefit firms seeking financing," *American Sociological Review*, 481–505; Watson, J. (2007), "Modeling the relationship between networking and firm performance," *Journal of Business Venturing*, 22(6): 852–874.

33  Blockson, L. C. (2003), "Multisector approaches to societal issues management," *Business & Society*, 42(3): 381–390.

34  Börzel, T. and Risse, T. (2005), "Public private partnerships. Effective and legitimate tools for transnational governance?," In: Grande, E. and Pauly, L. (eds.), *Complex Sovereignty. Reconstituting Political Authority in the Twenty First Century*, Toronto, ON: University of Toronto Press, pp. 195–216.

35  Ebrahim, A., Battilana, J. and Mair, J. (2014), "The governance of social enterprises: Mission drift and accountability challenges in hybrid organizations," *Research in Organizational Behavior*, 34, 81–100.

36  Cornforth, C. (2014), "Understanding and combating mission drift in social enterprises," *Social Enterprise Journal*, 10(1): 3–20.

37  Weiss, T. G. (2000), "Governance, good governance and global governance: Conceptual and actual challenges," *Third World Quarterly*, 21(5): 795–814.

38  Owen, J. (2003a), HIH Royal Commission, *The Failure of HIH Insurance Volume 1: A Corporate Collapse and Its Lessons, Commonwealth of Australia*, April: xxxiii and Owen, J. (2003b), *Corporate Governance – Level upon Layer*, Speech to the *13th Commonwealth Law Conference 2003*, Melbourne, 13–17 April, p. 2.

39  *Ibid.*

40  Kooiman, J., Bavinck, M., Chuenpagdee, R., Mahon, R. and Pullin, R. (2008), "Interactive governance and governability: An introduction," *The Journal of Transdisciplinary Environmental Studies*, 7(1): 1–11.

41  *Ibid.*

42  *Ibid.*; Zehavi, A. (2012), "New governance and policy instruments: Are governments going 'soft'," In: *Oxford: The Oxford Handbook of Governance.*

43  Dart, R. (2004), "The legitimacy of social enterprise," *Non-profit Management and Leadership,* 14(4): 411–424.

44  Kreutzer, K. and Jacobs, C. (2011), "Balancing control and coaching in CSO governance. A paradox perspective on board behaviour," *Voluntas: International Journal of Voluntary and Nonprofit Organizations,* 22(4): 613.

45  Cornforth, C. (1995), "Patterns of cooperative management: Beyond the degeneration thesis," *Economic and Industrial Democracy,* 16(4): 487–523.

46  Freeman, R. E. and Reed, D. L. (1983), "Stockholders and stakeholders: A new perspective on corporate governance," *California Management Review,* 25(3): 88–106.

47  Spear, R., Cornforth, C. and Aiken, M. (2009), "The governance challenges of social enterprises: Evidence from a UK empirical study," *Annals of Public and Cooperative Economics,* 80(2): 247–273.

48  Ebrahim, A., Battilana, J. and Mair, J. (2014), "The governance of social enterprises: Mission drift and accountability challenges in hybrid organizations," *Research in Organizational Behavior,* 34: 81–100.

49  Cornforth, C. (2014), "Understanding and combating mission drift in social enterprises," *Social Enterprise Journal,* 10(1): 3–20.

50  Feld, B. and Ramsinghani, M. (2014), *Startup Boards: Getting the Most out of your Board of Directors,* Wiley, p. 7

51  Carter, D. A., Simkins, B. J. and Simpson, W. G. (2003), "Corporate governance, board diversity, and firm value," *Financial Review,* 38(1): 33–53.

52  Hutton, J. (1999), *The Stakeholders Society,* Blackwell: London.

53  Spear, R., Cornforth, C. and Aiken, M. (2007), *For Love and Money: Governance and Social Enterprise.* National Council for Voluntary Organisations, UK.

54  *Ibid.*

55  Cornforth, C.J. and Edwards, C. (1998), *Good Governance: Developing Effective Board-management Relations in Public and Voluntary Organizations,* CIMA Publishing: London, UK.

56  Eisenberg, T., Sundgren, S. and Wells, M.T. (1998), "Larger board size and decreasing firm value in small firms," *Journal of Financial Economics,* 48(1): 35–54.

57  Feld, B and Ramsinghani, M. (2014), *Startup Boards: Getting the Most out of your Board of Directors,* Wiley, p. 7.

58  This article is worth reading on the gravity of the situation: Carson, B. (2015), "There's a dark side to startups, and it haunts 30% of the world's most brilliant people," *Business Insider,* dated 2 July, Available: https://www.businessinsider.com.au/austen-heinzs-suicide-and-depression-in-startups-2015-7 [Accessed 13 October 2018].

59  De Mol, E., Pollack, J. and Ho, V. T. (2018), "What makes entrepreneurs burn out," *Harvard Business Review,* dated April 4, Available: https://hbr.org/2018/04/what-makes-entrepreneurs-burn-out [Accessed 13 October 2018].

60  Maslach, C. and Jackson, S. E. (1981), "The measurement of experienced burnout," *Journal of Occupational Behaviour,* (2): 99–113.

61  Cardozo, B. L., Crawford, C. G., Eriksson, C., Zhu, J., Sabin, M., Ager, A. *et al.* (2012), "Psychological distress, depression, anxiety, and burnout among international humanitarian aid workers: A longitudinal study," *PloS one,* 7(9): e44948.

62  Shah, S. A., Garland, E. and Katz, C. (2007), "Secondary traumatic stress: Prevalence in humanitarian aid workers in India," *Traumatology,* 13(1): 59–70; WHO (2017), *Mental Health Atlas 2017.* Switzerland

63  WHO (2017), *Op. cit.*; World Health Organization (2010), *World Health Statistics*: Geneva.

64  Maslach, C., Schaufeli, W. B. and Leiter, M. P. (2001), "Job burnout," *Annual Review of Psychology,* 52(1): 397–422.

65  Eriksson, C. B., Bjorck, J. P., Larson, L. C., Walling, S. M., Trice, G. A., Fawcett, J. *et al.* (2009), "Social support, organisational support, and religious support in relation to burnout in expatriate humanitarian aid workers," *Mental Health, Religion and Culture,* 12(7): 671–686.

66  Cardozo *et al.* (2012), *Op. cit.*

67   Gilly, J.-P., Kechidi, M. and Talbot, D. (2013), "Resilience of organisations and territories: The role of pivot firms," *European Management Journal*, 32(4): 596-602; Meyer, A. D. (1982), "Adapting to environmental jolts," *Administrative Science Quarterly*: 515-537.

68   Grotberg, E. A. (1995), "Guide to promoting resilience in children: Strengthening the human spirit," *Early Childhood Development: Practice and Reflections*, 8, Bernard van Leer Foundation.

69   Almedom, A. M. (2005), "Resilience, hardiness, sense of coherence, and posttraumatic growth: All paths leading to "light at the end of the tunnel?" *Journal of Loss and Trauma*, 10: 259.

70   Luthar, S. S., Cicchetti, D. and Becker, B. (2000), "The construct of resilience: A critical evaluation and guidelines for future work," *Child Development*, 71(3): 543-562.

71   Ayala, J. C. and Manzano, G. (2014), "The resilience of the entrepreneur. Influence on the success of the business. A longitudinal analysis," *Journal of Economic Psychology*, 42: 126-135.

72   Baron, R. A., Franklin, R. J. and Hmieleski, K. M. (2016), "Why entrepreneurs often experience low, not high, levels of stress: The joint effects of selection and psychological capital," *Journal of Management*, 42(3): 742-768.

73   Jones, M. B. (2007), The multiple sources of mission drift. *Nonprofit and Voluntary Sector Quarterly*, 36(2): 299-307.

# MANAGING RESOURCES

## Chapter Objectives

➢ Identify and manage key resources.

➢ Differentiate between tangible and intangible values.

➢ Use strategies like storytelling, brand-building, and reputation management to drive intangible value.

➢ Control media and don't let media control you.

➢ **Cases:** Livox (assistive technology: Brazil), PT. Tirta Marta (environmental sustainability: Indonesia); The Qessa Academy (traditional storytelling culture: Afghanistan), and Clínicas del Azúcar (health, diabetes: Mexico).

## 5.1. Managing Tangible and Intangible Resources

A resource is defined as something a firm owns or can access. Resources can be human capital, time, infrastructure, patents, or finances. They often act as signals to the marketplace. For example, a successive round of funding raised from prominent actors can signal legitimacy and credibility in the marketplace.[1] Resources can be broadly classified as tangible or intangible resources, and they are sources of competitive advantage in the marketplace. A technology and a person with unique capabilities are all intangible resources. Tangible resources are things you can touch, see, and feel — money, products, infrastructure, etc. Many non-profit SEVs in early days struggle with financial assets. It is estimated that in USA, over 50% of non-profits have less than 1 month of cash reserve, putting them at financial risk.[2] The challenge lies in not letting overhead expenses get out of control. These are the cost of personnel in accounting, management, and human resource departments, the costs involved in fundraising expenses, including salaries, professional consultants, and special events, information management technology costs, and the costs of supplies and materials consumed for administration.

SEVs that find themselves in a cash crunch prefer to bootstrap. They may then look for volunteers instead of paid employees. Many volunteers work for a cause because of their passion and identify with the organization's values. While bootstrapping, founders may barter their expertise or assets (personal or organizational) for resources — it could be skills, office space, technology, free PR, and even in some case deferred payments. With respect to the cost of technology, to save costs, one option is to use open-source software[3] or frugal innovation.[4] Some types of resources are covered in Chapter 3 and in Exhibit 3.3. Exhibit 5.1 gives additional sources of funding SEVs can tap into. More methods are discussed in Chapter 6 under Business Models. Livox (see Case Study 5.1) is a for-profit SEV that uses its commercial arm to subsidize the not-for-profit arm to ensure it can be financially sustainable yet not dilute its mission.

Exhibit 5.1: **Common Funding Methods SEVs Can Tap Into**

| Funding Model | Advantages | Disadvantages |
|---|---|---|
| Grants | This is the most commonly used method. Often, it has a cascading effect. Grants are useful when piloting new initiatives that have a high-risk factor, or in developing assets. You do not have to repay but need to keep track of expenses. | Comes with strings attached and very often can lead to mission drift, or poor financial planning. Grants have their own objectives and timelines. You require a lot of time and expertise for grant-writing. Competition for grants are high — less than 8% chance of winning.[5] Grants are often given in instalments on completion and after review of promised milestones. |
| Micro-grants | Small funding usually through loans, networking foundations with mentoring. | You require time to network. The grants are often not enough for scaling — just for survival or sometimes program related. |
| Social investment/ impact investing | Where the principal and interest are returned and the lender is associated to cause-based funding. | May neglect financial aspects. Impact is defined and may need to be changed if conditions change. Communities may be exploited for financial returns if impact is not defined by communities but by investors and entrepreneurs. |
| Patient capital | Usually associated with high-risk, big-initiative projects. Principal is often paid back once SEV starts making a profit. While normal funds look at 4–6 year exits, in patient capital it may be 8–15 years. | They can be focused on scaling and put tremendous pressure on the organization and founders who may not have business experience. Investors may get impatient. |
| Loans | Depends if the SEV is trading successfully or has assets to cover capital expenditure. | Problem is that you must have assets. |
| Social impact bonds | Once objective is achieved, government pays back the lender with interest. | Dangers of *Payment by Results*. Requires true partnership between providers, investors, commissioners, and beneficiaries. |
| Equity investments | A share of the SEV in return for investments (has to be permitted by local laws). | If not planned properly, you can lose control of the direction the company is going. |
| Crowdfunding | Rather new, but harnesses technology to encourage small donations on a large scale. | You need to develop a good marketing pitch and use social media. |
| Initiative-based CSR funding | Adopt a pet project in different countries sponsored by a corporate honcho. | Need to network and funds may not be long term. |
| Fee for service | Sell the product or service. | Needs to meet market expectations. |
| Subsidy/barter | Negotiate a subsidy or barter services. | Need to be good at networking, negotiation, and delivering promised value. |

## Case Study 5.1: **Livox (Brazil)**

Founded by Carlos Pereira, Livox gives voice to the *people of determination* community who struggle to communicate. Due to a medical mistake, Pereira's daughter was born in 2007 with cerebral palsy, and she had difficulty in communicating. Stem cell treatment was available at a cost of US$40,000, but he had just US$3. He used a crowdfunding campaign to raise the money to treat her. Though she improved,  she still struggled to communicate. His desire to help her motivated him to learn computer engineering and to develop an app to talk to her.

In Brazil alone, his home country, there are 15 million people who have a problem communicating due to various reasons. World Health Organization has stated that those with disabilities face poor health, high rates of poverty, and fewer opportunities. It is estimated there are more than 1 billion people with disabilities. Livox uses artificial intelligence to learn and predict through machine learning what the user wants to communicate through touch, eyeblinking, or voice. For this, it interprets motor, cognitive, and visual disorders, by learning through the user's past history of usage with the app, by the way the user interacts with the screen. To develop the app, Carlos spent time with people in a rehabilitation center in Brazil, with various needs. Livox has more than 20,000 users in Brazil alone. Though its largest base is in South America, it is available in 25 languages and is being used across Chile, Peru, United Kingdom, Portugal, Jordan, and Saudi Arabia.

What stands out about Livox is its increasing appetite to maximize its impact of innovation. Pereira has begun to commercialize Livox in the United States through another edition, called Livox Bridge. The commercial application of Livox has been adopted across the medical sector to communicate with patients, in academia by schools, and by community welfare organizations. The cost of Livox without insurance is expensive, at US$10,000; however, by reaching a careful balance between commercial customers and those who desperately need it, Pereira has managed to deliver the product across Android-based platforms for a license fee as little as US$250 and free of cost for those under severe hardship. This non-profit arm called *Inclusion without Borders* received a US$550,000 grant from Google in 2015. In 2018, they raised US$60,000 from MIT and in 2019 they benefited from UNICEF's Innovation Fund. The price is important as disability may increase the chances of poverty, and those who face poverty may be more likely to plunge into further health problems. The profit arm of Livox works with its non-profit arm to improve lives by selling licenses of its software to governments, professional organizations, healthcare providers, and those who can afford it.

The key to Livox's success has been the decision to harness technology and intellectual property rights, without which the product would not have seen the light of day and the innovation would never have come to the market. Livox is also a member of several entrepreneurship networks such as the Schwab Foundation and Artemisia and partners with The Florida Hospital to advance research. They are able to bridge the gap that can make the difference for someone with a disability to lead a dignified life.

Intangible resources are non-physical things like innovation, knowledge, goodwill, reputation, image, culture, and networks.[6] It is estimated that up to 75–90% of a firm's value can be intangible assets.[7] Intangible value comes from many resources and can be classified based on the perspective from which you look at them. In structured and highly regulated markets, the legal framework may provide you with intangible assets based on your intellectual property rights, trade secrets, copyrights, and even reputation that you can defend in a court of law.[8] Past history can give you an advantage in the marketplace — for example, Gavi had an advantage because of their association with the Bill & Melinda Gates Foundation and the seed fund they were given. History can be an advantage when it can leverage previous associations with people (networks), brands, customers, distributors, etc. Human capital is a source of general and expert knowledge and skills, and at a cumulative level, it is a source of culture. In addition, intangible value comes from organizational capital (structure, databases, partnerships, culture).[9] In the case of PT. Tirta Marta, discussed below, founder Sugianto had many sources of value — a lot of it was intangible — the patents, the goodwill of the business, and the networks, but he also had the tangible value — the factory and the financial assets (see Case Study 5.2).

Drivers of intangible value are many and can be financial or non-financial. Non-financial drivers are innovation (a combination of human, intellectual, and relational and structural capital),[10] quality, customer relations, management capabilities, alliances, technology, brand value, employee relations, and environmental and community issues.[11] Brands are known to contribute 20% or more of the value of a firm.[12] The biggest challenge an SEV will have

## Case Study 5.2: **PT. Tirta Marta (Environmental Sustainability, Indonesia)**

The company was established in 1971 as a pioneer in film-based flexible packaging manufacturing for consumer goods. Sugianto Tandio studied in the USA and worked as a Senior Engineer at 3M in the USA. In 1994, he bought the family business and soon returned to Indonesia in 2000. He had spent many years in research and millions of dollars trying to find an eco-friendly  version of conventional plastic bags. Conventional plastic can take 500–1,000 years to decompose. He launched two patented eco-friendly inventions — OXIUM® (launched in 2010, is a natural additive to plastic that ensures rapid degradation) and ECOPLAS® (launched in 2016, is a biodegradable plastic polymer made from tapioca). ECOPLAS became the first *Fair for Life*-certified bioplastic in the world, registered in Switzerland. This has provided jobs for farmers of tapioca, as this only grows in the tropics. Sugianto says for every 5,000 tons of plastic manufactured, 50,000 farmers are employed. Using the family network, he was soon able to get 90% of Indonesian modern markets and convenience stores to stock OXIUM® plastic shopping bags. ECOPLAS® is cheaper than other bioplastics and found customers like Zara, Bata, and Billabong.

is on how to covert intangible assets to value that is of tangible benefits. If you have great relationships — perhaps you struggle with the following question: How can we get finance or regulatory approvals or buy-in from communities? Can the expertise you have gained working with a wicked problem be turned into an opportunity — say consultancy — that also becomes an additional form of revenue?

According to Verna Allee, this is a three-stage process that involves an exchange analysis, an impact analysis, and a value analysis[13]:

(1) As an intangible asset is a negotiable form of a good, you will need to negotiate its value (in monetary or barter terms).

(2) You need to manage the deliverable side of this intangible good to ensure expectations are met. This may mean articulating the benefits, but it may also mean explaining the behind-the-scenes process and hours that go into meeting the deliverables.

(3) Ensure there is a clear articulation of both intangible and tangible assets in the business model. Kaplan and Norton use strategy maps[14] to visualize the linkages between the two.

Value is understanding the perceptions of costs or sacrifices, and benefits from the stakeholder point of view.[15] This may differ based on the stakeholder group, but understanding value from their perspective is a useful exercise and will help you identify trigger points. Ideally, there are two strategies used to increase value, reducing costs or increasing benefits[16] (see Exhibit 5.2).

Exhibit 5.2: **Perceived Value (Examples)**

| Benefits | Costs |
| --- | --- |
| Product (core, augmented, and ancillary) | Monetary cost (for product/service) |
| Service | Monetary cost (installation, use, security, and insurance) |
| Social value (image, relationships, and sharing) | Transportation (time, money, and effort) |
| Symbolic value | Time (to find, buy, pay, learn, use, and dispose) |
| Interaction value (this may be positive or negative) | Psychic cost |
| Safety/security/credibility | Other fears associated with risk |

*Source*: Compiled from multiple sources.

Value may accrue or get lost in various stages of the customer journey.[17] This term, customer journey, is borrowed from design thinking where you look at the user experience and try and focus on pain points. Pain points are moments of truth where there are negative evaluations of the brand. Various words are used like touch point or service encounters, but they are similar.[18] Value can be created before the actual consumption of service or product brand, during its consumption, and after consumption.[19] For an SEV, the first challenge is to define what the brand is about (very often it is the founder and the people associated with the cause) and then to figure out the assets that lead to value.

It is also important to find ways to take tacit knowledge present in the system and create explicit knowledge, so we can use the information and it becomes valuable. For example, if you made a trip to raise funds. The money could be used for the cause, it becomes an accounting item but was it valuable? By documenting your insights and having a track of people you met, you may also be able to create value. Today, you don't just need to spend time writing, you can record with voice notes, photographs, and videos. You can go and update this log and show how the contact was useful (maybe after years), again reinforcing the need to invest in networks. You may have insights on what went wrong that can be used in future to avoid the same mistake. Though technology is becoming a big driver of value, we forget people also drive technology. SEVs should have a good plan to harness the value of people as a resource.

**A moment of truth is when a customer or beneficiary (or stakeholder) is at that interaction point when he or she makes an evaluation (positive or negative) of the brand with which they are interacting. It may be even before they consume the actual product or service, or even post-consumption, which means you must understand the customer journey.**

Often the signals of trust, which is an important outcome of value, may differ from beneficiary to donor. For donors, signals are previous accomplishments shared by the company, third-party evaluations, financial ratios, name recognition, word of mouth (especially family and friends), sincerity of appeal, stories, size of the organization, and celebrity endorsements.[20] For beneficiaries, it is really staying power, promises delivered, and trust. An interesting document to read is the *Overhead Myth*, an open letter signed by BB Wise Giving Alliance, Guidestar, and Charity Navigator.[21] A lot of the value recommended comes from (1) demonstrating ethical practices and sharing data about performance, (2) managing toward results and understanding true costs, and (3) educating funders on real cost of results (more about this on the Intervention Strategy Plan in Chapter 7). Rarely can one founder do all of this, so you really need a strong team.

## 5.2. **Power of People and Alliances**

### 5.2.1. *Power of People*

Staffing often becomes the biggest overhead for SEVs. Part of the dilemma arises because founders are unable to identify skills gaps, and candidates often have generic skills or education.[22] The Better Business Bureau standards recommend 65% of funds should be spent on program costs and 35% on fundraising, while Charity Navigator recommends less than one-third should be spent on program costs and less than 10% on fundraising.[23] Most of the program cost is spent on human talent cost.[24] To cut costs, SEVs will often depend on volunteers. However, volunteers may not always have the expertise required, and SEV leaders need to make an analysis of time to train and manage volunteers and the cost of hiring professional expertise. Traditional volunteers (who volunteer out of passion, or for the cause) may often be engaged in the back end or in repetitive tasks.[25] This can cause dissatisfaction and feelings of being unappreciated. In fact, turnover for non-profits is often around 15–20%.[26] One method being used to manage this problem is the recruitment of professional volunteers from the corporate sector[27] or even through academic partnerships. Traditional volunteers need more personal relationships than corporate volunteers.

Corporate volunteers also need an investment of time. First you will need to find corporate sponsors, then create and advertise volunteer opportunities that are meaningful to employees, create a staff–volunteer relationship, and then plan an onboarding and supervision model.[28] It was found that volunteers and paid staff interchangeability was limited to around 12% of tasks.[29] In some cases, SEVs might also want to look at online volunteers. The growth of online communities and contribution to open-source platforms is one trend worth exploring. Again, the method of attracting these types of volunteers is dependent on building a dedicated community. Online volunteers can be used for online advocacy, online assessment and consultancy, to source and recruit offline volunteers or even convert offline volunteers to online volunteers, and to manage knowledge online.[30] When hiring, people look for multipliers (see Exhibit 5.3). Multipliers are beneficial to the organization.

Exhibit: 5.3: **Theory Box: Multipliers**

| There are two types of people in any organization — multipliers and diminishers. It is the fundamental way they lead others. An SEV's management team must be able to hire multipliers for long-term success. | | |
|---|---|---|
| How would you | Multiplier: (people are smart and will figure this out) multiplies the intelligence of others | Diminisher: (they will never figure this out without me) diminishes the intelligence of others |
| Manage talent? | Develop | Use |
| Approach mistakes? | Explore | Blame |
| Set direction? | Challenge | Tell |
| Make decisions? | Consult | Decide |
| Get things done? | Support | Control |
| Types | The Talent Manager (attracts talent and uses them at the highest contribution point); the Liberator (creates an environment requiring peoples best thinking and work); the Challenger (defines an opportunity that encourages people to stretch); the Debate-Maker (drives sound decisions through rigorous debate); the Investor (gives other people ownership for results and invests in their success). | The Empire Builder (hoards resources and underutilizes talent); the Tyrant (creates a tense environment that suppresses peoples thinking and capability); the Know-it All (gives directives that showcase how much they know); the Decision-Maker (makes centralized abrupt decisions that confuse the organization); the Micro Manager (drives through their personal involvement). |

*Source*: Compiled from Wiseman and McKeown.[31]

As an organization evolves, so must employees and the mind-set of an organization. In the early years, validation of the idea and becoming self-sufficient are key focus areas for a founder. As an organization gets better in managing its resources and plans, the focus will shift to ensure that the cause is not diluted, especially as the organization grows in people and markets and if the founder leaves. With time, the purpose of the organization may get lost or the conditions in which you operated in may no longer be the same. This may lead to mission drift and worse, loss of values. Organizations must find ways to reinforce systems to ensure that values and governance are robust. This may require developing a competency framework[32] and retraining and skills upgrading. Also, it may be important to provide role models for what values you are trying to articulate. Nothing is stronger than leading by example. Older workers may have the experience and can mentor newer employees.[33]

Here, change management is important. A recent McKinsey article talks of the following four conditions to manage change successfully: (1) a purpose to believe in, (2) reinforcement of systems, (3) skills required for change, and (4) consistent role models.[34] The following are some basic good practices all SEVs should adopt irrespective of their size: (1) have a clear code of conduct that aligns to its values; (2) should determine what is the corporate culture of the organization; (3) all roles and responsibilities should ideally be defined — at least work on a task inventory and the required skills — this will help in recruitment planning, appraisals, or even talent management; (4) work on employee retention and succession planning as attrition is high; (5) have a volunteer management program; and finally (6) governance and compliance strategy, even if they cannot afford auditors.

### 5.2.2 *Public–Private Partnerships: The Strength of Strategic Alliances*

Strategic Alliances are partnerships to help organizations reach their goals. It is considered "a *voluntarily initiated cooperative agreement between firms that involves exchange, sharing, or co-development, and it can include contributions by partners of capital, technology, or firm-specific assets … (where the) governance structure of the alliance is the formal structure participants use to formalize it.*"[35] While there is often a shared understanding of the common goals, what is often under-evaluated is the uncertainty costs of coordination and appropriation (transfer of knowledge or other propriety knowledge or resources).[36] SEVs have to be able to articulate what they bring to the table, especially when they are focusing on pooling of resources to create the interdependencies needed to make a strategic alliance work.[37] This is challenging, especially for new SEVs. The private sector can be a tremendous source of resources, but historically keeps alliances with the non-profit sector at an arm's length, especially if they are still establishing their legitimacy. They prefer to work with established partners (for example, Unilever with World Wildlife Fund or Yum! Restaurants with World Food Program).[38] Research in the corporate sector finds that over 50% of alliances fail and those based on technical needs often dissolve faster, while reorganization allows continuation of the alliance in some form.[39] In the developmental sector, there is not much research on this topic, but projects fail, get caught in an audit fraud, or get abandoned and forgotten.

Public–private partnerships (PPPs) are a special type of strategic alliance. The concept of PPPs began as a movement linked to the privatization of public assets and management or processes and outcomes in purview of the public sector.[40] The World Bank adopts the following definition of PPPs — *A long-term contract between a private party and a government entity, for providing a public asset or service, in which the private party bears significant risk and management responsibility and remuneration is linked to performance.*[41] This implies a spectrum set between two extreme ends where the government entity or private entity own and operate the assets. PPPs can have combinations of ownership, involvement at the operational level, revenue generation and sharing, and risk sharing or mitigation (see Exhibit 5.4).[42] Privatization differs from PPPs, as in PPP, the public sector continues to have a role, but in privatization, there is permanent transfer of ownership of an asset from the public sector to the private sector.[43] In nationalization, the reverse is true. Private assets are made public. This is a worry any successful private sector organization needs to consider, especially in fragile economies and when regulations are sparse.

Exhibit 5.4: **Types of PPP**

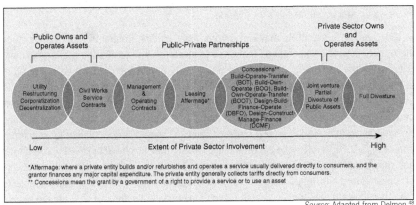

Source: Adapted from Delmon.[48]

Looking at PPPs from the point of view of the private sector, the private sector adopts a hybrid type of governance, in which as non-state actors (this includes NGOs, IGOs, and transnational corporations), they are involved in political steering and co-governance along with state actors for the provision of collective goods, and adopt governance functions that have formally been the sole authority of sovereign nation-states.[44] PPPs have become increasingly important since the 1992 World Summit for Sustainable Development in Rio de Janeiro[45] and is set in the Sustainable Development Goals.

PPPs are a type of strategic alliance, an outcome of the nature of the relationship between civil society, corporates, stakeholders, and governments. PPPs happen when *People and organisations from some combination of public, business and civil constituencies, who engage in voluntary, mutually beneficial, innovative relationships to address common societal aims through combining their resources and competencies.*[46] There are six possible areas of partnership: management reform, problem conversion, moral regeneration, risk shifting, restructuring public service, and power sharing.[47]

Basically, the objective of a PPP is to bring private sector efficiencies into the public domain. PPPs are not the same as public contracting, as the private entities bear more risk and responsibility. The contractual time arrangements vary from 1 to 3 years (service and management contracts) to lease, and concessions and build–operate–transfer models range from 8 to 30 years.[49] Initially, PPPs were seen as a government-led activity to get private sector involvement in the design, building, financing, and/or operation of existing or new infrastructure facilities and to improve services delivery and management of facilities that till then, were in the total jurisdiction of the public sector.[50] In the case of financing being offered by the public sector, a key question is affordability (who pays, when, and how do you manage the financial risks) and the legal and regulatory environment. Prison management has become a topic for privatization. While worldwide there are about 184 private prison facilities, USA has 158 and it is a US$1 billion growing business.[51] While governments have only saved 1% of total costs through privatization, the question remains — what is the purpose of a prison facility — incarnation or rehabilitation? Would it fall in the area of SEVs? Under which conditions? Would the public think differently it the focus was correctional facilities for minors?

In the case of SEVs, PPPs may not always have binding contracts but could include innovative, flexible collaborations that are inter-sectoral in nature, while the arrangement is formal — the terms are not binding to either party due to the transient nature of SEVs. In this case, these collaborations can be characterized by (1) jointly determined goals, (2) collaborative and consensus-based decision-making, (3) non-hierarchical and horizontal structures and processes, (4) trust-based and informal as well as formalized relationships, (5) synergistic interactions among partners, and (6) shared accountability for outcomes and results.[52] SEVs often begin with the problem that is characterized by complexity and may need proper framing to get public awareness and collaboration with a network of stakeholders and influencers, to reach a stage of action.[53] SEVs should be able to map their constituents' public benefit (which may provide legitimacy) with private benefit and aim for a high public benefit.[54] One way of creating value is storytelling. The Qessa Academy is a non-profit SEV dedicated to preserving the art of storytelling in Afghanistan (see Case Study 5.3).

## 5.3. **Create Value: Storytelling**

Storytelling is undervalued as a skill and for its ability to generate value. For resource-strapped entrepreneurs, stories are powerful tools to reach out to stakeholders. Research finds that the role of personal narratives help founders in resource acquisitions.[55] It is linked with leadership and motivation,[56] for fostering collaboration, teaching and problem sharing,[57] coping,[58] crisis resolution[59], and creating solidarity.[60] Stories are often used to collect evidence of impact of SEVs. Storytelling can be used for scenario analysis — the more authentic the stories are, the better the plan is.[61] The list goes on. The truth is that we are all irrational and stories appeal to us for sensemaking (see Exhibit 5.5). Sensemaking is an active process — giving information, meaning, and presenting associated responses.[62]

## Case Study 5.3: **The Qessa Academy (Afghanistan)**

Qessa Academy (translated from Dari, a type of Persian, as The Academy of Stories) is a school based in Kabul, Afghanistan. It is the first of its kind to train youth to preserve the culture of storytelling and provides them employment opportunities. There is a high rate of illiteracy (25%) in Afghanistan compounded by the long war. In the Afghan culture, the traditional storytellers are highly revered. The problem is that traditional storytellers are elderly, and the population demographics of the country are now mostly youth (68%).

In 2013, Qessa Academy opened its door to unemployed youth between the ages of 18 and 25 who were taught English, community development, and storytelling. The community development classes included topics like public health, environment, and human rights. The traditional stories (*qessah*) and folktales (*aufsanah*) focused on entertainment and education, while preserving the local heritage. The narratives were based on positive values.

The initial first-year students who finished the course (just 6) got an internship in Afghan foundations and Ministry of Education and performed publicly on radio and TV. The second year had 17 graduates. In a typical year, 20 students enroll in the Academy. Much of their mission is possible through grants. Qessa Academy uses the storytelling medium to disseminate technical information to illiterate audiences, particularly relating to public health, food security, irrigation, and mitigation of natural disasters.

Qessa Academy is a spin-off of Plain Ink, which was founded by Selene Biffi. Selene previously was involved with the United Nations in delivering education in Afghanistan, until her team came under attack by Taliban where 11 people were killed. Selene's determination brought her back to Afghanistan in a personal capacity to complete her project which was backed by the Afghan Ministry of Education. Plain Ink also works in rural communities in India to produce educational comics and children's books to engage communities and find local solutions to local problems. Plain Ink has distributed 7,000 comics on public health to those below the poverty line in India, and up to 80% of the students changed their habits after reading them. Plain Ink has gone on to build manpower in Italy where it has provided training on social entrepreneurship to over 1,000 young people, of which 50% have opened up a start-up.

Qessa focuses on positive stories that would give hope. For unemployed youth, the situation is not easy. Afghans live on less than US$2 per day, but the Talibans pay up to US$500 for new recruits.

Exhibit 5.5: **Theory on Irrationality**

*Irrationality can only be defined in terms of rationality* — Stuart Sutherland

Rational thinking has two forms — conclusions are drawn based on the knowledge one has that (1) is most likely correct or (2) most likely to achieve the end outcome. The assumption behind rational thinking is that there are laws governing the world that remain constant over time. So, while you can use rational means to achieve an end, there is probably no *rational end*. Irrationality is an action performed deliberately (while error is made voluntarily). We make irrational decisions for many reasons — the immediacy of salience (availability) of easy to remember information (stories that are meaningful linger longer than statistics), probably because of the emotions aroused in us. We may make wrong connections or assume wrong causes. There are a hundred causes that contribute to irrationality. For example, sometimes we fail to seek evidence that may be contradictory by ignorance or purposeful avoidance, to maintain our beliefs. Hence, humans are inconsistent in their decision-making and one thing is clear — we as humans value spontaneity as we link it to sincere emotions.

*Source*: Adapted from Sutherland. [63]

What makes a powerful story? While storytelling is a skill, most entrepreneurs would benefit from understanding the works of Joseph Campbell[64] who looked at the Hero's journey (see Exhibit 5.6, a rendition of Vogler's interpretation[65]). A story essentially has the following three stages:

Exhibit 5.6: **Stages of a Hero's Journey — Write Your Story Narrative**

| Act | Stage of a Journey | Your Story (Fill in) |
|---|---|---|
| Act I<br><br>Ordinary World | 1. Ordinary World — your life oblivious of your future quest. | |
| | 2. Call to Adventure (your trigger — what nudged you). | |
| | 3. Refusal, reluctance to undertake the journey (your doubts). | |
| | 4. Meeting with the mentor (or another artifact that persuades you). | |
| | 5. Crossing the Threshold (your point of no return). | |
| Act II<br><br>Special World | 6. Test, Allies, Enemies. | |
| | 7. The Big Test/Ordeal — the approach — what were your fears. Who had failed before. | |
| | 8. The Ordeal — the battle — how it played out. | |
| | 9. The Reward (what was the result, the benefit, and the win). | |
| | 10. The Road Back. | |
| Act III<br><br>Ordinary World | 11. Resurrection — the new, older, and wiser you. | |
| | 12. Return with the Elixir (Knowledge — what did you learn — what is now better). | |

(1) **Separation:** An ordinary person is called for an extraordinary journey. For SEV founders, a call may be the source of your inspiration — what motivates you.

(2) **Initiation:** This is the trials and tribulations phase. In the second stage, we see that though the Hero is reluctant, he is helped on to this journey by a person/event/thing (usually a mentor) and then he proceeds to the "other world". Often this stage is rarely solitary as help may come in unexpected ways — a partner, an investor, etc. The founder is able to conquer the challenges and prove he is now a Hero. However, he has still not returned to his world.

(3) **The Return:** The Founder returns to a more normal life, changed, wiser, and now master of two worlds. He now becomes the teacher. Stories are powerful methods to create intangible value and are often used in building brands.

The story of CDA (Case Study 5.4) is powerful — the name Clínicas del Azúcar translated from Spanish means *Sugar Clinics*. Developing a powerful brand that has a story and can communicate value is critical if you wish to scale.

## Case Study 5.4: **Clínicas del Azúcar (Mexico)**

Clínicas del Azúcar (CDA) is a chain of low-cost diabetes clinics. It was founded by Javier Lozano in 2010 and opened its first clinic in 2011. Javier's mother had type-II diabetes. Mexico ranks 5th highest in diabetes as a country. It is the second largest cause of death in Mexico after heart diseases. It is the first cause of amputations and blindness and in some cases has lead to suicides. Historically, you had to be wealthy if you wanted to be treated for diabetes, so, it quickly began being called *The Disease of the Rich*. You would need up to US$12,000 pesos monthly for treatment, if you were to visit a private clinic. Javier witnessed the inequality of treatment first-hand when he worked in the non-profit sector focusing on health and nutrition. His mother's struggle with the management of the disease with private insurance made him wonder about the difficulty for other people who could not even access care.

Javier got an MBA from MIT Sloan Management, and he was excited about using technology to solve this problem. He wanted to build something convenient and affordable. A one-stop shop for diabetes care. CDA's mission was to successfully reach patients at the bottom of the pyramid.

CDA has used the assembly-line concept in the health clinic. The treatment offered ranges from $300 to $600 pesos for consultation with a specialist, US$30–600 pesos for lab work, and $250–800 pesos for diagnosis to prevent complications. The annual subscription pricing is innovative in this sector. Treatment for 1 year would be less than one-third of what was being offered at that time. CDA allows flexible payments — weekly, biweekly, or monthly installments, as well as a full payment. The proprietary electronic system helps create a personalized treatment plan for each patient.

The business model has reduced appointment times by 80%, lowered diabetes complication rates by 60%, and reduced patients' annual costs by 75%. At the end of 2018, The International Finance Corporation (IFC), a member of the World Bank Group, announced an equity investment in CDA, which at that time became the largest chain of specialized diabetes clinics in Mexico. CDA's impact metrics include figures like penetration of patients in lower income segments and continuous improvements in blood sugar levels of those patients.

## 5.4. **Brand and Reputation**

Brands are intangible in nature and can be a powerful medium to communicate value. There are tangible elements in a brand like the name, logo, symbols, color, the product, or even the people that are associated with a brand. Founders must often make a choice whether the key element of the brand is the person or the brand itself that is represented by the product or service or the people. This crucial question will determine the longevity of the brand.

Combining the BrandZ[66] model, Brand Resonance pyramid,[67] and theory on loyalty bonds, it is obvious that there are several stages to develop a brand and build loyalty to the brand (see Exhibit 5.7).

Exhibit 5.7:  **Brand and Loyalty Bonds Strategy**

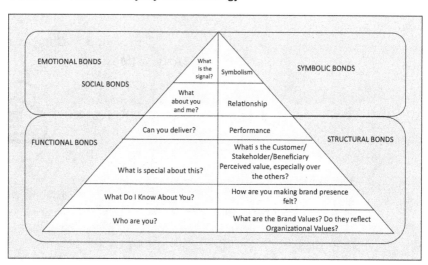

**Stage 1 — Brand Values:** This begins with your core values — what motivates you? What are you inherently about? What are the fundamental values and principles that your SEV or brand is defined by? Many researchers call this the brand essence. This is intangible in nature. It is the belief that will spread through the culture of the organization and influence your customers.[68] It means eventually that this belief will be defined by your customers and you need to audit to make sure your brand essence and values are being properly communicated.[69] It is essential you cross-reference this with your vision (the world you want to see) and your mission statement (what you do to make it happen).[70]

**Stage 2 — Brand Presence:** How do you make your presence felt? Here, you tangibilize the intangible through little points of interactions or *touchpoints*. It can be visual cues, auditory cues, verbal cues, etc. Some interaction points may be the technology, your employees and volunteers, other customers, and even places or events.[71]

**Stage 3 — Perceived Value:** This is in reference to competitive or substitute offerings (look at Exhibit 5.2). Value is intangible in nature. In marketing, we call this *augmented product benefits.*[72]

**Stage 4 — Performance:** It is an understanding of whether you can deliver what you are perceived to promise. Ideally, functional promises need to be met, but higher order promises — emotional, relationship, etc. — form much of the intangible value.

**Stage 5 — Brand Relationships or Associations:** Here, you can associate your brand with other brands to get a *halo effect*, a positive spillover of goodwill.[73]

**Stage 6 — Symbolism:** This is intangible, and you wish to understand what your beneficiary or customer feels by associating with you. Brand symbols can be explicit or implicit. This may impact Stage 2 of the brand and the Loyalty Bonds Strategy Model (Exhibit 5.7). Brand symbolism has a net positive effect on brand warmth (the warm fuzzy feeling you get when you think of your brand), which leads to a greater likelihood of endorsing a non-profit brand online.[74]

Often the bonds used to create loyalty in marginalized communities are social bonds and symbolic bonds (about hope), and the product and service satisfaction comes later (functional bonds). This is because trust is a rare commodity in these communities. Ideally, if you want to develop a proper long-term brand strategy, you begin from the bottom of the pyramid. Bonds that develop because of the structural reasons (have little choice in the matter), financial ties (price based), or functional promises (all about the product or service) will have to still grow symbolic, social, and emotional bonds, if they are to increase loyalty.

A brand differs from reputation, which is about the organization. It is defined as the stakeholder's overall evaluation of a company over time, based on the stakeholder's direct experiences with the company, any other form of communication and symbolism that provides information about the firm's actions, and/or a comparison with the actions of other leading rivals.[75] For reputation management, you will need to ask three basic questions as follows: (1) Who is the evaluator? (2) What is being assessed? (3) How does context influence the judgment? Brands can contribute to reputation[76] but this may not be necessarily so. SEVs with a cash flow problem should not waste too much time on brand development. However, that being said — you build brands and reputation by under-promising and over-delivering.

## You build brands and reputation by under-promising and over-delivering.

Non-profits are suffering from lack of public trust. Sadly the lowest public trust indicators seem to be for civil rights institutions, environment, education, and arts and culture.[77] SEVs need to regularly take stock of their inventory of trust (see Exhibit 5.8). Trust can be "rented"[78] by the alliances and partnerships with more reputable partners or stronger brands. Trust is also cultivated through a strong communication strategy, one of which is using media effectively.

Exhibit 5.8: **Building and Destroying Trust**

| Why do You Trust | Why Don't You Trust |
|---|---|
| (1) Reputation Built Over Time — "A good reputation and history of giving a high percentage of money collected to the charities." | (1) Greed and High Overhead — "That their CEOs are overpaid and a small portion of income goes to the intended targets." "When I see the leaders eating at expensive restaurants, driving big cars, wearing diamonds, and going on expensive trips." |
| (2) Honest and Transparent — "What makes me trust a charity is transparency. In that, I mean transparency in how the donations are allocated and exactly who gets what." "You know where the money is going and you see it working." | (2) Reputation and Bad News — "Rumors". "Having a bad reputation or being fairly new." |
| (3) Research, Rating, and Credentials — "Concrete proof that donations are used for their stated purpose." | (3) Lack of Honesty and Transparency —"Their vagueness of purpose". "Never were vetted and never heard of them." "Not knowing where all the monies donated go." |

*Source*: Adapted from Cha.[79]

## 5.5. **Managing Media**

One of the most important reasons for using media is awareness. A study in UK found that while 75% of those surveyed support social enterprises, only 21% actually know what they were about.[80] More awareness helps build credibility, legitimacy, reputation, and brand value. This of course can translate into a buy-in or sales. Media can also be helpful in crisis situations as it can give a more sympathetic perspective of events.

One of the challenges of managing media is that it requires an investment of resources. Especially as you go global with products, people, assets, or brands. You want to use media to create a positive frame of mind. Social media (Facebook, LinkedIn, Twitter, Instagram, Pinterest, and Snapchat) are increasingly being preferred by SEVs. Sometimes founders think social media is an easy method to communicate. Contrary to expectations, social media is not an easy tool to manage. It remains challenging as it requires an almost 24/7 approach to being connected, curated, and managed.[81]

If you do use social media, try and separate the founder brand and company or product brand on social media pages to minimize confusion between brands and perhaps personal opinions versus corporate opinions. Tools like *Hootsuite* are useful to do this. It is important to remember that the way you frame a message might determine its benefits (see Exhibit 5.9). The challenge for many founders is to not let the headiness of being a *celebrity* distract you from the purpose of the work. Media can also be a two-edged sword (see Case Study 4.4 of Chapter 4). Chapter 6 will also cover some techniques on crisis management that may be relevant to this section.

Exhibit 5.9: **Framing of Media Messages**

| What is Framed | Description | Example |
|---|---|---|
| Situations | Everyday living | Describe and define overall situations from daily life (slice of life). Documentary on White Helmets to bring awareness on Syria. |
| Attributes | Direct attention to focal attributes | Use of pictures, problems faced, past experience of the product, positioning to give product meaningfulness. UNHCR's Instagram account on refugees. |
| Choices | Showing alternatives (with biases toward a focal choice) | Focus on loss and risk. Smoking and ads on cancer. |
| Actions | Using persuasive techniques to act | Focusing on gains or goals. Education and focus on employment. |
| Issues | Debate or discussion | Alternate realities of social issues — example vaccines. Can use advocates or sponsors. |
| Responsibility | Find a reason for the situation | Can be uncontrolled or controlled, example alcoholism is a societal issue or an individual issue that requires medication? This also includes legal and moral responsibility. |
| News | Use current news and cultural reference points | For example, "climate change" can use celebrity endorsement. |

*Source*: Adapted from Hallahan.[82]

Because SEVs work in gray areas, explaining value is difficult. A study on social value[83] found the following six important qualities:

(1) **Audacity:** The ability to embrace big and bold solutions. Example: Case Study 2.3 of Chapter 2.

(2) **Connectivity:** Engaging deeply with the communities being served and creating buy-in among the many constituencies who can affect the outcomes. Example: Case Study 3.3 of Chapter 3.

(3) **Capacity:** Using data to understand trends, predict behavior, and improve. Example: Case Study 5.4 of Chapter 5.

(4) **Ingenuity:** Disrupting entrenched approaches with innovative solutions. Example: Case Study 2.1 of Chapter 2.

(5) **Tenacity:** Leveraging the time, relationships, sweat, and resources required to persevere. Example: Case Study 3.2 of Chapter 3.

(6) **Diversity:** Generating revenue or value and support from multiple sources. Example: Case Study 1.4 of Chapter 1.

Of course, a single organization can generate value on multiple fronts, but it is important to decide what you want to showcase. The most important thing is to figure out what works for you. Looking for mentors, investors, and collaborators? LinkedIn could be a good choice. If you are looking for crowdsourcing, you should definitely consider social media specific to what your target audience prefers. You should keep in mind that the half-life period of social media is very low. While no one knows the exact period, at the higher end, a half-life of a Tweet is 24 minutes versus 90 minutes for a Facebook post.[84]

Every SEV should consider creating a media strategy. There are several points to consider as follows:

(1) Who is your target audience? Different stakeholders may be comfortable with different types of media.

(2) What is your measurable objective? Do you want to look at likes, retweets, or even better, sales, enquiries, enrollments, etc.?

(3) What are the resources you are willing to put aside for this? This may include things like time but also money for events, travel for interviews, and hosting media.

(4) What types of media will you use? Make the list a wish list. With social media if you cannot be regular in posting or updating content, this will be a challenge.

(5) What have you learnt from your past experiences? Do a regular review and put up learnings. This will help you hone your media strategy better.

(6) What is your damage control plan? Do you have access to advisors or volunteers who can help?

In conclusion, resource management is an important topic and much needed if you wish to scale or even for long-term survival.

## 5.6. Managing Resources: A Recap

It is possible that an SEV may have more resources than they are aware. It is important to reflect and audit both intangible and tangible resources. This is important even in the bootstrapping phases, as barter is very common. For any stakeholder, perceived value is a function of costs and benefits. Understanding this is critical when you approach various stakeholders to get buy-in. It is simply an articulation of "What's in it for me?" This chapter highlights the power of storytelling, building a brand, and managing media.

## 5.7. Questions

### Question 1
Company x is a small SEV start-up. They have a high-tech platform but they don't have the manpower to manage it 24/7. Should they use barter of volunteerism? Would it matter if the tech platform was for medical outreach rather than as a social awareness tech platform?

### Question 2
Take any SEV you are familiar with — do a perceived value analysis for at least two stakeholders, one being the beneficiary.

### Question 3
Use the storytelling format in Exhibit 5.6 to write your own Hero's Journey.

## Question 4

For an SEV you are familiar with, use the Brand and Loyalty Bonds Strategy to find an area of improvement and a media strategy to enhance the brand.

## Question 5

A new start-up has created a technology product that helps social introverts get out of their comfort zone. It is a talking watch. They want to focus on elderly and teenagers who may not be getting the help they need and hence may end up with depression or worse be thinking of suicide. Looking at Exhibit 5.9, what frame would be beneficial for which stakeholder group? What medium would you use? How could you use the social value qualities of audacity, connectivity, capacity, ingenuity, tenacity, and diversity?

# Sources

### Case Study 5.1: Lixox (Brazil)

Compiled from Arthur, J. (2018), "#Innovate4Health: Livox gives disability a voice in brazil and beyond," *Medium*, dated 24 October, Available https://medium.com/innovate4health/innovate4health-livox-gives-disability-a-voice-in-brazil-and-beyond-cb5cbde93d34; MIT Solve (2019), *Livox*, Available: https://solve.mit.edu/challenges/teachers-and-educators/solutions/4677 [Accessed 11 April 2019] [Accessed 15 May 2019]; Global Innovation Exchange (2019), *Livox*, Available: https://www.globalinnovationexchange.org/innovation/livox [Accessed 20 April 2019]; Google Impact Challenge (nd), *Inclusion without Borders – Livox*, Available: https://www.google.org/impactchallenge/disabilities/grantees/inclusion-with-borders-livox.html; Harris, B. (2018), "The his man quit his job and built a whole company so he could talk to his daughter," *WEF*, dated 5 January, Available: https://www.weforum.org/agenda/2018/01/this-man-made-an-app-so-he-could-give-his-daughter-a-voice/ [Accessed 20 April 2019]; Lane, B. (2016), "This app helps the world's largest minority group to communicate and thrive," *Unreasonable Is*, dated 21 December, Available: https://unreasonable.is/an-app-that-helps-the-worlds-largest-minority-to-thrive/ [Accessed 20 April 2019]; Livox website: Available: http://www.livox.com.br/en/functionalities/ [Accessed 20 April 2019]; WHO (2019), *NVI Year in Review – 2018*, Available https://www.who.int/disabilities/en/ [Accessed 20 April 2019].

### Case Study 5.2: PT. Tirta Marta (Indonesia)

Endeavor (2013), *Sugianto Tandio*, Available: https://endeavor.org/entrepreneur/sugianto-tandio/ [Accessed 20 April 2019]; Global Business Guide (nd), *Tirta Marta*, Available: http://www.gbgindonesia.com/en/manufacturing/directory/2014/tirta_marta/interview.php [Accessed 20 April 2019]; Pt. TirtaMarta (2019), *About Us*, Available: http://www.tirtamarta.com/green-plastic-solutions/about-us/ [Accessed 20 April 2019]; Job Street (2010), "Sugianto Tandio: Saving the world 1 plastic bag at a time," Available: https://www.jobstreet.com.ph/career-resources/sugianto-tandio#.XLhdSy-B0lI [Accessed 20 April 2019]; Rottenberg, L. (2014), *Crazy is a Compliment: The Power of Zigging When Everyone Else Zags*, Penguin Randon House: New York; Sabarini, P. (2013), Sugianto Tandio: Making eco-friendly plastic, Jakarta Post, dated 14 January, Available: http://www.thejakartapost.com/news/2013/01/14/sugianto-tandio-making-eco-friendly-plastic.html [Accessed 20 April 2019]; Tandio, J. (2012), "Cassava: An Indonesian solution to the global waste problem: Sugianto Tandio at TEDxJakSel," TEDx, Available: https://www.youtube.com/watch?v=jON7MvJ1xOk [Accessed 18 April 2019].

### Case Study 5.3: The Quessa Academy (Afghanistan)

Selene Biffi (2019), LinkedIn Profile: https://www.linkedin.com/in/selenebiffi [Accessed 18 April 2019]; The Ink Blog (2017), "Selene Biffi talks about her dedication for creating economic and educational opportunities for Afghan youth," dated 27 February, Available: http://www.inktalks.com/blog/fellows-corner-selene-biffi/ [Accessed 20 April 2019]; UNESCO (2017), "Enhancement of literacy in afghanistan (ELA) programme," INESCO office in Kabul," Available: http://www.unesco.org/new/en/kabul/education/youth-and-adult-education/enhancement-of-literacy-in-afghanistan-iii/ [Accessed 21 April 2019]; Biffie, S. (2017), "PLAIN INK: Stories crafting a better world," *Changemakers*, Available: https://www.changemakers.com/globalgoals2015/entries/plain-ink [Accessed 20 April 2019].

### Case Study 5.4: Clínicas del Azúcar (Mexico)

*Clínicas del Azúcar* (2018), Available: http://www.clinicasdelazucar.com/ [Accessed 20 April 2019]; Endeavor (2019), *Javier Lozano*, Available: https://endeavor.org/entrepreneur/javier-lozano/ [Accessed 20 April 2019]; Federation Mexicana de Diabetes (2017), "Defunciones por diabetes en México," Available: Federación Mexicana de Diabetes, A.C.: http://fmdiabetes.org/defunciones-diabetes-mexico-2/ [Accessed 20 April 2019]; IFC (2018), "IFC Invests in Clínicas del Azucar to promote diabetes control in México," Available: https://ifcextapps.ifc.org/IFCExt/Pressroom/IFCPressRoom.nsf/0/2E5C35D61FDB34AD852583450052C70C [Accessed 20 April 2019]; International Diabetes Federation. (nd), Countries with the highest number of diabetics worldwide in 2017 (in millions)," *The Statistics Portal*, Available: https://www.statista.com/statistics/281082/countries-with-highest-number-of-diabetics/ [Accessed 19 May 2018]; Legatum Center for Development, MIT (2016), "Clínicas del Azúcar," *Youtube*, dated 8 June, Available: https://www.youtube.com/watch?v=-VpeH0oMoLg [Accessed 20 April 2019]; Lozanso, J. (nd), "Clínicas del Azúcar: Data-mining and co-creation of licensing model for low-cost specialized diabetes," *Changemakers*, Available: https://www.changemakers.com/makingmorehealth/entries/cl%C3%ADnicas-del-azúcar [Accessed 20 April 2019]; Social Impact Incentives (SIINC) (2017), Case Study: Clínicas Del Azúcar — To attract investment and create impact at scale, Available: https://www.roots-of-impact.org/wp-content/uploads/2017/06/SIINC-Case-StudiesCdA-FINAL.pdf [Accessed 20 April 2019].

# ENDNOTES

1   Bruton, G. D. and Rubanik, Y. (2002), "Resources of the firm, Russian high-technology startups, and firm growth", *Journal of Business Venturing*, 17(6): 553–576.
2   Guidestar provides some excellent resources in this topic for example: provhttps://learn.guidestar.org/products/us-nonprofits-financial-health
3   Kogut, B. and Metiu, A. (2001), "Open-source software development and distributed innovation," *Oxford Review of Economic Policy*, 17(2): 248–264. Look at the following article: Jones, J. E. (2017), "Open source software is philanthropy," *Stanford Social Innovation Review*, Available: https://ssir.org/articles/entry/open_source_software_is_philanthropy# [Accessed 15 April 2019]. Here are some additional sources: https://www.wildapricot.com/articles/199-free-or-cheap-online-nonprofit-tools.
4   Zeschky, M., Widenmayer, B. and Gassmann, O. (2011), "Frugal innovation in emerging markets," *Research-Technology Management*, 54(4): 38–45.
5   Society for Non Profits (nd), *Pros and Cons: Grants*, Available https://www.snpo.org/funding/grants.php [Accessed 17 April 2019].
6   Hall, R. (1993), "A framework linking intangible resources and capabilities to sustainable competitive advantage," *Strategic Management Journal*, 14(8): 607–618.
7   McDonald, M. (2009), "Linking intangible assets to shareholder value," *Journal of Digital Asset Management*, 5, 126–134.
8   Coyne, K. P. (1986), "Sustainable competitive advantage — What it is and what it is not," *Business Horizons*, Jan/Feb: 54–61.
9   Fernández, E., Montes, J. M. and Vázquez, C. J. (2000), "Typology and strategic analysis of intangible resources: A resource-based approach," *Technovation*, 20(2): 81–92.
10  do Rosário Cabrita, M. and Vaz, J. L. (2005), "Intellectual capital and value creation: Evidence from the Portuguese banking industry," *Electronic Journal of Knowledge Management*, 4(1): 11–20.
11  Kalafut, P. C. and Low, J. (2001), "The value creation index: Quantifying intangible value," *Strategy & Leadership*, 29(5): 9–15.
12  McDonald, M. (2009), *Op. cit.*
13  Allee, V. (2008), "Value network analysis and value conversion of tangible and intangible assets," *Journal of Intellectual Capital*, 9(1): 5–24.
14  Kaplan, R. S. and Norton, D. P. (2003), *Strategy Maps — Converting Intangible Assets into Tangible Outcomes*, Harvard Business School Press, Boston, MA.
15  Monroe, K.B. (1991), *Pricing — Making Profitable Decisions*, McGraw-Hill, New York, NY.
16  Ravald, A. and Grönroos, C. (1996), "The value concept and relationship marketing", *European Journal of Marketing*, 30(2): 19–30.
17  Rawson, A., Duncan, E. and Jones, C. (2013), "The truth about customer experience", *Harvard Business Review*, 91(9): 90–98.
18  Halvorsrud, R., Kvale, K. and Følstad, A. (2016), "Improving service quality through customer journey analysis," *Journal of Service Theory and Practice*, 26(6): 840–867.
19  Voorhees, C. M., Fombelle, P. W., Gregoire, Y., Bone, S., Gustafsson, A., Sousa, R. and Walkowiak, T. (2017), "Service encounters, experiences and the customer journey: Defining the field and a call to expand our lens," *Journal of Business Research*, 79: 269–280.

20  Give.Org (2018), *Donor Trust Report*, BBB Wise Giving, Available: https://www.give.org/docs/default-source/donor-trust-library/give-org-donor-trust-report.pdf [Accessed 1 April 2019].

21  The Overhead Myth (nd), Available: http://s5770.pcdn.co/wp-content/uploads/2014/10/Overhead-Myth_Letter-to-the-Nonprofits-of-America.pdf [Accessed 12 April 2019].

22  Lyon and Ramsden identify gaps in management, largely traditional. Lyon, F. and Ramsden, M. (2006), "Developing fledgling social enterprises? A study of the support required and means of delivering it," *Social Enterprise Journal*, 2(1): 27–41.

23  Sessoms, G. How Much Can a Non-Profit Legally Spend on Overhead?, Small Business, Available: https://smallbusiness.chron.com/much-can-nonprofit-legally-spend-overhead-72388.html [Accessed 12 April 2019].

24  Upholt, G. and Stahl, R. (2013), *The Nonprofit Talent Ratio*, Talent Philanthropy Project In Partnership with Research Center for Leadership in Action, NYU Wagner.

25  McDonald, C. and Warburton, J. (2000), "Responses to Change? Volunteering in non- profit welfare organisations in turbulent times," Paper presented at the Australia and New Zealand Third Sector Research Fifth National Conference, *Partnership & Activism*, 2–5 December, University of Western Sydney.

26  CIPD (2009), *Annual survey report 2009*, Available: https://www.educationandemployers.org/wp-content/uploads/2014/06/recruitment-retention-and-turnover-cipd.pdf [Accessed 13 April 2019].

27  Points of Light Foundation (2000), *The Corporate Volunteer Program as a Strategic Resource: The Link Grows Stronger*, Washington, DC: The Points of Light Foundation.

28  Zappalà, G., Parker, B. and Green, V. (2001), "The "new face" of volunteering in social enterprises: The Smith Family experience," *Background Paper No. 2*, Research & Advocacy Team, The Smith Family.

29  Handy, F., Mook, L. and Quarter, J. (2008), "The interchangeability of paid staff and volunteers in nonprofit organizations," *Nonprofit and Voluntary Sector Quarterly*, 37(1): 76–92.

30  Peña-López, I. (2007) "Online volunteers: Knowledge managers in nonprofits," *The Journal of Information Technology in Social Change*, Spring (1): 142–159.

31  Wiseman, L. and McKeown, G. (2010), *Multipliers: How the Best Leaders Make Everyone Smarter*, HarperCollins: NY.

32  Royce, M. (2007), "Using human resource management tools to support social enterprise: Emerging themes from the sector," *Social Enterprise Journal*, 3(1): 10–19.

33  Agarwal, D., Bershin, J. and Lahiri, G. (2018), "The longevity dividend: Work in an era of 100-year lives — 2018 Global Human Capital Trends," *Deloitte Insights*, Available: https://www2.deloitte.com/insights/us/en/focus/human-capital-trends/2018/advantages-implications-of-aging-workforce.html?zd_source=hrt&zd_campaign=2895&zd_term=sushmanbiswas [Accessed 18 April 2019].

34  Lawson, E. and Proce, C. (2003), "The psychology of change management," *McKinsey Quarterly*, Available: https://www.mckinsey.com/business-functions/organization/our-insights/the-psychology-of-change-management [Accessed 15 April 2019].

35  Gulati, R. and Singh, H. (1998), "The architecture of cooperation: managing coordination costs and appropriation concerns in strategic alliances," *Administrative Science Quarterly*, p. 781.

36  *Ibid.*, p. 781.

37  Thompson, J. D. (1967), *Organizations in Action: Social Science Bases of Administration*, New York: McGraw-Hill.

38  Rondinelli, D. A. and London, T. (2003), "How corporations and environmental groups cooperate: Assessing cross-sector alliances and collaborations," *The Academy of Management Executive*, 17(1): 61–76.

39  Li, L., Jiang, F., Pei, Y. and Jiang, N. (2017), "Entrepreneurial orientation and strategic alliance success: The contingency role of relational factors," *Journal of Business Research*, 72: 46–56; Ellis, C. (1996), "Making strategic alliances succeed," *Harvard Business Review*, 4: 8–9; Dussauge, P., Garrette, B. and Mitchell, W. (2000), "Learning from competing partners: Outcomes and durations of scale and link alliances in Europe, North America and Asia," *Strategic Management Journal*, 21(2): 99–12.

40  Linder, S. H. (1999), "Coming to terms with the public-private partnership: A grammar of multiple meanings," *American Behavioral Scientist*, 43(1): 35–51.

41  World Bank (2018), *Introduction*, PPP Knowledge Lab, Available: https://pppknowledgelab.org/guide/sections/1-introduction [Accessed 13 January 2018].

42  Delmon, J. (2010), "Understanding options for public-private partnerships in infrastructure," *Research Working Paper 5173*, Washington DC: World Bank.

43  Farquharson, E., Torres de Mästle, E., Yescombe, E. R. and Encinas, J. (2011), *How to Engage with the Private Sector in Public-Private Partnerships in Emerging Markets*, Washington DC: World Bank.

44  Schäferhoff, M., Campe, S. and Kaan, C. (2009), "Transnational public-private partnerships in international relations: Making sense of concepts, research frameworks, and results," *International Studies Review*, 11(3): 451–474.

45  Murphy D. F. and Bendell J. (1999), *Partners in Time? Business, NGOs and Sustainable Development*,. UNRISD: Geneva.

46  Nelson J. and Zadek S. (2000), *Partnership Alchemy: New Social Partnerships in Europe*, Copenhagen Centre: Copenhagen: 14.

47  Linder, S. H. (1999), "Coming to terms with the public-private partnership: A grammar of multiple meanings," *American Behavioral Scientist*, 43(1): 35–51.

48  Delmon, J. (2010), *Op. cit.*

49  Farlam, P. (2005), "Assessing public-private partnerships in Africa," *Nepad Policy Series*, Johannesburg: South African Institute of African Affairs.

50  Farquharson, E., Torres de Mästle, E., Yescombe, E. R. and Encinas, J. (2011), *Op. cit.*

51  Austin, J. and Coventry, G. (2001), *Emerging Issues on Privatised Prisons*, Washington D.C.: Bureau of Justice Assistance.

52  Brinkerhoff, D. W. and Brinkerhoff, J. M. (2011), "Public–private partnerships: Perspectives on Purposes, Publicness, and Good Governance," *Public Administration and Development*, 31(1): 2–14.

53  Waddock, S. A. and Post, J. E. (1991), "Social Entrepreneurs and Catalytic Change," *Public Administration Review*, 393–401.

54  Brinkerhoff, D. W. and Brinkerhoff, J. M. (2011), *Op. cit.*

55  Martens, M. L., Jennings, J. E. and Jennings, P. D. (2007), "Do the stories they tell get them the money they need? The role of entrepreneurial narratives in resource acquisition," *Academy of Management Journal*, 50(5): 1107–1132.

56  Forster, N., Cebis, M., Majteles, S., Mathur, A., Morgan, R., Preuss, J., ... and Wilkinson, D. (1999), "The role of story-telling in organizational leadership," *Leadership & Organization Development Journal*, 20(1): 11–17.

57  Haigh, C. and Hardy, P. (2011), "Tell me a story – a conceptual exploration of storytelling in healthcare education," *Nurse Education Today*, 31(4): 408–411.

58  *Ibid.*

59  Stephens Balakrishnan, M. (2011), "Protecting from brand burn during times of crisis: Mumbai 26/11: a case of the Taj Mahal Palace and Tower Hotel," *Management Research Review*, 34(12): 1309–1334.

60  Gill, R. (2011), "Using storytelling to maintain employee loyalty during change," *International Journal of Business and Social Science*, 2(15): 23–32.

61  Rasmussen, L. B. (2008), "The narrative aspect of scenario building – How story telling may give people a memory of the future," In *Cognition, Communication and Interaction*, Springer, London, pp. 174–194.

62  Thomas, J. B., Clark, S. M. and Gioia, D. A. (1993), "Strategic sensemaking and organizational performance: Linkages among scanning, interpretation, actions, and outcomes," *Academy of Management Journal*, 36: 239–270.

63  Sutherland, S. (1992), *Irrationality: The Enemy Within*, Constable and Company.

64  Cambell, J. (2004), *The Hero with a Thousand Faces*, Bollingen Series, Princeton University Press: NJ.

65  Vogler, C. (1985), *A Practical Guide to Joseph Campbell's the Hero with a Thousand Faces. Hero's Journey.*

66  BrandZ (nd), Available: https://brandz.com/article/value-drivers-model-how-do-brands-drive-value-growth-33 [Accessed 19 April 2019].

67  Keller, K. L. (2013), *Strategic Brand Management: Building, Measuring, and Managing Brand Equity*, Pearson Education Limited.

68  Newman, G. E. and Dhar, R. (2014), "Authenticity is contagious: Brand essence and the original source of production," *Journal of Marketing Research*, 51(3): 371–386.

69  Van Rekom, J., Jacobs, G., Verlegh, P. W. and Podnar, K. (2006), "Capturing the essence of a corporate brand personality: A Western brand in Eastern Europe," *Journal of Brand Management*, 14(1–2): 114–124.

70  Miltenburg, M. (2019), *Brand the Change*, BIS Publishers: Amsterdam

71   *Ibid.*

72   Kotler, P. (2012). Kotler on Marketing. Simon and Schuster.

73   Beckwith, N. E., Kassarjian, H. H. and Lehmann, D. R. (1978), "Halo effects in marketing research: Review and prognosis," *ACR North American Advances.*

74   Bernritter, S. F., Verlegh, P. W. and Smit, E. G. (2016), "Why nonprofits are easier to endorse on social media: The roles of warmth and brand symbolism," *Journal of Interactive Marketing*, 33: 27–42.

75   Gotsi, M. and Wilson, A. M. (2001), "Corporate reputation: Seeking a definition," *Corporate Communications: An International Journal*, 6(1): 24–30.

76   Geissler, U., and Einwiller, S. (2000), "Branding cyberpreneurs & challenges for communications management in the 21st century," In: Boyle, T. J., Hinrichs, B. and Klenke, K. (eds.), *Proceedings of the 18th AoM/IAoM Annual Conference*, Chesapeake, pp. 39–46.

77   Give.org (2018), *Op. cit.*

78   Choi, S.-Y., Stahl, D. O. and Whinston, A. B. (1997), *The Economics of Electronic Commerce*, Macmillan Technical Publishing, Indianapolis, Indiana, pp. 239–241.

79   Give.org (2018), *Op. cit.*

80   Jervis, J. (2013), "Social enterprises: Popular but confusing, says study," *The Guardian*, dated 8 January, Available: https://www.theguardian.com/social-enterprise-network/2013/jan/08/social-enterprise-popular-confusing-study [Accessed 15 April 2019]

81   Some interesting ideas are presented here: Corriveau, S. (nd), *Ways Social Enterprises Can Harness the Power of the Web*, Available: https://www.centreforsocialenterprise.com/social-enterprises-power-of-web/ [Accessed 20 April 2019].

82   Hallahan, K. (1999), "Seven models of framing: Implications for public relations," *Journal of Public Relations Research*, 11(3): 205–242.

83   Ukman, L. (2017), "What is social capital value and how do we measure it?," *WEF*, dated 1 May, Available: https://www.weforum.org/agenda/2017/05/how-to-measure-the-value-of-the-homeless-world-cup/ [Accessed 20 April 2019].

84   Rey, B. (2014), *Wiselytics*, dated 5 March, Available: http://www.wiselytics.com/blog/tweet-isbillion-time-shorter-than-carbon14/ [Accessed 20 April 2019].

# INTER-NATIONAL-IZATION: BRANDS, SOCIAL INNOVATION, AND POWER OF NETWORKS

## Chapter Objectives

➢ Differentiate the concepts of internationalization and globalization.

➢ Comprehend and use social innovation to manage scale.

➢ Identify the characteristics of global brands.

➢ Create a strategy using networks to internationalize.

➢ Define trust and design strategies to maintain trust with stakeholders.

➢ Explain and predict optimal crisis management techniques.

➢ **Cases:** Last Mile Health (health: Liberia), International Humanitarian City (humanitarian logistics: Dubai, UAE), Girl Effect (culture: Malawi, Rwanda, Ethiopia), and Oxfam (aid: Haiti).

## 6.1. **Internationalization and Globalization**

Unlike those firms that operate in the private goods market where success is often a function of the efficiency of markets, SEVs operate in the area of public goods where ideally no one should be excluded, everyone can have access, and ideally everyone should benefit.[1] This makes it more challenging to define success.

In some cases, SEVs may work with global public goods (see Exhibit 6.1), which are defined as public goods that cut across borders, generations, and populations, extending to at least more than just one group of countries and not discriminating against any population group or any set of generations, present or future.[2] There is a temporal dimension to working with public goods as they are universal and success may take many generations and require active partners across countries to make an impact. Based on the types of gaps presented in the discussion that follows — the jurisdictional gap, the participation gap, and the incentive gap Exhibit 6.1 — firms will need to decide an optimal strategy for scaling and accessing global markets.

There are two concepts that are often confused together. These are the concepts of internationalization and globalization. Internationalization is a process where the firm recognizes the place and the cultural dimensions needed to be included in its strategy. This traditional approach to crossing borders has been prevalent since the beginning of nation states, dominated by trade. A firm's decision to internationalize is based on many factors — profitable access to resources, access to new markets, overcoming trade barriers, and location advantages.[3] While we assume the world is increasingly getting homogenous and trade is crossing borders more easily, the reality is not true. Structurally, there are over 291 regional trade agreements in force out of 467,[4] and most agreements are at the bilateral level to facilitate trade interconnectedness.[5] Even the EU, which is the largest trade entity accounting for roughly 17% of global trade, conducts a staggering 76% of its trade within European borders. At the best it is "regional".

On the contrary, globalization assumes that markets are getting more integrated at a global level, whether through finance, supply chains, political ideologies, or consumers. This shifts our notion of spatiality and connectivity.[6] For-profit organizations associate internationalization with sales, but this is an irrelevant concept for SEVs because sales is not their primary purpose, and internationalizing can hurt the social purpose if it is too rapid or unfocused. In this case, the concept of internationalization for SEVs can be extended to the ability to not just sell products and services in the international markets but to include the process of raising funding from, gaining legitimacy, and getting access to resources like human capital and technology, from international markets. Three separate strategies can be used to drive the internationalization and globalization agenda of an SEV. These are innovation, branding, and networks.

Exhibit 6.1: **Theory Synopsis: Types of Global Public Goods**

There are three types of global public goods according to Kaul *et al.*[7]:

**Class 1:** *Natural global commons* include issues such as the ozone layer or climate stability, where the policy challenge is sustainability and the need for collective action to prevent overuse. Natural commons precede human-made activity.

**Class 2:** *Human-made global commons* encompass a range of diverse issues: scientific and practical knowledge, principles and norms, the world's common cultural heritage, and transnational infrastructure such as the Internet. These are considered stock variables: they have already been produced and are human-made. The Internet is a network-based human variable. Here, the challenges are under-use. There are three types of under-use: repression, lack of access, or entry barriers. For example, basic human rights as an example of a universally accepted norm, we see yet another type of underuse: repression.

**Class 3:** *Global policy outcomes* includes peace, health, and financial stability. These are also human-made. The collective action problem associated with these less tangible global public goods is the typical challenge of undersupply. Examples could be peace, health, financial stability, free trade, freedom from poverty, environmental sustainability, equity, and justice.

In the case of global goods, three gaps test an SEV's ability to scale and reinforce the need for networks. These gaps as per Kaul *et al.*[8] are as follows:

(1) **A jurisdictional gap:** Here the discrepancy arises because of the boundaries between global policy agendas and national policy-making agenda. To close this gap, you need to address gaps from the national-level policies to the international-level policies (regional and global levels) and then close the loop back to the national level.

(2) **A participation gap:** This arises when implementation often gets roadblocked at the stakeholder level, due to the fact that international cooperation is still primarily at the intergovernmental level. To close this gap, all actors, irrespective of whether governments, civil society, and business; all population groups across all generations; and all groups of countries need to be brought into the process. This may come down to bargaining power according to Coff (1999).[9] SEVs may need to ask questions such as the following: Can stakeholders act in a unified manner? What will it take to make them do so?

(3) **An incentive gap:** The benefits outlined, many of which are based on moral suasion, are considered not enough for states to cooperate or change regulations for the global public good. To close this gap, ideally there should

Exhibit 6.1: **(cont)**

be a transparent result or an evidence-based incentive loop to ensure that cooperation yields fair and clear results for all.

Types of Corporate Resource Allocations

| Social Orientation | Welfare | | Stakeholder Relationship Orientation | |
| --- | --- | --- | --- | --- |
| | | | Low | High |
| | | High | Agency Loss | CSR |
| | | Low | Process Improvement and all other | Direct Influence Tactics |

*Source*: Barnett (2007)[10]

Often private firms get involved in public goods through CSR or corporate social performance (CSP) programs. CSP is defined as "a business organization's configuration of principles of social responsibility, processes of social responsiveness, and policies, programs, and observable outcomes as they relate to the firm's social relationship",[11] but this is hard to measure as there is no market for CSP especially as the "rent" or returns accrued may not be easily visible. An interesting perspective is presented by Coff,[12] who states that organizations do not accrue rent, people do, and the firm is merely a nexus of contracts.

It is not easy to measure for CSR and its influence on corporate financial performance (CFP). Often social cause spending could be outside the purview of CSR, and about stakeholder influence. Hence, SEVs need to be careful and be realistic when managing networks. The simple truth is that often it is a WIN–WIN game. SEVs that are non-profit may benefit by relating to the CSR aspirations of for-profit firms, and for-profit SEVs may benefit by creating a strong social value strategy, or if they are mostly for-profit, they may focus on strong CSR strategies.

For example, if you look at Exhibit 6.2 on Last Mile Health and the factors that affect internationalization, you will find that in Case Study 6.1, the various partnerships (Gavi, the Vaccine Alliance, The Audacious Project, and Living Goods) were instrumental in fueling Last Mile Health's expansion into Africa. Of course the founders' personal networks may have also come to play. He is a graduate of John Hopkins Bloomberg School of Public Health and affiliated with Harvard Medical School. He also has roots with Africa as he left Liberia at the age of nine.

## Case Study 6.1:  **Last Mile Health (Liberia)**

It is estimated that more than one billion people don't have access to basic healthcare either because of access (they live in remote areas) or inadequate number of healthcare professionals. After the civil war ended in 2003, Liberia, with a population of 4 million had just 50 doctors. Last Mile Health (LMH) began in 2007 because they knew the despair of people who lived in remote communities. The  seven founders began with just US$6,000 in seed money, and their initial venture was called Tiyatien Health (rebranded Last Mile Health in 2013), meaning "justice in health". Raj Panjabi, co-founder and CEO of LMH, said, "*I think social change gets created in two ways. One is to solve problems that have already been defined and the other is to define the problem in the first place...Embracing the consciousness to actually understand the problem in the first place and communicate around it: that remote villages are a distinct issue for health care, period.*"

Raj reiterates, "*It turns out that blind spots in rural health care can become hot spots of disease.*" He gives the example of Ebola. When Ebola struck in 2013, (1) it took about 1 month to identify the disease by which time it had spread rapidly, (2) no vaccines were available as it was a neglected disease, (3) there were few specialist doctors on the ground in the country, and (4) few medical diagnostic centers. The disease quickly spread across Guinea, Liberia, and Sierra Leone. Patient zero was traced to an 18-month-old boy from a remote community in the Guinea rainforest who was assumed to have died from cholera-like symptoms on 26 December, 2013. By the time the officials were informed on 24 January 2014, the virus had spread. His family died, and eventually more than 11,300 people died resulting in the closure of borders, closing of schools, leaving broken families, and further wreaking havoc on an already fragile health system.

LMH identified the following three problems with primary health: (1) few interventions focus on last-mile communities, (2) community workers have minimal training and are often unsupervised, and (3) the supply chain, transportation, logistical, and performance management systems of Liberia are underdeveloped. There are over 1.2 million Liberians who cannot easily access a professional community health worker. LMH's 2017–2019 Strategic Plan says, "*The net result is a global health paradox: the people who have greatest need for primary health care are the least likely to receive it.*"

LMH works with the government to recruit, train, equip, manage, and pay laymembers of rural communities to provide 30 lifesaving health services to their neighbors. These frontline workers are equipped with a backpack and a smart device that can also help with diagnosis. The smart device is connected to the closest clinic, where medical professionals can support them. This allows early interventions. Word Health organization estimated that the world is facing a shortage of 18 million health workers. To combat Ebola, in 2014, Last Mile Health trained 10,000 community health workers in 500 villages. They also helped educate the population in things essential to prevent the spread of disease like the need for quick and safe burials of their loved ones.

The Liberian government has adopted the Last Mile Health model and expects that this will help it reach the 1.2 remote people of Liberia by the end of 2019. In 2018, a US$18 million partnership between Gavi, the Vaccine Alliance, The Audacious Project, Last Mile Health and Living Goods will reach out into Liberia, Uganda, and Kenya to further the reach of vaccines, capture data, and deploy 50,000 community health workers to serve 34 million people by 2021. Raj says, "*We as people are not defined by the conditions we face, no matter how hopeless they seem, we're defined by how we respond to them … I've seen the power of this idea to transform ordinary citizens into community health workers, into every day heroes.*" A model such as this needs to work with various stakeholders, it needs funding, needs technology (the smart devices helped not only reduce the load of the material the frontline medical workers carried but made it possible to seek support from the nearest clinic), needs policy entrepreneurs, needs ministry and community support. It made sure that the vulnerable had a chance of survival.

Exhibit 6.2: **Social Entrepreneurship (SE) Evolution: Variables that Affect Internationalization**

| Factor | Aspiring SE | Nascent SE | Baby SE | Established SE |
|---|---|---|---|---|
| | Social Bricoler | | Social Constructionist | Social Engineer |
| Focus | Micro (individual focus)/ apprenticeship | | Meso (focus on organization) | Macro (broader social/economic/ political context) |
| Time (Emerson, 2004) | Sporadic | 0–12 months | 12–60 months | 60+ months |
| Motives | Purpose-driven — novel idea/personal cause affiliation/ external market opportunity. | Purpose with provisions (operating costs) — agent of change (Top Management Team plays a big role). | Provisions with purpose (managing cash flow and capital) — organization is able to act as a catalyst of change. | Profit with purpose — sustainability of concept and lasting impact (commercialization of concept, scalability, systems and well-articulated business philosophy) Glocality — looking for smaller partners to create local impact. |
| Risks | Local community (personal/family risk) | Community, civil, legal, government (personal/family/ those directly associated with cause — activists and impact group). | Government-intergovernmental (personal/ organization) | International arena (personal and organizational) |

Exhibit 6.2: **(cont)**

| Factor | Aspiring SE | Nascent SE | Baby SE | Established SE |
|---|---|---|---|---|
| | **Social Bricoler** | | **Social Constructionist** | **Social Engineer** |
| Expectation | Some social impact — not independently audited | | Audited statements | Verified audited statement of accounts (financial and social impact) — accounting for capital investment; management of operating capital; some financial returns. |
| Firm evolution | Conventional non-profit | Non-profit with some earned income | Social enterprise — business with social responsibility. | Business with social responsibility — conventional business. |
| Funding | Personal (cash, time, volunteer time, goods in kind). | Family and friends seed capital/ community foundations (local, national, regional, and international) (cash, volunteer time, goods in kind, infrastructural/ logistics/ consultancy support). | Like-minded people/ major national foundations/ grants/subsidies: secondary capital (cash — systematic collection, volunteer time, goods in kind, infrastructural/ logistic/consultancy support/PR) (local, national, regional, and international). | Marketplace — mainstream: equity market; government (ex-carbon credits) (local, national, regional, and international). |
| Scope | Individual | Community | Local/regional — saturated national market. May start drawing international funds. | Regional/ international — millions of beneficiaries in multiple countries. Scalability comes in control, partnerships, and replication. |
| Impact | Small | | Social need [Gap] | Social deconstruction [redefinition] |
| Manpower | Self-reliance | Volunteers (self-minded, friends/ family) | Professional volunteers, hiring of some administrative staff. | Structure/business is more formal and roles become specialized. |

Exhibit 6.2: **(cont)**

| Factor | Aspiring SE | Nascent SE | Baby SE | Established SE |
|---|---|---|---|---|
| | **Social Bricoler** | | **Social Constructionist** | **Social Engineer** |
| Networks/ partnerships/ collaboration | Family/friends | Community | Stakeholders include regional and international mentors/legal becomes important. | Focus on partnerships and formal strategic alliances; competition/ political/ regulatory/ financial become more important; multiple stakeholders need to managed — beneficiaries/ supporters/firm stakeholders (employees/board, etc.); regulators need to manage media. |
| Market Focus | Positive change in the life of the beneficiary. | Positive change for a collection of individual beneficiaries. | Agent of change for society through education and culture. | Challenge existing norms [impact rules/regulations/ policies]. |
| | Harmony and co-existence awareness — PR | | Legitimacy — brand building — need for impact metrics and accounting metrics. | Reputation and relationship management (productive balance between mission and money; transparency) — need for accounting metrics. |

*Source*: Adapted from Balakrishnan and Lindsay.[13]

## 6.2. **Social Innovation**

As identified in the lifecycle of an SEV, the ability to innovate and adapt are critical not just for survival but also for growth. Innovation is the ability for a firm to look at old problems in new ways and find new processes or products to solve challenges in a sustainable way. Social innovations are innovative activities, services, or products that meet social needs.[14] This definition was mostly applicable for social businesses, but could be extended to for-profit SEVs. Social change has unintended side effects,[15] which means SEV founders must be cognizant of long-term effects and monitor side effects. The stages of social innovation are highlighted by the following model — ideation prompting, problem ascertain, prototyping and piloting ideas, business model and diffusing, scaling, and system evolving. Each stage requires an iterative process of innovation.

Anita Roddick founded Body Shop in 1976. Body Shop's rapid growth required more capital, and so the founder decided to float an IPO. She raised funds through the stock market in 1984, with 100% equity listed by 1986. But competition in this sector increased. As the share prices fell, Anita as CEO found that she was accountable for the firm's financial performance. In 1988, she had to step aside as CEO after 22 years.[16] In 2004, she was diagnosed with Hepatitis C. In 2006, Anita sold Body Shop to L'Oréal for £652 million though L'Oréal was known for animal testing and this was against Body Shop's ethos. In 2007, she died of Hepatitis C. While we like to think our founders, customers, and investors in the social goods sector are not motivated by emotions or money, this is rarely true. The rapid growth of Body Shop and the decisions to list on the stock market meant it was evaluated as a for-profit firm. What Body Shop did in terms of social innovation was bring a wider awareness to the global market about ethically produced cosmetics.

**Social innovations are elements of social change that create new social facts, namely impacting the behavior of individual people or certain social groups in a recognizable way with an orientation towards recognized objects that are not primarily economically motivated.[17]**

Creativity and innovation have a great deal to play in the survival, scale, growth, and internationalization of a firm (see Exhibit 6.3). On the one hand, you are looking for creative ways of addressing challenges, and on the other hand, you are innovating to make it work. This process is cyclical in nature and often needs several iterations. In the humanitarian sector, in-kind assistance or vouchers are commonly used to give refugees a method to buy daily essentials, but often cash is preferred because of its flexibility in usage. The downside of cash is that it can be stolen or used for wrong purposes. In Samoa, after Cyclone Evan, the World Bank experimented with an e-voucher system in 2014 to send relief via mobile phones using Digicel Samoa. The disadvantage of this method was that the mobiles had to have a specially registered chip. In Afghanistan, Bitcoin was used by the Digital Citizen Fund[18] to pay its women beneficiaries. By digitalizing payments, the Bill & Melinda Gates Foundation argue that financial inclusion would be the ultimate goal as 80% of the poor (earning less than US$2 per day) have access to a bank account.[19] With each experiment, the ability to learn from what works and what did not can be used to improve the next iteration of innovation. For the humanitarian sector, this meant e-payment preparedness — whether the other actors like the target population, governments, humanitarian actors, and private sector, who were necessary for sourcing, managing, and transfer of the money, were ready.[20]

A good part of the social innovation process is failure. Strategic failure is intelligent failure, which has the following four goals: (1) to focus on processes rather than outcomes; (2) to legitimize intelligent failure; (3) to achieve and sustain individual commitment to

Exhibit 6.3:   **Theory Synopsis: Innovation and Creativity**

Innovation and creativity are often confused. Creativity requires originality (newness or novelness) and a degree of effectiveness.[21] Newness need not be fully original, but can involve the regeneration or new combinations of existing knowledge or materials.[22] The effectiveness part of creativity is the ability to deliver value. Creativity should, or could, change or transform existing domains, and hence is a subjective judgment of its potential.[23] The challenge lies with the question — value to which target audience? In the process of encouraging creativity in an organization, the social judgment of value needs to be streamlined to separate personal creativity (person) from organizational creativity. Because creativity is often associated with sporadic and abstract concepts, it is most applicable in the ideation stage, though this is not technically true as creativity has been considered a heuristic — a process that can be used also to discover a problem, rather than an algorithmic (goal-oriented).

Researchers and scholars have defined innovation as the general process of creating something different, which occurs with the conversion of existing knowledge and ideas into a new benefit, such as new or improved processes or services.[24,25] Innovation is inexplicably related to change — either to take advantage of changing environments or to influence the environment.[26] The nature of innovation is to bring in or to create something new, or change what is existing or improve the existing, where the aim of innovation is to succeed, differentiate, or compete.[27] Either way, you require adaptable and resilient people and organizations since innovation depends on the acceptance of new ideas, services, products, processes, systems, or structures.[28] Newness should also not be confused with blue-sky thinking,[29] as it can be looking at old problems from different angles or even taking what is available and applying it in another context or modifying it. Innovation is embedded in the process of learning and discovery.[30] Innovation also has been separated from creativity in the sense that *"Invention is the creative act, while innovation is the first or early employment of an idea by one organization or a set of organizations with similar goals."*[31] Western scholarly debates on creativity and innovation begin with the fact there is no clear definition of these terms.[32] Further, innovation seems the bigger concept than creativity.

*Source:* Extracted from Moonesar *et al.*[33]

intelligent failure through organizational culture and design, and (4) to emphasize failure in management systems rather than individual failure.[34] Failure is an opportunity to learn, course correct, and try again. This is commonly called a "pivot" (see Exhibit 6.4). To pivot successfully, you need more than an individual; ideally, you need a team, a structure, and a system. If you are looking outside your organization to raise capital, be advised that big investors are rarely willing to bet on just one individual and prefer teams who may also collectively excel in creativity and innovation. If you work in the global market, the skills you might need are that of a "glocal citizen" — a person who *develops enterprise-wide citizenship strategies that harmonize, or integrate, local action with global themes and commitments.*[35]

Exhibit 6.4: **Theory Synopsis: Pivot**

A "pivot" is the change in some business model elements based on the rigorous testing of the hypothesized business model using a series of minimum viable products (MVPs), which represent the smallest set of features/activities needed to rigorously validate a concept. The feedback from these tests is used to pivot.[36] It is more about product–market fit than about problem–solution.[37]

The Startup Genome Report found that startups that pivot once or twice compared to those startups that pivoted more than 2 times or not at all, were 52% less likely to scale prematurely, more likely to raise 2.5× more money and have 3.6× better user growth.[38]

However, value is created by addressing a pain point.[39] The key barriers to a successful pivot are (1) customer interaction (who do you choose, how valid is the feedback, and how do you contain the spread of noise associated with the MVP), (2) looking beyond customer problems to create sustainable value that gives you a competitive advantage, and (3) market sizing as this will allow you to scale at a rate that is sustainable.[40]

## 6.3. **Global Branding**

A global brand can be based in a country but should be perceived to embrace the international market. With the *death of distance*, an increasing number of firms, thanks to services which may not be as confined to a location for production, a new class of firms called "born globals"[41] have been created. Born globals are rapidly able to internationalize and sell a significant share of their products in at least three continents in the first few years of their life. These new firms are able to tap into the flow of capital or money, goods and services, information or ideas, people or labor, and technology.[42] This is leading to firms with bases in multiple parts of the world, and their unified brand recognition across countries is increasingly seen as an advantage. In the NGO sector, strong brands are more likely to get donations.[43] In reality, brands may need to "glocalize", which is the ability to have consistent global values, yet adapt the product for the local market. This scenario is more likely true for SEVs as the challenges of each community may require fine-tuning.

**A brand is a promise that the customers and the stakeholders believe in. Included in the brand promise are the brand values and the brand deliverables. It is better to under-promise and over-commit than vice-versa.**

Research finds that global brands consistently outperform the market even in difficult times and can act as business accelerators during times of growth and as insulators during periods of downturn.[44] From a market perspective, global brands have a higher premium[45] and are perceived as having a higher quality, prestige, credibility, and an increased tolerance toward price premiums.[46] For SEVs, the dilemma is about how many scarce resources to divert for the development of a global brand away from the core programs. This is not an easy decision but should be embraced with the long-term vision of where the SEV wants to be. Below is a checklist of five questions to consider if you decide to position your SEV as a global brand.

1. *Differentiating between a corporate brand and product brands*

Nestle, a 150-year-old Swiss brand, is a transnational corporation. This classification is based on its assets, sales, and employment overseas.[47] Nestle has a presence in 191 countries, with over 2,000 brands under its umbrella. The corporate brand, Nestle, is also considered as one of the top 100 global brands, with just one of its portfolio brands, Nescafe, being ranked higher. Most of its other brands are local or regional brands. Investors may look at the corporate brand, but local beneficiaries and customers will look at the product brand first, and the corporate brand as a guarantee or endoser. Many SEVs don't think ahead of the future and this may be challenging when you want to scale. SEVs could decide to dominate at a global level in a narrow niche they are operating in — take, for example Gavi, the Vaccine Alliance whose name suggests the area of operation and whose key audience is the stakeholders they deal with.

The challenge with SEVs who use global consumers to provide the financial resources to fund their operations is that they must be able to show that they are a global brand. With TOMS' Buy One Get One (BOGO) model,[48] the consumers of TOMS products came from all over the world. Initially, it was easy to associate BOGO with shoes and the beneficiaries as children in Latin America. Since then, TOMS has diversified and the global value delivered has morphed to bags, eyewear, and more beneficiary markets (save the animals, childbearing mothers). What is the brand value of TOMS? What is the role of a corporate brand and a product brand in this case?

The BOGO models face challenges on the ground in individual markets. VisionSpring began in 2001 to provide eyeglasses to those in need. They began in El Salvador and began expanding across Latin America using their own sales force. But when they entered into India in 2003, the model was no longer cost-effective and they had to change using a partnership hub and spoke model, where income from higher end products were used to subsidize products meant for low-income partners which were sold by *vision entrepreneurs*. According to Jordan Kassalow, founder of VisionSpring, what is important for the SEV scale is a strong understanding of the legal structure of the country of operation.[49] All these examples highlight the importance of understanding both the corporate brand and product brands. When both morph, you might have issues of perception (what is TOMS about) or about value or jurisdiction (VisionSpring and its partners).

2. *Where are your sales or funds coming from?*

Global brands are those for-profit organizations where 25–75% of sales are outside the home region.[50,51,52,53] AC Neilsen assumes that these brands also have a total revenue of at least US$1 billion. Ideally, sales should be from outside the home country and from three separate continents.[54] Regional brands have sales from mostly bordering countries or similar countries.[55] But SEVs don't always deal in sales — so in this case we should look at funding.

For SEVs, they have a choice on whether to position themselves as local, regional, or global brands. Grameen Bank is a Bangladeshi brand and many of its funders were foreign governments giving aid to less developed countries. One of the challenges in obtaining funds from diverse sources may be mission drift.[56] There have been tighter regulations on NGOs receiving foreign funds in places like India,[57] Israel, Russia, Ethiopia, Hungary, Nigeria, and Ethiopia, for example.[58]

For those SEVs selling services or products, they may need to understand the "Made in" perception. There may be a higher equity attached to less developed countries for social goods, which is the reverse perception of high-tech and more sophisticated category of goods. SEVs must also look at their contribution to host countries or beneficiary countries. TOMS has created 700 jobs in Ethiopia, India, and Kenya (their beneficiary markets), where they have a sizeable presence.[59]

3. *Brand orientation — Global or international, or "placeless"?*

By default, brands are perceived to be anchored to places. However, with the internet, advances in travel and communications, brands can also be perceived as placeless.[60] Depending on the cause of the SEV, place may be an advantage — especially for those embedded in the communities or whose beneficiaries are limited by geography.

Placelessness may have an advantage for those using e-commerce to connect to the world. You might be able to tap into global communities and leverage the internet to scale services (think Wikipedia).

Tree Change Dolls is a small family-run business based in Tasmania. They sell recycled upscaled dolls around the world through Etsy. While it is a tiny SEV and does not have a global supply chain as it sources used dolls from thrift shops, its sales through Etsy, an international distribution system allows it to tap into the world. It has an international customer base and has won international recognition.

For those for-profit SEVs which want to be acquired, or are looking for an exit from their business venture, it is important to consider brand origins for future mergers and acquisitions. You are really deciding about the heritage of your brand and the impact this has on brand values. While research is limited, one study finds that there is no difference in performance between firms that stress global standardization as a strategy versus other strategies.[61]

4. *How can you communicate "globalness"?*

There is limited research on whether globalness would be an advantage for SEVs. Based on research from the for-profit sector, it has been found that consumers make assumptions on available information, so perceived globalness may be more important than actual globalness. Perceived brand globalness can be defined as the extent to which there is a belief by consumers that a *brand is marketed in multiple countries.*[62] Globalness is important when an SEV is planning to franchise, source funds from the global market, or wants to develop international legitimacy for the cause (refer to Case Study 2.1 in Chapter 2).

For those SEVs who decide to position themselves as global brands, in order to bridge *the global share of heart gap,*[63] they should invest in a brand strategy where they have some standardized brandscapes that make brand recognition in multiple countries easy.[64] A brand can be a global brand with a local cultural positioning, for example, the Singapore Girl in Singapore Airlines.[65] In some cases, brand values may be related to heritage and cultural nuances (for example, Jordan River Foundation — an SEV that sells cultural handicrafts made in Jordan by disadvantaged communities). The IDEA framework is useful when looking at brands in the non-profit sector. "IDEA" stands for brand *integrity,* brand *democracy,* brand *ethics,* and brand *affinity* (see Exhibit 6.5).[66]

Exhibit 6.5:  **Brand IDEA Explained**

Brand *integrity* means that the organization's internal identity is aligned with its external image and that both the identity and image are aligned with the organization's mission.

Brand *democracy* means that the organization trusts its members, staff, participants, and volunteers to communicate their own understanding of the organization's core identity.

Brand *ethics* means that the brand itself and the way it is deployed reflect the core values of the organization.

Brand *affinity* means that the brand is a good team player, working well alongside other brands, sharing space and credit generously, and promoting collective over individual interests.

*Source:* Adapted from Kylander and Stone.[67]

5. *Creating brand communities*

Brand communities can be used to advocate causes and create a sub-culture that can help leverage existing values in the marketplace. Brand communities may be positioned as cosmopolism, iconic symbols of global culture representing quality, the global myth, or social responsibility.[68] This strategy takes advantage of using like-minded people to "*serve as a passport to global citizenship, a vehicle for participation in a global world, and a pathway to belonging to the global world.*"[69]

The Giving Keys uses key-shaped jewelry with motivational words to help end homelessness. Their brand community actively uses social media like Instagram to share stories. This is done using the hashtag #thegivingkeys and to pay it forward. By the end of 2018, they had created 152,166 hours of work for people transitioning out of homelessness (or 70+ jobs).[70] The company is based in Los Angeles, and its beneficiaries are in Los Angeles, but their customers are global, from whom they collect motivational stories. In some cases, brand communities may refer to key stakeholders that are also strategic alliance partners, like the case of Gavi, the Vaccine Alliance.[71]

In Germany, the zero-packaging movement begun with creation of the supermarket "Original Unverpakt". The movement is slowly gaining movement and tackling the problem of food waste and recycling.[72] It is crossing borders as the threat of single-use plastics is a menace all over the world. The movement has started a trend back to the simpler way of life. In a more educated and sustainability conscious Europe, this is a trend that is slowly gaining global momentum through loyal brand communities.

**A global brand hence can be defined as a viable brand that can be a product, place, service, corporation, etc. that has sales or consumption outside the origin country of the brand, in excess of 50%, available in at least three continents.**

SEVs must decide on the level of brand "globalness" and Exhibit 6.6 gives some ideas. Brand globalness can be applied to the SEV corporate brand or the products or services it sells

Exhibit 6.6:  **Brand Typology**

| Brand type/ Characteristic | Pure Local | Pure Regional | Pure Global |
|---|---|---|---|
| Brand | Local meaning | Regional meaning, representation, halo branding and alliances. Can have local heritage. | International meaning, representation, halo branding and alliances. Can have local heritage. |
| Product and promotion | Local adaptation | Regional adaptation and standardization | Glocal (global + local) |
| Availability | Nationally | Regionally (similar countries or bordering countries) through direct/indirect representation. | Internationally at least in three continents through direct/indirect representation. |
| Sales | More than 50% domestic. In case of brands that are not "for-profit", it may mean consumption of brand is more than 50% within the home country. | More than 50% from regional sales. In case of brands that are not "for-profit", it may mean consumption of brand is more than 50% outside the home country and within the region. | More than 50% from global sales. In case of brands that are not "for-profit", it may mean consumption of brand is more than 50% outside the home country. |
| Website | Locally focused — language, content, etc. | Regionally focused — language, content, etc. | Globally focused, with regional/individual country representation if necessary. |

Exhibit 6.6:  **(cont)**

| Brand type/ Characteristic | Pure Local | Pure Regional | Pure Global |
|---|---|---|---|
| Customer | National | Regional | International across the globe, global citizenship |
| Supply chain | Local | Regional | Worldwide |
| Government | Local or national | Regional | Works with governments in multiple countries, across at least three continents looking for administrative or economic arbitrage. |

*Source*: Adapted from Balakrishnan *et al.*[73]

(which maybe different brands). There are advantages in separating the company brand and product brand as you can "sell" or franchise the product or service brand without having to give away the parent brand, but this may require additional funding, a resource that many SEVs don't have. Always use the SEV mission as a decision point. Are you diverting valuable funding away from your cause?

## 6.4. **Role of Networks in Internationalization and Scale**

Theories on born globals,[74] new international ventures, and the expedited Uppsala model[75] all show that managing networks for small firms or startups can lead to faster internationalization. Internationalization is defined as *a combination of innovative, proactive and risk-seeking behavior that crosses national borders and is intended to create value in organizations.*[76] SEVs must be able to deliver returns to not just the founders, but external investors and stakeholders such as business angels, crowdfunders, venture capitalists, foundations, and governments. These returns can be in the form of finance, new jobs, economic growth,[77] legitimacy,[78] or power. Since small firms lack resources, networks can become a valuable to access other resources or get help to monitor, control, or influence stakeholders. The network effect can contribute up to 70% to firm valuation.[79]

Many SEVs become dependent on key stakeholders for resources. The key to managing uncertain environmental conditions is this ability of a firm to grow across markets and to take advantage of new opportunities wherever they arise. This could be by leveraging research and development (IPs),[80] training, and the stock of knowledge and learnings the firm possesses.[81] At the simplest level, this may mean joining a cluster[82] and taking advantage of proximity to other organizations in similar stations (see Case Study 6.2).

Networks are about relationships or linkages (contractual, emotional, social, financial, political), which determine a "flow" of resources through influence.[83] It is measured through density, which is the relative number of ties that link actors together. It is calculated as a ratio of the number of relationships that exist in the network (stakeholder environment) to the total number of possible ties if each network member were tied to every other member.[84] These ties can be either at a personal or an organizational level and can be direct or indirect ties. If the density is

## Case Study 6.2: **International Humanitarian City, (Dubai, UAE)**

International Humanitarian City (IHC) was formed in 2003 by His Highness Sheikh Mohammed bin Rashid Al Maktoum, Vice-President and Prime Minister of the United Arab Emirates and Ruler of Dubai, through the merger of Dubai Aid City (DAC) and Dubai Humanitarian City (DHC). It is the one and only non-profit, independent, humanitarian free-zone authority in the world. IHC is a non-religious, non-political, and nonprofit organization.

It currently hosts close to 87 entities, representing UN organizations, international non-governmental organizations, intergovernmental organizations, and commercial companies who work in the field of delivering aid in both situations of crises and to support long-term economic development. The IHC model is based on the proven Dubai free-zone model. IHC provides a secure environment that fosters partnerships, social responsibility, and global change.

IHC plays a vital role in terms of logistics to support troubled spots in the MENA region and East Africa through warehousing and transport of emergency response goods. In 2017 alone, they had managed 20 airlifts and two sea shipments, dispatching US$18 million worth of relief items, reaching 12 countries.

During an emergency response, all organizations try and respond with supplies within the first 48–72 hours. One of the biggest challenges in a humanitarian crisis situation is predicting stock. Often IHC partners will find that they do not have adequate supplies. In 2018, IHC launched The Humanitarian Logistics Databank, which will address the long-standing issue about the coordination of aid shipments and allow for greater transparency on data on aid at local, regional, and international levels, collating information at ports, airports, or other entry points on food, medicine, and shelter. This should decrease bottlenecks and increase collaborations. In fact, one representative reiterated that because they were all in one place during an emergency, they would talk with each other informally and can tell their respective HQs about what stock the other partners had to facilitate coordination between organizations at the HQ level.

high, the ties between the actors are more, leading to more information exchange,[85] shared behavioral expectations,[86] possibly more coalitions,[87] innovation,[88] and greater internationalization.[89]

Centrality is another method of measuring networks.[90] It is the relative position of an actor with respect to the network, relative to others. It is measured by the number of direct ties to other actors, the independent access to other actors, and the control over other actors. Based on the level of centrality, actors can act as communicators (well connected) or gatekeepers (brokers between actors).[91] By visualizing networks and by looking at mentorship, board members, former employees, sources of investment, sources of inspiration, suppliers, distributors, and founders (for example, Endeavor has done some interesting work in this area for conventional startups),[92] you will get a sense of centrality and relationships you need to develop to be successful.

Networks help you manage risks, provided they are the right people or entity and there is not too much reliance on a single person or entity.[93] There are many types of risks that SEVs can face, but the main ones arise either because of newness or smallness. For example, (1) the founding team finds themselves quickly out of depth with the new roles and the unfamiliar environment, as their resources get stretched thin, or (2) the founders don't have the networks that can offer them a base of influence on the environment.[94] In a global landscape, risks can come from the external uncontrollable environment (think of Chid Liberty in Liberia), from the supply chain (and its disruption), investors (SEVs dependent on grants face uncertain funding), other players in their impact space, or their beneficiaries, which all can impact their global reputation.

### 6.4.1. *Strategies to Manage Networks*

A study on high-growth versus slow-growth firms [95] finds that the key differences observed between them were the level of commitment to growth, growth-oriented vision, and participation in interorganizational relationships. Surprisingly, it was not the level of emphasis on planning or goal-setting variables. There are three stages to managing networks for growth as follows:

- **Stage 1:** Assessing what networks you are missing;
- **Stage 2:** Sorting networks;
- **Stage 3:** Building relationships with networks.

**Stage 1:** The starting point is identifying the risks the SEV is exposed to. Founders with related background, knowledge, experience, or education in the field already have an advantage to grow the organization.[96] Even before managing networks, it is important to audit what are the resources SEVs have access to or lack. At one extreme, resources can be considered tangible, discrete, and property based (they are called simple resources like finance which can be quantified into numbers). At the other extreme, resources can be considered intangible, systemic, and knowledge based (these are called complex resources like skills and capabilities or reputation).[97] Resources can be considered instrumental (give access to other resources like finance, which is used to pay salaries) or utilitarian or functional (for example, property where physical offices are based). Some resources may be easily available and others may be scarce, and those firms that own them would get a competitive advantage.

For simplicity's sake, resources can be divided into the following categories: human, social, financial, physical, technological, reputational, and organizational. One study finds that firm survival increases to the degree to which human capital was non-transferable and non-appropriable at the level of founders more than employees, which comes back to the founding team member's strengths.[98] Once you audit the founding team member's strengths and weaknesses, you can benchmark against industry standards, other stakeholders operating in the same industry or market, and then look at existing structural holes. Structural holes are the new networks you will need to develop. Identifying vulnerable points are future opportunities for SEVs founders. By diversifying the expertise levels of networks, you broaden your support system and increase innovation by avoiding network failures.[99] Exhibit 6.7 presents a checklist that founders can consider when planning their SEV networking strategy.

Exhibit 6.7: **Types of Risks (Assessment)**

| Category | International Market Risks | Your Evaluation (High/Medium/Low) | | |
|---|---|---|---|---|
| Market | • Likelihood of beneficiaries accepting your service/product (local/regional/national/international market) over competing products/services. | H | M | L |
| | • Likelihood of the retail chain/intermediary recommending/ stocking your product/service (local/regional/national/ international market) over competing products/services. | H | M | L |
| | • Likelihood of customers paying money for your service/ products (local/regional/national/international market) over competing products/services. | H | M | L |
| Funding | • Likelihood of you raising money from the market (local/ regional/national/international market). | H | M | L |
| | • Period of finding raised. | H | M | L |
| | • Likelihood of the funding raised to cover future needs (at least for goal that is met) (local/regional/national/ international market). | H | M | L |
| | • Likelihood of the funding raised to come with no strings attached, or what is the cost of capital? | H | M | L |
| Human resource | • Likelihood of you finding talent (capabilities, skills and *relevant* experience) from the market (where — local/ regional/national/international market and the cost of acquiring talent — volunteers, paid, skilled). | H | M | L |
| | • Likelihood of you retaining talent for the duration needed to achieve your goals (and how will you manage expectations?). This includes founder or key employee turnover. | H | M | L |
| | • Likelihood of you developing talent for future roles and responsibilities. | H | M | L |
| | • Likelihood of your employees adhering to the values articulated in the vision of your organizations (and what are your fail-safe mechanisms). | H | M | L |

Exhibit 6.7: **(cont)**

| Category | International Market Risks | Your Evaluation (High/Medium/Low) | | |
|---|---|---|---|---|
| Technical | • Likelihood of you developing and retaining your IP (protecting at the following levels — local/regional/national/ international market and raising funding for development, protection and maintenance). | H | M | L |
| | • Likelihood of finding and the ability to manage the security risks, upgrades, and data protection needed with open-source software or when you work with suppliers. | H | M | L |
| | • Likelihood of you funding the access to much needed technology platforms. | H | M | L |
| Suppliers | • Likelihood of you finding reliable and ethical suppliers (paid or donated). | H | M | L |
| | • Likelihood of you finding a supplier who can manage production variability and costs. | H | M | L |
| Business Model | • Likelihood of you borrowing an existing successful business model (from the local/regional/national/international market) and adapting it successfully with minimum downtime. | H | M | L |
| | • Likelihood of your business model adding value to your beneficiaries, investors, and regulators and other important stakeholders. | H | M | L |
| | • Likelihood of you having a strong governance model that is accountable and transparent to key stakeholders based on the resources you have in hand. | H | M | L |
| | • Likelihood of you having developed a strong communication strategy (internal and external). | H | M | L |
| Legitimacy (to be done at the local, regional, national, and international levels) | • Community acceptance. | H | M | L |
| | • Likelihood of you winning an award. | H | M | L |
| | • Likelihood of getting positive media coverage at local, regional, national, and international level. | H | M | L |
| | • Likelihood of you being invited to join a reputable association that gives you legitimacy. | H | M | L |
| | • Likelihood of conducting successful trails or publishing a paper that validated your process/product. | | | |

**Stage 2:** In this stage, you will sort your networks. A good tool that can be used is the one developed by Woolthuis *et al.*[100] for the SI Policy framework. Networks are sorted based on types of risks which are as follows:

(1) **Infrastructural system failures:** Is there an opportunity to find an existing non-competing player who could share resources? An example of how UNICEF used this is

highlighted with their relationship with Kuehne+Nagel. Many grants are in-kind and can also take the form of CSR. In 2017, UNICEF procured US$3.46 billion in supplies and services for children in 150 countries and areas, and for emergency supplies, through Kuehne Foundation from Kuehne+Nagel, which provides logistics support. Another example for humanitarian logistics for UNICEF is being based in IHC, Dubai.

(2) **Institutional system failures:** Is there a failure or an area of threat from hard institutional failures — rules, regulations, or the legal system? There may be an opportunity to develop networks with actors in a position to influence the policy environment or support the organization (lawyers, politicians, and policemen), or even charities that provide free advice or consultation required in those "gray" areas. One example is employment opportunities for convicts. Because employment is difficult, this leads to a vicious cycle of repeat offense. The Forward Trust (UK, formerly Blue Sky set up in 2005) employs only ex-offenders for 6 months in ground maintenance and waste management, reducing re-offense rates. They work with Veolia, a UK leader in environmental solutions.[101]

Sometimes the risks come from soft institutional failures like culture, social values, or the "informal, unwritten" rules and customs that dominate the systems. Here, expertise can come through networks with actors already established in the environment, trainers, and even local people. When Sougha, an initiative based in the United Arab Emirates, was being set up to train women artisans in local handicrafts in the rural areas of UAE, it began approaching potential beneficiaries door to door. By first getting acceptance from the grandmothers, who then were able to convince their sons and encourage their daughters, granddaughters and daughters-in-law to take up the handicrafts, they were able to scale and create legitimacy.[102]

(3) **Network failures:** These can come from overdependency on "too strong" networks that may lead to groupthink[103] or blindness in decision-making or "too weak" networks that may leave you overexposed, as there is an inadequate use of complementarities or interactive learning that could lead to innovation. A study on networks and alliances found that senior management played a key role. The skills they needed to develop were the ability to network, ability to develop strong ties, and get access to prestige.[104]

(4) **Capability failure:** These are failures that may arise when, for example, the organization does not have social media skills, accounting skills, financing skills, etc. Network actors need to be found that can support or advice the SEV. The missing actors can come from beneficiaries, customers, private sector (suppliers, startups, large international organizations, etc.), knowledge institutions (universities, technical institutes, etc.), and third parties (banks, legal consultants, PR firms, etc.). For example, in 2019, Google gave Nextleaf Analytics (SEV operating in the health and vaccine cold chain data analytics segment) an AI grant and consulting and coaching experience. This was a competitive grant involving 2,600 organizations. Networking is not easy and should be planned.

SEVs also benefit by sorting their networks based on priority and type of relationship they require (strong or weak ties). For this, the SEV must understand their role in the ecosystem. Timothy Rowley[105] calls these roles: (1) the compromiser, where the job is to pacify and bargain with influential stakeholders; (2) the commander, where the SEV will control information and influence behavior, acting as a gatekeeper; (3) subordinate, where the

SEV will fall in line with the well-organized structure and established norms; and finally (4) the solitarian, where the SEV can avoid stakeholder scrutiny as the ecosystem is not densely populated and it dwells in the periphery.

**Stage 3:** Managing relationships is a question of time, commitment to the relationship, and the value both partners receive. Though networks are often based on personal relationships, many of the existing theories on loyalty are applicable. Relationships are built on trust, credibility, incentives, or structurally binding contracts. Those networks that are trust based may have more commitment than those that are forced or dependent on incentives.[106] For example, is the motivation to endorse your SEV an outcome of fear of loss of income? Is the relationship bound by family ties? Is your friend on your board and how will this affect transparency and governance? (see Case Study 6.3).

## Case Study 6.3: **Girl Effect, UK: Creating Grassroots Change**

The Nike Foundation initially launched the Girl Effect in 2003 to focus on adolescent girls, and in 2004, it became a foundation. The objective is to build youth brands and mobile platforms to empower girls to change their lives. Girl Effect did this by creating a grassroots cultural brand and measuring changes in attitudes and behaviors through the consumption of the branded radio  talk show, magazine, digital, or self-starting club. Four elements — knowledge, attitudes, behaviors, and norms (KABN) — are closely monitored. *"KABN is our religion. We're accountable to our investors,"* she says. Notice the words — investors, not donors, because *"there's no return on an investment but there is a return on impact."*

The first youth brand Ni Nyampinga was launched in November 2, 2011 in Rwanda and was made for girls, by girls. The name means "a girl who is beautiful inside and out, who makes wise decisions". The brand gained popularity through a unique mix of inspiring entertainment, storytelling, and education using a multimedia platform using magazine, radio, and mobile.

In terms of funding, as a Nike spin-off, they are supported by Nike Foundation, NoVo Foundation, and the UK's Department for International Development; but they also have sponsors from both the technology and telecommunication sector. In addition, they work closely with governments. In terms of networks, NoVo foundation's Co-Presidents are the Buffetts (of Warrren Buffett fame). They collaborate with UN Foundation, the Coalition for Adolescent Girls, International Center for Research on Women, Population Council, and the World Bank.

In early 2019, Ni Nyampinga was one of three new brands that were developed to tap into the cultural fabric — the others are Yegna in Ethiopia and Zathu in Malawi. The impact is real and strong, for example, within 5 years, Ni Nyampinga as a brand was more well-known than Coca Cola.

## 6.5. **Crisis Management**

Managing an SEV means you need to deal with constant uncertainty. A crisis is at one end of the spectrum of uncertainty. Uncertainty is associated with doubt or a situation where risk arises in assessing the probabilities of outcomes, but not knowing the outcome itself, or the inability to see the future.[107] A crisis on the contrary is defined as a low-probability, high-impact situation which stakeholders can perceive as socially or personally threatening and hence a threat to the survival of the organization.[108] During this stage, time, information, and resources are scarce and emotions run high as cognitive functions are limited. A crisis can be divided into several stages (see Exhibit 6.8). In such circumstances, an SEV should predict risks, plan for them, monitor and minimize risks during an event, and after the event, try and restore the new level of normalcy. Crises provide excellent opportunities for change through learning.

Exhibit 6.8:   **Theory Synopsis: Deconstructing a Crisis**

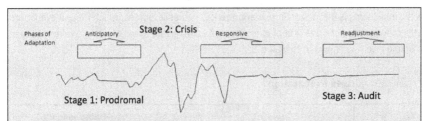

A crisis can normally be defined in three stages: Prodromal stage, crisis stage, and audit stage (post-crisis recovery period).

**Stage 1 — Prodromal characteristics:** This is the stage before the onset of the actual crisis and it can take years. An organization has the ability to plan for future crises, and this includes policies, preventive measures, and creative scenario planning to take control early of in the crisis and minimize risks.[109] The goal is to have a policy or structure in place to allow the organization to take control early to mitigate risks. The increasing frequency of "black swans"[110] makes this more challenging. The SEV as a team should build adaptability, basing decisions on the priority of values.[111]

**Stage 2 — Crisis characteristics:** An actual crisis itself has four stages as follows: (1) the jolt (actual event); (2) The point of no return; (3) acute stage (full impact felt); and (4) chronic (clean-up) stage. The focus during a crisis is to see how the organization can resolve the crisis as quickly as possible with minimum damage, taking into account organizational values and stakeholders.[112] Human life should always be a priority over and above everything else. This stage is often complicated by the fact that decisions become reactive. Often there is no precedent to follow, information is low, and the situation itself rapidly escalates, resulting in tremendous stress on people, structures, and the system.[113] At this stage, transparency is key, so communication plays a key role. This can be done by setting up information flows as

Exhibit 6.8: **(cont)**

---

the formal structure gets perished,[114] protecting the brand promise at an integrated level, and leveraging networks.[115]

**Stage 3 — Audit characteristics:** Once a crisis is past, it is time for the organization to pick up the pieces, heal itself and its stakeholders, move forward and use the learnings to prepare for future crisis.[116] Because much of what is considered the stakeholders experience is a perception of reality,[117] it is vital that the organization does have positive media[118] and combat perception of indifference.[119]

---

*Source:* Adapted from Stephens Balakrishnan.[120]

## 6.5.1. *Crisis Resolution*

Ideally, you should not wait for a crisis to happen in order to prepare for a crisis. The challenge with small teams is the lack of time, manpower, and other resources, which make it even more imperative to predict crisis and plan for them. It is important to look for crisis vulnerability at multiple levels as shown in Exhibit 6.9.

Exhibit 6.9: **Crises Preparation**

| Crisis Levels | Internal | Immediate ecosystem | Industry | Transboundary (industry and nation) and other uncontrollable factors |
|---|---|---|---|---|
| Types of issues (examples) | Theft, breakdown in product/ service promise, inappropriate employee behavior, sudden vacuum in key positions due to death/illness, working capital. | Competitor threat, supplier failure, distribution failure, threat from beneficiary community, and threat from other stakeholders. | Industry crisis that can lead to fall out on all players (regulations, credibility, etc.). | Media crisis (social media precipitated); Failure in a closely allied industry (banking that may affect finance); Natural disasters, terrorism, epidemics, etc. |

Once a crisis occurs, organizations must take quick stock on their exposed areas and put together a plan of action. For example, if the SEV is heavily dependent on social media, you must have an idea of influential social media influencers you can reach out to help manage the crisis. It helps if you already have an existing relationship with them rather than wait for a crisis to happen to contact them.[121]

The first and most important rule in any crisis is saving human life (employees, beneficiaries, immediate actors in the vicinity) at all costs. For SEVs that operate in fragile countries, being taken hostage, kidnapping, and death are often not unusual. Managing situations like this requires expertise and training.[122]

The second objective is to conserve and save resources. These may be investments in infrastructure, goods, and even reputation. What is critical? What are priorities? For reputation management during a crisis, constant communication is required and the objective is not to lose sight of the goals.

Crisis communication is key to managing and responding to a crisis and involves communication not just with the public but also with both internal and external stakeholders. As a crisis progresses, accurate information to make decisions becomes scarce and this increases uncertainty and heightens emotions. Based on the type of crisis, stakeholders attribute different levels of responsibility with the organizations involved, and hence, the response may have to accordingly differ.[123] The classic communication strategies available for response are of three types — denying, diminishing, and bolstering/deal strategies (see Exhibit 6.10).

Exhibit 6.10:  **Types of Communication Strategies**

| Coombs Response Strategy | Types of Communication Strategies |
|---|---|
| **Denying strategies** | |
| Attack accuser | Attack the accuser/counter message. |
| Denial | Disregard for crisis; denial that the organization is involved; denial of event; evasion of responsibility. |
| Scapegoat | Scapegoat (blame someone else). |
| Reactive response | Outrage management (minimalistic approach — focus on where outrage is). |
| **Diminishing strategies** | |
| Excuse | Excuse (denying intent to do harm or inability to control events); partial acknowledgment of crisis. |
| Minimize events | Reducing offensiveness of event, or diminish it/responsibility. |
| Justification | Justification — standards being used are not appropriate. |
| No comment | Refusal to confirm or deny. |
| Reframing | Change the context and distract; spinning negative to a positive. |
| **Rebuilding/deal strategies** | |
| Reassure | Reassurance management. |
| Compensation | Corrective action or rebuild; compensation (in kind). |
| Apology | Mortification; apology; full acknowledgment of crisis; full apology (full responsibility and asks forgiveness). |
| Proactiveness in information | Proactive news breaking; updates on current state/conditions/ where to get information, etc.; precaution advocacy. |
| Escapism | Changing name, logo, or slogan; changing target audience. |
| Move on | Take corrective action to prevent recurrence of same event. |

Exhibit 6.10:  **(cont)**

| Coombs Response Strategy | Types of Communication Strategies |
|---|---|
| **Rebuilding/deal strategies (contd.)** | |
| Move on: Re-legitimization | Legitimizing and emphasis on fairness of the process. |
| Image restoration | Rebuilding reputation by gaining trust. |
| **Bolstering/Deal responses** | |
| Reminder | Creating isolation of the event/people/cause; reminder (reinforce past good works). |
| Ingratiation | Ingratiation (praise stakeholders); collaboration with credible partners/including (social) media using #; hosting events or opinion leaders to generate Word of Mouth responses (secondary crisis communication response). |
| Victimage | Redemption of guilt (reminding stakeholders that you are also a victim); creating empathy; and creating reassurance. |
| Reframing | Spinning negative to a positive. |

*Source*: Compiled from multiple sources.[124]

When using social media to respond to a crisis, one study found that Tweets with native videos, a video link, a text link, a photo, and a plain text worked effectively, in that order of impact.[125] Because the variety of responses is huge and time during a crisis is always limited, SEVs should explore what can be done prior to a crisis to make sure they have a game plan. Look at the Oxfam Case Study, as the head of Oxfam, how would you respond? (see Case Study 6.4).

## 6.6. **Transparency**

While scandals are unfortunately very common in both the non-profit[126] and the for-profit sector (think of The United Way charity scandal versus Enron), they impact the third sector harder as it is a trust-based business and results are not easy to ascertain. The third sector works with public trust, government trust, and in the case of partnerships, private sector trust. Often money donated in smaller sums (think pennies and change) is difficult to trace, and then it becomes harder to account and hence hold people responsible. Raising money for one cause and diverting it to another expense is not acceptable. SEV founders often don't have management experience, but this is not an excuse for poor management. Scandals lead to tighter regulations. Regulations such as the Sarbanes–Oxley Act of 2002 were enacted post scandals (in USA). Although these are only applicable to the public corporation, private organizations sometimes slip under the radar. Though there are acts that are applicable to non-profits (Nonprofit Integrity Act in California), the fact remains that if the third sector does not regulate itself, the government will step in.

The concept of transparency, especially with the spate of recent scandals, highlights the importance of the process SEVs must manage to keep trust and legitimacy. Based on an extensive review on the topic, it involves availability and access to real-time data, sharing or disclosure of timely data, feedback opportunity using the data, and identifying the extent to which the principle of operation and objectives of the firm are observable.[127] The ethics of transparency is

## Case Study 6.4: **Crisis: Oxfam, Haiti**

Oxfam was embroiled in a crisis. On 8th of February 2018, staff including the country director of Haiti were accused of sexual misconduct. Oxfam held an internal audit in the face of public exposure and three men were allowed to resign, four were sacked. The exposure in Haiti resulted in workers in Chad coming forward with similar allegations for 2006. At this point, when the Charity Commission launched an enquiry, the Deputy Chief Executive of Oxfam resigned saying she was deeply sorry. Celebrity patrons like Minnie Driver and Desmond Tutu withdrew their support. By then it was 16th of February, only 8 days had passed. According to *The Guardian*, the chief executive of Oxfam GB, Mark Goldring, claimed that the attacks were "out of proportion to the level of culpability" and accused critics of an anti-aid agenda. On 19th of February, it was found out that a 2011 enquiry was held into the Haiti sex abuse. By 16th of May, the Chief Executive, it was reported, "stands down". It is estimated Oxfam may have lost 7,000 regular donors. The right to work in Haiti was suspended, and it was estimated that the lawsuits were worth £16 million and would result in aid program cuts. In the previous year, in 2017, Oxfam raised over £400 million from donors (private and governments) and helped 11.6 million people across the world. How would you have handled this crisis? What were the communication methods you can see that oxfam used? Were these methods successful?

dependent on managing the boundaries between regulations and the principles behind why transparency is important in the first place (dependence) (see Exhibit 6.11). Transparency is based on the perceived quality of intentionally shared information[128] and the process through which one can gauge the necessary aspects and status of an operation at all times.[129]

**Perceived Quality of Information:** There is a tendency to make information too complicated or too simple, which may lead to incorrect assumptions. For SEVs that build their business model on assumptions using the theory of change, there are dangers in oversimplification. To improve transparency, the following guidelines must be considered:

(1) Is the data/information accurate? What is the precision of the data (especially with political and economic data that may be lagged or distorted)?

(2) Is the source of the data reliable?

(3) Is the data following the best practice?[130]

(4) Is the data easily observable? Can the data be validated (audited by an independent third party?)

(5) Is the data presented in a meaningful way to help understand decisions?

(6) Is the data clear and simple and the correct measure of the objectives that help with evaluation?

Exhibit 6.11: **Relations of Dependence and Regulation between Ethical Principles and Information**

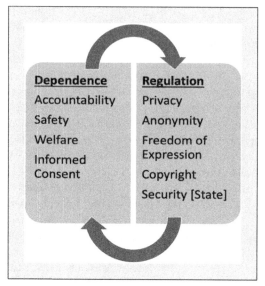

| Dependence | Regulation |
|---|---|
| Accountability | Privacy |
| Safety | Anonymity |
| Welfare | Freedom of Expression |
| Informed Consent | Copyright |
| | Security [State] |

*Source*: Adapted from Turilli and Floridi.[131]

**Process of Disclosure:** Disclosure is defined as the stakeholder perception of information received, whether it is relevant and timely.[132] The disclosure of information revolves around the concept of availability of data and the openness a firm has with respect to sharing or accessing data. There are two scenarios where firms may keep secrets, and these are called sanctioned secrets (which are considered legitimate by its stakeholders like IPs) or unsanctioned secrets (which are considered illegitimate by its stakeholders, fraud, and misrepresenting data).[133] As stakeholders are international and many in number, those SEVs operating in the global public goods market will find that the level of complexity in transparency increases and requires more resources to manage oversight and communication. Managing multiple stakeholders is key to managing perceptions.[134] One of the toughest periods where transparency comes into play is during a crisis. Transparency is important to develop trust and should be a part of good governance which is discussed in Chapter 4. This has been a problem for the NGO sector and there is no doubt they will be held to increasingly higher standards.

## 6.7. **Internationalization: A Recap**

Based on the scaling strategy, SEVs will have to decide the level of internationalization they want. This may affect brand decisions (global, local, or regional). Since time is an important consideration, firms need to be able to innovate and leverage their networks to their advantage. One way to determine a networking strategy is to audit the risks and find networks that can close those structural holes. But whatever you do, SEVs need to be prepared that crises are a reality of a firm's lifecycle and contingency plans go a long way in mitigating the risks. Some communications strategies are given above. The role of perceived transparency in communication can go a long way in maintaining and keeping existing relationships.

## 6.8. **Questions**

### Question 1
Red Cross found out one of its employees used the official twitter account for a personal tweet:[135] The message said "Ryan found two more 4 bottle packs of Dogfish Head's Midas Touch beer... when we drink we do it right #gettingslizzerd" — How would you answer? Red Cross deleted the tweet and used this message *"We've deleted the rogue tweet but rest assured the Red Cross is sober and we've confiscated the keys."* The employee also responded, *"Rogue tweet frm @RedCross due to my inability to use Hootsuite...I wasn't actually #gettingslizard but just excited! #nowembarrasing."* Do you think they handled it well? What communication strategy did they use?

### Question 2
Last Mile Health approached you to help position their brand — do you think it is global? Why? How do you think it should be positioned? Do you think urban pockets of poverty can benefit from Last Mile Health?

### Question 3
Pick a local SEV and help them manage their networks using Exhibit 6.7.

### Question 4
Look at the Sauti Kuu Foundation (Kenya and Germany)[136] — if they decided to internationalize, how would you suggest they use networks to do so? Should they go regional first?

### Question 5
Look at the UN list of tabled allegation https://conduct.unmissions.org/table-of-allegations. How would you plan for crises of this nature? What are some of the interventions that are needed?

# Sources

### Case Study 6.1: Last Mile Health (Liberia)

Compiled from various sources: Dreifus, C. (2017), "Dr. Raj panjabi goes the last mile in liberia," *New York Times*, dated 31 July, Available: https://www.nytimes.com/2017/07/31/health/raj-panjabi-last-mile-health-liberia.html [Accessed 13 January 2019]; Last Mile Health website; Gavi (2018), "New initiative to bring vaccination to over 8 million people across Africa," dated 15 August, Available: https://www.gavi.org/library/news/press-releases/2018/new-initiative-to-bring-vaccination-to-over-8-million-people-across-africa/ [Accessed 13 January 2019]; Last Mile Health (2019), "Centre for health market innovations," Available: https://healthmarketinnovations.org/program/last-mile-health [Accessed 13 January 2019]; Chater, R., van Niekerk, L. and Lim, J. (2016). *Last Mile Health, Liberia.* Social Innovation in Health Initiative Case Collection. [Online] WHO, Geneva: Social Innovation in Health Initiative, Available: https://socialinnovationinhealth.org/2016/11/04/case-study-last-mile-health/ [Accessed 14 January 2019]; Last Mile Health Strategic Plan 2017–2019, Available: https://www.dropbox.com/s/uk7keg8olxw4l9p/LMH_StrategicPlan_Final.pdf?dl=0 [Accessed 13 April 2019]; Philanthropy News Digest (2018), "Last mile health, living goods launch community healthcare initiative," dated 29 January, Available: https://philanthropynewsdigest.org/news/last-mile-health-living-goods-launch-community-healthcare-initiative [Accessed 10 January 2019]; Skoll Foundation (2017), "Last mile health," Available http://skoll.org/organization/last-mile-health/ [Accessed 10 January 2019]; Itkowitz, C. (2017), "This harvard doctor has a plan to save 30 million lives by 2030," *Washington Post*, dated April 26, Available: https://www.washingtonpost.com/news/inspired-life/wp/2017/04/26/how-this-harvard-doctor-plans-to-use-a-1-million-prize-to-solve-global-health-crises/?noredirect=on&utm_term=.add3e37aa7b9 [Accessed 13 January 2019].

### Case Study 6.2: International Humanitarian City (Dubai, UAE)

Compiled from various sources: Interviews conducted with IHC representatives on 14 January 2019; IHC 2018. The Official Website of HRH Princess Haya Bint Al Hussein, https://princesshaya.net/english/interests/humanitarian/ [Accessed 1 January 2019]. IHC 2019. Official Website: http://www.ihc.ae [Accessed 1 January 2019]; IHC (2018), "International humanitarian city launches pioneering platform to revolutionise global relief efforts," dated 11 February, Available: http://www.ihc.ae/international-humanitarian-city-launches-pioneering-platform-to-revolutionise-global-relief-efforts/ [Accessed 1 January 2019].

### Case Study 6.3: Girl Effect, UK: Creating Grassroots Change

Compiled from various sources: Atlas of the Future (2019), "Girls built Rwanda's biggest media brand — Ni Nyampinga — Girl effect," Available: https://atlasofthefuture.org/project/ni-nyampinga-girl-effect/ [Accessed 14 April 2019]; Harriman Steel (nd), "Girl effect: Ni Nyampinga," Available: http://www.harrimansteel.com/girl-effect-ni-nyampinga/ [Accessed 13 April 2019]; Johnston, A. (2018), "Girl effect: What social change means, and why it matters," *London Business School*, dated 29 January, Available: https://www.london.edu/faculty-and-research/lbsr/girl-effect-what-social-change-means-and-why-it-matters [Accessed 13 April 2019]; Kanani, R. (2014), "The nike foundation on unleashing the 'Girl Effect'," *Huffington Post*, dated 20 June, Available: https://www.huffingtonpost.com/rahim-kanani/nike-foundation-girl-effect_b_850551.html [Accessed 13 April 2019]; Nike Foundation Press Release (2008), "NIKE, NoVo Foundation commit $100 million to the girl effect," Available: https://philanthropynewsdigest.org/news/nike-novo-foundation-commit-100-million-to-the-girl-effect [Accessed 13 April 2019]; The New York Times (2012), ""Ni Nyampinga," a new platform for Rwandan girls' voices," dated 16 January, Available: https://www.newtimes.co.rw/section/read/38600 [Accessed 14 April 2019].

### Case Study 6.4: Crisis: Oxfam, Haiti

Compiled from various sources: Gayle, D. (2018), "Timeline: Oxfam sexual exploitation scandal in Haiti," *The Guardian*, 15 June, Available: https://www.theguardian.com/world/2018/jun/15/timeline-oxfam-sexual-exploitation-scandal-in-haiti [Accessed 14 April 2019]; Hopkins, N. (2018), "Oxfam to axe jobs and aid programmes in £16m cuts after scandal," *The Guardian*, dated 15 June, Available: https://www.theguardian.com/world/2018/jun/15/oxfam-warns-staff-urgent-savings-16m-haiti-scandal [Accessed 14 April 2019].

# ENDNOTES

1 Gibelman, M. and Gelman, S. R. (2001), "Very public scandals: Nongovernmental organizations in trouble," *Voluntas: International Journal of Voluntary and Nonprofit Organizations*, 12(1): 49–66.

2 Kaul, I., Grungberg, I. and Stern, M. A. (1999), "Global public goods," *Global Public Goods*, 450–546.

3 Buckley, P. and Casson, M. (1976), *The Future of the Multinational Enterprise*, London, UK: MacMillan Press.

4 WHO (2019), *Regional Trade Agreements – Facts & Figures*, Available: https://www.wto.org/english/tratop_e/region_e/region_e.htm [Accessed: 2 February 2019].

5 Maluck, J., Glanemann, N. and Donner, R. V. (2018), "Bilateral trade agreements and the interconnectedness of global trade." *Frontiers of Physics*, Available: https://doi.org/10.3389/fphy.2018.00134 [Accessed 13 April 2019].

6 Scholte, J. A. (2002), "What is globalization? The definitional Issue–again," *Coventry, Centre for the Study of Globalisation and Regionalisation (CSGR), Department of Politics and International Studies, University of Warwick*.

7 Kaul, I., Grungberg, I. and Stern, M. A. (1999), *Op. cit.*

8 *Ibid.*

9 Coff, R. W. (1999), "When competitive advantage doesn't lead to performance: The resource-based view and stakeholder bargaining power," *Organization Science*, 10(2): 119–133.

10 Barnett, M. L. (2007), "Stakeholder influence capacity and the variability of financial returns to corporate social responsibility," *Academy of Management Review*, 32(3): 794–816.

11 Wood, D. (1991), "Corporate social performance revisited," *Academy of Management Review*, 16: 691–718.

12 Coff, R. W. (1999), *Op. cit.*

13 Balakrishnan, M. S. and Lindsay, V. (2013), "The rise of the global social entrepreneur: A conceptual framework," In: *55th Academy of International Business Annual Conference, Bridging the Divide: Linking IB to Complementary Disciplines and Practice*, Istanbul, Turkey, 3–6 July.

14 Mulgan, G. (2006), "The process of social innovation," *Innovations: Technology, Governance, Globalization*, 1(2): 145–162.

15 Gillwald, K. (2000), "Konzepte sozialer Innovation," *WZB paper: Querschnittsgruppe Arbeit und Ökologie*, Berlin, Available: http://bibliothek.wzb.eu/pdf/2000/p00-519.pdf [Accessed 13 April 2019].

16 New York Times (1998), *Body Shop Chief To Step Down*, dated 13 May, Available https://www.nytimes.com/1998/05/13/business/international-business-body-shop-chief-to-step-down.html [Accessed 10 April 2019].

17 Kesselring, A. and Leitner, M. (2008), "Soziale innovationen in Unternehmen," Study compiled by order of the Unruhe Stiftung: Vienna, Available: http://www.zsi.at/attach/Soziale_Innovation_in_Unternehmen_ENDBERICHT.pdf [Accessed 14 April 2019], p. 28.

18 Haig, S. (2017), "Afghan entrepreneur empowers women through bitcoin," *Bitcoin*, dated 13 August, Available: https://news.bitcoin.com/afghan-entrepreneur-empowers-women-through-bitcoin-in-afghanistan/ [Accessed 12 April 2019].

19 Bill & Melinda Gates Foundation (2014), "*The opportunities of digitizing payments*," Available: http://siteresources.worldbank.org/EXTGLOBALFIN/Resources/8519638-1332259343991/G20_Report_Final_Digital_payments.pdf [Accessed 4 November 2018].

20 IRC (2016), "*Making electronic payments work for humanitarian response*," Available: https://www.rescue.org/sites/default/files/document/469/makinge-paymentsworkforhumanitarianresponse-final1.pdf [Accessed 12 April 2019].

21 Runco, M. A. and Jaeger, G. J. (2012), "The standard definition of creativity," *Creativity Research Journal*, 24(1): 92–96.

22 Stein, M. I. (1953), "Creativity and culture," *Journal of Psychology*, 36: 31–322.

23 Csikszentmihalyi, M. (1996). *Creativity: Flow and the Psychology of Discovery and Invention*. NY: Harper Perennial, p. 28.

24 McNabb, D. E. (2006), *Knowledge Management in the Public Sector: A Blueprint for Innovation in Government*, ME Sharpe.

25 Mulgan, G., Tucker, S., Ali, R. and Sanders, B. (2007), "Social innovation: What it is, why it matters and how it can be accelerated," Available: http://eureka.sbs.ox.ac.uk/761/1/Social_Innovation.pdf [Accessed 21 August 2018].

26 Damanpour, F. (1991), "Organizational innovation — A meta-analysis of effects of determinants and moderators," *Academy of Management Journal*, 34(3): 555–590.

27 Baregheh, A., Rowley, J. and Sambrook, S. (2009), "Towards a multidisciplinary definition of innovation," *Management Decision*, 47(8): 1323–1339.

28 Thompson, V. A. (1965), "Bureaucracy and innovation," *Administrative Science Quarterly*, 10: 1–20.

29 Van de Ven, A. (1986), "Central problems in the management of innovation", *Management Science*, 32(5): 590–607.

30 Dosi, G. (1990), "Finance, innovation and industrial change," *Journal of Economic Behavior & Organization*, 13(3): 299–319.

31 Becker, S. W. and Whisler, T. L. (1967), "The innovative organization: A selective view of current theory and research," *The Journal of Business*, 40(4): 463.

32 Amabile, T. M. (1983), "The social psychology of creativity: A componential conceptualization," *Journal of Personality and Social Psychology*, 45(2): 357–367.

33 Extracted from Moonesar, I. A., Stephens, M., Batey, M. and Hughes, D. (2019), "Innovation & creativity: A case of government of Dubai," In: Stephens, M., El Sholkamy, M., Moonesar, I. A. and Awamleh, R. (eds.), *Future Governments*, Emerald Group Publishing: UK.

34 Sitkin, S. B. and Pablo, A. I. (1992), "Reconceptualizing the determinants of risk behavior," *The Academy of Management Review*, 17(1): 9–38.

35 Post, J. E. (2000), *Meeting the Challenge of Global Corporate Citizenship* (research paper), Boston, MA: Boston College Center for Corporate Community Relations, p. 16.

36 Eisenmann, T. R., Ries, E. and Dillard, S. (2012), "Hypothesis-driven entrepreneurship: The lean startup," *Harvard Business School Entrepreneurial Management Case No.* 812-095.

37 Nobel, C. (2011), "Teaching a 'lean startup' strategy," *HBS Working Knowledge*, pp. 1–2.

38 Marmer, M., Herrmann, B. L., Dogrultan, E., Berman, R., Eesley, C. and Blank, S. (2011), "Startup genome report extra: Premature scaling," *Startup Genome*, 10: 1–56.

39 Blank, S. (2005), *The Four Steps to the Epiphany: Successful Strategies for Products that Win*, Texas: K&S Ranch.

40 Nirwan, M. D. and Dhewanto, W. (2015), "Barriers in implementing the lean startup methodology in Indonesia — Case Study of B2B startup," *Procedia-Social and Behavioral Sciences*, 169: 23–30.

41 Cavusgil, S. T. and Knight, G. (2015), "The born global firm: An entrepreneurial and capabilities perspective on early and rapid internationalization," *Journal of International Business Studies*, 46(1): 3–16; Oviatt, B. M. and McDougall, P. P. (2005), "Toward a theory of international new ventures," *Journal of International Business Studies*, 36(1): 29–41.

42 Knight, J. and de Wit, H. (eds.) (1997), *Internationalisation of Higher Education in Asia Pacific Countries*, European Association for International Education.

43 Paco, A., Rodrigues, R. G. and Rodrigues, L. (2014), "Branding in NGOs — Its influence on the intension to donate," *Economics and Sociology*, 7(3): 11–21.

44 Chehab, A., Liu, J. and Xiao, Y. (2016), "More on intangibles: Do stockholders benefit from brand values?," *Global Finance Journal*, 30: 1–9; Interbrand (2017), *Best Global Brands 2017*. Available: http://interbrand.com/best-brands/best-global-brands/2017/ranking [Accessed 20 November 2017]: 51; Johansson, J. K., Dimofte, C. V. and Mazvancheryl, S. K. (2012), "The performance of global brands in the 2008 financial crisis: A test of two brand value measures," *International Journal of Research in Marketing*, 29(3): 235–245; Millard Brown (2017), *Most Valuable Brands*, Available: http://brandz.com/admin/uploads/files/BZ_Global_2017_Report.pdf [Accessed 1 November 2017], p. 17.

45 Steenkamp, J. B. (2014), "How global brands create firm value: The 4V model," *International Marketing Review*, 31(1): 5–29.

46 Davvetas, V. and Diamantopoulos, A. (2016), "How product category shapes preferences toward global and local brands: A schema theory perspective," *Journal of International Marketing*, 24(4): 61–81; Johansson, J. K. and Ronkainen, I. A. (2005), "The esteem of global brands," *Brand Management*, 12(5): 339–354; Özsomer, A. (2012), "The interplay between global and local brands: A closer look

at perceived brand globalness and local iconness," *Journal of International Marketing*, 20(2): 72-95; Steenkamp, J. B. E., Batra R. and Alden, D. L. (2003), "How perceived brand globalness creates brand value," *Journal of International Business Studies*, 34(1): 53-65; Swoboda, B., Pennemann, K. and Taube, M. (2012), "The effects of perceived brand globalness and perceived brand localness in China: Empirical evidence on Western, Asian, and domestic retailers," *Journal of International Marketing*, 20(4): 72-95; Yu, L. (2003), "The global-brand advantage: Research indicates that buyers are more likely to perceive value in global brands (Marketing)," *MIT Sloan Management Review*, 44(3): 13-14.

47  According to the transnationality index calculated by UNCTAD, 2002.

48  For more on BOGO, read Marquis, C. and Park, A. (2014), "Inside the buy-one give-one model," *Stanford Social Innovation Review*, Winter, pp. 28-33.

49  Punia, K. (2013), "VisionSpring & #8211; helping people see the world in a better way, literally," *YourStory*, 1 August, Available: https://yourstory.com/2013/08/visionspring-helping-people-see-the-world-in-a-better-way-literally/ [Accessed 2 February 2019].

50  Steenkamp, J. B. E. (2014), *Op. cit.*, p. 7.

51  Knight, G. A. and Cavusgil, S. T. (1996), "The born global firm: A challenge to traditional internationalization theory," *Advances in International Marketing*, 8: 11-26.

52  Luostarinen, R. and Gabrielsson, M. (2006), "Globalization and marketing strategies of born globals in SMOPECs," *Thunderbird International Business Review*, 48(6): 773-801.

53  Rennie, M. W. (1993), "Born global," *The McKinsey Quarterly*, Autumn: 45.

54  Crick, D. (2009), "The internationalisation of born global and international new venture SMEs," *International Marketing Review*, 4(5): 453-476.

55  Lopez, L. E., Kundu, S. K. and Ciravegna, L. (2009), "Born global or born regional? Evidence from an exploratory study in the Costa Rican software industry," *Journal of International Business Studies*, 40(7): 1228-1238.

56  Zahra, S. A., Gedajlovic, E., Neubaum, D. O. and Shulman, J. M. (2009), "A typology of social entrepreneurs: Motives, search processes and ethical challenges," *Journal of Business Venturing*, 24(5): 519-532.

57  The Economic Times (2019), "NGO crackdown has foreign fund inflows plunging 40% since Modi govt era: Report," dated 10 March, Available: https://economictimes.indiatimes.com/news/politics-and-nation/ngo-crackdown-has-foreign-fund-inflows-plunging-40-since-modi-govt-era-report/articleshow/68342585.cms [Accessed 13 April 2019].

58  Krebs, R. R. and Ron, James (2018), "Why Countries should welcome, not fear, foreign funding of NGOs," *Lawfare*, dated 13 May, Available: https://www.lawfareblog.com/why-countries-should-welcome-not-fear-foreign-funding-ngos [Accessed 12 April 2019].

59  TOMS (2019): Available: https://www.toms.com/production.

60  Miyoshi, M. (1993), "A borderless world? From colonialism to transnationalism and the decline of the nation-state," *Critical Inquiry*, 19(4): 726-751.

61  Samiee, S. and Roth, K. (1992), "The influence of global marketing standardization on performance," *The Journal of Marketing*, 1-17.

62  Steenkamp, J. B. E., Batra R. and Alden, D. L. (2003), "How perceived brand globalness creates brand value," *Journal of International Business Studies*, 34(1): 53-65.

63  Pitta, D. A. and Franzak, F. J. (2008), "Foundations for building share of heart in global brands," *Journal of Product & Brand Management*, 17(2): 64-72.

64  Bengtsson, A., Bardhi, F. and Venkatraman, M. (2010), "How global brands travel with consumers: An examination of the relationship between brand consistency and meaning across national boundaries," *International Marketing Review*, 27(5): 519-540.

65  Alden, D. L., Steenkamp, J. B. E. and Batra, R. (1999), "Brand positioning through advertising in Asia, North America, and Europe: The role of global consumer culture," *The Journal of Marketing*, 75-87.

66  Kylander, N. and Stone, C. (2012), "The role of brand in the nonprofit sector", *Stanford Social Innovation Review*, Spring, Available: https://ssir.org/articles/entry/the_role_of_brand_in_the_nonprofit_sector [Accessed 12 April 2019].

67  *Ibid.*

68  Holt, D. B., Quelch, J. A. and Taylor, E. L. (2004), "How global brands compete," *Harvard Business Review*, 82(9): 68–75.

69  Strizhakova, Y., Coulter, R. A. and Price, L. L. (2011), "Branding in a global marketplace: The mediating effects of quality and self-identity brand signals," *International Journal of Research in Marketing*, 28(4): 342–351.

70  The Giving Keys: https://www.thegivingkeys.com/pages/impact.

71  Coviello, N. E. and Munro, H. J. (1997), "Network relationships and the internationalization process of small software firms," *International Business Review*, 6: 361–386; Moen, O. and Servais, P. (2002), "Born global or gradual global? Examining the export behavior of small and medium-sized enterprises," *Journal of International Marketing*, 10(3): 49–72.

72  For more on Original Unverpackt: https://original-unverpackt.de/ueber-original-unverpackt-2/.

73  Stephens Balakrishnan, M., Hamzaoui Essoussi, L., Papadopoulos, N., Richter, U. and Balasubramanian, S. (2018), "The relevance of 'globalness' in brand-fit strategy," In: *60th Academy of International Business Annual Conference*, Minneapolis, USA, 26–28 June.

74  Cavusgil, S. T. and Knight, G. (2015), *Op. cit.*; Oviatt, B. M. and McDougall, P. P. (2005), "Toward a theory of international new ventures," *Journal of International Business Studies*, 36(1): 29–41.

75  Verbeke, A., Amin Zargarzadeh, M. and Osiyevskyy, O. (2014), "Internationalization theory, entrepreneurship and international new ventures," *Multinational Business Review*, 22(3): 246–269.

76  McDougall, P. P. and Oviatt, B. M. (2000), "International entrepreneurship: The intersection of two research paths," *Academy of Management Journal*, 43(5): 902–906.

77  Gerschewski, S., Rose, E. L. and Lindsay, V. J. (2014), "Understanding the drivers of international performance for born global firms: An integrated perspective," *Journal of World Business*, 50(3): 558–575.

78  Mason, C., Kirkbride, J. and Bryde, D. (2007), "From stakeholders to institutions: The changing face of social enterprise governance theory," *Management Decision*, 45(2): 284–301.

79  Harihahran, A. (nd), "All about network effects," *Andreesen Horowitz*, Available: https://a16z.com/2016/03/07/all-about-network-effects/?fbclid=IwAR2BIVNmoqOX8fvwSG709N_FdXA7z9KbOtvyXLDdTcKp2w44XKgimsSoBvQ [Accessed 18 January 2019].

80  Acedo, F. J. and Jones, M. V. (2007), "Speed of internationalisation and entrepreneurial cognition: Insights and a comparison between international new ventures, exporters and domestic firms," *Journal of World Business*, 42(8): 236–252.

81  Ratten, V., Dana, L. P., Han, M. and Welpe, I. (2007), "Internationalisation of SMEs: European comparative studies," *International Journal of Entrepreneurship and Small Business*, 4(3): 361–379.

82  *Ibid.*

83  Rowley, T. J. (1997), "Moving beyond dyadic ties: A network theory of stakeholder influences," *Academy of Management Review*, 22(4): 887–910.

84  *Ibid.*

85  Oliver, C. (1991), "Strategic reponses to institutional processes," *Academy of Management Review*, 16: 145–179.

86  *Ibid.*

87  Mintzberg, H. (1983), *Power in and around Organizations*, Englewood Cliffs, NJ: Prentice-Hall.

88  Gilsing, V., Nooteboom, B., Vanhaverbeke, W., Duysters, G. and van den Oord, A. (2008), "Network embeddedness and the exploration of novel technologies: Technological distance, betweenness centrality and density," *Research Policy*, 37(10): 1717–1731.

89  Solberg, C. A. and Durrieu, F. (2006), "Access to networks and commitment to internationalisation as precursors to marketing strategies in international markets," *Management International Review*, 46(1): 57–83.

90  Freeman, L. C. (1979), "Centrality in social networks: Conceptual clarifications," *Social Networks*, 1: 125–239.

91  *Ibid.*

92  Endeavor, (2014), *The New York City Tech Map*, Available: http://nyctechmap.com/ [Accessed 14 January 2019].

93  Marcum, T. M. and Blair, E. S. (2011), "Entrepreneurial decisions and legal issues in early venture stages: Advice that shouldn't be ignored," *Business Horizons*, 54: 143–152.

94  Stinchcombe, A. L. (1965), "Social structure and organizations," In: March, J. G. (ed.), *Handbook of Organizations*, Rand McNally, Chicago, IL: 14; Freeman, J., Carroll, G. R. and Hannan, M. T. (1983), "The liability of newness: Age dependence in organizational death rates", *American Sociological Review*, 48: 692-710; Baum, J. A. C. (1996), "Organizational ecology," In: Hardy, C. C. and Nord, W. (eds.), *Handbook of Organizational Studies*, Sage: London, pp. 77-114.

95  Barringer, B. R., Jones, F. F. and Neubaum, D. O. (2005), "A quantitative content analysis of the characteristics of rapid-growth firms and their founders," *Journal of Business Venturing*, 20(5): 663-687.

96  *Ibid.*

97  Brush, C. G., Greene, P. G. and Hart, M. M. (2001), "From initial idea to unique advantage: The entrepreneurial challenge of constructing a resource base," *Academy of Management Perspectives*, 15(1): 64-78.

98  Pennings, J. M., Lee, K. and Witteloostuijn, A. V. (1998), "Human capital, social capital, and firm dissolution," *Academy of Management Journal*, 41(4): 425-440.

99  Carlsson, B. and Jacobsson, S. (1997), "In search of useful public policies: Key lessons and issues for policy makers," In: Carlsson, B. (ed.), *Technological Systems and Industrial Dynamics*, Kluwer Academic Publishers, Dordrecht.

100  Woolthuis, R. K., Lankhuizen, M. and Gilsing, V. (2005), "A system failure framework for innovation policy design," *Technovation*, 25(6): 609-619.

101  More about the Forward Trust: https://www.forwardtrust.org.uk/news-and-updates/the-forward-trust-formerly-blue-sky-wins-major-charity-award-for-ground-breaking-partnership/.

102  Al Nahyan, S. S. S. and Stephens, M. (2018), *Empowering Women in Remote Communities and Safeguarding Heritage: The Case of Sougha, a Khalifa Fund Initiative, Case Study*, MBRSG Case Study.

103  Esser, J. K. (1998), "Alive and well after 25 years: A review of groupthink research," *Organizational Behavior and Human Decision Processes*, 73(2-3): 116-141.

104  BarNir, A. and Smith, K. A. (2002), "Interfirm alliances in the small business: The role of social networks," *Journal of Small Business Management*, 40(3): 219-232.

105  Rowley, T. J. (1997), "Moving beyond dyadic ties: A network theory of stakeholder influences," *Academy of Management Review*, 22(4): 887-910.

106  Curasi, C. F. and Kennedy, K. N. (2002), "From prisoners to apostles: A typology of repeat buyers and loyal customers in service businesses," *Journal of Services Marketing*, 16(4): 322-341.

107  Courtney, H. (2001), "Making the most of uncertainty," *McKinsey Quarterly*, 4: 39-47.

108  Pearson, C. M. and Clair, J. A. (1998), "Reframing crisis management," *Academy of Management Review*, 23(1): 59-76.

109  Darling, J. R. (1994), "Crisis management in international business: Keys to effective decision making," *Leadership and Organization Development Journal*, 15(8): 3-8; Fink, S. (1986), "Crisis forecasting," *Management Review*, 75(3): 52-57; Lerbinger, O. (1997), *The Crisis Manager: Facing Risk and Responsibility*, Lawrence Erlbaum Associates, Hillsdale, NJ; Tew, P. J., Lu, P., Tolomiczenko, G. and Gellatly, J. (2008), "SARS: Lessons in strategic planning for hoteliers and destination marketers," *International Journal of Contemporary Hospitality Management*, 20(3): 332-346.

110  Taleb, N. N. (2010), *The Black Swan: The Impact of the Highly Probable*, New York: Random House.

111  Stephens Balakrishnan, M. (2016), "Managing uncertainty in emerging markets: Lessons from the MENA region," In: Merchant, H. (ed.), *Handbook of Research on Emerging Markets*. USA: Edward Elgar Publishing, pp. 317-354; Stephens Balakrishnan, M. (2012), "Managing in uncertain times," In: Balakrishnan, M. S., Michael, I., Rogmans, T. and Moonesar, I. A. (eds.), *Actions and Insights: Middle East North Africa (Vol. 2): Managing in Uncertain Times*. UK: Emerald Group Publishing, pp, xvii-xxxix.

112  Darling, J. R. (1994), *Op. cit.*; Smith, D. (1999), *Exploring the Barriers to Learning Around Crises*, mimeo, Centre for Risk and Crisis Management, University of Sheffield, Sheffield.

113  Dearstyne, B. (2007), "The FDNY on 9/11: Information and decision making in crisis," *Government Information Quarterly*, 24(1): 29-46; Garcia, H. F. (2006), "Effective leadership response to crisis," *Strategy & Leadership*, 34(1): 4-10; Wang, W.-T. (2009), "Knowledge management adoption in times of crisis," *Industrial Management & Data Systems*, 109(4): 445-462.

114 Smallman, C. and Weir, D. (1999), "Communications and cultural distortion during crisis," *Disaster Prevention and Management*, 8(1): 33–41.

115 Stephens Balakrishnan, M. (2011), "Protecting from brand burn during times of crisis Mumbai 26/11: A case of the Taj Mahal Palace and Tower Hotel," *Management Research Review*, 43(12): 1309–1333; Tew, P. J., Lu, P., Tolomiczenko, G. and Gellatly, J. (2008), *Op. cit.*

116 Tew, P. J., Lu, P., Tolomiczenko, G. and Gellatly, J. (2008), *Op. cit.*; Ritchie, B. W. (2004), "Chaos, crises and disasters: A strategic approach to crisis management in the tourism industry," *Tourism Management*, 25: 669–683.

117 Ashcroft, L. (1997), "Crisis management — public relations," *Journal of Managerial Psychology*, 12(5): 325–332.

118 Vassilikopoulou, A., Siomkos, G., Chatzipanagiotou, K. and Triantafillidou, A. (2009), "Hotels on fire: Investigating consumers' responses and perceptions," *International Journal of Contemporary Hospitality Management*, 21(7): 791–815.

119 Garcia, H. F. (2006), *Op. cit.*

120 Stephens Balakrishnan, M. (2016), *Op. cit.*

121 An interesting paper on managing blog influencers can be found here: Liu, B. F., Jin, Y., Briones, R. and Kuch, B. (2012), "Managing turbulence in the blogosphere: Evaluating the blog-mediated crisis communication model with the American Red Cross," *Journal of Public Relations Research*, 24(4): 353–370.

122 Vecchi, G. M., Van Hasselt, V. B. and Romano, S. J. (2005), "Crisis (hostage) negotiation: Current strategies and issues in high-risk conflict resolution," *Aggression and Violent Behavior*, 10(5): 533–551.

123 Coombs, W. T. and Holladay, S. J. (1996), "Communication and attributions in a crisis: An experimental study in crisis communication," *Journal of Public Relations Research*, 8(4): 279–295.

124 Domschat, L., Stephens, M. and Sayani, H. (2019), "Communication to protect brand image during a terrorism crisis," *Forthcoming paper*.

125 Luege, T. (2017), "Links I liked: Twiplomacy, Rohingya left in the dark, facebook shares more crisis data," *Social Media for Good*, Available: http://sm4good.com/2017/11/30/links-i-liked-twiplomacy-rohingya-left-in-the-dark-facebook-shares-more-crisis-data/ [Accessed 22 January 2019].

126 Gibelman, M. and Gelman, S. R. (2001), "Very public scandals: Nongovernmental organizations in trouble," *Voluntas: International Journal of Voluntary and Nonprofit Organizations*, 12(1): 49–66.

127 Schnackenberg, A. K. and Tomlinson, E. C. (2016), "Organizational transparency: A new perspective on managing trust in organization-stakeholder relationships," *Journal of Management*, 42(7): 1784–1810.

128 *Ibid*.

129 Klotz, L., Horman, M., Bi, H. H. and Bechtel, J. (2008), "The impact of process mapping on transparency," *International Journal of Productivity and Performance Management*, 57(8): 623–636.

130 For example, budgets can follow OECD Best Practices of Budget Transparency: see Blöndal, J. R. (2006) as cited by Caamaño-Alegre, J., Lago-Peñas, S., Reyes-Santias, F. and Santiago-Boubeta, A. (2013), "Budget transparency in local governments: An empirical analysis," *Local Government Studies*, 39(2): 182–207.

131 Turilli, M. and Floridi, L. (2009), "The ethics of information transparency," *Ethics and Information Technology*, 11(2): 105–112.

132 Williams, C. C. (2008), "Toward a taxonomy of corporate reporting strategies," *Journal of Business Communication*, 45(3): 232–264.

133 Anand, V. and Rosen, C. C. (2008), "The ethics of organizational secrets," *Journal of Management Inquiry*, 17: 97–101.

134 Read the paper on Transparency International's approach to measuring corruption. Andersson, S. and Heywood, P. M. (2009), "The politics of perception: Use and abuse of Transparency International's approach to measuring corruption," *Political Studies*, 57(4): 746–767.

135 Collier, M. (2017), "How the Red Cross defused a potential social media crisis situation," Available: http://www.mackcollier.com/red-cross-social-media-crisis-situation/ [Accessed 22 January 2018]. If you are looking for a good guide on how to use social media during a crisis here is one: http://sm4good.com/2017/10/11/red-cross-and-un-release-guide-on-how-to-use-social-media-in-emergencies/

136 Sauti Kuu Foundation: https://sautikuufoundation.org/en/how-it-began/

# MEASURING IMPACT AND CONTROL

## Chapter Objectives

➢ Identify and understand the importance of impact metrics.

➢ Plan an intervention strategy.

➢ Find methods to translate metrics to financial numbers for comparison, better control, and increasing investment chances.

➢ Understanding the difficulties of auditing for control and accountability.

➢ Explaining the importance of separating the organization from the person.

➢ **Cases:** @ThisIsOurLane & #ThisIsMyLane movement (crowd-sourced advocacy — gun control: USA), Beacon of Hope (sustainability, education, tolerance: UAE/impact: refugees around the world), IKEA Foundation (refugee: Netherlands (headquarters)/impact: Jordan), Lucky Iron Fish (health: Canada/impact: Cambodia); and THE 99 (tolerance: Kuwait/impact: global).

## 7.1. Introduction

While you were briefly introduced to the theory of change in the previous chapters, you will delve into it in detail to understand how to identify relevant impact metrics for your SEV and develop a process of monitoring and evaluation. The SEV environment is dynamic, and this means that interventions may (most likely) not go as planned. You can scale vertically (going deep) or horizontally (go wide) and this in both ways may seem like a dilution of purpose. Hence, the North Star for your decisions on SEV strategy should be the goal you set out. The challenge for any SEV or any organization working on social values is that it is tough to take something intangible and convert it into tangible objectives.

One of the challenges facing the business world is the debate on value versus profits. This debate was given a new twist with the concepts of shared value outlined by Porter and Kramer in 2011.[1] They found a way to introduce societal progress into the profitability and competitiveness arena that businesses operate in. The idea at that time was considered different, as it highlighted the importance of introducing metrics to track social impacts and tie them to their economic interests at the business level. Will the dual purpose dilute social impact? For-profit stakeholders may worry that dual purpose will dilute economic impact.

## 7.2. **Why Impact Metrics Matter**

Social impact is defined as "*Intended and unintended consequences (psychological or physiological or social) of planned interventions to human populations of any public or private actions that alter the ways in which people live, work, play, relate to one another, organize to meet their needs, and generally act as a member of society. A positive value is created when it is over and above normal trends and impact lives positively.*"[2] Several points need to be highlighted as follows:

(1) Planned interventions can have intended and unintended consequences.

(2) The outcomes need not be just economic ones; they can be psychological, or physiological, or social.

(3) It is vital to track the various ways people live, work, play, relate to one another, organize to meet their needs, and generally act as a member of society.

(4) You can only consider yourself successful when your intervention impacts lives positively.

(5) You need to discount the effect of normal trends and other interventions to know if you were successful.

Measuring social impact is not easy, but many SEVs only measure them after they begin working on communities or create interventions which may not give them a good baseline of data to track change. Look at Case Study 7.1 on the impact of NRA and explain with the definition of social impact what the areas of concern are.

## 7.3. **Planning for a Change Intervention**

In an ideal situation, SEVs should begin planning interventions after a good understanding of the ecosystem and the problem they are solving. There are two fundamental questions they must ask:

(1) Do I have the right root problem or in other words, how do I know that I am not looking at the symptom of a problem?

If a problem is defined by the symptom, the ability to correct the issue will be unlikely. Root cause analysis is a tool we use in business situations, especially in the *kaizen* way of thinking,

## Case Study 7.1: **#ThisIsMyLane Movement & @ThisIsYourLane**

Take, for example, a scenario where people fear for their lives. Well, you might think — let us give them guns and teach them to shoot. But when you don't get rid of the inherent paranoia or teach them how to lock their weapons, you end up with a "shoot first ask response later" or accidental shootings, or worse, another paranoid generation that never grew up in the same situation! The National Rifle Association Foundation's (USA) mission is "preserving the core of our American values and traditions in our steadfast effort to Teach Freedom." In fact, according to the "Donor Bill of Rights and Policy on Privacy," NRA states that it *"was established to assure that philanthropy merits the respect and trust of the general public and that donors and prospective donors can have full confidence in The NRA Foundation."* Veiled ignorance is not valid for SEVs who must look at impact (intended or intended) in measuring impact.

In the USA, doctors began clashing with the NRA, which is a powerful gun industry lobby, for the ban of assault weapons. The doctors uploaded casualty pictures of victims of gun attack on Twitter using the hashtag #thisismylane on the twitter site @thisisourlane. The stories are devastating, but they chronicle these victims. In the USA, it is estimated that 35,000 people die each year by gun-related incidents and two-thirds of them are suicides. This makes USA the country with the highest self-inflicted fatalities in the world (670 people per week or 3.1 per 100,000 people) from gunshot injuries. In Europe, the statistic is 1 out of 100,000 due to stringent gun control laws. This campaign was started by a doctor who was a victim of a stray bullet as a 17-year old. While this is a social movement, it brings home the fact that gun-related avoidable deaths are real. They impact other people than those the NRA sells to. Whose responsibility is to audit SEVs? The SEV? The beneficiaries? The donors and other involved stakeholders? The public? The government? What is missing?

which involves continuous improvement.[3] It involves asking the question "Why". The approach is exemplified in this quote, *"The basis of Toyota's scientific approach is to ask why five times whenever we find a problem ... By repeating why five times, the nature of the problem as well as its solution becomes clear. The solution, or the how-to, is designated as "1H.[4]""* Thus, "Five whys equal one how" (5Ws = 1H). This way, the structural relationships are identified until you reach the root cause of the problem (see Exhibit 7.1).

Exhibit 7.1: **Problem Identification**

To perform the five Whys analysis, adhere to the following steps:

(1) State the core problem that needs to be addressed.

(2) Identify the possible causes for that problem (the first "why"). If various reasons are found, categorize them and use rich data to support it (anecdotes and facts). Here, you could explore surface symptoms (unhappiness, poverty, etc.), human variables (abusive partner), and environment (lives in a flood-prone area), for example.

(3) Rate each cause based on the likelihood that it led to the problem.

(4) Move forward with the top-rated cause and identify the possible causes for that problem (the second "why") following steps 2–3.

(5) Repeat this till the root cause of the problem is identified — the factors are identified.

(6) Draw a connection circle map to identify cause–effect relationships and identify any ladder of inferences in your system of operation. A ladder of inference is a belief that forms from what people see or observe that gets reinforced over time.

(7) From all of the factors identified, work on the one that is most in your control.

This process may also need to look at (1) events that show evidence there is a problem in the form of symptoms; (2) patterns and trends — which may be a function of rules, practices, and cultures; (3) underlying structures — institutions, laws, and regulations; and (4) mental modes, which is a function of beliefs, attitudes, and behaviors. SEVs may have to decide which area they wish to work in. Often an essential job of an SEV is to change perceptions [or reframe] to increase disruptions to *status quo* and acceptance of something new.

Ideally, you will have come up with a process that looks like this.

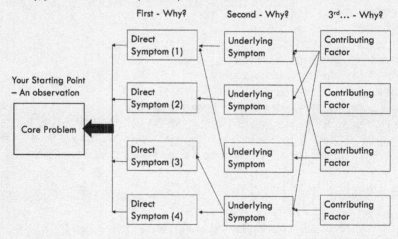

Exhibit 7.1: **(cont)**

A direct symptom (suicide) could be due to depression (underlying symptoms). The underlying symptoms and factors can be (1) inadequate help — no one to reach out to, (2) not enough mental health practitioners, (3) not enough education on the topic for others to recognize depression, (4) not enough money to pay for mental health, and (5) a belief that if they ask for help they are perceived as weak which may be reinforced by society. An iceberg visual helps you understand what is going on. Of course, cross-referencing it with experts and other data sources ensures the decision is not a biased one.

**Obvious Problem (events, what you observe)**

Patterns (historical), trends (data from other sources that can reinforce what you are observing)

Structures (Society, Institutions, Regulations & Laws, etc)

Mental Modes (beliefs, attitudes, behaviours (individual & collective)

(2) Do I have the right solution? (Will it solve the problem in a sustainable and ethical manner and create no other negative impact?)

For this, a good journal paper to read is the one by Card[5] who finds the root problems with the 5Ws and also with the solution in the example given below:

**Problem:** The Washington Monument [the monument in question was in reality, the Lincoln Memorial] is deteriorating.

Why? Harsh chemicals are being used to clean the monument.

Why? The monument is covered in pigeon droppings.

Why? Pigeons are attracted by a large number of spiders at the monument.

Why? Spiders are attracted by a large number of midges at the monument.

Why? Midges are attracted by the fact that the monument is the first monument to be lit at night.

**Solution:** Turn on the lights one hour later.

The facts of this popular story are incorrect, as the monument in question was being damaged by water being used to clean the swarm of midgets that died on impact by being attracted to the light.[6] But it serves as a caution against oversimplification. When the lights were switched on later, though the midges decreased by 85%, an unintended side effect was that tourists were unhappy. Many had driven long distances and were unable to take a picture with the dimly lit monument. Being such a vast majority, when they complained, the authorities eventually switched the lights back on as per the original schedule. Attitude and behaviors of the people involved (even though the problem was the building preservation) needed to be addressed.

Assuming you did manage to (1) identify the root cause of the problem and (2) decide which area you wished to make an impact (structures that foster the problem, people who are impacted by the problem (victims)), you still need to identify the institutions that can help or make the problem worse, people who cause the problem, or even people who are transmitting the problem. Social media can play a strong role as was seen in the spread of false news on measles vaccines that led to the measles outbreak in USA in 2019.

The next job is to identify the correct solution. Here, you need to be ruthlessly clear what you want to do. The 7Ws are useful — who is the target of your intervention, what do you intend to do, when will you do it (and how frequently), where will this take place, why is it necessary, in what way will you do these interventions, by what means will you ensure it is done and done well.

### The ancient philosophers' questions are useful:

> Quis — who,
>
> quid — what,
>
> quando — when,
>
> ubi — where,
>
> cur — why,
>
> quem ad modum — in what way,
>
> quibus adminiculis — by what means,
>
> quomodo — how.

There are three types of results that can be identified as follows[7]:

(1) **Impact:** These are direct changes in the well-being of the target person, family, or community. It can take the form of funding, services, products, etc. Here, you would need to decide the various levels at which impact can take place: individual, family, community, organization, society, national, or international levels.

## Case Study 7.2: **Beacon of Hope (UAE)**

Beacon of Hope was established in 2016 as a non-profit in the UAE by Sheikha Shamma bint Sultan bin Khalifa Al Nahyan. It uses educational material to address sustainability challenges while promoting a culture of empathy and unity across borders. It distributes a solar rechargeable box to children in refugee camps and impoverished areas in Yemen, Jordan, Iraq, Liberia, Morocco, Tanzania, Somalia, Djibouti, USA (in the Bronx area), and Puerto Rico. The kit needs to be assembled by the recipients, which is a learning opportunity in STEM subjects. Light is essential for refugees who often live in dire conditions. It gives them security when night falls and a chance to study when natural daylight fades. It also reduces the adverse impact that kerosene lights have on their health and removes the risk of burns or destructive fire. Included with the material is a teacher resource pack so that the concept of "light" is integrated within the classroom at different grades and in various subjects.

There are over 10,000 beneficiaries. The box was developed by university students from Khalifa University in UAE and has gone through several iterations. A new Beacon of Hope kit that will target the UN Sustainable Development Goals is being developed, which is an outcome of a hackathon. Each box has a message from an Emirati youth to the beneficiary. An example of one of the messages is, "*I hope you like this gift of light. It was fun to make and yours to keep it will help you find your way in the dark and help you find your way to hope.*" This UAE initiative was also represented at the UN Solution Summit and was one of 10 solutions chosen among 1,000 solutions presented to the UN Foundation.

As mentioned by the organization, "*Our initiative targets 3 main focus areas that are essential to the healthy development & growth of children. Our 'beacon-in-a-box' solar light kit is unique because it is quirky & interesting & unlike anything that child has seen in the environment they grew up in, it is stimulating because they get to see what is usually under the hood, they make it with their own hands & they can teach others how to make it. We could hand out ready-made solar lamps, but at the end of the day, what did the child learn? Did they feel helpless receiving a gift from international strangers? Or did they feel accomplished to make their own light with the help of those strangers who at the end of the day become their favorite new friends in the process of learning about renewable energy & building a personal solar powered light?*"

(2) **Influence:** These are changes in policies, regulations, systems, practice, or public opinion. Some strategies in this area can be research, technical assistance, system or policy analysis, advocacy, legislative intervention, information dissemination, and stewardship.

(3) **Leverage:** These are changes in the institution system looking at collective impact. It will involve collaboration with both private and public sectors organizations.

Many SEVs begin at one level, and with time, they find that they have spillover to other levels (see Case Study 7.2). For example, Sulabh started at the family and community level, but was able to get national traction, change laws, and make a difference internationally in how sanitation was approached in impoverished areas. Gavi, on the contrary, was very international from the beginning with its global agenda at the top.

## 7.4. The Intervention Strategy Plan

To create a strategy for social change, many SEVs use the theory of change (TOC) or the logic model (logframes).[8] Carol Weiss, a proponent of TOC, during a roundtable on community change sponsored by Aspen Institute, stressed that SEV programs are difficult to evaluate because the assumptions that inspire them are poorly articulated, the founders are unclear about the change process, and hence evaluation becomes hard for these complex initiatives.[9] The Social Impact Strategy Model is given in Exhibit 7.2, which is a combination of TOC and logframes. Though you interpret the model from left to right (inputs to long-term goal), in reality when designing your Social Impact Strategy Model, you work from right to left (begin first with the long-term goal and end with inputs and assumptions).

Exhibit 7.2:  **Social Impact Strategy Model**

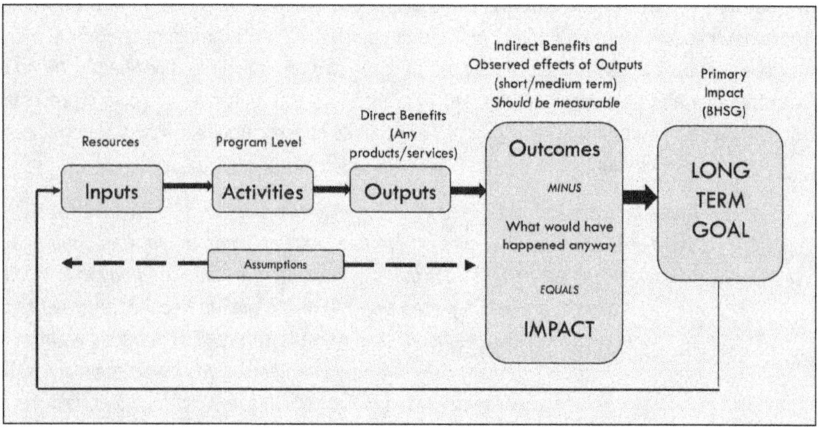

## 7.4.1. *Step 1: Long-term Goal*

Ideally, the long-term goal should capture the problem you are trying to solve. You would need to address the steps outlined in Exhibit 7.2 on problem identification. This also requires you to have a strong understanding of context as defined by *The Open Book of Social Innovation*,[10] which recommends the following steps:

(1) **Mapping needs of the community:** To find hierarchies, bottlenecks, and opportunities;

(2) **Mapping capacities:** To help plan manpower resources, leverage and develop local talent, and increase synergy with existing players;

(3) **Mapping physical assets:** To plan finances and identify gaps in infrastructure, human resources, supplies, and limit future liabilities;

(4) **Mapping systems:** To plan operations keeping in mind the embedded formal and informal contexts to develop reputation and legitimacy;

(5) **Mapping flows:** Understand the flow of goods, people, and information to control factors crucial to the SEV model;

(6) **Mapping expertise:** Expertise may lie outside the SEV and partnerships and networks may give access to capabilities and knowledge.

The goal is long-term. One technique that can be used is to find a Big Hairy Audacious Goal (BHAG — pronounced *Bee-hag*).[11] A Big Hairy Audacious Goal looks 10–30 years into the future and is translated into a vivid description that has three characteristics — passion, emotion, and conviction.[12] Ideally, it should be a quantitative goal (to help audit progress), but in some cases, it is qualitative. It motivates people and helps focus on organizational efforts and resources. A vision reflects purpose and aspirations, but a goal must be something reachable. For example, the idea of a moonshot[13] (NASA's 1960s mission to get a man on the moon). A moonshot refers to a goal that requires thinking on the "edge of tomorrow" and reflect an ambition that has simplicity, clarity, significance, and technical feasibility or plausibility.[14]

There is, of course, an element of uncertainty that it cannot be achieved, but you will know what needs to motivate the organization (and other stakeholders) forward. It must make every employee fired up with a drive to succeed and must be part of the benchmark metrics. It must be imaginable (so not so lofty or unachievable that it becomes a fairy tale). Some SEVs may have by design, short- or medium-term goals and plan on their own obsolescence, but this is not normal.

Somewhere in this process, an SEV must also articulate their core ideology (values and purpose) with which the organization is to be built. Having too many (more than five) reflects dilution of values with other things like operating practices. Values should never change and should be the ethos of the organization. The core purpose explains the reason why the SEV exists and why its people work there — it should capture the "soul of the organization".[15] Core purpose should ideally not be confused with a goal which is more measurable. Core purpose reflects a vision of how you would like to make change occur (ideal state).

For example, Gavi, the Vaccine Alliance's mission is "Saving children's lives and protecting people's health by increasing equitable use of vaccines in lower-income countries".[16] In the case of UNHCR, they are guided by core values to ensure the protection and participation of refugees — as individuals, families, and communities in decisions that affect their lives and respect for fundamental human rights, social justice, and human dignity, and respect for the equal rights of men and women (which is reaffirmed in its other values).[17] In terms of importance, values should be easy to remember and adhere to. Why do you think people join the UNHCR (or ideally should be the reason)? This will help you later as you build your organizational culture and spirit, help with hiring decisions, and training programs.

### 7.4.2. *Step 2: Outcomes*

An SEV answers the following question: "What happens because of our activities?"[18] Outcomes are measurable and need to be articulated at various program levels. They are often indirect benefits or observed effects of outputs and/or activities. For example — by creating vaccine access to children in underdeveloped areas, and protecting people's health, you can prevent/reduce childhood deaths and increase productivity.

A good theory of change will need to understand normal change (deadweight, attributions, and displacements) and the difference your interventions will make. Deadweight is the normal change that would have happened anyway due to external factors. So the vaccine effect on productivity needs to be separated from those diseases that are not vaccine preventable. This often means that SEVs must have a reasonable track of baseline indicators to be able to declare with certainty their intervention was the reason for the change. If they did not collect this information, proxies could be used, including qualitative information, to calculate baseline.

SEVs should be able to calculate attribution, which is the effect of other players' interventions in the ecosystem. For example, education and sanitation may also help in reducing mortality and increasing productivity by decreasing sickness.

Finally, drop-off is a measure that calculates how long your impact lasts. In cases of attitudes and behaviors, if there is a drop-off period of 6 months, then you know you will have to reinforce this to ensure that the effect stays. Ideally, SEVs must budget for all of these to ensure control and good governance.

### 7.4.3. *Step 3: Outputs*

Not all SEVs will have outputs, but as more for-profit SEVs are created, this needs to be considered. An output is a product or service that can be ideally "sold" or "gifted" in the marketplace (see Case Study 7.3). In this case, while IKEA was raising funds for a cause, the UNHCR could calculate the output as the kilowatts of power generated. The outcomes are well-being, psychological and physical safety, job opportunities, and improved educational results for refugees or it can be in the amount saved from an already stretched UNHCR budget that was redirected to other causes. The activities were the three campaigns held across IKEA stores. For TOMS, outputs could be the number of shoes sold and hence gifted. The outcomes could be healthy feet, or educational opportunities. For the Beads of Change, could be the handicrafts sold, the outcomes could be empowerment, economic likelihoods etc.

### 7.4.4. *Step 4: Activities*

The question at this stage an SEV needs to answer is: What is it we do?[19] Once you know the impact and outcomes, you need to plan program-level activities for each that will help you get the desired results. Activities are cost centers, so this needs to be calculated carefully, keeping in mind the resources you require and any drop-off effects. Most interventions require time and need a minimum period of "energizing" to ensure the activities create the maximum impact. This could translate into set-up, training, alignment of key stakeholders, and even prepping the community, so there is an acceptance of the intervention. When Ruwwad-Al-Tanmeya began their work in a disfranchised community in Amman, Jordan, they decided their first activity was to be accepted by the community. Much of their early investment activities were understanding the needs of the community, working on a wish list important for the community, and delivering on those promises. They set up a center in the community so they could be part of the community.

### 7.4.5. *Step 5: Resources*

The question at this stage an SEV needs to answer is: What are we investing in?[20] Each activity needs to be budgeted, to calculate resources — people, money, supplies, services, and even

## Case Study 7.3: **IKEA Foundation, Azraq Jordan Refugee Camp (One of the Initiatives)**

In the Azraq Jordan refugee camp, the IKEA Foundation invested €30.8 million in renewable energy through UNHCR, under the "Our Brighter Lives for Refugees" campaign. IKEA raised funds through three campaign periods over 2014–2015 where for every lamp or bulb sold during those periods, the IKEA Foundation donated €1 to UNHCR. More than 300 stores in 40 countries participated. UNHCR set up a solar-powered farm in Azraq to help cover the energy needs of all the refugees living in the camp. In Phase I, in May 2017, clean energy free of charge was provided to some 20,000 Syrian refugees, and Phase 2 would cover 36,000 refugees. UNHCR hopes to reduce $CO_2$ emissions by 3,500 tons per year, which would otherwise be generated from fossil fuel consumption. They distributed solar lamps and installed solar-powered streetlights to increase safety for refugees around the campsite. This resulted in a savings of US$1.5 million a year for UNHCR (which was spent on energy needs) and now could be re-invested in other critical programs. There is a definite improvement in daily life in the desert — for example, psychological well-being and safety, preservation of food (since it can now be refrigerated), provided job opportunities, and allowed children to study after dark. It is an example of PPP cooperation between a host government, a private organization, and UNHCR. The unused energy is redirected to the national grid.

infrastructure. Decisions need to be made around choices — Should you use volunteers or hire professionals? Lease or buy infrastructure? Share services or create your own? Invest in monitoring or control impact? These are just some decisions SEVs need to take, and this requires a strong understanding of the pros and cons. The long-term goal should help with making these decisions, but then, the SEV must also be able to raise funds required. Here, it is crucial for SEVs to understand their area of accountability.[21] Resources available at any point of time will determine the scalability and thus the reach in terms of beneficiaries. You should be able to answer the following key questions: What is the best way for the organization or project to contribute? What should its role be (position, capacity, added value) with the resources it has available? How should they document the change process with the resources they have available?

### 7.4.6. *Step 6: Assumptions*

While this has been placed as the last step, it is one of the most critical stages, as an Intervention Strategy Plan is predicated by assumptions. Take, for example, if I teach self-defense to women, they will be safer (the underlying assumption is that if they learn self-defense, they know how to use it and that it will not aggravate the predator to be more violent). This involves three assumptions as follows: (1) they can learn, (2) they know how to use it effectively, and (3) it will not result in a more aggravated response from the assailant. When I am considering the funds I need, I will have to budget for a place and people to teach (maybe even transportation, marketing, etc.), time (how long will it take before I can see results), and monitoring to understand the impact (and perhaps also education campaigns in the community). By monitoring my assumptions, I will know if they are correct or you may need to modify the theory of change. The robustness of your strategy will increase when you move away from opinion-based to evidence-based information, implicit causal links to explicit causal relationships, oversimplified representation accuracy to a sufficiently detailed representation, innovative precedence to a tested method, and participation that is open and shared with external stakeholders.[22]

Assumptions can be made about (1) context and the actors and factors at play; (2) pathways of change; and (3) conditions for and quality of implementation. This must be followed by a risk analysis where each assumption must be checked for being valid and the consequences if it was wrong.[23] Assumptions can also be tested in a scenario analysis activity as follows: (1) identifying the assumptions (explicit or implicit), and determining which among the two is the basis of operation; (2) imagining what plausible alternative explanations or perspectives might explain what is happening if the initially identified assumptions, in fact, did not hold true; and (3) exploring what evidence would be needed to ascertain which options, among the defined assumptions and plausible alternative hypotheses, is best borne out empirically.[24]

### 7.4.7. *Step 7: Putting it All Together — Visualizing and Narrating*

The next step is the hardest part as you must capture the essence of your Intervention Strategy Plan as a narrative that is easy to understand and to be able to visualize the steps to help you track the process. On the 16th of August 2013, the European Parliament (EP) tweeted: "*Everyone knows that a picture is worth a thousand words... Even better if it's a picture with words...*" It is clear that infographics, pictures with metrics — help bridge the chasm between stakeholders to get everyone aligned. This is needed to create a shared understanding of an SEV's objectives and values.[25] Data can be tedious and complicated, but it does not need to be, according to Hans Rosling, who highlights the need to look beyond the numbers.[26]

**"The purpose of computing is insight, not numbers". Likewise for visualization, "The purpose of visualization is insight, not pictures".[27]**

Exhibit 7.3: **Free Software Example for Visualizing and Storytelling**

Loopy: Free open-source software, https://ncase.me/loopy/

VUE: Free open-source software, http://vue.tufts.edu/about/index.cfm

Lucid Chart: free, https://www.lucidchart.com

YEdGraph Editor: https://www.yworks.com/products/yed

Resonant: https://resonant.kitware.com

Ganttpro: https://ganttpro.com

Google Data Studio: https://marketingplatform.google.com/about/data-studio/

[Keep in mind some are in beta testing so may not free for long.]

There is a vast amount of scientific evidence supporting visualization. If the process of understanding requires effort, it will drop engagement.[28] SEV needs to find a way to visualize their Intervention Strategy Plan and come up with a narrative. Different types of free software exist as shown in Exhibit 7.3, and this is helpful for SEVs on a tight budget.

Visualization alone is not enough, SEVs must have a powerful narrative accompanying their Intervention Strategy plan, and storytelling is one technique being used currently very successfully in organizations, where there are multiple stakeholders and for the broad public. Storytelling can encourage sensemaking,[29] communicate values,[30] convey a multiplicity of viewpoints,[31] help create trust in complex situations,[32] and reinforce and build the brand[33] among others. Stephen Denning[34] identified eight different narratives presented in Exhibit 7.4.

Exhibit 7.4:   **Narrative Patterns**

| If your objective is | You will need a story that | In telling it, you will need to | Your story will inspire such phrases as: |
|---|---|---|---|
| Sparking action (springboard stories) | Describes how a successful change was implemented in the past, but allows listeners to imagine how it might work in their situation. | Avoid excessive detail that will take the audience's mind off its own challenge. | "Just imagine ..."; "What if ... ?" |
| Communicating who you are | Provides audience-engaging drama and reveals some strength or vulnerability from your past. | Provide meaningful details but also make sure the audience has the time and inclination to hear your story. | "I didn't know that about him!"; "Now I see what she's driving at!" |
| Transmitting values | Feels familiar to the audience and will prompt discussion about the issues raised by the value being promoted. | Use believable (though perhaps hypothetical) characters and situations and never forget that the story must be consistent with your own actions. | "That's so right!"; "Why don't we do that all the time!" |
| Communicating who the firm is — branding | Is usually told by the product or service itself, or by customer word-of-mouth or by a credible third party. | Be sure that the firm is actually delivering on the brand promise. | "Wow!"; "I'm going to tell my friends about this!" |
| Fostering collaboration | Movingly recounts a situation that listeners have also experienced and that prompts them to share their own stories about the topic. | Ensure that a set agenda doesn't squelch this swapping of stories — and that you have an action plan ready to tap the energy unleashed by this narrative chain reaction. | "That reminds me of the time that I ..."; "Hey, I've got a story like that." |
| Taming the grapevine | Highlights, often through the use of gentle humor, some aspect of a rumor that reveals it to be untrue or unreasonable. | Avoid the temptation to be mean-spirited — and be sure that the rumor is indeed false! | "No kidding!"; "I'd never thought about it like that before!" |
| Sharing knowledge | Focuses on mistakes made and shows, in some detail, how they were corrected, with an explanation of why the solution worked. | Solicit alternative — and possibly better — solutions. | "There but for the grace of God ... "; "Gosh! We'd better watch out for that in future!" |

Exhibit 7.4: **(cont)**

| If your objective is | You will need a story that | In telling it, you will need to | Your story will inspire such phrases as: |
|---|---|---|---|
| Leading people into the future | Evokes the future you want to create without providing excessive detail that will only turn out to be wrong. | Be sure of your storytelling skills. (Otherwise, use a story in which the past can serve as a springboard to the future.) | "When do we start?"; "Let's do it!" |

*Source*: Adapted from Denning.[35]

## 7.5. **Translating Impact into Financial Metrics**

On the one hand, there is a rising debate on even whether everything, should be translated into financial numbers like GDP which is used to monitor developmental progress.[36] But the reality is that investors still want to know what their "returns" are, and though they may be happy with lives saved or children educated, by translating these numbers into common currency of our times, the financial investments may be validated. Investors that provide seed capital primarily judge the impact of an SEV based on the financial health of an organization, besides the social value created. A standard method used is the Social Return on Investment (SROI) tool. SROI allows you to calculate the value using proxy measures and claim statements like, for every US$1 investment into the program, we delivered a health saving of US$X. It is especially useful for fundraising.

$$SROI = \frac{Tangible + Intangible\ Value\ to\ the\ Community\ of\ Impact}{Total\ Resource\ Investment}$$

SROI can be based on future impact (forecast) or past impact (evaluative).[37] A key caution is (1) to avoid double counting of outcomes and (2) to be realistic. When looking for proxies, you can ask the beneficiaries how they value the service if equivalent examples are not available. If you are delivering water purifiers free of cost — one way to measure the value of interventions is the cost of purifying water. Equivalent options is in terms of carbon footprints for the example where methods use fossil fuels or burning wood. You could extend this concept to increased health benefits, hence, saving in healthcare expenditure. If you wanted to look at families, you might be challenged in calculating the value of the intervention for the resources a caregiver of a sick person spends taking care of the person. It could be estimated in terms of productivity (how many hours of work did they lose? How much money is lost from the time they would have invested in working?). What happens if the caregiver is not working? Hence, calculating value may need some creativity, yet it needs to be plausible, backed by evidence. At this stage, gather experts and look and benchmark with other SEVs even if they are in different ecosystems.

As in the case of Lucky Iron Fish (see Case Study 7.4) you could look at the impact of the consumption of iron on health (hence savings on health expenditure), earnings (from less sick days or days spent to care for a sick person), or increased productivity (increased earnings from feeling healthier). Of course, the easiest will be to see if anemia did decrease. You would need to know baseline and see if any other interventions were simultaneously in play.

## Case Study 7.4: **Lucky Iron Fish**

Lucky Iron Fish is a Canadian SEV whose goal is solving iron deficiency and anemia, a problem that affects 2 billion people worldwide according to the World Health Organization. Anemia causes a wide variety of problems, making people susceptible to a wide range of diseases and illness and in extreme cases, death. Christopher Charles had visited Cambodia in 2008 as a Masters student, and he found that this problem was a widespread problem there. The standard way of solving the problem, supplements, or tablets were not working either because of unavailability or expense involved. Charles was inspired by previous research that cooking in iron pots could aid the intake of iron. A product was initially designed as a block of iron that could be added to the cooking pot. But there was a low acceptance until the product was redesigned in the shape of a lucky fish with a smile, making it culturally acceptable. If people used the product three times a day (by putting it with the boiling water), in daily cooking, they should have got at least 75% of the required daily iron intake. The trials proved positive. In 2012, Gavin Armstrong, a doctoral candidate, was so inspired by the idea, he expanded the scope of his study to commercialization, registered the product as the Lucky Iron Fish® and registered a company with Charles and their supervisor (who was common to both).

He secured funding for research from the Government of Canada (C$500,000 = US$386,608) and his university (C$180,000) for more research, to make the fish more long-lasting. They raised funding for R&D and for distributing the fishes free in Cambodia through grants and a "buy one give one" program. The SEV won an award for product design at the 2015 Cannes International Lions Festival, a 2015 Design for Asia award, and US$880,000 from the Bill & Melinda Gates Foundation for research. They were twice recognized by Clinton Global Initiative University and got a shout-out by Oprah. They are in the certified top 10% of B-Corporation businesses worldwide.

There were problems in their Intervention strategy. The first was when they began the company, they went door to door in Cambodia hoping to sell the fish, but they were only able to sell one fish a month. There were two things to factor in, the first was that the company had no trust in the communities, and second, the government was handing out free supplements that many people were not consuming. The assumption that the water was relatively clean was found to be untrue. In some cases where the water was contaminated by arsenic, the iron intake was negligible. The SEV had to work with local partners active in the ecosystem. Another research paper claimed that the underlying reason for the deficiency was genetic, for example, Hemoglobinopathy E, where smaller than normal red blood cells are present. If that were the case, the iron fish would need augmentation for iron intake. What are elements of TOC you see in this case study?

## 7.6. **Control**

No matter how great your Intervention Strategy Plan, you might find three errors cropping up:

(1) Planned goals or impacts were not reached because the implementation deviated from the plan. This could be because of lack of control, interventions from other stakeholders you did not foresee, or unforeseen situations. For example, the Ebola epidemic setback Gavi's vaccine plans in those countries and disrupted the regular immunization schedule.

(2) Targets were not reached because an assumption made proved false, or the situation changed, rendering the conjecture inaccurate. It is therefore critical that evaluations should not only measure outcomes but also test assumptions. Looking at the case of the Lucky Iron Fish, the assumption is that the person cooking uses the fish three times a day. A proper intervention may need to combine this strategy with a reinforcement intervention to ensure everyone is using the fish the right way.

(3) Targets were not reached because the theory itself was incomplete, not specific enough, or had leaps of faith — because all the necessary preconditions were not identified?[38]

So where does control come in? Most SEVs need to work on a robust (1) internal control system and (2) external control. Internally, they need to track organizational processes, allocation of resources, and manpower expenditures. They need to know how everything that contributes to the impact. It is very tempting to be enchanted by media and prizes and external recognition but sometimes, especially when there are limited resources, these activities are draining and take away from the impact.

A founder of an SEV (school for handicapped children) in the remote mountains of the Himalayan range found that he had to go to his native country every year — a very wealthy nation — for three purposes: (1) healthcare, (2) fund-raising, and (3) taxes. Unfortunately, there were few qualified staff or training facilities at the remote high-altitude location, and he trained the staff to the best of his abilities. As he got older, the trips away became longer, as acclimatization took time, unfortunately, when he returned from one such trip, he found that the person left in charge of the facility had physically abused the children. What are some measures of control he could have put in place, so the school functioned as he wanted in his absence? Control measures need a risk assessment to help manage unplanned for contingencies like this. While it is easy to say, the school was in a very remote area.

Accounting is one method of control, but often limited to managing finance, not culture or behavior. So, from best management practices, roles and responsibilities need to be clearly assigned. Many SEVs, especially small startups, find that the job roles of employee's morph in the early years. This makes control harder. Culture needs to be reinforced, making sure values are clearly stated and known. Values are often implied and not explicit, allowing a way out for employees. Many SEVs depend on volunteers, and this also makes control harder. Secondary PTSD is not uncommon for employees operating under challenging situations like humanitarian crises, though strangely little research exists.[39] SEVs should factor psychological counselling and stress management into their budgets and timelines to ensure no breakdowns occur. Other methods of managing control is through the board or the advisory board. The board often acts as an interface with the external environment, co-opting various key stakeholders.

Control of the external environment is impossible, as all SEVs can do is influence. But they can monitor and adapt. Ideally, SEVs should look at other players in their ecosystem (their area of expertise and their community) and at other players in similar ecosystems (at a regional, national, and international level). A method for external control is to audit *vis-à-vis* best practices, for example, a B-Corporation certification, an ISO 26000, or a quality assurance system. Transparency on how much money is spent for the cause versus administration and marketing can be benchmarked with other enterprises (for example, an SEV can look at Charity Navigator).

All these methods help SEVs minimize the adverse and unintended effects of their interventions and make sure their intended interventions contribute to the intended goal. Since environments are dynamic, people change, and more players come in, it is alright to change the goal and the strategy as the purpose of the SEV is to do good and do good well. Of course in the end, you may need to know when one path is closed and how to channelize all of the good through another (see Case Study 7.5).

## Case Study 7.5: **THE 99 (Kuwait)**

THE 99 was a venture of Teshkeel Media Group. The idea came to its founder, Dr. Naif Al Mutawa in 2003. He believed that he could bring religious tolerance and understanding of Islam by creating a cartoon series for children. The cartoon would introduce heroes and heroines from countries around the world to children from all over the world by embracing THE 99 virtues of Allah, which were named in the Koran. It would celebrate tolerance for diversity and the greater good. But the journey was difficult, and finally the venture closed down. At its height, THE 99 was a successful comic book series, had a cross-over comic with the Justice League, merchandising, a planned theme park, an animated series, and was recognized by President Obama. The venture had signed a 26-part animation deal with Endemol in 2009 (the production house behind successful series like Big Brother, Star Academy, and Deal or No Deal) and The Hub in 2010 (co-owned by Discovery and Hasbro). Unfortunately, Islamophobia put a stop to the release of the series. However, Naif managed to get his documentary out in 2011 titled, Wham! Bam! Islam! Netflix then truck a deal and released his series in 2012. One of the biggest challenges Naif had was to convince ople that what he was doing was not the propaganda of the religion. In fact, in March 2013, a local a was issued against Naif in Kuwait and then in 2014 from the Grand Mufti of Saudi Arabia and the er Council of Clerics. Naif refused to run from Kuwait, returning without police protection, as he had ts there (he ran a clinic). Eventually, the fatwa was dropped. THE 99 airs in over 70 countries. While the e as it was conceived does not exist, the impact is felt. In 2013, Marvel introduced the first Pakistani eroine, Kamala Khan, DC then introduced Nightrunner, a French–Algerian sort-of Batman and then an American Green Lantern Corps character called Simon Baz. Naif now spends his time in his clinic and ages social entrepreneurs.

## 7.7. **Business with Purpose: A Journey**

Building a business with purpose is a journey. The dual goals of an SEV — profits and purpose — make the journey that much harder. However, there are many resources to draw on and the path is well-trodden. It is hoped that this book contributes in some small way to your journey into the amazing world of social entrepreneurship. As highlighted by the Sustainable Development Goals, partnerships are key. Not-for profit entrepreneurs should look at for-profit entrepreneurs and learn from them on how to run a business operation. Without cash flow and good management practices, your venture will fail. For-profit entrepreneurs should look at great social enterprises. Without a value-embedded business operation, you may leave the world in a worse off place — there is so much good that can be done, and there are great role models out there.

## 7.8. **Questions**

### Question 1
Create an Intervention Change Strategy for your SEV or one from the marketplace. Look at methods to creative brainstorming.

### Question 2
Funders or grant organization often want Social Metrics. Read the paper by Kasper and Marcoux.[40] What are some of the tensions? What are the metrics that are detrimental to the cause? Explain.

### Question 3
Do you think the growth of social impact indicators and increasing standards and legislations may make social ventures all about the money and not about the change? Debate the pros and cons considering many social ventures begin with good intensions and as a hobby. Compare the Bill & Melinda Gates Foundation, the Chan Zuckerberg Initiative to your local neighborhood SEV or initiative. Where is the fine line?

### Question 4
Reflect on an SEV and identify some barriers to their progress. Were any of these barriers a function of wrong assumptions? Very often, assumptions are reinforcing and may be consequences of the choice of the decision. Behavioral economics may provide interesting insights in this topic. A paper that you could read is that by Kahneman.[41] How could you apply these concepts rationally to the SEV problems?

### Question 5
What are the resources you should budget for control in an SEV dedicated to a cause like the Sprout Pencil, a pencil when used that can be planted and grows (https://sproutworld.com) versus a cause fighting domestic violence (http://adullamsocialenterprises.org/domestic-abuse-awareness/). What metrics are presented? What more needs to be done?

### Question 6
Jeff Bezos highlights key philosophies he believes in for his company — do the same for your SEV.

## Culture

A word about corporate cultures: for better or for worse, they are enduring, stable, hard to change. They can be a source of advantage or disadvantage. You can write down your corporate culture, but when you do so, you're discovering it, uncovering it — not creating it. It is created slowly over time by the people and by events — by the stories of past success and failure that become a deep part of the company lore ...

One area where I think we (Amazon) are especially distinctive is failure. I believe we are the best place in the world to fail (we have plenty of practice!), and failure and invention are inseparable twins. To invent you have to experiment, and if you know in advance that it's going to work, it's not an experiment. Most large organizations embrace the idea of invention, but are not willing to suffer the string of failed experiments necessary to get there ...

## Decision-Making

One common pitfall for large organizations — one that hurts speed and inventiveness — is "one-size-fits-all" decision making.

Some decisions are consequential and irreversible or nearly irreversible — one-way doors — and these decisions must be made methodically, carefully, slowly, with great deliberation and consultation. If you walk through and don't like what you see on the other side, you can't get back to where you were before. We can call these Type 1 decisions. But most decisions aren't like that — they are changeable, reversible — they're two-way doors. If you've made a suboptimal Type 2 decision, you don't have to live with the consequences for that long. You can reopen the door and go back through. Type 2 decisions can and should be made quickly by high judgment individuals or small groups. ...

First, never use a one-size-fits-all decision-making process. Many decisions are reversible, two-way doors. Those decisions can use a light-weight process. For those, so what if you're wrong? I wrote about this in more detail in last year's letter.

Second, most decisions should probably be made with somewhere around 70% of the information you wish you had. If you wait for 90%, in most cases, you're probably being slow. Plus, either way, you need to be good at quickly recognizing and correcting bad decisions. If you're good at course correcting, being wrong may be less costly than you think, whereas being slow is going to be expensive for sure.

Third, use the phrase "disagree and commit." This phrase will save a lot of time. If you have conviction on a particular direction even though there's no consensus, it's helpful to say, "Look, I know we disagree on this but will you gamble with me on it? Disagree and commit?" By the time you're at this point, no one can know the answer for sure, and you'll probably get a quick yes.

Fourth, recognize true misalignment issues early and escalate them immediately. Sometimes teams have different objectives and fundamentally different views. They are not aligned. No amount of discussion, no number of meetings will resolve that deep misalignment. Without escalation, the default dispute resolution mechanism for this scenario is exhaustion. Whoever has more stamina carries the decision.

## Proxies

As companies get larger and more complex, there's a tendency to manage to proxies. This comes in many shapes and sizes, and it's dangerous ... A common example is process as proxy. Good process serves you so you can serve customers. But if you're not watchful, the process can become the thing. This can happen very easily in large organizations. The process becomes the proxy for the result you want. You stop looking at outcomes and just make sure you're doing the process right ...

Another example: market research and customer surveys can become proxies for customers — something that's especially dangerous when you're inventing and designing products. "55% of beta testers report being satisfied with this feature. That is up from 47% in the first survey." That's hard to interpret and could unintentionally mislead ... I'm not against beta testing or surveys. But you, the product or service owner, must understand the customer, have a vision, and love the offering. Then, beta testing and research can help you find your blind spots. A remarkable customer experience starts with heart, intuition, curiosity, play, guts, taste. You won't find any of it in a survey ...

The thing I have noticed is when the anecdotes and the data disagree, the anecdotes are usually right. There's something wrong with the way you are measuring it.

# Sources

### Case Study 7.1: #ThisIsMyLane Movement & @ThisIsYourLane

Compiled from various sources: NRA (2018), From the website: https://www.nrafoundation.org/about-us/ [Accessed 30 November 2018]; Pane, L. M. (2018), It's a Twitter war: Doctors clash with NRA over gun deaths https://www.boston25news.com/news/its-a-twitter-war-doctors-clash-with-nra-over-gun-deaths/876600964 [Accessed 30 November 2018]. Twitter site @ThisIsOurLane

### Case Study 7.2: Beacon of Hope

Compiled from various sources: Interviews, Lowry, W. (2018), "Beacon of Hope UAE is bringing light to the world," *The National*, dated 25 October, Available: https://www.thenational.ae/uae/watch-beacon-of-hope-uae-is-bringing-light-to-the-world-1.784294 [Accessed 22 May 2019]; Quote from Beacon of Hope (2019), Global Innovation Challenges, Available: https://www.globalinnovationexchange.org/innovation/beacon-of-hope-uae [Accessed 22 May 2019]; Website: https://www.beaconofhopeuae.com/.

### Case Study 7.3: IKEA Foundation, Azraq Jordan Refugee Camp (One of the Initiatives)

Compiled from various sources: IKEA Foundation (2018), "Brighter Lives for refugees 25 November 2015–18 January 2016," Available: https://www.ikeafoundation.org/campaigns/brighter-lives-for-refugees/ [Accessed 30 November 2018]. See videos available on this site: https://www.ikea.com/gb/en/this-is-ikea/people-planet/people-communities/good-cause-campaigns/brighter-lives-for-refugees/ UNHCR (2016), "IKEA brighter lives for refugees campaign raises 308 million euros," Available: https://www.unhcr.org/en-us/news/press/2016/1/569ca2de6/ikea-brighter-lives-refugees-campaign-raises-308-million-euros-renewable.html https://www.unhcr.org/en-us/news/latest/2017/5/591bfdbb4.html https://www.ikeafoundation.org/campaigns/brighter-lives-for-refugees/ [Accessed 30 November 2018].

### Case Study 7.4: Lucky Iron Fish

Compiled from various sources: Charles, C. V., Dewey, C. E., Daniell, W. E. and Summerlee, A. J. S. (2011), "Iron-deficiency anaemia in rural Cambodia: Community trial of a novel iron supplementation technique," *European Journal of Public Health*, 21(1): 43–48; Luck Iron Fish website: https://luckyironfish.com/pages/our-journey; Roxby, P. (2015), "Why an iron fish can make you stronger," *BBC*, dated 17 May, Available: https://www.bbc.com/news/health-32749629 [Accessed 2 December 2018]; Schatz, R. D. (2015). "How a social entrepreneur overcame his 'arrogant failure' and won kudos from oprah," Forbes, dated 18 October, https://www.forbes.com/sites/robindschatz/2015/10/18/how-a-social-entrepreneur-overcame-his-arrogant-failure-and-won-kudos-from-oprah/#23a1aa742044 [Accessed 1 May 2018]; Wieringa, F. T., Dahl, M., Chamnan, C. *et al.* (2016), "The high prevalence of anemia in Cambodian children and women cannot be satisfactorily explained by nutritional deficiencies or hemoglobin disorders," *Nutrients*, 8(6): 348. Published 2016 Jun 7. doi:10.3390/nu8060348.

### Case Study 7.5: THE 99

Adapted from: Stephens Balakrishnan, M. (2016), "THE 99: The journey of Dr. Naif Al-Mutawa," In: Balakrishnan, M. S. and Lindsay, V. (eds.), *Actions and Insights: Middle East North Africa* (*Vol. 5*): *Social Entrepreneurs*, UK: Emerald Group Publishing, pp. 328–357.

# ENDNOTES

1 Porter, M. E. and Kramer, M. R. (2011), "The Big Idea — Creating shared value," *Harvard Business Review* (January–February).
2 "Maas and Liket (2011), "Social impact measurement: Classification of methods," In: Burrit, R. (ed.), *Environmental Management Accounting, Supply Chain Management and Corporate Responsibility Accounting*, USA: Springer.

3  Ohno T. (1998), *Toyota Production System: Beyond Large-Scale Production*. Portland, OR: Productivity Press.

4  *Ibid.*, p. 123.

5  Card, A. J. (2017). "The problem with '5 whys'," *BMJ Qual Saf.* 26(8): 671–677.

6  Gross, J. A. 5 "Whys folklore: The truth behind a monumental mystery," *The KaiZone*, 2014. http://www.webcitation.org/ 6jHDZM1Gc [Accessed 25 July 2016].

7  Adapted from the Annie E. Casey Foundation (nd), Making Connections Initiative, Available https://www.aecf.org/work/past-work/making-connections/ [Accessed 1 December 2018].

8  While a Logframe (short for Logical Framework Approach) is often used as a management tool in the development sector for planning, monitoring, and evaluation, a TOC differs in the assumption that complex problems make the social change process complex and requires many intermediate steps, feedback loops, and various stages. Change is rarely linear, and often because of multiple stakeholders, a dialogue is critical for successful interventions.

9  Weiss, Carol (1995), "Nothing as practical as good theory: Exploring theory-based evaluation for comprehensive community initiatives for children and families in 'new approaches to evaluating community initiatives'," Aspen Institute.

10 Murray, R. *et al.* (2010), *The Open Book of Social Innovation*, The Young Foundation: NESTA.

11 Collins, J. C. and Porras, J. I. (1996), "Building your Company's Vision," *Harvard Business Review*, 74(5), 65–77.

12 Collins, J. C. and Porras, J. I. (1996), *Op. at.*

13 A term used to refer to goals that require thinking on the "edge of tomorrow."

14 McGahan, A. M. (2017), "Moonshots achieving breakthrough innovation in established organizations," *Harvard Business Review*, December.

15 Collins, J. C., and Porras, J. I. (1996), *Op. at.*

16 Gavi (2018), Mission, Available: https://www.gavi.org/about/mission/ [Accessed 1 December 2018].

17 UNHCR (2004), Code of Conduct and Explanatory Notes, https://cms.emergency.unhcr.org/documents/11982/32382/UNHCR+Code+of+Conduct/72ff3fdf-4e7c-4928-8cc2-723655b421c7 [Accessed 1 December 2018].

18 Allen, W., Cruz, J. and Warburton, B. (2017), "How decision support systems can benefit from a theory of change approach. Environmental management," The final publication is available at Springer via https://dx.doi.org/10.1007/s00267-017-0839-y]

19 Ibid.

20 Ibid.

21 Dhillon, L. and Vacca, S. (2018), "Refining theories of change," *Journal of MultiDisciplinary Evaluation*, 14(30): 64–87.

22 *Ibid.*

23 Hivos ToC Guidelines (2015), *Theory of Change Thinking in Practice*, Netherlands.

24 Brookfield, S. (2012), *Teaching for Critical Thinking: Tools and Techniques to Help Students Question their Assumptions*, San Francisco, CA: Jossey-Bass.

25 Weiss, C. H. (1995), "Nothing as practical as good theory: Exploring theory-based evaluation for comprehensive community initiatives for children and families", In: James Connell *et al.* (eds.), *New Approaches to Evaluating Community Initiatives: Concepts, Methods, and Contexts*, Washington, DC: Aspen Institute.

26 Rosling, H. (2006), "The best Stats you have ever seen," *Ted Talk*, Available: https://www.ted.com/talks/hans_rosling_shows_the_best_stats_you_ve_ever_seen?language=en [Accessed 2 December 2018].

27 Card, S. K., Mackinlay, J. D., Shneiderman, B. and Kaufmann, M. (1999), *Information Visualization: Using Vision to Think*, Academic Press, USA. ISBN: 1-55860-533-9.

28 Song, H. and Schwarz, N. (2008), "If it's hard to read, it's hard to do: Processing fluency affects effort prediction and motivation," *Psychological Science*, 19: 986–988. Available at: http://sitemaker.umich.edu/norbert.schwarz/files/08_ps_song___schwarz_effort.pdf.

29 Boje, D. M. (1991), "The storytelling organization: A study of story performance in an office-supply firm," *Administrative Science Quarterly*, 36(3): 106–126.

30  Swap, W., Leonard, D., Shields, M. and Abrams, L. (2001), "Using mentoring and storytelling to transfer knowledge in the workplace," *Journal of Management Information Systems*, 18(1): 95–114.

31  Abma, T. A. (2003), "Learning by telling storytelling workshops as an organizational learning intervention," *Management Learning*, 34(2): 221–240.

32  Grisham, T. (2006), "Metaphor, poetry, storytelling and cross-cultural leadership," *Management Decision*, 44(4): 486–503.

33  Stephens Balakrishnan, M. (2011), "Protecting from brand burn during times of crisis: Mumbai 26/11: A case of the Taj Mahal Palace and Tower Hotel," *Management Research Review*, 34(12): 1309–1334.

34  Denning, S. (2006), "Effective storytelling: Strategic business narrative techniques," *Strategy & Leadership*, 34(1): 42–48.

35  *Ibid.*

36  See more recent discussions on this topic. A good starting point is WEF Blog by David Pilling (2018), 5 ways GDP gets it totally wrong as a measure of our success, dated 17 January, https://www.weforum.org/agenda/2018/01/gdp-frog-matchbox-david-pilling-growth-delusion/[Accessed 2 December 2018].

37  A useful resource is The SROI Network (2012), A guide to Social Return on Investment, Available: http://www.socialvalueuk.org/app/uploads/2016/03/The%20Guide%20to%20Social%20Return%20on%20Investment%202015.pdf [Accessed 2 December 2018].

38  Dana, H. T., Heléne, C., Eoin, C. and David, C. C. (xxxx), *Theory of Change*, ActKnowledge, NY: USA; Guskovict, K. L. and Potocky, M. (2018), "Mitigating psychological distress among humanitarian staff working with migrants and refugees: A case example," *Advances in Social Work*, 18(3): 965–982.

39  Strohmeier, H. and Scholte, W. F. (2015), "Trauma-related mental health problems among national humanitarian staff: A systematic review of the literature," *European Journal of Psychotraumatology*, 6(1), 28541.

40  Kasper, G. and Marcoux, J. (2014), "The re-emerging art of funding innovation," *Stanford Social Innovation Review*, Spring, Available: https://ssir.org/articles/entry/the_re_emerging_art_of_funding_innovation [Accessed 14 April 2019].

41  Kahneman, D. (1994), "New challenges to the rationality assumption," *Journal of Institutional and Theoretical Economics*, 18–36.

42  Bezos, A. (2015), Shareholder letter. Available: https://ir.aboutamazon.com/static-files/f124548c-5d0b-41a6-a670-d85bb191fcec; Bezos, A. (2016), Shareholder letter, Available: https://blog.aboutamazon.com/company-news/2016-letter-to-shareholders; Bort, J. (2018), "Amazon CEO Jeff Bezos explains his famous one-character emails, known to strike fear in managers' hearts," *Business Insider*, dated 21 April, Available: http://www.businessinsider.com/bezos-explains-his-dreaded-one-character-emails-2018-4 [Accessed 24 May 2019].

Printed in the United States
By Bookmasters